SARBANES-OXLEY

Sarbanes-Oxley

Building Working Strategies for Compliance

TERENCE SHEPPEY

AND

ROSS McGILL

palgrave
macmillan

First published 2007 by
PALGRAVE MACMILLAN
Houndmills, Basingstoke, Hampshire RG21 6XS and
175 Fifth Avenue, New York, N.Y. 10010
Companies and representatives throughout the world

PALGRAVE MACMILLAN is the global academic imprint of the Palgrave Macmillan
division of St. Martin's Press, LLC and of Palgrave Macmillan Ltd. Macmillan® is a
registered trademark in the United States, United Kingdom and other countries.
Palgrave is a registered trademark in the European Union and other countries.

ISBN-13: 978–0–2300–0678–2
ISBN-10:   0–2300–0678–7

This book is printed on paper suitable for recycling and made from fully managed
and sustained forest sources.

A catalogue record for this book is available from the British Library.

A catalog record for this book is available from the Library of Congress.

10   9   8   7   6   5   4   3   2   1
16 15 14 13 12 11 10 09 08 07

Printed and bound in Great Britain by
Antony Rowe Ltd, Chippenham and Eastbourne

Contents

List of figures   *xii*

List of tables   *xiv*

Preface   *xvii*

About the authors   *xix*

List of abbreviations   *xxi*

PART I The Sarbanes-Oxley Act   **1**

1   **What is Sarbanes-Oxley?**   **3**

Introduction   3

SOX at a glance   4

Practical compliance summary   5

2   **Background and Legislative Trends**   **7**

Background   7

Trends in regulation   9

Trends in financial services   10

Regulatory pressure   11

The effect of the Act: is it working?   12

Current trends   14

Positive skepticism   16

Practical compliance summary: looking forward   16

3   **Perspectives for the Financial Sector**   **19**

The response to regulation   19

Practical compliance summary   25

4   **An Overview of the Act**   **27**

Introduction   27

Structure and sections of the Act   28

Titles: quick summary   28

Sections of the Act   28

Title I: Public Company Accounting Oversight Board   28
Title II: Auditor independence   36
Title III: Corporate responsibility   40
Title IV: Enhanced financial disclosures   46
Title V: Analyst conflicts of interest   51
Title VI: Commission resources and authority   52
Title VII: Studies and reports   52
Title VIII: Corporate and criminal fraud accountability   53
Title IX: White-collar crime penalty enhancements   56
Title X: Corporate tax returns   57
Title XI: Corporate fraud accountability   58
Timetable to compliance   60

PART II The Requirement: SOX and the Financial Sector   63

5   Why are Financial Services Affected?   65
Overview of the financial sector   65
Reputation as a capital asset   69
Reputation and best practice   69
Compliance models for the finance sector   74
Practical compliance summary   77

6   The Public Face: Financial Reporting   78
Reporting and compliance   78
Financial reporting and compliance   79
Financial reporting assertions   80
Sources of information   81
"True" and "fair"   81
Publicized compliance   82
Auditing of financial statements   82
Reporting standards   83
Transaction standards: SWIFT   86
Technical standards: XBRL   88
Improving reporting   91
Practical compliance summary   91

7   The Impact of Cost   93
The cost of compliance   93
Cost–benefit analysis   94
Cost and complexity   95
Ongoing costs   96
The true cost of compliance   98
Diverted costs   100

Cost examples   101
Auditor costs   103
Practical compliance summary   103

8   Responsibility   **105**
Introduction   105
Summary of key issues for senior executives   105
Executive responsibility   106
Evaluation and assessment   107
Ethical behavior   108
The role of non-executive directors   108
The responsibility cascade   109
Audit committee   110
Practical compliance summary   113

9   Internal Auditing   **114**
Internal auditing   114
Executive action   115
IT audit planning   116
Auditing models: control self-assessment   121
Auditing tools   123
Practical compliance summary   125

10 External Auditing   **127**
Who is to do the audit   127
Types of audit: certification audit   128
Ensuring the organization meets the audit requirements   128
The role of the CPA in auditing for the Act   129
Preparing for an audit   129
Audit process   130
Steps in the auditing process   131
Ongoing auditing   132
Statement of applicability for the Act   132
External audit reporting   133
PCAOB summary   137
Practical compliance summary   141

Part III Practical Compliance   **143**

11 Building the Strategy   **145**
The strategic nature of compliance   145
Approaches to compliance   146
State of compliance   149

Compliance and risk 154
Preparing for compliance 157
Industry best practice 163
Practical compliance summary 165

12 The Compliance Process 166
The compliance process 166
The compliance process: strategic and tactical 167
The compliance process: systematic and pragmatic 172
Mapping the compliance cycle to business 176
Applying the compliance cycle to processes 177
The compliance process in context 177
Practical compliance summary 179

13 Compliance with Section 302 181
Documentation for demonstrating compliance 181
Practical compliance summary 186

14 Compliance with Section 404 188
The special challenges of Section 404 188
Section 404: Management assessment of internal controls 188
Content of management's internal control report 189
Critical success factors (CSFs) for Section 404 189
Project management lifecycle 191
Implementing a Section 404 project 192
Practical compliance summary 194

15 Compliance with Other Relevant Sections 195
Sections 802 and 1102 195
Section 103: Auditing, quality control, and independence
standards and rules 198
Section 201: Services outside the scope of practice of auditors;
prohibited activities 199
Section 409: Real-time issuer disclosures 199
Practical compliance summary 201

16 Compliance in the Supply Chain 202
Compliance in the extended enterprise 203
The significance for intermediaries, underwriters, and others
in the chain 204
SAS 70 in the supply chain 204
Outsourcing functions in the supply chain 206
Practical compliance summary 206

17   Internal Controls   **207**
Introduction   207
Disclosure controls and procedures   208
Scoping internal controls   210
Internal controls   211
Measurement criteria   215
Practical compliance summary   221

18   Documentation, Testing, and Evaluation   **223**
Documentation for demonstrating compliance   223
Regulatory requirements for documentation   224
Documentation, email, and compliance   226
Risk management: documenting controls with a control matrix   228
Evaluation and testing   229
Testing controls   229
Management assessment   232
Practical compliance summary   235

19   Process and the Organization: Policies and Behavior   **236**
The idea of a process   236
What constitutes a process?   236
Process mapping and flowcharting   237
Compliance and process   238
Business processes in financial services   242
Corporate governance   245
Behavior   246
Internal policies   247
Practical compliance summary   248

Part IV Securing the Organization for Compliance   **251**

20   Risk Management   **253**
Risk assessment   253
Treating risk   254
Risk and the Act   254
Business risk   255
Implications of the Act   256
Risk factors   256
Risk management   260
Extending the scope of the Act   265
Changing behavior   267
The financial function and risk management   269
Practical compliance summary   270

21	**Intellectual Capital**	**271**
	Intellectual property	271
	IT and the business: the value of information	272
	Documents and records: the risk of intellectual property loss	274
	Practical compliance summary	276
22	**Information Security**	**277**
	Using ISO 17799 as a framework for compliance	277
	Documentation	278
	Statement of applicability	278
	ISO 17799 controls for compliance	278
	Management approval	293
	Practical compliance summary	296
	Part V Solutions for Compliance: Joining the Dots	**297**
23	**Frameworks for Compliance: COSO and COBIT**	**299**
	COSO: an introduction	299
	The five components of COSO	300
	Performance measures	308
	COBIT	311
	IT governance	316
	Precursors and other models	326
	The COBIT project	327
	Definitions	327
	Documentation	331
	Developing the framework	331
	Control objectives and principles	332
	Summarizing the system	334
	Practical compliance summary	334
24	**Methodologies and Frameworks**	**342**
	Supporting compliance	342
	ITIL	343
	Six Sigma	344
	ISO 17799	347
	CMMI	349
	What methodologies, frameworks, and standards have in common	350
	Practical compliance summary	351
25	**Professional Service Providers and Best Practice**	**353**
	The major players: the Big Four	353
	Practical compliance summary	359

26   The Benchmark Solution   360

An ideal solution?   360
Benchmarks in general   360
Ongoing processes and flexibility   363
Timescales   364
Benchmarking and the compliance process   364
Sample COBIT model mapped to a generic finance company   368
Internal auditing in practice   372
Practical compliance summary   380

Appendix A A summary of practical compliance   381
Appendix B Vendor solutions   399
Compliance at the desktop   400
Unstructured communications   401
Preventive compliance   403
Useful contacts for compliance solutions and components   404

Bibliography and References   *406*
Index   *409*

Figures

2.1 Regulatory pressure model   12
2.2 Do you agree that Sarbanes–Oxley will restore investor confidence in US listed companies?   13

3.1 Technology waves, user adoption, and regulatory focus   23

5.1 Controls and monitoring: the broker's title   72

7.1 Cost versus complexity   96
7.2 Maintaining the cost of ongoing compliance   98

8.1 The responsibility cascade   111

9.1 IT audit feedback to risk assessment   120

10.1 The audit process   133

11.1 The strategic compliance process   146
11.2 The compliance iceberg   147
11.3 Passive linear compliance   150
11.4 Active linear compliance   150
11.5 Cyclical compliance   151
11.6 The sliding window   154
11.7 The compliance chain   157
11.8 Inputs to preparation for the compliance process   159

12.1 The compliance process   169
12.2 The compliance process and management   176
12.3 The compliance engine   177
12.4 The compliance process in context   178

14.1 Planning the compliance timetable   192

16.1 A financial services supply chain   202

17.1 Management mapped to compliance responsiblities   207
17.2 Section 404 as a subset of disclosure controls   208
17.3 Management decisions on disclosure   209
17.4 Control deficiencies   218

19.1 Process and layers of control   239

20.1 Risk areas and characteristics   257

23.1 COBIT and compliance   315
23.2 Enterprise and IT governance in context   317
23.3 The COBIT project   328

24.1 Before and after variances using Six Sigma techniques   346

26.1 Benchmarking and compliance   362
26.2 FinOrg relevant internal management bodies   370

A.1   Compliance process road map   382

Tables

4.1   Sections of the Act   29
4.2   Structure of the Act: titles and descriptions   30
4.3   Timetable for accelerated filers—larger companies   61
4.4   Timetable for non-accelerated filers—smaller companies
      and foreign companies   61

5.1   Sample compliance map by sector   76

7.1   Invisible costs of compliance   100

8.1   Impact on senior executives of the Sarbanes-Oxley Act   106
8.2   Requirements for a code of ethics for senior executives   109

10.1 Example reports in the PCAOB standard   134

11.1 A preparatory assessment checklist   162

12.1 The PDCA method   174
12.2 Applying PDCA to the compliance process   175

13.1 Section 302 and practical compliance activities   182
13.2 Advantages and disadvantages of reuse   185

14.1 Summary of Section 404 requirements   190

15.1 Section 802   196
15.2 Section 1102   197
15.3 Section 103   198
15.4 Section 201   200
15.5 Section 409   200

17.1 A comparison of sections 302 and 404   210

17.2	Summary of PCAOB internal controls	215
17.3	Summary of PCAOB policies and procedures	216
17.4	A control deficiency	217
18.1	Controls: frequency of application	231
22.1	A comparison of ISO 17799 and the compliance process	279
22.2	Sample incident management process	283
22.3	Incident management and the statement of applicability	284
22.4	Control objective: information security policy	285
22.5	Sample control objectives and controls	286
22.6	Sample implementation of controls	290
22.7	Controls and risk	291
22.8	Controls and user access	292
22.9	User responsibilities	293
22.10	Correct processing	294
22.11	Testing options	295
22.12	Business continuity	295
23.1	Control environment indicators	302
23.2	Control environment actions for practical compliance	303
23.3	Risk assessment levels	304
23.4	General controls	306
23.5	Application controls	307
23.6	Information quality indicators	309
23.7	Monitoring indicators	310
23.8	Performance measures	311
23.9	COBIT key goal indicators	318
23.10	COBIT critical success factors	321
23.11	Key performance indicators and measurement methods	322
23.12	COBIT maturity model and compliance	323
23.13	COBIT framework requirement overlaps	330
23.14	Planning and organization summary	335
23.15	Acquisition and implementation summary	337
23.16	Delivery and support	338
23.17	Monitoring summary	341
26.1	FinOrg domain planning and organization	371
26.2	FinOrg strategic information technology plan control objectives	373
26.3	FinOrg acquisition and implementation	375
26.4	Delivery and support	377

A.1   What is Sarbanes-Oxley?   383
A.2   Background and legislative trends   383
A.3   Perspectives for the financial sector   384
A.4   Why financial services?   385
A.5   Financial reporting   386
A.6   The impact of cost   387
A.7   Responsibility   388
A.8   Internal auditing   389
A.9   External auditing   389
A.10 Building the strategy   390
A.11 The compliance process   391
A.12 Compliance with Section 302   392
A.13 Compliance with Section 404   392
A.14 Compliance with other sections   393
A.15 Compliance in the supply chain   393
A.16 The impact of cost   394
A.17 Documentation, testing, and evaluation   394
A.18 Process and the organization: policies and behavior   395
A.19 Risk management   395
A.20 Intellectual capital   396
A.21 Information security   396
A.22 COSO and COBIT   396
A.23 Methodologies and frameworks   397
A.24 Professional service providers and best practice   397
A.25 The benchmark solution   398

B.1   A cross-section of solutions available on the market   405

Preface

The Sarbanes-Oxley Act, more than any other recent piece of legislation, has captured the imagination of corporations across the United States. It is a development in US law that increasingly affects non-US as well as US firms which trade as listed companies. This international dimension is significant as international companies decide on how they are to come to terms with its requirements. There is a particular relevance to the financial services industry, not just because of the fundamental applicability of corporate governance to the firms themselves, but because they have experience of working in a heavily regulated environment. They face issues of compliance on a daily basis. Yet the emphasis of the Act on penalties and the towering presence of the US Securities and Exchange Commission (SEC) casts a worrying shadow across publicly listed companies. The central questions these companies ask are:

■ Are we affected by the Act?
■ If so, how are we affected?
■ How do we do something about it?

In reality the first two questions are quickly answered, but the third question is not so easily addressed. While this book looks at all these questions, its special focus is on the third.

Since its inception there has been much regulatory activity surrounding Sarbanes-Oxley, largely focused on the practicalities of compliance. Whilst there has been some shift in the attitude of the SEC on the burden of compliance for smaller companies and non-US entities, nevertheless the requirements remain substantial, and for most companies daunting. This book is an examination of how compliance is achieved and maintained; what solutions have evolved since the Act first became the concern of boardrooms, and how financial services have responded to the challenge of the staged sections of the Act. In particular this book explores the strategies and tool sets that have led companies to successfully manage compliance, and suggests effective measures for implementation.

Part I looks at the Act itself, and takes a view on why those of us involved in financial services with responsibility to implement regulatory compliance should consider the Act as a significant and relevant piece of legislation. It also looks the background and trends that create the context for the Act.

Part II examines in more depth the implications of the Act, understanding the importance of public reporting, the impact of the cost of compliance, and the responsibilities of everyone to respond to this regulation.

Part III explores how we can develop a solution that leads to effective compliance while maintaining the interests of the organization. In particular it addresses the critical consideration that compliance is not a one-off project, but a process that delivers the intention of legislators to change the way companies behave, from board level to the customer interface.

Part IV furthers this exploration by considering the nature of the information economy, how the compliance effort is centered on risk, and how the exercise can be modeled on security, so that a compliance solution secures the organization against the implications of non-compliance.

Part V draws these threads together, by considering the frameworks and methodologies that offer a practical basis for developing the compliant organization.

Each chapter tackles a specific topic that contributes to the central consideration of compliance, and includes a summary of practical tips and best practice that builds a body of ideas for managing the compliance process.

Whether compliance is seen as a burden and a negative cost to the business, or an opportunity to invest in improving business practice and policy rollout, this book offers a response based on what has worked and is currently available to the senior executives and those responsible for compliance, who are faced with a climate of increased regulation and who have to deal with the demands of the Act.

DISCLAIMER

The views and opinions expressed in this book are solely those of the authors. Although the authors have made every effort to ensure the complete accuracy of the text, they do not accept any legal responsibility whatsoever for consequences that may arise from errors or omissions or any opinions given. Nothing in this book is, or is intended to constitute, the provision of absolute or definitive advice. Readers are strongly advised to take professional independent advice on these matters.

About the authors

Terence Sheppey has had a successful career spanning 20 years in networking, communications, consultancy and partnership management. Terence is now the Managing Director of Precision Texts Ltd, a publishing and documentation consultancy. Since the 1980s, Terence has held management roles in major American and British hardware companies such as UB Networks, Newbridge, and European software vendors. He has global experience developing operational and business support systems for service providers from China through South-East Asia, Europe, and North America. As a consultant with Cap Gemini Ernst & Young, Terence provided knowledge management expertise and infrastructure advice to major finance companies. In the late 1990s he held the post of Director of Alliances for specialist workflow and billing software companies, globally managing integration partners, HP, IBM, KPMG, Logica, and Cisco, and speaking at major conventions in Europe and Asia.

Recognized for showcase projects and cited for outstanding contributions with many companies, Terence has considerable experience of the technical environments in which modern financial institutions operate, and has a profound grasp of the practical solutions needed to manage change and compliance. He has distilled this experience into technical guides for a variety of audiences, and contributed specialist articles to many publications. The author is currently working on a series of guides for finance and health sector compliance managers on the implications of the Sarbanes–Oxley regulations. His published works include *The New Global Regulatory Landscape*, co-authored with Ross McGill.

Ross McGill graduated with Honors in Materials Science and Education in 1978. Since graduating, he has held key management posts with major international companies. He ran his own consultancy practice helping financial services firms become more competitive and efficient. Ross has since worked for ten years in the wholesale financial services sector, and was until 2002 Group Managing Director of five software companies. He is particularly well known in the industry for his public work with the

Society for Worldwide Interbank Financial Telecommunications (SWIFT), the US Treasury, IRS and global custodians dealing with the practical effects of new regulatory structures. He now works as director of marketing for Globe Tax Services Inc, leading business process outsourcing of withholding tax processing in the United Kingdom, and EMEA, where he advises financial intermediaries on best practice in business process enhancement.

Ross was co-chair of the SWIFT Market Practice Group on US 1441 NRA regulatory issues for ISO standard messaging, and co-chaired an Operational Impact group with the IRS, US Treasury and Deloitte & Touche LLP from 1999–2001. Ross also serves as the UK expert representing service bureaux on the ISO20022 Securities Evaluation Group (SEG) Committee TC68. Ross's published works include *International Withholding Tax: A Practical Guide to Best Practice and Benchmarking; Relief at Source: An Investor's Guide to Minimizing Internationally Withheld Tax*, and in 2005 *The New Global Regulatory Landscape*, co-authored with Terence Sheppey.

Abbreviations

AAA	American Accounting Association
ADR	American Depositary Receipts
ADS	American Depositary Shares
AICPA	American Institute of Certified Public Accountants
Basel II	Revised International Capital Framework (Basel Committee on Banking Supervision)
BI	business intelligence
BPM	business process management
BS	British Standard
BSI	British Standards Institute
CAAT	computer assisted audit techniques
CBI	Confederation of British Industry
CCO	chief compliance officer
CCTA	Central Computer and Telecommunications Agency
CEO	chief executive officer
CFO	chief financial officer
CIO	chief information officer
CMMI	capability maturity model integration
COBIT	Control Objectives for Information and Related Technology
CO	compliance officer
COSO	Committee of Sponsoring Organizations of the Treadway Commission
COTS	commercial off-the-shelf software
CP	compliance process
CPA	Certified Public Accountant
CSA	control self-assessment
CSF	critical success factors
CTF	compliance task force
CTO	chief technology officer
CXO	executive officers
DRS	direct registration system
EDGAR	Electronic Data Gathering, Analysis and Retrieval for SEC filings
EDI	electronic data interchange

ERM	enterprise risk management
ERP	enterprise resource planning
FASB	Financial Accounting Standards Board
FCPA	Foreign Corrupt Practices Act
FEI	Financial Executives Institute
FMCG	fast-moving consumer goods
FSA	Financial Services Authority
GAAP	generally accepted accounting principles
GAO	General Accounting Office
IAS	International Accounting Standards
IASB	International Accounting Standards Board
IASC	International Accounting Standards Committee
IFRIC	International Financial Reporting Interpretations Committee
IFRS	International Financial Reporting Standards
IIA	Institute of Internal Auditors
ILM	information life cycle management
IM	instant messaging
IMA	Institute of Management Accountants
IP	intellectual property, internet protocol
IOSCO	International Organization of Securities Commissions
ISF	Information Security Forum
ISMS	information security management system
ISO	International Standards Organization
ITGI	IT Governance Institute
ITIL	IT Infrastructure Library
KGI	key goal indicator
KPI	key performance indicator
KYC	know your customer
LOB	line-of-business
MiFID	Markets in Financial Instruments Directive
MPG	market practice group
MUG	message user group
NACD	National Association of Corporate Directors
NASD	National Association of Securities Dealers
NASDAQ	National Association of Securities Dealers Automated Quotations
NYSE	New York Stock Exchange
OECD	Organization for Economic Co-operation and Development
PDCA	plan–do–check–act
PCAOB	Public Company Accounting Oversight Board
RCA	root cause analysis
RFID	radio frequency identification
ROI	return on investment
SAC	Standards Advisory Council
SAG	Standing Advisory Group

SAS	Statement of Auditing Standards
SEC	US Securities and Exchange Commission
SEI	Software Engineering Institute
SIA	Securities Industry Association
SLA	service level agreement
SOD	segregation/separation of duties
SOX	Sarbanes-Oxley Act (2002)
SSO	single sign-on
STP	straight through processing
SWIFT	Society for Worldwide Interbank Telecommunications
TQM	total quality management
UAT	user acceptance test
XBRL	eXtensible Business Reporting Language

PART I

The Sarbanes-Oxley Act

CHAPTER 1

What is Sarbanes-Oxley?

INTRODUCTION

The Sarbanes-Oxley Act, also known as the Public Company Accounting Reform and Investor Protection Act, is a development in US law that affects both US and non-US firms seeking to comply with corporate governance initiatives. Often known under the abbreviation SOX, the act is so named after the architects of the Act, Senator Paul Sarbanes and Representative Michael Oxley. As legislation it was passed in 2002, with implementation of its sections and clauses coming into force in stages from 2004 onwards.

The Act applies to companies registered on the New York Stock Exchange (NYSE) or NASDAQ. It also applies to US and non-US firms whose shares are traded as American Depositary Receipts (ADRs). There are currently nearly 2,000 issued ADRs.[1] There is particular relevance to the financial services industry not just because of the fundamental applicability of corporate governance to the firms themselves, but because these firms act on behalf of many thousands of institutional shareholders which have similar concerns over both the companies they invest in, and the duty of their custodians.

This means that there are issues of compliance, risk management, and fiduciary duty that apply to these firms and to the financial institutions that are involved in their affairs. Investors in these firms are increasingly aware of the significance of these regulatory requirements. This is especially so as ownership of ADRs, originally intended for US persons, is global.

Perspectives

Since its inception there has been much regulatory activity surrounding Sarbanes-Oxley, largely focused on the practicalities of compliance. While there has been some shift in the attitude of the SEC on the burden of compliance for smaller companies and non-US entities,[2] the requirements remain and are substantial. The activities of compliance are now "mission

critical" for major financial institutions, many of which may not have sufficient secure and accountable systems for managing the life cycle of their
information. Without these in place, demonstrating compliance to the Act
is very difficult.

A concept we revisit throughout this book is the need for the organization to ensure that its interests are placed at the heart of the compliance
effort. The considerable investment in resources should have a measured
benefit, and every activity throughout the process should be considered for
its ultimate value for the company. Without this guiding principle the
compliance effort remains just that, an effort rather than a purposeful exercise in delivering improvements. The perspective of the organization
should be paramount. From this viewpoint other interests, such as that of
the shareholder and the market, coincide in the compliance process. By
responding to regulation through compliance, the company is responding
to their interests. Ideally, all can emerge winners. Such synergy is fundamental to the Act's intention. It is, after all, more than the execution of
effective financial reporting. Its focus is on how well a board of directors
fulfill their duties, how well the company as a whole behaves within the
strictures of good governance, and how transparent are its financial activities. There is no contradiction between being an entrepreneurial and fast-
moving market maker, and a fully compliant organization.

If it is the case that a company has to comply with the Act, and do so
with some enthusiasm, how does it achieve compliance at a minimal cost
and for maximum benefit? Chapter 11 explores this possibility by building
a strategy that encompasses the interests of the company as a whole in
becoming complaint; and Chapter 12 demonstrates a model that can carry
the ongoing nature of compliance forward. From the outset it is vital that
the greater scope of the Act is understood. Key to this is understanding
what is required of a company, and in part this understanding is based on
the experience, knowledge, and expertise traditionally represented by auditors and consultants that specialize in this market. The Act exists within a
context, and it is as well to understand the background and key trends in
financial services that affect how companies approach compliance.

SOX AT A GLANCE

What is the Sarbanes-Oxley Act of 2002?

■ Sarbanes-Oxley (SOX) is a US law passed in 2002 to strengthen
corporate governance and restore investor confidence. The Act
derives its short title from the sponsorship of US Senator Paul
Sarbanes and US Representative Michael Oxley.

- The law applies to US and non-US public companies with securities registered with the SEC under the Securities Exchange Act.[3]
- The law was passed in response to a number of major corporate and accounting scandals and misdemeanors in the United States.
- The legislation establishes standards in accounting and reporting practices for all US public company boards, their management and public accounting firms. It extends and amends the Securities Exchange Act of 1934.
- The Act consists of 11 "titles" that address issues from reporting requirements, internal controls to criminal penalties for non-compliance. It establishes an oversight board to administer the Act and allied standards and recommendations.
- The titles cover a range of governance issues, including control over internal company trade such as loans to senior executives, the responsibilities of senior executives in maintaining systems of control over periodic and non-periodic financial reporting, the roles of audit committees and external auditors, and the provision of protection for whistleblowers.
- The real challenge of the Act is for a company to demonstrate compliance by supporting claims that its systems of control over financial reporting are working well. This includes documenting processes, archiving communications, and maintaining systems of control over the recording of transactions and business activity.
- Deterrence is the chief weapon of the Act. This deterrence operates at the personal level: for the chief executives of the organization threatened with large fines and potential imprisonment up to 20 years; at the company level: loss of share value through impact on brand image, market perception, and investor confidence. The severity of the punitive measures highlights the importance of the Act against the backdrop of general legislation.

PRACTICAL COMPLIANCE SUMMARY

The key concerns for those companies affected by the Act are centered on:

- understanding how the Act affects the company
- exploring the best ways to respond to the Act by:
  - understanding what compliance means

- examining the options available for implementing an effective compliance program.
- deciding on and initiating an effective compliance process
- investigating what solutions are available and select appropriate solutions
- applying industry best practice to compliance efforts.

NOTES

1. American Depositary Receipts (ADRs) are certificates of ownership of American Depositary Shares (ADSs). While these terms are often used interchangeably, an ADR can consist one or more ADSs. The latter represents the shares of a non-US company held by a custodian bank in the company's home country. ADRs are, under US law, US securities and subject to US securities regulations.
2. In spring 2005, the SEC extended the deadline for non-US companies, or 'foreign private issuers', to comply with the amendments to SEC rules under the Act. These amendments require non-US companies to comply with Section 404 of the Act on or after July 15, 2006 (extended from July 15, 2005). This also applies to senior executive certifications of their internal controls in annual reports. The SEC responded to overseas events, such as the need for non-US companies in the European Union to comply with International Financial Reporting Standards in 2005.
3. All references made to the Exchange Act refer to the Securities Exchange Act (1934). Some of the Sarbanes-Oxley amendments also apply to the Securities Exchange Act (1933).

CHAPTER 2

Background and Legislative Trends

BACKGROUND

The history of the scandals and corporate misdemeanors of the early years of the twentieth twenty-first century is now well known. By 2003, the spectacular financial failures of high-profile public companies, management and auditors indulging in "creative accounting" brought the level of SEC enforcement activity to record levels. Multi-billion dollar restatements and resulting bankruptcies of companies such as Enron and WorldCom led directly to the Act. The latter provided tools for the SEC to deter repetitions of these corporate frauds and to punish those who abuse public trust.

The consensus that emerged as to why and how these events occurred has centered on a belief that boards of directors cannot be trusted to manage the affairs of their companies unsupervised by regulatory control. It assumes that the rules and voluntary codes of ethics that operate at this level are not sufficient to deter those with access to company funds from abuse in that position; further, that regulation through heavy punitive measures is the best and most effective response.

The auditing profession has been seen to be tainted as well, when firms take equity in their clients as part of their compensation. Auditors were perceived as willing accomplices in the process of projecting probity to achieve the appearance of better financial results, rather than as gatekeepers for accurate financial disclosure. Creative accounting that distorts GAAP was employed to cloak fraudulent activities. The SEC was tasked with studying and reporting on the trends that led up to the Act and the scandals that launched it. By 2002, the US General Accounting Office reported that 10 percent of all listed companies restated their financial results in the period 1997–2002.[1] In 2001 alone, there were 225 restatements. Many of these were NYSE listed companies and revenue recognition was a key area of concern. With the Act, SEC enforcement moved on to an era of faster response and a new approach based on expected cooperation from investigated companies. The focus shifted onto individuals and those responsible at the highest levels, notably the board of directors. It took Enron to uncover the extent of this failing among senior executives.

In the period leading up to the Act, the SEC was beginning to adjust its message to corporates, pushing ideas that placed responsibility for action back on the organization through:

- self-policing—through procedures to allow for the reporting of fraud and misconduct, especially related to periodic auditing
- self-reporting— with immediate disclosure of misconduct to regulators and the public
- self-healing—where acknowledged weaknesses are tackled as a priority with energy and resources.

This emphasis was followed through in the Act with the onus on executives to institute systems that could find problems, report them, and fix them.

Enron and WorldCom

The events at Enron Corp. were chief among those that set regulators down the path to the Act. The US Justice Department set up an Enron Task Force, and the SEC brought a joint action with this body in the US courts, focusing on senior individuals and fraudulent practice that deliberately misled analysts about Enron's real financial circumstances. The actions covered off-balance-sheet activities and sham transactions. It was clear that nothing could happen without the collusion of auditors who were charged with signing-off audits, so Merrill Lynch & Co, Inc. were dragged into the mire for aiding and abetting securities fraud. The case broadened to include other senior individuals at Enron, as the SEC uncovered overstated earnings and fraudulent asset sales. The scandal, when it broke, was all the more devastating because of Enron's widely admired and previously perceived virtuous role as the flagship of sound entrepreneurial practice. PricewaterhouseCoopers LLP (PwC) and its affiliate Pricewaterhouse-Coopers Securities LLC were caught violating auditor independence rules over a period of five years (1996–2001). Each aspect of the case added a dimension that was to help shape the substance of the Act. Then the storm broke on Arthur Andersen LLP. This firm was found guilty of obstruction of justice in relation to conduct of the Enron case. The firm did not survive the debacle and ceased to practice.

The events around WorldCom Inc. indicated that the Enron affair was not a one-off. Action was initiated against WorldCom as it announced its intention to restate financial results for its current quarter (in 2002) and all the quarters of the previous year. WorldCom was accused of fraud, overstating its earnings, and violating GAAP[2].

In a way the actions taken at WorldCom set the scene for the Act:

- Investigations were started into corporate governance policies.
- Training for management and staff on best practice was mandated.
- A senior figure was appointed to oversee the monitoring of regulations to avoid future violations.

These are all points of practice encouraged by the Act, and a trend had been established. In 2001 the SEC outlined some key assumptions about good corporate practice that had been found wanting in subsequent investigations:

- Public companies, in particular, must have effective, active compliance programs.
- These companies must be responsible for disclosing publicly any failings.
- Failings should be fixed, and cooperation is the behavior expected in investigations.

The scene was set for a move to tighten up regulation. In 2002, Congress took action by formulating and passing the Act.

TRENDS IN REGULATION

The Securities and Exchange Commission

No discussion of the Act, compliance with it or exploration of how the Act has come about can avoid the central role of the US Securities and Exchange Commission, generally know as the SEC or the Commission.

> The primary mission of the U.S. Securities and Exchange Commission (SEC) is to protect investors and maintain the integrity of the securities markets.

So opens the introduction to the SEC mandate on its website. In this state-ment is contained the whole thrust of the Act and its antecedents in the Acts of 1933 and 1934, the US Code and many other legislative measures. These have all been introduced to ensure that the financial system and the markets on which so much reliance is placed are maintained as the engine of the US economy. The Sarbanes-Oxley Act is really another piece of legislation within this tradition. The Act is a mechanism for ensuring that the SEC has an up-to-date, effective legislative response to the corporate disasters at the opening of the new millennium. In this context, the text of the Act makes constant references to the clauses and sub-clauses where it updates, replaces, or modifies existing SEC regulation. The apparent trend, then, is towards not so much more legislation, but legislation with more bite. The Act is there to restore confidence in the markets and rebuild trust in financial systems.

That the substance of the Act is not entirely new is clear when we consider these precedents. The amendments and additions to the Securities and Exchange Commission Acts are part of the picture. It has been observed that the requirements of the Act have strong parallels with, and are closely related to, the requirements of the Foreign Corrupt Practices Act, the COSO model being a common factor.

International Organization of Securities Commissions

In a broader context, the work of the SEC has extended through the International Organization of Securities Commissions (IOSCO).[3] It is an indication of how regionalization has evolved to globalization. This body evolved following its inception in 1974 from an inter-American regional association into a global body. In 1984, securities regulators from France, Indonesia, Korea, and the United Kingdom joined. It is now a recognized international standard-setter for securities markets. Its wide membership regulates more than 90 percent of the world's securities markets—over 100—and it acts as the world's most important international cooperative forum for securities regulatory agencies. In 1998 it adopted a set of Objectives and Principles of Securities Regulation (IOSCO Principles), now used as the international regulatory benchmarks for all securities markets. In 2003 it added a comprehensive methodology (IOSCO Principles Assessment Methodology) for objectively assessing the level of implementation of the IOSCO Principles. IOSCO provides comprehensive technical assistance to its members, in particular those that regulate emerging securities markets. By 2005 the organization had established its focus on:

- growing membership
- cross-border cooperation
- reducing global systemic risk
- protecting investors
- ensuring fair and efficient securities markets.

IOSCO also consults widely with the international financial community and in particular with the financial services industry. It is one of several examples of the development of global bodies working closely with regional and geographically based regulatory regimes.

TRENDS IN FINANCIAL SERVICES

The financial services sector is subject to many trends, of which regulation is a particularly significant one. However, as it is an information economy sector, one noted area of development is in the growth of the importance of business intelligence (BI), which now encompasses the management of data, information and intellectual capital. The central role of reporting for compliance is reflected in the interests of BI as a discipline for generating reliable value in reports and deriving value from the information pulsing through the modern financial corporation.

Within BI there is a special focus, strictly relevant to compliance, on the need to ensure data is accessible and certifiable. Surveys have indicated a list of key desirables for the industry:

- Information must be of a certain quality and accuracy.
- Information must reflect enterprise interests and values as well as line-of-business (LOB) interests and values.
- There must be greater access to quality data for everyday decision making.

A recognized driver that has fuelled a growth in BI solutions and functions is regulation. The push towards compliance has driven financial institutions to move quickly and make major investments in data infrastructure and data governance.

BI has flourished around some specific developments, notably the way compliance has forced companies to explore risks in a more coordinated manner at an entity-wide level. This has led to a number of developments:

- the "pre-staging" of data from across the enterprise in a common format that enables it to be integrated for reports and analysis
- an emphasis on the quality of data for specific uses, where data is certified against many criteria
- the bigger view consolidated through a "dashboard"—reflecting the status of an organization's data, either in real time or periodically.

These elements contribute to the data-centric organization's focus on intellectual capital. This is especially so for financial institutions that operate rapid, flexible data analysis and transaction exchange.[4]

REGULATORY PRESSURE

These trends are accelerated by regulatory pressure. All management within financial institutions is caught in a "pressure" system (Figure 2.1). Through the Act, regulators are pushing hard at companies at board level, and the board is transferring that pressure through its management structure. The IT function is caught between budget, requirement, and capability, while having to provide information intelligence and data to the business. In turn it presses its management for more budget to meet unanticipated capital and operational costs of compliance. The pressure for budget returns to the board, reinforces the reality of the requirements, and opens spending in areas that have been held back. While this pressure model is not unique to regulation, nevertheless the quality and threat of external scrutiny and punishment is ensuring a new severity of the pressure. It is also the case that the return on investment at board level can only be realized when behavioral changes are realized throughout the organization.

Generally, the profile of information as an asset has been a trend in itself. This is realized by a sharp increase in the presence of information strategies at the highest levels of the company. Information architectures and information security management systems (ISMS) ensure that the security of the organization is tightly linked with the significance of intellectual capital for financial services. It is another part of the jigsaw for full compliance.

THE EFFECT OF THE ACT: IS IT WORKING?

The Act has been in existence for a number of years, and many companies have made considerable investments in compliance. What evidence is there that the Act is rebuilding investor confidence in the economic

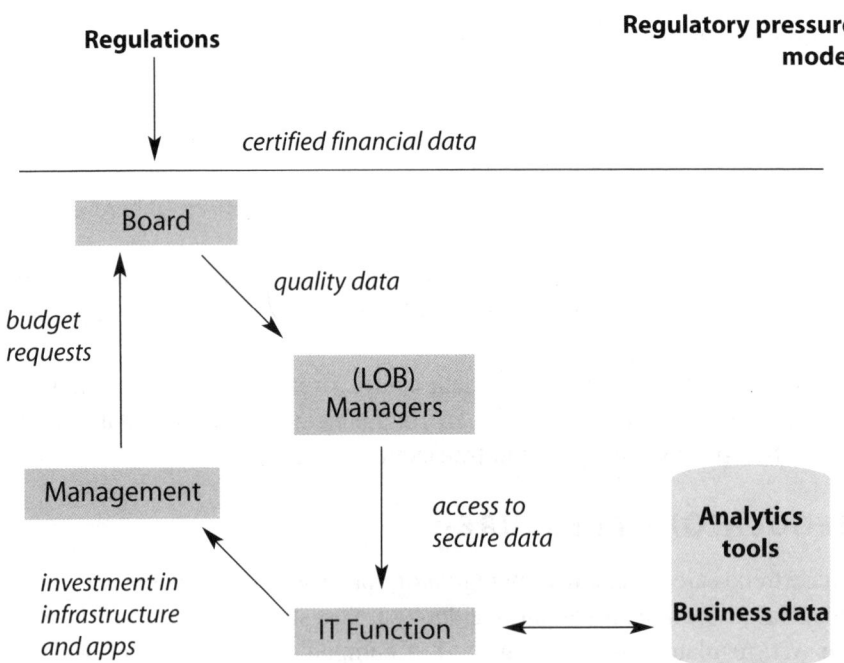

Figure 2.1 Regulatory pressure model

system? There is an inbuilt assumption that if legislation is passed, especially tough legislation, things will automatically get better. It seems to be a reasonable assessment until we consider the real objective of the Act—to change corporate behavior, not simply to get listed companies to file proper financial statements and reports.

In January 2004, GTNews published the results of an international survey of 134 senior finance and treasury professionals (GTNews 2004). The results were then analyzed by the organization type and location of the respondent. They were asked among other things how far they agreed or disagreed that the Sarbanes-Oxley regulations were likely to restore investor confidence in US listed companies and whether such corporate governance initiatives would benefit best practice in treasury functions (Figure 2.2).

At the time, their findings were not encouraging for regulators. Over half (57 percent) of respondents indicated that they did not believe the Act would restore investor confidence in US listed companies. Analyzed by type, all agreed that it was asking too much for the Act alone to achieve this considerable objective. The common sentiment was that such a transformation could only be achieved through a change in behavior, sought by the Act, and enshrined in codes of corporate ethics. A salient observation was the failure of non-executive directors to thwart corporate misdemeanors. Coupled with the occurrence of scandal in already heavily regulated industries, such as financial services, the prognosis for improvement was gloomy. This view might seem to be a little pessimistic. Even at the time of the survey, there was strong support for extending such legislation to jurisdictions across the globe. There also appeared to be divergence in the way

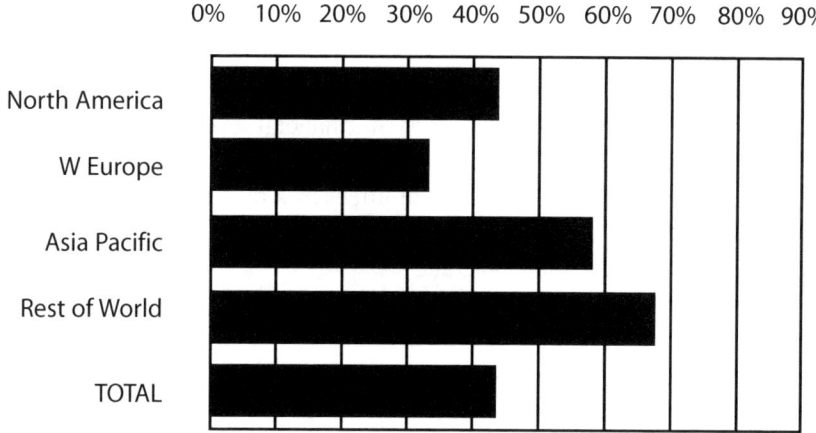

Figure 2.2 Do you agree that Sarbanes-Oxley will restore investor confidence in US listed companies?

banks and other corporations viewed the value of the Act. As entities that rely on information when borrowing and lending money as well as when investing in customers, banks may value full disclosure. Corporations see themselves as disclosing competitively sensitive information. Banks also have a head start with investments in quality internal control systems. However, there is a trend that the Act is part of: a trend towards good corporate governance. This is a broadly positive trend, and is seized upon as such by some lead players in industry, as well as the regulators.

Criticisms continue to note that the Act has an apparent narrow focus on financial misstatement whilst seeking a much broader behavioral transformation. In a sense the financial statement is an easier objective, and it is viewed as a constructive base for establishing that most elusive of all objectives: trust. However, uncovering and publishing misstatements can be destructive and a strong disincentive to comply; and then again non-compliance carries heavy penalties. The mix of carrot and stick is difficult to get right.

CURRENT TRENDS

Although predicting the future is difficult, the present and near future is a little more tractable, and for compliance with the Act the picture is colored by a fair amount of optimism. A recent survey in 2006, from Oversight, garnered the opinion of financial executives in the United States and identified a number of trends, which contribute to a view that compliance with the Act generates many benefits for financial organizations. The message here is that despite its cost, the Act is achieving its objective of supporting the healing process for corporate integrity and investor confidence, at least in US public markets. The greatest measured increment in benefits were found in:

- the Act's ability to improve the accuracy of financial reports
- improved individual accountability in financial reports
- reduced errors in financial operations
- more empowerment for audit committees as a result of more and better information
- decreased risks of financial fraud
- a strengthened view of companies for investors.

What these results reflect is the enterprise-centric view of regulation, where compliance delivers benefits to the organization; this contrasts with the regulator-centric view, where enforcement delivers public benefits. From this list we can identify some important trends that pervade the compliance process.

Increased shareholder value

■ A market-value effect, where investors appreciate the effort to be compliant since they can identify the organization as an ethical business.
■ A broader market-wide impact, building overall confidence in the securities and financial markets.

Compliance costs

■ The cost of compliance with requirements of the Act is acknowledged as a burden that affects stock prices.
■ An effect of such spending is a reduction in the size of dividends.
■ The subsequent year costs are higher than expected, notably driven by Section 404, where uncertainties abound on the detail of compliance.
■ The impact of capital spending plans varies, from compliance having little or no effect on capital spending plans, to a reduction in these plans because of compliance costs.

Small-capitalized companies, non-profit and private companies

A majority of the Oversight survey respondents believed some elements of the Act will be adopted by private companies and non-profit organizations not directly addressed by the scope of the Act. Such companies are seen to be responding to the Act, either through anticipation of the need to govern themselves, or as players in a supply chain for larger corporates that are affected and which require compliance from suppliers to manage their risks. The general assumptions that underline this were:

■ Because of the benefits of compliance, it is believed that non-profit organization stakeholders demand the same accountability and controls that apply to public companies.
■ A majority of financial executives asserted that Section 404 should apply to all public companies regardless of size.
■ Smaller companies should have their controls independently audited.

Some of this is in contrast to the debate over the application of the Act to smaller companies, especially non-accelerated public filers, and the compliance burden it places on them.

Automation and the role of continuous monitoring

A major trend for compliance and financial operations in general is the growth in the importance of continuous monitoring of financial processes. This is coupled with real-time transaction inspection, and the automation of manual controls for compliance to reinforce the efficiency of the overall control environment. Continuous monitoring is particularly significant for auditors and sections of the Act such as 404.

The benefits of this trend to automation in the monitoring of real-time transactions are that it provides financial executives with more predictable and versatile control environments, reduces errors in financial processes, and automates control testing and hence effectiveness. All this leads to increased confidence in financial reports, makes some headway in reducing compliance maintenance costs, and starts to address another troublesome issue: the risks associated with the segregation of duties.

Segregation of duties

The cost of enforcing the segregation of duties (SOD) across business processes has been positioned as a limitation on the effective longer-term implementation of Section 404. Many existing systems are still not able to match the requirements of the Act. The major challenges within this trend are various:

- keeping job definitions and the changing status of staff current and matched to access rights
- handling SOD in remote and smaller offices
- managing the special requirements of specialists and power users.

Access and control to information according to job profile and responsibilities is a critical control area. This is likely to see expanded interest as ID technologies, such as RFID, make inroads within financial services.[5]

POSITIVE SKEPTICISM

One aspect of surveys and projections is the way they sharpen our awareness of what is and what is not possible, regardless of regulatory carrots and sticks. When we discuss practical compliance we are focused on the reality that pervades most institutions and firms in the financial sector. This reality insists that an ideal state of compliance is illusory, and when we come to define our response to the Act and our approach to compliance, we must maintain a degree of "positive skepticism" about what can be achieved.

PRACTICAL COMPLIANCE SUMMARY

Looking forward

Trends change, and those that remain consistent tend to shift direction, sometimes reversing within a year or so. The near-future trends we have discussed are still effective guides to what might make a difference to the compliance process.

For the immediate future the goals for compliance with the Act, and to ensure improvements in the overall quality of financial reporting, focus on:

- Reducing costs internally—through automation and best use of assets and resources.
- Reducing costs externally—including reducing a reliance on consultants.
- Improving the support of the IT function—by automating manual processes where possible, while reducing the quantity of key controls to increase manageability.

The compliance process, as we will see, has these imperatives built in to its overall approach.

NOTES

1. According to the US General Accounting Office (GAO), in a landmark study in 2002 (US Senate 2002), it was found that financial statement restatements increased significantly from 92 in 1997 to 225 in 2001—an increase of approximately 145 percent. The trend was predicted to rise to more than 170 percent by the end of 2002.
2. The Generally Accepted Accounting Principles (GAAP) are an internationally recognized set of accounting principles, standards, and procedures that companies use to compile financial statements. GAAP are required of companies so that investors can be confident financial statements conform to a reasonably consistent standard.
3. For more information on IOSCO (the International Organization of Securities Commissions), check the website www.iosco.org.
4. Check 21 is a case in point. Check 21 is a US federal law that is designed to enable banks to handle more checks electronically to make check processing faster and more efficient. It became effective on October 28, 2004. Estimates believe that full implementation of Check 21 has hidden complications that could have annual revenue implications of $1 billion or more.
5. Radio frequency identification (RFID) is a technology that "tags" data when collecting and storing information. This tag is also known as an "electronic label," and consists of a chip component with an antenna which enables it to be read faster than traditional bar codes and to hold much more data. It carries a unique serial code or ID. Originally used to track animals, this capability has spread to tracking packages, as advocates believe the technology will drive improvements in the efficiency of supply chains. Libraries are expanding these

options for books and other materials. Financial services are looking at the potential, and so great is it that there are concerns about personal security, and calls for regulation in business use. Prototypes are appearing in financial services, and ideas explored include managing customer relations in the bank branch by embedding RFID tags in check books or bank cards for identification on repeat visits, tracking and managing physical documents as they move around the back office, and using tags to trigger credit or debit payments at the point of sale. The tags could even be embedded in high-value banknotes to counteract counterfeiting. There are instances of RFID chips embedded in staff, to track and monitor their use of systems.

CHAPTER 3

Perspectives for the Financial Sector

THE RESPONSE TO REGULATION

Generally, even when regulation appears to be global and uniform, financial service firms tend to be conservative in their approach. Compliance is organized at departmental level, around the software tools and resources to hand. A concerted enterprise-wide response involving all departments is unusual.[1] Despite the time frames built into regulation, the sector has a history of taking its time over responding. However, the US government has not always led by example: US 1441 NRA Regulations, of fundamental impact to every financial intermediary outside the United States, were first mooted in Congress over 25 years ago, yet only came to fruition in the year 2000.

When we consider a typical response of the sector to regulation, one response has been that of defiance, using a range of tactics:

- group attempts to delay imposition
- legal attempts to thwart imposition
- operational attempts to claim that the industry was "not ready."

There is some evidence for the success of such approaches. With the US NRA regulations, the "not ready" response was tried successfully for three years before the IRS chose to impose regulations unilaterally on the financial services community. While the 1441 NRA regulations have some relevance to the Act (see McGill and Sheppey 2005), they are more illustrative of an approach to regulation that helps condition responses when it comes to managing compliance.

In recent years, the sector has become more vocal, even forming loose associations of single interest groups within and external to trade associations.[2] An underlying issue for many of these groups is the concern that the industry is being over-regulated as a reaction to perceived failures of processes and controls within individual firms, rather than widespread systemic issues requiring regulatory control.

There is variation in the degree to which the financial services community is prepared to support, and capable of supporting, the reporting and notification requirements of the Act. Now, more than in the recent past, those in the financial services community are able to address regulation by minimizing their effort based on the reuse of other compliance efforts. They also benefit greatly from developments in technology.

IT and financial services

Financial markets are the beneficiaries of major changes in communications infrastructures. These now transport data electronically around the world, enabling extremely complex transactions, and allowing counterparties with different roles in a transaction to complete in near real time. The openness and accessibility of such systems carries its own risk, mainly from data loss and unauthorized disclosure. Information security is more significant than ever.

At this level, of the practical management of information within complex systems, the Act is similar to any other legislation. It focuses on the integrity of information at a time when there is so much of it, and information is vulnerable both at source, in terms of its accuracy, and in use, through advice and transactions.

IT systems have the security of data as a key objective embedded in operational methodologies, and maintain systems monitoring and exception reporting so that events can be trapped and reported. However, the reality of financial services is that such systems are fragmented in their application, and their technology might not be up to date. A global custodian bank disclosed recently that over 40 percent of its instructions from clients and counterparties were still arriving by thermal fax. But the pull of automation is strong, and the largest banks and brokers have invested in automating key processes, and are continuing to spend billions of dollars. Their reasons are commercial, driven by narrowing profit margins and the need to reduce costs.

Automation is a fact of life for the sector. The reduction in main street outlets is a result of growth in telephony and online banking. Many insurance investments are also made through the internet. These technologies assume a degree of automation to match the timescales of near real-time transactions. Below the global banking level, at regional and local levels, the degree of automation rapidly falls off, although it is still a significant cost element in the business.

While the size of an organization is a factor in IT investment, technology enables the smaller players to compete product to product with larger organizations, notably in the retail market. Technology is lowering the barriers to entry to financial service markets. Although the more mature organizations have a greater ability to respond initially, emerging players have an advantage because they have a clean sheet to work from, and can benefit from the experience of the mature market. Fragmentation lies in the middle-ground markets, where lack of IT investment creates a gap. This competitive landscape is changing rapidly and the focus is ever more on business processes. Financial service organizations have to streamline where they can to build in a competitive edge; they have to exploit economies of scale where they can.

This "mixed" picture, with a mixture of applications that enable automation and those that reinforce re-engineered manual processes, delivers a mixed capability. The requirements for timely disclosure of information are dependent on automation and speed. Many financial institutions recognize the need to automate processes because of the business benefits in control, reduced risk and cost, and faster delivery of products and services. Regulators are caught between the predictability of older technologies and the promise of new ones. National cultures and resistance to technological innovation can have a significant effect; consider the resistance to national identity databases in the United Kingdom, and the conflicting requirements of anti-terrorism laws and the need to maintain data privacy in Europe and the United States. There are some advantages to manual systems—especially for effective information security strategies and internal controls—yet most know your customer (KYC) documentation, if it is to be used by multiple parties, must be moved manually. This in turn can sometimes create more risk than it removes. Storage and retrieval of information is a focus for the Act, yet the financial services sector as a whole relies on the movement of information just as much as its storage.

Retail and wholesale

A further perspective is the difference between retail financial services and wholesale financial services. The retail financial service sector is focused on banking, savings, direct investment, pensions, and other financial instruments, sold to individuals through institutions as well as intermediaries. Wholesale financial services tend to deal with investors as groups, funds, and institutional investors, serviced by a complex web of intermediaries around the world.

Retail financial services are akin, in today's market conditions, to a fast-moving consumer goods (FMCG) market. Sales and marketing methodologies, as well as back-office processing, have commoditized something that used to be delivered through personal service. This has had major ramifications as commoditization has led to a focus on cost reduction, and FMCG-style marketing.

Cost reductions have driven retail financial services inevitably towards outsourcing models using low-cost supply chains, in locations such as

India or China. Sales and marketing techniques have packaged products as fast and "off the shelf"; these would previously have taken a significant time to move. Again, these possibilities are underscored by technological innovations in call centers and global communications.

Making the connection

Firms continue to move back-office processing into low-cost markets without thought to the implications of the risks inherent in non-compliance. The need for an entity-wide view of the risks associated with compliance to legislation such as the Act is critical to the decision-making process that undertakes these projects. Often a compliance project will originate from the board, and operate in parallel with, but without any connections to, another project also initiated by the board that contradicts some the risks being mitigated by the compliance effort. There is a need to ensure that:

- the risks of regulation are understood
- projects, in their risk analysis phase, thoroughly highlight risks
- a combined risk matrix is worked through as a basis for decision making.

A problem of scale

The dangers of FMCG-style product packaging of financial services are well observed in the endowment mis-selling scandals of the latter part of the twentieth century, and the Equitable Life-type scenarios and pension 'black holes' of the early twenty-first century. Compliance in such a complex environment is a real challenge, as the volume of transactions presents the organization with issues of scale and diversity. The IT function struggles to handle the volumes of storable information, and to ensure that it can be accessed, while regulators insist on storage and retrieval.

There is a potential for "systemic error," where a policy implementation affects large numbers of customers and exception reporting fails to identify errors, often because they are not seen as errors. At this point risk and liability can increase dramatically.

Current responses to regulation, like many project-oriented activities within larger organizations, are often "siloed:" resources are managed "locally" to address immediate issues. This is another cost management exercise as much as a response to entity-significant legislation. The emphasis of the Act, in contrast, is on entity-wide issues, often systemic, to ensure that controls and reporting are broadly based enough to catch systemic error. Cost dominates the general response of the sector: the cost of compliance seems to be ever increasing, and this trend is likely to continue into the foreseeable future.

Control over regulation

Many view regulatory affairs as something over which they have little or no direct control. Pressure groups and community associations have limited effect, and are often thought only to mitigate the broader political sweep as it applies to them. However, there has been a move towards "balanced regulation," whereby cooperation with the regulated is valued as much as the need to regulate. The Public Company Accounting Oversight Board (PCAOB) has shown itself willing to pay more than lip service to consultation within the industry.[3] Self-regulation has long been an approach adopted in the United States and the United Kingdom. This is particularly effective in regimes where the markets are mature and sophisticated enough to operate their own associations, and police their members and listees effectively. The position of regulators regarding technology is also relevant. We see instances, and the Act is an example, where certain developments in technology have encouraged regulators to make requirements that depend on the implementation of technology. Because technology makes something possible, there is a requirement to meet that possibility, regardless of whether this is in fact feasible. Section 409 of the Act comes close to this. Figure 3.1 illustrates this in the context of the adoption curve for new technologies. In the past regulators

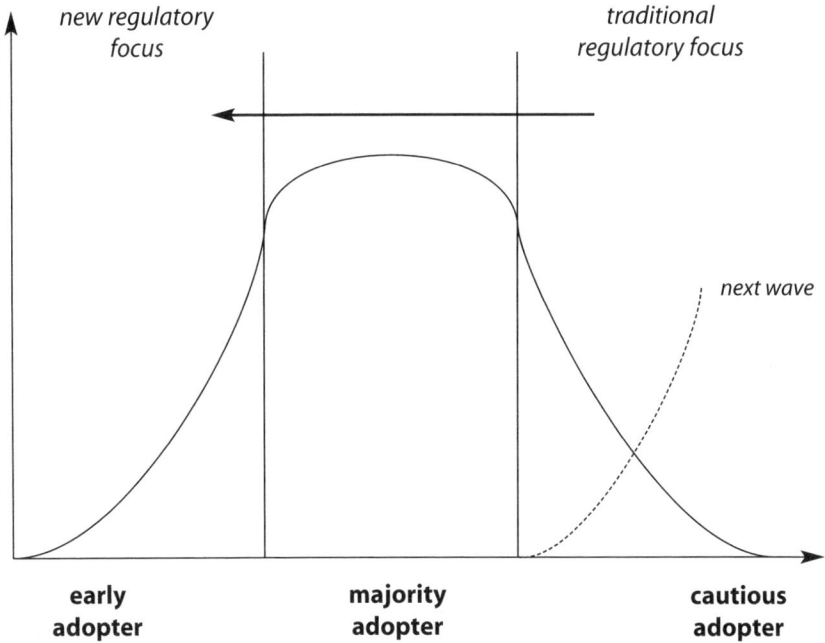

Figure 3.1 Technology waves, user adoption, and regulatory focus

have tended to be at the end of the curve of the technology wave; now there is a drive to be at the "early adopter" phase. Traditionally, the financial services sector has a mixed history when it comes to technology; it has been a cautious implementer. Now there is pressure from many sources, not just compliance, to implement new technologies that can generate competitive advantage in a rapidly changing market.

The symptoms of all this regulatory pressure tend to be seen in the documentation process. It is through documentary requirements that most regulators seek to demonstrate their control and look for evidence of compliance. At first sight the Act appears to be specific in its remit: periodic and non-periodic financial reports. However, the application of the Act is broad, and it is not specific about the detail of controls and documentation, only that there should be a system of control that is demonstrably effective, and that the processes controlled are documented.

The balance to be struck between manual and automated systems, the carefully managed life cycle of information, its security and the need to be flexible in delivery, is a unique issue for every affected organization. Controlling the response to regulation for the benefit of the organization is critical. Each will find its own way to compliance. However there are general rules and key processes that can be followed to achieve a solution that meets each unique circumstance, though no one solution is perfect.

Being wary of the Act is a reasonable stance, since the wording has to be worked over to tease out the wider implications. Nevertheless, a positive approach is warranted. The Act, disarmingly, asks no more of an organization than what it should be delivering anyway as an effective and efficient listed business: proper, reliable, truthful and transparent financial reports, generated by effective systems, in line with good corporate governance practice.

Financial sector organizational challenges

The challenges for the financial sector are quite specific and in line with those faced by any listed company. Some additional issues arise because of the complexity of the supply chain, and these are illustrated later. At this stage we can identify common practical issues that need to be addressed as part of the process of becoming compliant with the Act. In particular, it is important to ensure that the organization is in real-time control of the whole compliance effort. This means understanding the Act, understanding the organization and bringing the two together in a controlled and positive way, anticipating issues and dealing with them systematically. This last point ensures that compliance decisions are also positive business decisions. Shifting the perception from onerous cost to beneficial investment, builds a program that is risk-driven, not driven by departmental needs or constrained by software tools. The advantages are many, and these can be transformed into business benefits. Substantial operational and capital cost benefits can be gained by simply ensuring that thinking moves from a siloed business model to a more integrated one, as well as considering the way this will improve the creation and implementation of policies, procedures, and processes. Overall, the compliance activity can be advantageous.

Reducing unit costs of business processes is a major challenge for financial services into the mid-term, a view held by many executives now scrutinizing their obligations under the Act to see how they can best exploit them for business benefit. A key attribute that will allow the compliance effort to support a competitive stance is the attitude that allows strategic rethinking of business processes and the way they are managed. This may mean reviewing business re-engineering from a process-oriented perspective rather than a product-driven approach. However the issue is approached, the first stage is to understand the Act and what it requires of all levels of the financial sector business.

PRACTICAL COMPLIANCE SUMMARY

> ■ Establish clear lines of communication within the organization regarding compliance from top to bottom.
> ■ An informed workforce is a compliant one.
> ■ Ensure there is no confusion over the separation of roles and associated responsibilities.
> ■ Develop a program that initiates, drives, and maintains a state of compliance.
> ■ Develop a cross-functional approach to meeting the Act. Separation of functions and uncoordinated responses will ensure the compliance edifice is weakened by too many inter-departmental "cracks."
> ■ Maintain real-time control of the whole compliance effort.
> ■ Establish the balance between manual and automated processes. These processes will largely be in place, but the system of internal control will need to reflect this balance.

NOTES

1. This is explored later. The Act has encouraged firms to think across departmental borders; COSO and COBIT both attempt to address this directly.
2. For example, the Group of Thirty (G30). This is a private, non-profit international body established in 1978. It represents business and the public sector, with academic links. Its principles are to spread an understanding of international

economic and financial issues, to explore the implications of decisions taken in the public and private sectors, and to broaden awareness of the choices available to policy makers. For more information see www.group30.org.

3. The PCAOB has been mandated to consult over the implementation of the Act. In the summer of 2006 the PCAOB's Standing Advisory Group (SAG) met to discuss the role of company-level controls in audits, and auditor involvement in management's assessment process. This follows other attempts by the PCAOB to be flexible in the face of sector demands on some of the ambiguities of the Act. For more information on the PCAOB and the SAG, see www.pcaob.com.

CHAPTER 4

An Overview of the Act

INTRODUCTION

This section does not seek to replicate the text of the Act, which is widely available from a number of sources.[1] Nor does it intend to be a complete commentary on the history and development of the legislative process. It does, however, intend to emphasize those parts of the Act that are most relevant to the compliance effort. It also summarizes sections and indicates their "compliance scope." This references the individuals, functions, and types of organizations affected by the sections.

A first observation is that the Act does not exist independently of its circumstances; as such its intentions are set in a broader context. If there are any doubts that the Act was a reactive response to a set of circumstances peculiar to a period in US financial and social history, we need only consider its primary intention, best identified by the statement at the beginning of the text of the Act itself:

> To protect investors by improving the accuracy and reliability of corporate disclosures made pursuant to the securities laws, and for other purposes.

The founding principle is that the Act serves to further the interests of investors and those who support those interests, by placing a burden of transparency in financial practice on those organizations in which investors place their trust. This concept is central to the element of trust that underpins the financial services industry and on which markets rely to maintain liquidity. It is a principle that the SEC has sought to maintain and propagate since the Wall Street crash in the 1930s. This is the context in which the Act operates as a persuasive mechanism, and it carries a moral authority to insist on compliance. Without trust, the financial system itself is exposed to unpredictability on a scale that could be disastrous.

To understand the key points of the Act in terms of what it says and what it intends to achieve, we need to:

- examine the Act and comment on its main requirements
- establish who is affected by the Act, as organizations or individuals
- realize how it directly affects these individuals and organizations.

To understand the balance of requirements, we first consider the way the Act is structured.

STRUCTURE AND SECTIONS OF THE ACT

The structure of the Act divides the text into "sections" and "titles." The titles are then subdivided into further "sections." Table 4.1 highlights the most significant aspects of these sections. Once the contents, definitions and Commission (SEC) rules and enforcement references are established, the body of the Act follows in its "titles."

TITLES: QUICK SUMMARY

In all there are 11 titles, covering a range of topics, as outlined in Table 4.2. This summarizes the content of the title and provides a general description of the detail.

SECTIONS OF THE ACT

The outline of the Act in Table 4.2 provides a reference basis for exploring the Act in more detail. This is not a blow-by-blow account of the Act, but a thorough summary of the provisions most relevant to compliance, and the channeling of energies and resources to a practical end.

TITLE I: PUBLIC COMPANY ACCOUNTING OVERSIGHT BOARD

Section 101: Establishment; administrative provisions

The first of these sections, 101, sets out the composition of the Public Company Accounting Oversight Board (PCAOB). It must have five members, including two certified public accountants (CPAs). These members are appointed by the SEC with the approval of the Chairman of the Federal Reserve Board and the Secretary of the Treasury.

Section 102: Registration with the Board

The Act details the required professional status of those who deal with it,

Table 4.1 Sections of the Act

Section	Title	Overview
Sec. 1	Short title; table of contents.	This section notes that the Act has a short title, the "Sarbanes-Oxley Act of 2002." A popular shorthand is the near-acronym SOX. For our purposes SOX is used as a convenient short form.
Sec. 2	Definitions.	This section defines terms and concepts referenced in the body of the Act, including concepts such as audits, security, reports; legal entities such as persons, issuers; authorities and bodies such as states, the commission, accounting firms, the board, and its rules; and a range of other concepts such as securities laws and professional standards:
		• audit • exemption authority • audit committee • professional standards • audit report • public accounting firm • board • registered public accounting firm • commission • issuer • rules of the board • non-audit services • security • person • securities laws • associated with an public • state accounting firm • conforming amendment
Sec. 3	Commission rules and enforcement.	This section elaborates on the way the Act is to be interpreted for action. It heads this section with the significant regulatory action: The Commission shall promulgate such rules and regulations, as may be necessary or appropriate in the public interest or for the protection of investors, and in furtherance of this Act. The critical area of enforcement is addressed next. The Act notes that "in general:" A violation by any person of this Act, any rule or regulation of the Commission issued under this Act, or any rule of the Board shall be treated for all purposes in the same manner as a violation of the Securities Exchange Act of 1934 (15 U.S.C. 78a et seq.). This reinforces the common links and references to SEC laws and its authority over the Act and establishes the Act as an extension of existing regulation or law.

Table 4.2 Structure of the Act: titles and descriptions

Title	Description	Overview
Title I	Public Company Accounting Oversight Board	Sections 101–109. This title covers the creation and remit of the Public Company Accounting Oversight Board (PCAOB), already introduced in Section 2 (5) "The term 'Board' means the Public Company Accounting Oversight Board established under section 101." This body is central to any discussion on practical approaches to the Act since it has been the reference body for recommending the best practice models to adopt to ensure compliance.
Title II	Auditor independence	This details Sections 201–209, covering services outside the scope of practice of auditors. It covers the need to vary audit partners, avoid conflicts of interest in the choice of auditors through rotation, and the nature of auditor reports. It details conforming amendments to SEC legislation. The US-centric nature of the Act is highlighted by a reference to considerations for (US) State regulatory authorities.
Title III	Corporate responsibility	Sections 301–308 introduce key issues that generate a great deal of compliance activity. These include the role and function of audit committees under the Act; the central idea of corporate responsibility for financial reports (302). It mandates behavioral issues such as the conduct of audits, the use of bonuses and profits and senior executive constraints and penalties. It also deals with rules of responsibility for attorneys.
Title IV	Enhanced financial disclosures	Sections 401–409 focus on how information about the company is made public and the controls in place to ensure that information is accurate, fair and representative. This title also drives compliance activities since it focuses on disclosures in periodic reports, disclosures of transactions involving management and principal stockholders, and the critical step of management assessment of internal controls (404). Behavioral issues are again introduced through a requirement for a code of ethics for senior financial officers, and the expertise of the board. The SEC notes it will check on certain issuers with a regular and systematic review, and no affected company will be reviewed in this way 'less frequently than once every three years'. This title has, as its final Section (409), another significant requirement that generates compliance activity: that the organization will 'disclose to the public on a rapid and current basis' any additional information 'concerning material changes' in the financial status of the issuer.

Table 4.2 continued

Title	Description	Overview
Title V	Analyst conflicts of interest	The single section of this title, 501, mandates the treatment of securities analysts by registered securities associations and national securities exchanges. It outlines issues around conflicts of interest in the role of advising on as against advertising investments.
Title VI	Commission resources and authority	Sections 601–604, equip the Commission with sufficient funds and resources to pursue the interests of the Act. Much of this title amends sections of the Securities Exchange Act of 1934. It comments on the suitability and qualifications of those involved in auditing activities and of brokers.
Title VII	Studies and reports	Sections 701–705 state the need for studies that illuminate the factors that have led to the consolidation of public accounting firms since 1989, and the consequent reduction in the number of firms capable of providing audit services to large national and multi-national business organizations that are subject to the securities laws; a study of the role and function of credit rating agencies in the operation of the securities market; a study to determine the number of securities professionals found to have aided and abetted a violation of the Federal securities laws; a review and analysis of all enforcement actions involving violations of reporting requirements; and a study on whether investment banks and financial advisers assist public companies in manipulating their earnings and clouding their true financial condition.
Title VIII	Corporate and criminal fraud accountability	Sections 801–807 cover criminal penalties under the United States Code[2], for the destruction, alteration, or falsification of records in Federal investigations and bankruptcy, to include fines and imprisonment for "not more than 20 years," or both. A review of federal sentencing guidelines for obstruction of justice and criminal fraud and provisions to protect employees of publicly traded companies' staff who "whistleblow" on their companies by providing evidence of fraud. It also covers the introduction of criminal penalties for defrauding shareholders of publicly traded companies; these penalties being fines or imprisonment of "not more than 25 years, or both."

Table 4.2 continued

Title	Description	Overview
Title IX	White-collar crime penalty enhancements	Sections 901–906 on white-collar crime penalty enhancements refer mostly to the United States Code for attempts and conspiracies to commit criminal fraud offenses, for mail and wire fraud and violations of the Employee Retirement Income Security Act of 1974. A final section in this title focuses again on corporate responsibility for financial reports, and amends the US Code. The failure of corporate officers (the CEO and CFO) to certify periodic financial reports means the offenders "shall be fined not more than $1,000,000 or imprisoned not more than 10 years, or both." If they "willfully" certify any statement which does not match all the requirements of Section 906 they shall be fined "not more than $5,000,000, or imprisoned not more than 20 years, or both."
Title X	Corporate tax returns	Section 1001 simply states that the Federal income tax return of a corporation should be signed by the CEO.
Title XI	Corporate fraud and accountability	Sections 1101–1107 are mostly concerned with definitions and amendments to the US Code. These cover tampering with records or impeding an official proceeding, and the prohibition of individuals from serving as company officers or directors. One amendment is striking, in that it upgrades fines from $1,000,000, to $5,000,000, and $2,500,000 to $25,000,000. The imprisonment period is amended from not more than 10 years to 20 years. The biting edge of the Act is expressed in these sections. This title also reinforces the protection of informants against retaliation, by threatening perpetrators with fines "under this title or imprisoned not more than 10 years, or both."

including registration for these bodies and the appropriate fees (a registration fee and an annual fee), and funding for the operational existence of the Board itself. To maintain itself the Board can also establish an annual accounting support fee, funded by issuers such as the public companies audited.

Section 103: Auditing, quality control, and independence standards and rules

The PCAOB defines and maintain controls and standards for the auditing

Section 102 compliance table

Description	Compliance scope
The Act requires that a public accounting firm register with the Board if it is to engage in auditing activities with a company (issuer) covered by the Act.	Auditors

process critical to the perception of transparency in financial reporting. The Board has the responsibility of instituting "auditing, quality control, ethics, independence, and other standards relating to the preparation of audit reports for issuers."

Although this ensures that accountants meet their obligations under the Act, the creators of the Act have built in obligations to respond to feedback from the market under regulation. To manage an overall standard of quality control for the auditing process, the Board insists on an audit standard that matches that required by Section 404(b). This reinforces the importance for public companies to use a framework for internal controls that is either an adoption of, or a closely modeled alternative to, that of COSO.

Section 103 compliance table

Description	Compliance scope
The Board can carry out inspections of accounting firms and impose disciplinary measures and penalties.	Auditors
Public accounting firms are expected to include in their documents and records management the maintenance of auditing records "for a period of not less than 7 years."	Auditors
The Board is expected to cooperate with professional and advisory groups for standards setting. It can adopt existing or new standards and take them as models for modification if necessary and report on this annually to the Commission (SEC).	The PCAOB
The Board requires a partner review for approval of audit reports.	Auditors

Section 104: Inspections of registered public accounting firms

This section determines the frequency of the controlling quality reviews. Auditors should prepare accordingly, however they are affected.

Section 104 compliance table

Description	Compliance scope
Auditors that report on more than 100 companies are inspected annually, others are inspected every three years.	Auditors

Section 105: Investigations and disciplinary proceedings

In maintaining the confidentiality, security and protection of Board activities, this section deals with the use of information gathered by the PCAOB in its activities. Hearings on disciplinary action will not be made public unless there is a pressing need to do so, and the use of penalties is defined where quality controls and standards fail.

Section 105 compliance table

Description	Compliance scope
All the documentation received by the Board will be "confidential and privileged" although it can be made available to the SEC and, under US jurisdiction, federal and state agencies.	PCAOB

Section 106: Foreign public accounting firms.

The Act recognizes the use of foreign accounting firms. These may not have direct representation or interests in the United States. Section 106 (d) rules on a "foreign public accounting firm," which is "a public accounting firm that is organized and operates under the laws of a foreign government or political subdivision thereof."

Section 106 compliance table

Description	Compliance scope
If the accounting firm audits a US company it has to register with the Board.	Non-US auditors
Foreign accounting firms that carry out any audit work for a US related company, such as a foreign subsidiary of that company, that provides input to the financial reporting of the US listed company and which is included in the reporting interests of a US auditing firm.	Non-US auditors

Section 107: Commission oversight of the Board

This section is important in that it once again asserts the importance of the relationship between the Act and the SEC, and its historic legislation. The Act states that:

> The Commission shall have oversight and enforcement authority over the Board, as provided in this Act. The provisions of section 17(a)(1) of the Securities Exchange Act of 1934 ... and of section 17(b)(1) of the Securities Exchange Act of 1934 ... shall apply to the Board as fully as if the Board were a "registered securities association" for purposes of those sections 17(a)(1) and 17(b)(1).

The relationship is alluded to time and again, emphasizing that the Act operates in a pre-existing legal context. The actions of the PCAOB can be challenged and changed by the SEC, which can scrutinize its findings and penalties.

Section 107 compliance table

Description	Compliance scope
The Act's oversight body is responsible to the SEC for enforcing and establishing an operational basis for the successful application of the Act.	PCAOB
When it imposes sanctions the Board must notify the SEC of its actions.	PCAOB

Section 108: Accounting standards

The standards that are to be observed by accounting bodies engaged in this auditing process are to be those of industry best practice.

Section 108 compliance table

Description	Compliance scope
The Board is to use accounting standards recognized by the SEC as "generally accepted" within the industry.	PCAOB

Section 109: Funding

This section deals with PCAOB administration of budgets, including annual budgeting, sources of funds, their use, recoverable items of budgetary expenditure, general fundraising, and allowable fees for activities relating to the Act.

TITLE II: AUDITOR INDEPENDENCE

Auditing is one of the key functions covered in detail by the Act. It is the activity that, in the eyes of investors, protects their interests; it assures them that the company cannot hide financial figures or massage results to suit its interests. It is not surprising then that the Act lays great store by the perceived and actual independence of the auditing arm. The whole of Title II is dedicated to this important topic.

Section 201: Services outside the scope of practice of auditors; prohibited activities

An auditing firm must to be seen to be independent and neutral in its dealings with a company. It cannot simultaneously provide auditing services and other services to the same public company. Performing or assisting in internal audit services is a particular issue. Major consultancies have built a bread-and-butter business off the back of outsourced work on internal audit projects, and acted as external auditors. The separation of these functions has had a big impact on the way such consultancies operate, leading to internal reorganization to meet the demands of the Act. The PCAOB leaves this area open to further refinement, although it does indicate that it can amend the strictures of this section on a case-by-case basis, with the flexibility to exempt individuals as well as organizations. This area of the Act is expected to evolve. Overall, those auditing firms that need to provide services that conflict with the Act under these provisions can petition the client's audit committee for permission to perform "non-audit services." The pre-approval process is defined in this and the following sections.

Section 202: Pre-approval requirements

The Act allows a registered public accounting firm to "engage in any non-audit service, including tax services," that is not listed previously if the function is "pre-approved" by the audit committee of the issuer. The Act includes waivers.

Section 203: Audit partner rotation

To further the separation of responsibilities that can lead to inappropriate

Section 201 compliance table

Description	Compliance scope
A public accounting firm cannot simultaneously provide auditing and other services to the same public company. Such "prohibited activities," or kinds of activities, would constitute such a breach. They include: • bookkeeping or operational accounting activities • designing and implementing information systems for financial operations • valuation or assessment of financial options and actuarial services • performing or assisting in internal audit services. Other prohibited parallel activities include: • performing management activities and functions on behalf of the client company • providing broker, dealer, legal and investment services.	Auditors

Section 202 compliance table

Description	Compliance scope
A registered public accounting firm may "engage in any non-audit service, including tax services," that is not listed previously (in Section 201) if the function is "pre-approved" by the audit committee of the issuer. This requirement is waived if "the aggregate amount of all such non-audit services provided to the issuer" is less than 5 percent of the total amount of revenues from that issuer in any fiscal year, the services were "not recognized" by the client company as non-audit services at the time of engagement, or were approved "prior to completion of the audit."	Auditors

behavior, the Act forbids whoever acts as the lead audit partner, or the part-ner who reviews the audit, from having been involved in this way in audits for a client in any of the five previous fiscal years.

Section 204: Auditor reports to audit committees

This Section amends the SEC 1934 Act, Section 10A, placing responsibility on the auditing firm to disclose practices in the relationship between client and auditor.

Section 203 compliance table

Description	Compliance scope
The "lead (or co-coordinating) audit partner" or the audit partner responsible for reviewing the audit, is barred if involved in audits for the client in any of the five previous fiscal years.	Auditors

Section 204 compliance table

Description	Compliance scope
The auditor has to report to the audit committee of the client all "critical accounting policies and practices to be used" and "all alternative treatments of financial information."	Auditors

Section 205: Conforming amendments

This section provides some definitions, relating to the issuer audit committee and "registered public accounting firm," of items previously defined in Section 2 of the Act. It also details a number of amendments to the SEC 1934 Act, Section 10A.

Section 205 compliance table

Description	Compliance scope
Definitions that supplement those of section 2.	Auditors Audit committee

Section 206: Conflicts of interest

Section 206 protects transparency by furthering the separation of responsibilities for senior executives in their relationship with auditing firms.

Section 206 compliance table

Description	Compliance scope
A senior officer of an (issuer) client cannot have been employed by the client's audit firm during the year proceeding the audit.	Senior executives (issuer)

Section 207: Study of mandatory rotation of registered public accountants

The US Comptroller General is obliged to carry out a study on the effects of the mandatory rotation of audit firms and must submit a report to the Committee (PCAOB) within a year of the passing of the Act. The definition of "mandatory rotation" concerns the limit on the period, in years, in which a particular registered public accounting firm may be the auditor for an issuer.

Section 207 compliance table

Description	Compliance scope
The US Comptroller General is obliged to carry out a study on the effects of the mandatory rotation of audit firms.	US Comptroller General, PCAOB

Section 208: Commission authority

This short section addresses Commission regulations relating to the implementation of changes to the SEC 1934 Act, Section 10A. It also tightens the provisions covered in the preceding sections by applying the need for auditor independence found in the SEC 1934 Act, section 10A.

Section 208 compliance table

Description	Compliance scope
Auditor independence—It shall be unlawful for any registered public accounting firm, or associated individual, to prepare or issue an audit report if they have engaged in a prohibited activity under subsections (g) through (l) of section 10A of the Securities Exchange Act of 1934.	Auditors

Section 209: Consideration by appropriate State regulatory authorities

In a clear US-centric directive, US State regulators are to make up their own minds whether the PCAOB standards are to be applied to small and mid-size non-registered accounting firms.

Section 209 compliance table

Description	Compliance scope
This section notes that the standards applied under this Act should not be presumed to be applicable for small and medium sized non-registered public accounting firms.	US States

TITLE III: CORPORATE RESPONSIBILITY

A central belief behind the Act is that corporate behavior in general is perceived to be poorly regulated. The atmosphere in which the Act was passed meant that assumptions about weaknesses in corporate behavior were damaging not only to the companies involved and the securities markets in which they operated, but to the confidence of the population in general in their economy. The emphasis on corporate responsibility, then, elevates the importance of this title. Consequently the sections of this title are the primary focus of discussions on the real implications of the Act.

Section 301: Public company audit committees

The audit committee of the public company is a key entity in the process of making financial reporting open and transparent. This section ensures that this committee will be "independent" and drawn from, and responsible to, the board of directors. It makes clear that the issuer should properly fund the operation of the audit committee, and goes on to list the responsibilities of the audit committee in relation to auditing under the terms of the Act.

Section 302: Corporate responsibility for financial reports

This section marks a major focal point for developing compliance responses. It addresses the responsibilities of executives in public companies in providing financial reports. These reports are the most "visible" manifestations of corporate activity, and provide key information for investors. This is one of the key sections that emphasize the importance of board-level involvement in compliance processes because of the direct accountability directors bear. The conditions in this section are evaluated quarterly.

Section 301 compliance table

Description	Compliance scope
National securities exchanges and national securities associations are not to list the securities of issuers not complying with paragraphs (2) through (6) of this Section. The SEC has to provide "appropriate procedures" for such issuers to help them address any issues that result on non-listing in this way.	SEC, National Securities Exchanges and National Securities Associations [x301]
The issuer audit committee, as a committee of the board of directors, is responsible for appointing, paying, and managing external auditors; the auditors must report directly to the audit committee.	Audit committee (issuer)
The audit committee must establish procedures for managing (receiving, retaining, and treating) complaints "regarding accounting, internal accounting controls, or auditing matters"; as well "confidential, anonymous submission" of concerns on "questionable accounting or auditing matters".	Audit committee (issuer)
Appropriate funding must be arranged to cover auditor and external advisor costs.	Audit committee (issuer)

Section 302 compliance table

Description	Compliance scope
The Section mandates that the "principal executive officer or officers and the principal financial officer or officers, or persons performing similar functions" certify in periodic reports that they have reviewed the report. 302 (a) (1).	Executive officers (CEO and CFO) (issuer)
The report must not contain any "untrue statement of a material fact or omit to state a material fact" which is "misleading". 302 (a)(2).	Executive officers (CEO and CFO) (issuer)
The financial statements, along with financial information included in the report, "fairly present in all material respects" the financial status of the issuer for the period of the report. 302 (a)(3)	Executive officers (CEO and CFO) (issuer)

Section 302 compliance table continued

Description	Compliance scope
The signing officers are held responsible for "establishing and maintaining" internal controls. 302(a)(4)(A).	Executive officers (CEO and CFO) (issuer)
The signers must ensure they have designed internal controls to ensure that the company and its subsidiaries provide suitable "material information." 302(a)(4)(B).	Executive officers (CEO and CFO) (issuer)
The signers must have "evaluated the effectiveness of the issuer's internal controls 90 days prior to the report." Section 302(a)(4)(C). They must also include their "conclusions about the effectiveness of their internal controls" based on their evaluation. Section 302(a)(4)(D). *This responsibility links to Section 404, "Management assessment of internal controls."*	Executive officers (CEO and CFO) (issuer)
There is also a requirement to disclose to auditors and the audit committee, all "significant deficiencies" in the design or operation of internal controls. This is especially so if these deficiencies could affect the issuer's ability to record, process, summarize, and report financial data. They must also identify to the auditors any "material weaknesses" in these controls. 302(a)(5)(A).	Executive officers (CEO and CFO) (issuer)
Similarly, they disclose any fraud, "whether or not material", that involves management or other employees who have a significant role in the issuer's internal controls. Section 302(a)(5)(B).	Executive officers (CEO and CFO) (issuer) Staff involved in internal control compliance
The signing officers must also detail any important changes to internal controls or highlight factors related to internal controls that could affect them after the evaluation has taken place. They should provide information on how such "significant deficiencies" and "material weaknesses" have been treated. Section 302(a)(6).	Executive officers (CEO and CFO) (issuer)
This Section reinforces the comprehensive international scope of the Act. "Foreign re-incorporations have no effect". The requirements of the Act cannot be avoided by moving the corporate HQ, typically to a country external to US legislation. 302(b).	Affected foreign companies

Section 303: Improper influence on conduct of audits

The Act makes it illegal for anyone to coerce, influence, or manipulate an auditor, which by inference protects the auditor. It does raise the issue of controls and oversight within the auditor firm to avoid such potential vulnerabilities.

Section 303 compliance table

Description	Compliance scope
Auditors and accountants undertaking audits are protected from "any action to fraudulently influence, coerce, manipulate, or mislead."	Officer or director, or any other person acting under their direction (issuer)

Section 304: Forfeiture of certain bonuses and profits

This Section establishes a requirement for the reimbursement of funds within an issuer, and addresses the public issue of how misconduct by senior executives affects their remuneration from the companies they have either fraudulently deceived or fraudulently manipulated.

Section 304 compliance table

Description	Compliance scope
In the circumstances when an affected company has to issue an "accounting restatement due to the material noncompliance of the issuer," which results from financial reporting misconduct of some kind, the chief executive officer and chief financial officer of the issuer shall reimburse the company for any bonus or other incentive or equity-based compensation they received; and profits they may have realized from the sale of securities during that 12-month period. The SEC can exempt individuals in certain circumstances.	CEO, CFO (issuer)

Section 305: Officer and director bars and penalties

This section is a series of amendments to increase the point at which the degree of "fitness" of those appointed as officers is acceptable. The wording replaces "substantial unfitness" by "unfitness."

Section 306: Insider trades during pension fund black-out periods

This section is one of the largest, and provides considerable detail on its subject. It is divided into a number of sub-sections that deal with black-out periods and the trade of equities by senior executives and directors:

- Generally it is unlawful for a director or executive officer to trade equity securities of the issuer, other than an exempted security, during a black-out period if the equity was acquired in connection with service or employment as a director or executive officer.
- Any profit realized in violation of this sub-section can be recovered by the issuer.
- The Commission (SEC) shall issue rules to clarify the application of this sub-section, noting exemptions under the Internal Revenue Code (1986) and other circumstances. These circumstances are specified.
- The term "black-out period" means any period of more than three consecutive business days during which not less than 50 percent of the equity is temporarily suspended, and excludes a regularly scheduled period in which the participants and beneficiaries may not trade in equities.
- The term "individual account plan" has the meaning provided in section 3(34) of the Employee Retirement Income Security Act of 1974.
- When a director or executive officer is subject to these requirements in connection with a black-out period, the issuer must notify the director or officer and the SEC of the black-out period.

Further details outline obligations under individual accounts plans and other plans, and the content of notices on the black-out period. The section includes penalties for plan administrators, and plan amendments. The provisions of this section, including its amendments, take effect 180 days after the date of the enactment of the Act. The section talks of "good faith compliance," which in anticipation of further actual requirement details shall be treated as compliance.

Section 306 compliance table

Description	Compliance scope
This prohibits the purchase or sale of stock by officers and directors and other insiders during blackout periods. When this applies it must be notified to the SEC.	Executive officers, directors (issuer), and the Commission (SEC)

Section 307: Rules of professional responsibility for attorneys

This section establishes the requirement for the Commission to draw up effective guidelines for attorneys and legal representatives in reporting non-compliances. The emphasis is on "reporting up" through the organization, to the audit committee or to the board. The generality of this reporting has caused concerns that this might encourage a tendency to report everything, or "over-report" to cover the legal entity from later investigation and penalty. This presents company officers with everyday dilemmas. How does a legal officer report inaction by the board of directors once it has been alerted to non-compliance? At what point should he or she change from reporting up to reporting out to external regulators? The wording also involves the CEO, the audit committee, and the board in a chain of responsibility for making known a material violation, or failing this becoming non-compliant.

Section 307 compliance table

Description	Compliance scope
The Commission must publicize rules covering the expected standards of professional conduct for attorneys. An attorney must report evidence of a material violation of securities law or a breach of fiduciary duty to the chief legal counsel or the chief executive officer of the company or equivalent. If there is no appropriate response, then the attorney must report this to the audit committee or to the board of directors.	SEC, CEO, audit committee, board, legal staff (issuer)

Section 308: Fair funds for investors

This section addresses the way "disgorgement funds" are handled. It lays the foundation for funds won in pursuit of relevant SEC 1934 breaches to be used for the "benefit of the victims of such violations."

TITLE IV: ENHANCED FINANCIAL DISCLOSURES

The central role of financial disclosure in establishing credibility and transparency for the operations of a public company ensures that the Act gives it some attention. Title IV has several significant sections that consider the integrity of financial disclosures through reporting, and mandate how best to adapt the organization to meet its challenges.

Section 401: Disclosures in periodic reports

Section 401 focuses on "material correcting adjustments" identified by the registered accounting firm, which should be included in a financial report. The reports are now not just simple statements of a financial position but periodic statements of anything that can affect the operation, and therefore the likely profitability, of the organization. This is a specific investor-centric provision. These reports should disclose "all material off-balance sheet transactions" which can have a "material current or future effect on the financial condition of the issuer." The SEC mandates that pro forma financial information must be presented so as not to "contain an untrue statement." After outlining the disclosures required, it emphasizes that information should be comprehensive, provided where necessary, and accurate.

The SEC is required to study and draw up a report on the state of off-balance sheet transactions included in company reports so as to make recommendations for "improving the transparency and quality of reporting off-balance sheet transactions in the financial statements and disclosures required to be filed by an issuer with the Commission."

Section 401 compliance table

Description	Compliance scope
The SEC is to investigate and make recommendations on the comprehensive nature of company periodic reports; especially studying the way off-balance sheet transactions are included.	SEC

Section 402: Enhanced conflict of interest provisions

Abuse of the privileged position of senior executive status by misusing company funds was at the heart of the corporate scandals that formed the background to the Act. In keeping with this sensitivity about financial misuse by those involved with the production or approval of financial reports, this section addresses the extending of credit to any director or executive officer, loans for senior executives, and "prohibition on personal loans to directors."

Section 402 compliance table

Description	Compliance scope
An issuer (as defined under the Act), cannot arrange, extend, or maintain credit as a personal loan for a director or executive officer, bar some exemptions.	Senior executives (issuer)

Section 403: Disclosures of transactions involving management and principal stockholders

This section further amends the SEC 1934 Act, and rules on disclosures of stock transactions by directors, officers, and any owner holding a greater than 10 percent interest in a public company. It also sets the timing for these disclosures.

Section 403 compliance table

Description	Compliance scope
Directors, officers, and principal stockholders who are the beneficial owners of more than 10 percent of any class of any equity security must file this holding with the Commission and, if necessary, with an exchange. These statements are to be filed electronically and made public on a corporate website.	Senior executives, issuer stockholders

Section 404: Management assessment of internal controls

Section 404 is a key section shaping the way the Act is perceived. It is a driver for the way the financial industry is responding to compliance with the Act, greatly influencing the way compliance projects are being introduced and financed.

The principle is that management has to provide assurance, in the annual report, that the company's system of generating information for the financial report is adequately monitored through a system of internal controls.

This assessment is examined by the auditors who prepare the annual report, and they must "attest to, and report on" this assessment. The rules and guidelines that govern this process are to be provided by the PCAOB. The conditions of this section are evaluated quarterly, with an annual internal control report.

Section 404 compliance table

Description	Compliance scope
This section tasks the SEC with prescribing rules for annual reports to include an "internal control report." Management is responsible for "establishing and maintaining" an "adequate" internal control structure" and "procedures for financial reporting." The report must include "an assessment" of the "effectiveness" of the "internal control structure and procedures of the issuer for financial reporting." For "internal control evaluation and reporting," the registered public accounting firm that prepares or issues the audit report for the issuer must "attest to, and report on," the internal control assessment made by the management of the issuer. This attestation is subject to the standards for attestation engagements issued or adopted by the Board.	SEC, PCAOB, management (issuer)

Section 405: Exemption

This section exempts companies registered under Section 8, Registration of Investment Companies, of the Investment Company Act of 1940 from Sections 401, 402, and 404.

Section 406: Code of ethics for senior financial officers

The Act is necessarily part of a larger legislative and regulatory picture covered by the concept of corporate governance. Assumptions about governance relate to behavior and actions based on an ethical framework. This section points up the need for a formal declaration of ethical standards, for the financial function to address "ethical" issues, and brings the substance of the Act back to the larger context of corporate misdemeanor and "bad" behavior.

Section 406 compliance table

Description	Compliance scope
Each issuer must disclose whether or not, and if not, the reason, it has adopted a code of ethics for senior financial officers. Code of ethics means standards necessary to promote honest and ethical conduct, full, fair, accurate, timely, and understandable disclosure in the periodic reports and compliance with applicable governmental rules and regulations.	CFO and senior financial staff (issuer), SEC

Section 407: Disclosure of audit committee financial expert

The Act obliges the SEC to issue rules to ensure at least one member of the company audit committee is a "financial expert," as defined by the Commission. This is a move deemed "appropriate in the public interest and consistent with the protection of investors."

Section 407 compliance table

Description	Compliance scope
An issuer has to disclose whether or not its audit committee has at least one member who is a financial expert, and if not, the reasons. A financial expert is defined as a person with experience as a public accountant or auditor, or a principal financial officer, comptroller, or principal accounting officer of an issuer. The section also expects experience with internal accounting controls; and an understanding of audit committee functions.	Audit committee, SEC

Section 408: Enhanced review of periodic disclosures by issuers

Further, the Act obliges the SEC to review, on a periodic basis, the reports of certain affected companies, the criteria for these companies being detailed in this section.

Section 408 compliance table

Description	Compliance scope
The SEC must conduct regular and systematic reviews of financial reports (including 10-K) "for the protection of investors." The reviews must consider issuers that have issued material restatements of financial results, volatility in their stock price compared with other issuers, large market capitalization, disparities in price to earning ratios, issues that affect any material sector of the economy, and other relevant factors. They are not to be reviewed less frequently than once every three years.	SEC

Section 409: Real-time issuer disclosures

Although it is one of the shortest sections of the Act, 409 does carry some weight when considering practical compliance. In fact it may present the greatest challenge of all, depending on the compliance maturity of the organization, and there is a longer-term raft of projects based on its requirements. It is an amendment to the Securities Exchange Act, 1934, Section 13 (Periodical and Other Reports), adding a sub-section (l).

The key concept here is "real time." The ability to respond to the earlier sections on a periodic basis, either quarterly or annually, is perfectly achievable, even for poorly automated systems. However, this section moves into new territory, and mandates the company to produce ad hoc reports on issues that affect or potentially affect the financial health of the company. This is far more of a challenge.

Section 409 compliance table

Description	Compliance scope
The affected company, or issuer, must disclose to the public "on a rapid and current basis" any extra information about "material changes" in the financial condition or operations of the company. This must be "in plain English." The information may include trend and qualitative information and graphic presentations.	Affected company (issuer)

The remaining titles of the Act address issues that are common to many regulatory instruments. They look at conflicts of interest for analysts engaged in the securities markets, determine how information sources such as studies and reports are created and used, and outline the role and authority of the SEC, and its resources in relation to the Act. They also focus on the punitive considerations and measures necessary for the enforcement of the Act, and the general terms of corporate accountability over fraud and tax issues in so far as they are affected by the Act.

For the purposes of this book, those titles will be discussed that have value for the general discussion, and there is not an exhaustive review of all items.

TITLE V: ANALYST CONFLICTS OF INTEREST

Section 501: Treatment of securities analysts by registered securities associations and national securities exchanges

Through the rules in this section, the SEC, a registered securities association, or national securities exchange, must adopt rules that address conflicts of interest that arise when securities analysts recommend equity securities in research reports and public statements. The section mandates protection of securities analysts, and separation of activities to ensure their protection from pressure in pursuit of their professional judgments within a firm. It discourages "retaliation" against securities analysts who might produce adverse reports that could affect the relationship of a broker or dealer with an issuer. It covers periods when brokers or dealers who have participated, or are to participate, in a public offering should not publish or distribute research reports on such securities. A "securities analyst" is defined as any person working for a registered broker or dealer who prepares a research report, regardless of his or her actual job title.

Section 501 compliance table

Description	Compliance scope
This section seeks to establish safeguards within brokers or dealers to assure that securities analysts are separated by "informational partitions" within the firm from the "review, pressure, or oversight" of those who might potentially bias their judgment. It discourages "retaliation" against securities analysts. It looks for a disclosure of conflicts of interest in securities analysts' reports.	Registered securities associations

TITLE VI: COMMISSION RESOURCES AND AUTHORITY

Section 601: Authorization of appropriations

This covers amendments to the Securities Exchange Act of 1934 regarding funds authorized to be appropriated to the Commission.

Section 602: Appearance and practice before the Commission

This section addresses qualifications for those appearing before the Commission, to reinforce the requirement for quality in conduct and competence.

Section 603: Federal court authority to impose penny stock bars

This Section covers amendments to the Act of 1934 regarding penny stocks.

Section 604: Qualifications of associated persons of brokers and dealers

This section introduces amendments and conforming amendments to the Securities Exchange Act of 1934 and Investment Advisers Act of 1940, on those involved as brokers, dealers, and investment advisers.

TITLE VII: STUDIES AND REPORTS

Section 701: GAO study and report regarding consolidation of public accounting firms

This Section requires the Comptroller General to identify the reasons leading to the consolidation of public accounting firms since 1989, and the consequent reduction in the number of firms capable of providing audit services to large national and multi-national business organizations that are subject to the securities laws.

The impact of this situation is the chief concern, and the Act is initiating efforts to find solutions to increase competition and the number of firms capable of providing audit services to large national and multi-national business organizations. Unusually, the Act specifies some of the impacts, such as a decrease in competition among public accounting firms; higher costs, a lower quality of delivered services, a reduction in auditor independence, and considerations of the likely impact of Federal or State regulations on competition among public accounting firms.

Section 702: Commission study and report regarding credit rating agencies

The Act requires the Commission to study the role and function of credit rating agencies in the operation of the securities market, including its activities in evaluating issuers, its significance for investors, its assessments of risk, and issues surrounding becoming a credit rating agency.

Section 703: Study and report on violators and violations

As part of the ongoing investigative remit of the Act, the SEC is tasked with generating a study of "securities professionals," such as accounting firms and their staff, investment bankers, investment advisors, brokers, legal representatives, and dealers, who have been found to have "aided and abetted a violation of Federal securities laws." This indicates the active dimension to the Act, in keeping with its "securities laws with teeth" approach.

TITLE VIII: CORPORATE AND CRIMINAL FRAUD ACCOUNTABILITY

Section 801: Short title

This Section simply establishes a short title: the Corporate and Criminal Fraud Accountability Act of 2002.

Section 802: Criminal penalties for altering documents

Section, 802 along with sections 302, 404, and 409, can be said to be on the critical shortlist of those most read by interested companies, consultancies, and solutions vendors. Much of this refers to the US Code, and amendments to it. The significance of this section is that any document or record that is relevant to a federal investigation or a commission investigation based on non-compliance to the Act must be made available. For it to be destroyed "knowingly" with the intention to obstruct or impede an investigation is regarded as a felony. A miscreant can be fined under this title, imprisoned for not more than 20 years, or both. Further, audit work papers have to be maintained for a period of five years from creation.

Most significantly from a compliance perspective, the nature of documentation and records is expanded to include:

- memoranda
- correspondence
- communications
- electronic records.

In fact it includes anything that is created, sent, or received in connection with an audit or review and carries "conclusions, opinions, analyses, or financial data" relevant to the audit or review.

With this potential cache of data the sources of information have increased, and so has the job of ensuring all relevant data is captured and made available. Title XI, Section 1102 revisits this issue.

Section 802 compliance table

Description	Compliance scope
This section highlights the value the SEC places on its sources of information. In Federal investigations those who deliberately alter, destroy, change, conceal, or falsify, any "record, document, or tangible object" with the intent to "impede, obstruct, or influence" the investigation can be fined, imprisoned for up to 20 years, or both.	Staff of company under investigation (issuers)
All audit records and review work papers must be retained or for at least five years from the end of the fiscal period in which the audit or review was concluded.	Auditors
The SEC must expand the rules and regulations relating to the retention of relevant records that form the basis of an audit or review.	Auditors, SEC
Wilful violation of any rule or regulation under this section will lead to fines and up to ten years imprisonment, or both.	Affected company staff (issuer), auditors, SEC

Section 803: Debts nondischargeable if incurred in violation of securities fraud laws

This Section consists of amendments to the US Code.

Section 804: Statute of limitations for securities fraud

This Section consists of amendments to the US Code.

Section 805: Review of federal sentencing guidelines for obstruction of justice and extensive criminal fraud

This section aligns the Act with the US Code.

Section 806: Protection for employees of publicly traded companies who provide evidence of fraud

As well as amending the US Code, this section introduces whistleblower protection for employees of publicly traded companies. This section attempts to reinforce the data available to it by engaging as many sources of information as possible to reach non-compliances, misdemeanor, and company fraud. One such source is the employee who "whistleblows" on wrongdoing but needs protection in order to be able to disclose the information.

Section 806 compliance table

Description	Compliance scope
No company, company officer, employee, contractor, subcontractor, or agent may "discharge, demote, suspend, threaten, harass, or in any other manner discriminate against" an employee because of a lawful act done by the employee in assisting an investigation.	Affected company, its officers and employees (issuer)
The employee can pursue his or her defense through the courts for damages, reinstatement, back pay and compensation, including litigation costs, expert witness fees, and reasonable attorney fees.	

Section 807: Criminal penalties for defrauding shareholders of publicly traded companies

The importance of securities frauds in the run-up to the introduction of the Act is highlighted by this section, which strengthens the penalties available for anyone who "knowingly executes, or attempts to … defraud any person in connection with any security of an issuer." It also includes anyone who tries to "obtain, by means of false or fraudulent pretenses, representations, or promises, any money or property in connection with the purchase or sale of any security of an issuer." Such a person can be fined under this title, or imprisoned for up to 25 years, or both. The penalty for this fraudulent activity is marginally greater than the other draconian penalties under the Act. Generally there are only a few individuals within an organization who can successfully manage such a fraud, and these are senior executives.

Section 807 compliance table

Description	Compliance scope
Anyone committing fraud related to securities can be fined, or imprisoned for up to 25 years, or both.	Chief executives; company staff

TITLE IX: WHITE-COLLAR CRIME PENALTY ENHANCEMENTS

Section 901: Short title

This section states that it may be referred to as the White-Collar Crime Penalty Enhancement Act 2002.

Sections 902 (Attempts and conspiracies to commit criminal fraud offences) and 903 (Criminal penalties for mail and wire fraud) consist of amendments to the US Code.

Section 904: Criminal penalties for violations of the employee retirement income security act of 1974

This Section amends the Employee Retirement Income Security Act of 1974 by increasing a range of fines and lengths of imprisonment.

Section 905: Amendment to sentencing guidelines relating to certain white-collar offences

This section directs the US Sentencing Commission authorized under the US Code, to ensure that its approaches to sentencing "reflect the serious nature of the offenses and the penalties set forth in this Act." It notes the increase in serious fraud offenses discussed, and the requirement to modify sentencing "to deter, prevent, and punish such offenses." It suggests that "guidelines and policy statements" should be examined so that they match the severity of sentencing suggested by the changes made in the Act, and generally be consistent with other directives and sentencing policies.

Section 906: Corporate responsibility for financial reports

Financial statements filed with the SEC must be certified by the CEO and CFO. This section stipulates penalties for officers who certify and submit financial reports to the SEC that do not conform to that standards set, or do not fairly present in all material aspects the financial conditions and results of operations of the issuer. These are subject to a fine of not more than $1 million, imprisonment for not more than ten years, or both. If the officer, however, "willfully" certifies the same, the penalty climbs to a fine of $5 million, imprisonment for not more than 20 years, or both.

This section captures the interest of senior executives more than any other, because of its specific penalties and the nature of them. The inclusion of "willfully" appears to distinguish one penalty from another. How this is decided in practice is not yet clear. Like much legislation it will be clarified through case law. The conditions of this section are evaluated quarterly.

Section 906 compliance table

Description	Compliance scope
The filed periodic report must include a written state-ment by the chief executive officer and chief financial offi-cer of the issuer, that the report fully complies with the requirements of the Securities Exchange Act of 1934 (sections 13(a) or 15(d)) and that it fairly presents, in all material respects, the financial condition of the issuer.	CEO, CFO (issuer)
This section states that knowingly signing the report when it does not comply with all the requirements of this section means a fine of up to $1,000,000, or imprisonment for up to ten years, or both. If the signer "willfully certifies" the statement, knowing it does not comply, then he or she can be fined up to $5,000,000, or imprisoned for up to 20 years, or both.	CEO, CFO (issuer)

TITLE X: CORPORATE TAX RETURNS

Section 1001: Sense of the Senate regarding the signing of corporate tax returns by chief executive officers

The sole section in this title simply states that the tax return for a corpora-tion should be signed by the chief executive. The brevity of this section implies that tax is a well understood issue. Again the Act ties the signature to corporate responsibilities under law.

Section 1001 compliance table

Description	Compliance scope
The federal income tax return of a corporation should be signed by the chief executive officer.	CEO (issuer)

TITLE XI: CORPORATE FRAUD ACCOUNTABILITY

Section 1101: Short title

This section states that this title may be referred to as the Corporate Fraud Accountability Act of 2002.

Section 1102: Tampering with a record or otherwise impeding an official proceeding

A significant penalty clause is added as an amendment to the US Code. It reinforces earlier sections by strengthening punishments for tampering with evidence in the context of corporate fraud investigations. It again underlines the importance of documents as evidence. The section implies guilt by referring to whoever "corruptly" tampers with evidence, as opposed to accidentally or unintentionally altering (and so on) such evidence.

Section 1102 compliance table

Description	Compliance scope
Whoever intending to reduce the value of or make unavailable by altering, destroying, mutilating, or concealing "a record, document, or other object"; or obstructing an official proceeding, can be fined, or imprisoned for up to 20 years, or both.	Company staff (issuer)

Section 1103: Temporary freeze authority for the Securities and Exchange Commission

This section enables the Commission to gain a temporary order if, "during the course of a lawful investigation" of an issuer of publicly traded securities "or any of its directors, officers, partners, controlling persons, agents, or employees," it looks as if the issuer will make "extraordinary payments (whether compensation or otherwise)" to any of these people. The Commission will look to have the payment(s) escrowed. The recommended conditions of this order are detailed.

Section 1104: Amendment to the Federal sentencing guidelines.

This section prompts for the US Sentencing Commission to review sentencing guidelines applicable to securities and accounting fraud and related offenses; consider new sentencing guidelines for officers or directors of publicly traded corporations who commit fraud and related offenses; and submit to the US Congress an explanation of its actions and recommendations. This sentencing is to "reflect the serious nature of securities, pension, and accounting fraud and the need for aggressive and appropriate law enforcement action to prevent such offenses."

Section 1104 compliance table

Description	Compliance scope
The US Sentencing Commission is requested to review its sentencing policies and revise them in line with the Act, especially for officers of issuers who commit fraud and related offenses.	CEO, CFO, and senior executives (issuer)

Section 1105: Authority of the Commission to prohibit persons from serving as officers or directors

This section prohibits "any person who has violated section 10(b) or the rules or regulations" from acting as director or senior executive of an issuer, if the person is seen to be unfit to serve as an officer or director. This is made within the context of references and amendments to the Securities Exchange Act of 1934, and the Securities Act of 1933.

Section 1105 compliance table

Description	Compliance scope
The Commission has the ability to bar from executive office, anyone not seen to be fit to hold that office.	CEO, CFO, and senior executives (issuer)

Section 1106: Increased criminal penalties under Securities Exchange Act of 1934

The Securities Exchange Act of 1934 is amended to show revised figures for penalties under the Act so that "$1,000,000, or imprisoned not more than 10 years" becomes "$5,000,000, or imprisoned not more than 20 years"; and "$2,500,000" becomes "$25,000,000."

Section 1107: Retaliation against informants

A final section with a generalized amendment to the US Code that adds that anyone "knowingly" and "with the intent to retaliate," harms a person, including through his or her livelihood, because he or she has supplied information "relating to the commission or possible commission of any Federal offense," can be fined, or imprisoned up to ten years, or both.

TIMETABLE TO COMPLIANCE

The Act has put pressure on companies through an aggressive compliance timetable. Over time this has been eased to allow companies to be better prepared. One reason for delay cited by companies is the lack of specific skills in the market.

Phased filing requirements

This summary of compliance deadlines indicates the years in which the SEC "phased" the program for implementing the filing requirements for 10-K and 10-Q reports, with the number of days allowed for reports to be filed. The first table is for "accelerated filers." An "accelerated filer" is generally a US listed company with a market capitalization over $75 million that files annual reports with the SEC.

NOTES

1. A searchable version of the Act is available from a number of websites. The version used throughout this text is that published by the PCAOB, Public Law 107-204 July 30, 2002. 107th Congress, The Sarbanes-Oxley Act of 2002, version H.R. 3763.
2. The US Code is a formal compilation of the general and permanent laws of the United States. It is divided by subject matter into 50 "titles," and published by the Office of the Law Revision Counsel of the US House of Representatives every six years, with interim releases and supplements to keep it up to date. A number of amendments by the Act have updated the Code since 2002.

Table 4.3 Timetable for accelerated filers—larger companies

| Statements filed by November 15 | | | |
For fiscal years ending on or after	Days after end of year (10-K) filing	Days after end of quarter (10-Q) filing	Phase
December 15, 2002	90	45	Year 1
December 15, 2003	75	40	Year 2
December 15, 2004 *	60	35	Year 3

* Later postponed to 2005. The November 15 deadline for Section 404 still holds.

Table 4.4 Timetable for non-accelerated filers—smaller companies and foreign companies

| Statements now filed by July 2005 | | |
For fiscal years ending on or after	Days after end of year (10-K) filing	Days after end of quarter (10-Q) filing
December 15, 2005	60	35

Foreign companies' statements now filed by July 2006.

The Requirement: SOX and the Financial Sector

CHAPTER 5

Why are Financial Services Affected?

OVERVIEW OF THE FINANCIAL SECTOR

A main concern for financial services is the preservation of the structure of trust that results from good governance and transparency in the operation of markets. Regulatory compliance is a demonstration of this desire to engender trust. If we consider the financial sector as a whole and sketch some of its main features, the significance of compliance becomes clear. One of the main sectors of an economy is that covered by the financial sector. Any economy has a number of interrelated but separable sectors that dominate its activities. These consist of "households and non-profit institutions and serving households," "non-financial corporations," "financial corporations," "general government," and "rest of the world." The financial sector is largely represented by financial corporations, which in turn can be subdivided into:

- monetary financial institutions
- insurance corporations and pension funds
- other financial intermediaries and auxiliaries.

A financial system—the typical manifestation of this sector—consists essentially of financial institutions using financial markets to channel resources from lenders to borrowers. The core business of these institutions is to lend and borrow funds. Their central role in this process, and their balancing act in maintaining large holdings of financial assets and liabilities, reflect their role as intermediaries. They are, as we have seen, prime players in the information economy.

Markets and intermediaries

Financial markets are the environments in which these institutions come together. Through the markets all elements of the economy raise capital and settle debts. Much of the development of markets has been driven by the need to smooth this interplay, and reduce the critical costs inherent in the transaction process. Transaction costs and imbalances in privileged access to, and use of, information cause friction for a system of smoothly functioning financial transactions. One way to address this is represented by increasing abstraction: developing tradable equity or bonds, as debt, and the proliferation of financial instruments. This specialization has led to capital markets which have greatly stimulated lending, and the growth of specialists, as brokers, bringing together buyers and sellers and reducing search costs through exploiting specialist information.

However, this information process does not directly address adverse selection and moral hazard, although their effects can be ameliorated by financial intermediaries. The latter reduce transaction costs so that the risk is reduced for small savers, and this serves to stimulate this market. A striking example is the success of banks, as financial intermediaries, in handling the bulk of non-business funds. The control of information, its acquisition and disclosure, is essential for efficient market operations. Over time, regulation has ensured these qualities. It is the failure of trust in such a system that Sarbanes-Oxley seeks to treat.

Direct and intermediated finance: transformation

The difference between direct and intermediated finance through organized markets is that the transaction chain for the latter is longer and hence more costly; gains must balance and outweigh costs. Transformation is the process where the intermediary transforms assets from high to low risk, by taking small-size, low-risk, and high-liquidity claims, and acquiring larger, high-risk, and illiquid claims; focusing on the maturity, risk, and size of the claims.

As examples of intermediaries, banks manage the differences in the state of their liabilities over the longer term against their assets in the shorter term. In essence they borrow "short" and lend "long." Since loans carry a higher risk of default than deposits, banks manage risk through a number of strategies:

- filtering risk on loans
- diversifying and pooling risks
- managing their capital adequacy to address potential losses according to prudence and legislation, such as Basel II.

A key value for the market is the way in which intermediaries are able to aggregate funds generated by lenders into the larger amounts needed by borrowers. Through economies of scale, costs are reduced for contracted lending and borrowing.

However, financial intermediaries find themselves in a special situation. This is based on their legal status in relation to their client on the one hand, and their source of funding on the other. The most cost-efficient relationship is for the intermediary to hold a limited power of attorney on behalf of the client. This is by no means common for several reasons. Many clients insist on signing their own documents for personal, regulatory, or control reasons, and many intermediaries do not wish to have power of attorney because of the implied risk associated with the type of relationship.

However, there is risk and liability in whichever model is adopted. Even without a power of attorney, the service provided by an intermediary may imply a level of skill and knowledge that transfers liability to the intermediary even in the face of disclaimers of such liability,. This is the so-called "presumed expert" rule. Most intermediaries have a mix of clients, and so are in the worst possible position from a cost and complexity perspective. They must keep accurate records detailing their clients' financial transactions and the nature of the relationship they have with clients. This can lead to errors that can significantly affect the value of a client's portfolio. If there are a significant number of errors in the system, or if the errors create large discrepancies not identified because of systemic reporting inadequacies, there is a reputational risk to the intermediary if these issues become public.

This presents some exemplary issues for compliance:

- If the client is a US-listed company, the degree to which its financial reporting has been compromised as a result of the acts or omissions of its intermediary is relevant.
- If significant errors are found, and result in the intermediary's financial reporting containing a misstatement, generating a reputation risk and fiscal liabilities, to what extent will the intermediary be subject to the Sarbanes-Oxley Act ?

The intermediary's liability and reputation, and the significance of these under the Act, are determined by the degree to which it is clear about its role. It must determine whether its activities are truly "in loco client" or as an agent of the client.

Information and adverse selection

Banks are also effective at minimizing the adverse effects of "asymmetrical information." They avoid adverse selection through their greater knowledge of the market, its conditions, and the players involved in transactions. They are often in a position to buy good risks, since they have intimate knowledge of participants, such as those who bank with them. Fundamentally banks profit from their access to, and control of, information. This information underpins viability and edge in the market. Information, its use, abuse, and disclosure are central to the interests of the Act.

Moral hazard

Moral hazard, where the borrower acts in a way that might reduce the chances of the loan being repaid, is a danger for any lender. Restrictions through covenants to limit such activities, or compulsory loan protection, are mechanisms for controlling this risk. There may be some additional costs, but it is worth it if the risk is reduced. A non-traded loan may carry special advantages, which restrict the exchange of information about the trade. The lender seeks to be assured that the bank uses the deposit and monitors its use at a minimum risk to all involved. The bank is even seen as performing a public service. However, against the backdrop of the Act, it might be argued that this is not a sufficient system of protection.

Changing relationships

In more recent years the distinction between a lender, a borrower, and an intermediary has become ever more gray. Even in the classical model, the relationships between financial institutions can be extremely complex. It is often assumed that the relationship for example at market level is 1:1 for counterparty banking. In 2001 it was common for a non-US financial firm to have up to ten banking relationships in the United States, based on a variety of differentiating factors. After 2001, this number dropped significantly because of the increased costs of compliance to other regulations, but the situation still remains complex. Relationships also blur the differences between types of financial institution, particularly in wholesale banking, where brokers are beginning to engage in custody services in an effort to leverage the critical market information they hold. On the retail side, mortgage brokers are engaging in classical banking activities, and often demutualizing to achieve this. Finally at the equity level, it is not uncommon to find custodians and brokers with both client funds and proprietary funds under management. Unfortunately, it is very often the case that the attention given to proprietary funds is much higher than that given to client funds in many areas of fiscal management.

Most of these firms, in this complex arena, are at different levels of automation in the race to reduce costs for competitive advantage. Such differentiation creates errors in many areas, and leads to significant risk. That risk can be fiscal, but is often hidden. Fines imposed on financial institutions are rarely publicized to the degree they might be. Consequently compliance failures have not historically fallen foul of the provisions of the Act. That is likely to change, and financial firms will increasingly have to consider whether a failure under one set of regulations puts them at risk under the Act, with the consequences for their reputations in the market.

REPUTATION AS A CAPITAL ASSET

Overall, financial intermediaries act as a stimulant to the flow of funds in the economy through the services they offer. They have a fundamental role in the health of the economy and the market mechanisms that support it. Given this function it is additionally important for these organizations to be seen as beyond reproach within the scope of the Act. We are not yet at the point of "complete markets," with minimal transaction costs. We live in the age of "incomplete markets," and the role of the intermediary is significant. There is also a trend that values the reputation of the borrower as a fundamental influencing factor in the financing process. As borrowers go directly to the capital markets for their funds, bypassing banks, their reputation becomes ever more a capital asset, which must be protected.

As a capital asset, reputation should be highlighted as a risk for non-compliance. One view of reputation looks at a company's track record, its profitability, and how good it is at repaying loans. However, the link to market value and share value is significant. Reputation is linked to the perception of value, which is not necessarily the same as actual value. We have seen this relationship stretched a number of times in the last decades, notably during the dot.com boom, where companies with small actual value had inflated capitalized market values through exaggerated share values, and established companies with substantial actual value had relatively small market values.

REPUTATION AND BEST PRACTICE

The value of reputation is also associated with best practice. The difficulty here is who decides what good practice is, and how it changes over time. The financial services sector suffers from an intensely competitive approach: actual company practice might not be visible in the way that standards-based activities such as messaging standards are. There are a number of examples of how differences in practice can create problems that directly affect compliance efforts:

- Back-office practice is often the result of years of incremental change. The drivers for this practice are rarely compliance or global efficiency, and it often has more to do with tactical workarounds.
- Practice can vary by market as well as by the type of financial institution.
- Legal best practice is a gray area subject to interpretation. Sometimes this is based on domestic rather than international knowledge, with the potential for damage to reputation.

Two examples illustrate these points and indicate some unexpected aspects of transactions that could fall foul of the Act. They describe policies and procedures that are current. There is no right or wrong conclusion to be drawn, since reputation is, at heart, a subjective issue. Nevertheless the overlap between policy and actual procedure, and the way compliance and reputation interlink, can make a difference to an investor's perception.

Scenario 1: The trader's bonus

The first example considers a typical trade and corporate actions cycle, initiated by a trader on behalf of a client. The trader has a contract with a broker consisting of a basic salary package and a bonus element. The bonus element is calculated on the value of the trader's portfolio—its performance. That performance has at least two elements, one of which is the impact on the client's portfolio value from securities held "long" in the market. These will deliver some form of corporate action in due course, often a cash dividend. To put the issue in context, the proportion of yield delivered through dividends has risen and is likely to continue to rise, and the proportion of assets held cross-border has also risen, and is also expected to continue to rise.

Cash dividends from securities held long will constitute a significant issue for a trader, as they add value to the portfolio and the bonus. Where the dividend is from a cross-border investment, however, the income to the client's account will have withholding tax deducted at source. In Switzerland, for example, the statutory rate is 35 percent, so any income to the client's account will be 35 percent lower than the gross dividend declared by the issuer. Many clients, depending on their residency and legal status, are entitled to recover anything up to the full 35 percent of that withheld tax. The normal practice is for a trader to have his or her performance calculated based on the net dividend, on the presumption that any over-withheld tax has been recovered.

Two issues arise from this practice. First, it can take anything from months to years to actually recover such tax, and second, many brokers do not pursue tax reclaims on behalf of their clients. Normal practice is that the trader is credited with the net after tax recovery on day one—irrespective of whether any of the tax is ever actually recovered to the client's account. Assuming that, as in most cases, it will not be recovered, the trader's bonus is actually based on an inflated valuation of the portfolio.

This scenario is not illegal. A trader is entitled to negotiate the best deal possible in an aggressive market, and a broker is entitled to make whatever arrangements necessary to motivate the trader to perform. A compliance analysis at this level would find no reportable issue.

Following through, the bonuses paid are aggregated into the financial reports and signed off by the CFO. The default expectation of any reasonable person, such as a shareholder, would be that any performance bonus paid to a trader is based on the actual delivered benefit to a portfolio, and not an inflated figure, and that it should be credited not on day one, but in line with the actual cash flow. If the broker has no formal process for recovering over-withheld tax, it equally cannot say that there is a technical "receivable," that is, an entitlement. While the double tax treaty might assert such an entitlement in theory, the lack of a recovery process would surely lead a compliance officer to conclude that the money credited to the trader's account had no real likelihood of ever being actually realized.

There are several concerns expressed in the following questions:

- Has the nature of the remuneration of traders been made sufficiently transparent within the accounts?
- How much more cash would have been available for shareholders if traders had been remunerated on real performance as opposed to inflated performance?
- Are there ways that the board could improve the operation of the business?
- What else do those interested not know?

The Act is about avoiding impropriety by having mechanisms and controls that effectively identify potential problems. In the above case, the issue would be reported up the chain to an authorized person.[1] At this level, the practice would be assessed for its potential risk, to reputation or otherwise. At the lower level, the practice is identified as reportable because it is clear that the issue could affect the validity of higher-level financial reporting, and in the worst case, cause an issue at share-price level.

Whether this issue would be reported to shareholders under Sarbanes-Oxley would depend on the degree to which the management felt able to defend the practice if it was disclosed. The nature of such risks and how these are affected by the Act are the substance of compliance efforts. It does seem that a financial assertion could be made that is misleading. What would be the auditor's response to discovering this practice? Throughout this example, we assume that working internal controls are in place and operating effectively.[2] Whether they are the correct controls, and designed well enough, is another issue, and would directly affect any management assessment of their effectiveness.

Scenario 2: The broker's title

The scenario of the trader's performance highlights how, even with effective controls, monitored processes may still generate risk. Controls and monitoring are part of the issue, especially when we consider the broker's title. In Figure 5.1 we have an arrangement that is not particularly uncommon:

- The client is a French resident fund that is exempt from withholding tax.
- Broker A is a US-listed entity subject directly to the Act.
- Broker B is a UK-resident brokerage firm, a corporate entity.
- The issuer is a Swiss corporate entity.

Swiss statutory withholding tax on dividends is 35 percent. US entities are generally entitled to reclaim at a treaty rate of 15 percent on Swiss-sourced income, subject to documentation and a filed claim.

The situation outlined above occurs when shares purchased by a client or on its behalf are held "long." When a dividend is declared and distributed as a corporate action, the beneficial owner of the income will receive this dividend, net of taxes withheld in Switzerland. If, for example, the dividend were SFr10.00 on one million shares, the beneficial owner would receive SFr6,500,000, the balance being in the hands of the Swiss tax authority. This is standard market practice. The question arises who is the beneficial owner. Some brokers operate a policy of "taking title" to shares that they buy on behalf of their clients. Some do not. To do so poses an issue. The contract with the client states that the broker takes title.

When the broker receives the dividend, net of 35 percent tax, the broker presumes that, as the holder of the title in the shares, it can recover the difference between the 35 percent withheld by the Swiss tax authority and the 15 percent tax rate. The broker might, or might not, physically file the reclaim concerned, but the client's account must be credited. This would include the net dividend, plus the value of the reclaim that the broker is "entitled" to. So the client in this example would receive SFr 6,500,000 plus SFr 2,000,000, a total of SFr 8,500,000.

Internally all the procedures have been agreed and the client contract specifies the arrangement. From a regulatory viewpoint the above scenario appears to cause no conflict. However, some issues do arise:

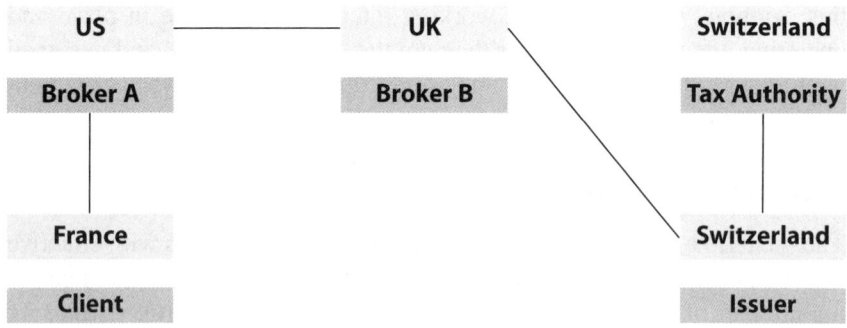

Figure 5.1 Controls and monitoring: the broker's title

- A foreign tax authority would not equate "title" with "beneficial ownership." For this authority the claim of title, would, on audit or enquiry, result in the broker being deemed to be fiscally transparent. A simple question can clarify this: while you claim to be the beneficial owner of the shares, is there any other entity that will receive money from you as a payer, based on or related to this transaction? Clearly, the answer is yes. The client will be credited with a dividend and also an amount representing a tax reclaim.
- It is also likely that that the client gave instructions for the purchase of the shares. The client paid for them and received the dividend, so the client is the beneficial owner of the shares as far as the foreign tax authority is concerned.

This introduces two major issues for the broker and client:

- The broker has essentially filed a false claim for a tax refund to which it was not entitled, because it was knowingly not the real beneficial owner.
- The client, in this example, is exempt from withholding tax, so the broker has credited it with a tax recoverable which does not match its entitlement. The fund should have received the full 100 percent of the dividend instead of 85 percent.

Generally, this kind of issue receives little attention. Because the broker files the reclaim based on a claim to be the beneficial owner, without an audit, the tax authority takes the word of the financial institution, and the client often does not know enough about withholding tax to spot the issue.

Compliance issues

So how are the players in this case affected under the Act? As a US-listed entity, Broker A is directly subject to the Act. From this follows a number of observations:

- Broker A's financial reporting will include income net of tax to which it was not entitled. Thus the CFO will be attesting to a financial statement that is not accurate.
- Monitoring mechanisms did not reveal a cross-border taxation issue. This could create:
  - risk, as a result of an audit by the tax authority
  - a lawsuit from the client and/or the tax authority
  - liability, as reparation to clients and damages and punitive fines.
- If such a practice was widespread across Broker A and ongoing, its share price could be damaged by revelations about the probity of such practices.

The position of Broker B appears to be unaffected by the Act.

The nature of the relationships between such institutions and the services they provide each other can be complex. A major consequence is that the ramifications of the Act may be difficult to predict, particularly for financial services. The United States particularly has been shown to have a very broad view of its jurisdictional powers. In a real-life parallel case in 2004, two directors of Lloyds TSB were wanted for questioning by the US authorities in relation to a bonus payment of $2 million. The transaction was deemed to be subject to US anti-money laundering rules, even though the transaction itself was evidently between two non-US financial entities and took place outside the United States. The critical factor was the way the two entities arranged their cross-border payments. Transactions passed through an account at a mutual counterparty bank in New York, and because of this, the transaction was deemed to be subject to US jurisdiction. Even though no allegation of wrongdoing was ever claimed, and no allegation has been filed by the employers of the two individuals concerned, nevertheless the directors were required to answer questions in the United States.

The potential for precedent is clear:

- If the transactional example above had taken place between two non-US brokers, both would probably believe that while the process might have left some issues to be resolved, it would not come under US jurisdiction and thus Sarbanes-Oxley.
- If the payment of the dividend and the "reclaim" funds passed through a US bank account on its way from Broker A to Broker B, it is likely that the transaction would be deemed subject to US jurisdiction.

Many non-US companies assume that the provisions of the Act do not affect them. Yet, as in the examples above, many transactions are international in nature, and involve US intermediaries and services at some point. The exact implications are not always easy to untangle from the legal requirements and precedents of separate jurisdictions. However, there is enough significant doubt to make it wise to assume that for the future well-being of the firm, some attention should be paid to the Act, and its requirements should be factored in risk assessments and policies.

COMPLIANCE MODELS FOR THE FINANCE SECTOR

One advantage the financial sector has over many other affected sectors under the Act is its experience of being regulated and its familiarity with the concept of compliance. In this sense, developing and maintaining a compliance process may not be a new experience. However, every set of regulations has its own focus. While other regulations may have led to work that can be reused, nevertheless the financial reporting aspect of the Act is very specific and also very large in its implications for the organization as a whole.

Are there significant differences, or even any differences, in the way organizations within the finance sector should approach compliance with the Act? If we consider the industry as whole, there are a number of specialist vertical sectors, each with its own focus. Some companies manage multiple sector functions; some manage just the one:

- financial intermediaries
- retail banking
- wholesale and investment banking—international banking
- building societies
- finance houses (non-bank credit companies)
- investment institutions
- pension funds
- life assurance companies
- investment trusts
- unit and OEICs (open-ended investment companies)
- financial markets
- foreign exchange
- equities
- international bonds
- fund management
- commodity
- insurance
- derivatives.

In principle, the compliance process applies to all entities across the industry, and despite their differences, there are enough common activities and interests to warrant a standard approach to compliance. A useful strategy is a two-step process: first establish a compliance program using a reference model, and second, be aware of differences in the ways models are applied across the sector for various organizations. Make the compliance program company-specific.

Compliance mapping

In the compliance process, at an early stage, each organization should consider the appropriate sets of controls it needs as a player in a vertical sector. As a part of the process we need to map these control areas, identifying controls and standards that will contribute to the compliance plan.

Table 5.1 introduces a compliance map with some sector samples. This table is a simplified version of what can become a complex matrix. The compliance regimes associated with various regulations and standards bodies, whether mandated or voluntary, have common elements, such as monitoring activities, transparency, general corporate and IT governance recommendations, and ethical codes. They also have regime-specific requirements.

If there is time and sufficient resources, consolidating the efforts on applicable compliance regimes within a single compliance process is an ideal. The nature of regulation is that is it often unpredictable, being reactive to events. Moves to make regulation more proactive, or predictable, are gaining ground. However, being largely behavior-oriented and originating from separate bodies with differing agendas, these regulations are difficult to forecast in detail. Nevertheless, any efforts to standardize on a common compliance program will generate cost benefits as well as organizational efficiencies. Reference models, such as COSO and COBIT for a business-oriented approach, ITIL for IT governance, and Six Sigma and CMMI for processes, are useful frameworks from which to build a consolidated compliance process. Although the compliance process and its associated compliance cycle espoused later in the book is specific to the Act, nevertheless its principles would work as a basis for such a consolidated approach.

Table 5.1 Sample compliance map by sector

Type	Relevant standards	Controls
Retail banking	SEC, regional local banking standards, SOX.	Client credit rating loan and account management history
Wholesale and investment banking, international banking	SEC, investment banking standards and codes of practice, SOX, internationally observed codes and standards	Company references Client company due diligence
Building societies	Mutual fund and mortgage regulations, SEC and SOX	Loan processing Credit assessment
Finance houses (non-bank credit companies)	Credit monitoring standards, SEC and SOX	Market risk Client risk

PRACTICAL COMPLIANCE SUMMARY

- Define the sector specifics for the organization and tailor compliance to its needs.
- Combine the information interests of the organization with information security.
- Develop a program that ensures reputation is factored into the compliance risk assessment.
- In particular look at key processes, and identify points at which geographies and jurisdictions overlap or conflict and develop processes, while considering effective controls to manage these.
- Build a picture of all relevant compliance regimes the organization is subject to, and identify the common elements to prepare processes that can consolidate efforts, such as controls.

NOTES

1. The Act mandates in Section 307 that attorneys report issues up through the management structure. This led to speculation that staff would "over report," in case they missed anything or were liable in the event of an investigation. This also implied "reporting out" if management at the most senior level refused or neglected to act on known issues that could affect transparent financial reporting. A practical way of addressing this from the "whistleblower" aspect of the Act, contained in Section 806, is to ensure that the compliance process, at the strategic level of defining guidelines, establishes effective processes and ownership to enable staff to report in accordance with the Act.
2. The definition of "operating effectively" for internal controls is dealt with in Chapters 17 and 18.

CHAPTER 6

The Public Face: Financial Reporting

REPORTING AND COMPLIANCE

Financial statements or reports are at the heart of compliance activities. As evidence of an organization's business activities and state of health, they are key record of its presence and value in the market. From this all other evaluations flow, especially the valuation of its capitalization and its suitability as an investment. A good financial report can increase the value of the company, and a bad financial repot can adversely affect the same value. The simplicity of this also summarizes the significance of the Sarbanes-Oxley Act. A company that can demonstrate its compliance demonstrates its likely financial integrity. This demonstration underpins its trustworthiness. The figures may dip and the actual value might drop, but the perception of being a sound operation may be enough to ensure that it remains a good investment.

However, a company identified as being in poor shape as far as compliance is concerned, despite a relatively good performance, might suffer a dent in its reputation. This can badly affect the perception of trust. Financial reports, as the most public indicators of the state of a company, directly address this. In addressing the reliability of reports, the Act seeks to ensure good practical corporate behavior. This explains the emphasis placed on senior executives. Financial reports, interim and final, are the stuff of their world. It is they who are directly associated with these statements. It is to them that the Act looks when it comes to assessments of compliance of the company as a whole. It is they who are directly tasked with ensuring transparency, and it is they who are penalized for failures.

For the purposes of our understanding of the compliance effort, a "typical" financial statement and its standards are outlined here. The financial statement will include a number of financial assertions about the business, which are contained in:

■ a balance sheet, detailing assets of a business

- a statement of income for the period covered
- a statement of expenditure for the period covered
- a profit and loss statement
- a cash flow statement
- a statement of other gains and losses not detailed in any of the above statements
- a statement detailing movements in equity that are not included in the income statement or the general profit and loss account
- a statement of retained earnings
- additional information that might be relevant for understanding the performance and state of the business, and key management decisions.

Internationally, public companies issue statements that conform to certain standards to make them intelligible to a discerning investing public. Specialists understand the minutiae, while key indicators are clearly identified for any potential investor or shareholder to use as the basis for making investment decisions. This interest in the health of a company extends to all its stakeholders, including employees and trade unions, tax authorities, banks, suppliers of goods and services, and customers in general. Companies are required to publish financial statements annually, and some listing agencies insist on quarterly periodic reports. The detail in these reports may vary according to national regulatory control.

FINANCIAL REPORTING AND COMPLIANCE

The reporting arena is larger than it at first appears: it is the distillation of all the business activities of the organization, summarized in text and figures, and represents the value of the organization. It is the tip of an information iceberg. From our review of intellectual capital, information assets, even compliance status, we see that the value of the organization is more than just financial figures. Indeed, the financial reporting process touches on:

- financial statement reporting
- the overall company performance
- forecasting and planning
- insights into the company structure and its operation
- personnel information
- executives' advice and guidance for the market, including executive knowledge of the organization and the market in which it operates
- admissions of deficiencies.

Although the periodic annual and quarterly reports are the primary focus of reporting activity, they are not the only reports to consider. Under Section

409 of the Act, there is a requirement to report variations in the state of the health of the business between reports; in particular, events must be reported that could make a difference to the way an investor perceives the company. These ad hoc reports can be especially demanding if the systems are not in place to identify, highlight, prioritize, and escalate them for publication.

FINANCIAL REPORTING ASSERTIONS

Risk identification and management is a core function for the business, an issue we return to frequently. The financial report is as much a statement or assertion about the risk control of the business as it is about disclosing figures. The subtext of the financial report for investors is reassurance that their investment is not at risk; and for new investors, that the company is a low-risk option. This is an assertion about the business. However, the term "assertion" carries a specific weight. It is commonly used interchangeably with "statement," but the nature of an assertion is that it has to be proven before it becomes a statement. A statement implies that it is a fact—a disputed fact perhaps, but a fact nevertheless. There is a range of assertions which contribute to a risk assessment. Assertion typically implies risk; after all, there is no such thing as a risk-free business. The Committee of Sponsoring Organizations (COSO)[1] lists a number of assertions about financial reports:

- Existence: that business items, assets as well as liabilities, and the responsibilities associated with these items, all do exist.
- Rights and obligations: that the organization does have rights to its assets, and asserts these rights publicly; and that it does have liabilities, and these are also publicly stated on the published balance sheet.
- Evaluation: that any assets and liabilities, expressed as income through revenue and outgoings, are reported quantitatively in financial statements in line with GAAP.
- Presentation and disclosure: that items in financial statements are described accurately, and fairly reported as reasonable assertions about the state of the business.
- Occurrence: this is akin to "existence." Transactions and economic activities describe events that actually happened during the period covered by the report.
- Completeness: that all relevant economic events that occurred during the financial year or period covered by the report have been recorded in financial statements. Nothing relevant in terms of assets and liabilities has not been disclosed. The picture is as complete as possible for the statements made.

Assertions in a financial report are subject to validation through the work of external auditors, and these financial assertions are also in line with those of the PCAOB.[2]

SOURCES OF INFORMATION

In principle, financial statements are consolidated accounts of the business. This information comes from many sources within the business, and if the business is international there may be a number of published statements reflecting the state of the subsidiaries and local entities. Whatever the final shape, they will contain most of the statements listed above, and the information that feeds these consolidated statements is derived ultimately from business functions. The processes and workflows that generate this data are embedded within the business and reflect its activities. The Act insists on an effective system of controls that monitor and check these processes to ensure that the flow of information is reliable and effective, and the statements that result are a reliable and not misleading representation of the state of affairs. In a system of internal control, the information sources are live records and stored records; the importance of record keeping and access to records becomes central to compliance. The nature of these internal systems is explored later.

A trend noted earlier is the move towards automation. This extends to the exchange of information, especially between a listed company and regulating body. An example is the application of eXtensible Business Reporting Language (XBRL) to financial reports.

"TRUE" AND "FAIR"

While we can choose what medium to use to deliver information, and it may appear to be consistent and context-rich, there is still the question of whether it is true. The broad requirement is that financial statements should be "true" and either "fair" or "correct." In the language of the Act, Section 302 notes that "the financial statements, and other financial information included in the [periodic financial] report, fairly present in all material respects the financial condition and results of operations of the issuer as of, and for, the periods presented in the report."

The exact nature of "fairly present" is part of the vagueness in terminology that the Act uses at critical moments. This has the advantage of not closely defining a potentially complex legal concept; it is also deferential to other definitions, notably those contained in other SEC regulations. This is a point we revisit when discussing "deficiencies" and "weaknesses." The importance of context, in order for data to provide meaning and value, is a constant theme in communicating effectively. This is true for the financial report. The importance of providing good "context" material is paramount for investors making decisions; this is also true for managers internally making compliance decisions. Information in general, and statistics in particular, are subject to presentation and interpretation. The Act expects responsible individuals to make their best efforts when assessing systems to use for reporting, and to provide quality information. This is an important part of corporate governance. However, recognizing the power of presentation is an important step in promoting the company. This is particularly the case when the financial report is pushed through the filter of marketing.

PUBLICIZED COMPLIANCE

It is understandable and valid for the publication of a financial report to be treated as a marketing event. It is an excellent opportunity to communicate directly with existing shareholders and new investors, and portray the company in the best possible light. This creative side of reporting has sometimes made it possible to de-emphasize unwelcome news and highlight positive aspects of the period in review. The Act cuts across the bows of adventurous marketing, and has returned the focus to the facts and figures. It has also bolstered the eagerness of company boards to emphasize their investment in, and observance of, good corporate practice. Corporate governance and ethics often have a section all to themselves. If the company has a clean bill of health in terms of compliance, this is now the vehicle for letting the market know.

Since compliance is now seen as a necessary positive in the report, the financial report is an opportunity to detail the efforts and investment being made in the compliance process, with some attention paid to the process itself and how the company is establishing an ongoing regime. It sends a clear signal that whatever the fallibilities in the way the company operates, it is serious about ensuring stakeholders are protected.

AUDITING OF FINANCIAL STATEMENTS

Auditing is central to practical compliance. In this context, an external, independent auditor will audit the company's statements. The accuracy of the statements is certified by the company's directors. External auditors review the financial statements of a company and offers an opinion on whether they are a "true" view of the company's financial health, within the limits of the audit. This allows standards to be monitored and conformance to general rules to be verified.

In view of the onus placed on auditors, it has been observed by many companies that their relationship with established auditors has changed. Whereas before the Act, senior executives might look to external auditors for advice, for example on the best way to comply with legislation, they now find auditors are reluctant to provide such advice. The language has changed, as auditors become more guarded about what they say, since their attestations on management assessments are now a potential risk. Audit reports have always been contentious. In the past these reports provide valuable comments on the state of the business. Inadvertently, the constraints of the Act may have much reduced the value of the auditor in this context.

REPORTING STANDARDS

The Act, in Section 108, notes that: "In carrying out its authority under subsection (a) and under section 13(b) of the Securities Exchange Act of 1934, the Commission may recognize, as 'generally accepted' for purposes of the securities laws, any accounting principles established by a standard setting body." The Act makes several references to "generally accepted" accounting standards. Given the importance of these standards to financial reporting, it is relevant to summarize them here.

Periodic financial reports are generally governed by the formats in Form 10-QSB/A, and are either a quarterly report under Section 13 or 15(d) of the Securities Exchange Act of 1934, or a transition report between specific dates. They are filed accordingly. While these formats are not a standard, they do conform to a "standard" approach. In addition to the structure discussed earlier, they include "Management's discussion and analysis of financial condition and results of operations," which includes a summary overview of the condition of the company, its strategy in the market, and a section on liquidity and capital resources. There is a section on "Quantitative and qualitative disclosures about market risk," and a section entitled "Other information," which covers legal proceedings, directors' dealings, and so on. All in all the format provides a substantial snapshot of the state of the company, of value to shareholders, potential investors, and regulatory bodies. The amendments of the Act are largely amendments to the SEC Act and these reporting requirements. This report is at the very sharp end of the whole discussion.

Form 10-Q

Forms 10-Q and 10-K are the reports that most publicly traded companies file with the SEC on a quarterly (Q) or annual (K) basis. Currently, Form 10-K must be filed with the SEC within 90 days of the end of the company's fiscal year. A company's Form 10-K is available on the SEC's EDGAR database; it is one of the noticeable aspects of modern financial reporting that it is largely done electronically, underlying points made elsewhere about the significance of e-commerce and electronic regulation. Under its "Rule as to use of Form 1O-Q," the SEC states that "Form

10-Q shall be used for quarterly reports under Section 13 or 15(d) of the Securities Exchange Act of 1934 .... A quarterly report on this form ... shall be filed within the following period after the end of the first three fiscal quarters of each fiscal year, but no quarterly report need be filed for the fourth quarter of any fiscal year." It then goes on to detail conditions of reporting for "accelerated filers." It notes that "Form 10-Q also shall be used for transition and quarterly reports .... Such transition or quarterly reports shall be filed in accordance with the requirements set forth in Rule 13a-10 or Rule 15d-10 applicable when the registrant changes its fiscal year end."

Form 8-K

This report is really a supplementary report in support of the picture painted by Form 10-K. It is used to report material events or corporate changes previously not been reported by the company in a quarterly or annual report. On March 16, 2004, the SEC adopted changes to Form 8-K that increased the number of events reportable on the form. Eight items were added to the report, and two were introduced from the periodic reports. The time companies have to file the Form 8-K was also reduced to four business days, from five or 15 according to the type of the event. Like Forms 10-K, Forms 8-K are listed on the SEC's EDGAR database. For Form 8-K, reportable events relate to changes in the way the company operates, changes in board-level personnel, changes to the company's financial year, and other significant changes to the financial operation.

GAAP

GAAP is an acronym for generally accepted accounting principles. There are several variants of these generally accepted principles, US GAAP and UK GAAP being examples. It is also the case that GAAP represents a set of accounting principles and procedures rather than standards. These principles and procedures are rules used by companies to compile their financial statements. GAAP is a combination of authoritative standards, established by policy boards, and commonly accepted ways of recording and reporting accounting information. Thus GAAP is really a mixture of principles and best practice. In the United States and other countries (like England) using a common law system, the government does not legislate for accounting standards; it allows the industry to determine best practice. However, the Securities and Exchange Commission (SEC) in the United States does mandate that GAAP be followed by public companies, and historically the SEC promoted private standard-setting bodies through the American Institute of Certified Public Accountants (AICPA) and the Financial Accounting Standards Board (FASB).

The aim of GAAP is no surprise in the context of the Act. The principles are imposed on companies so that investors have a minimum of consistent information in financial statements. GAAP covers the way of addressing certain aspects of accounting such as revenue recognition, which is critical to the way a company reports on a quarterly basis, and balance sheet classification. Investors expect companies to follow GAAP rules. However, since GAAP is essentially a recommendation, it is not a guarantee of accurate information. It points to principles that govern a process, and is an indicator of good intent.

Since there are international GAAP variants, differences in the sets of principles have evolved.[3] There are considerable efforts being made to converge standards at all levels within financial activities. Reporting standards are part of this process. In particular the International Accounting Standards Board (IASB), which develops International Financial Reporting Standards (IFRS) that have been adopted globally and by the European Union, is attempting to unify standards.

International Financial Reporting Standards (IFRS)

In 2001, the US-based International Accounting Standards Committee (IASC) Foundation became the parent of the IASB, based in London. This assumed accounting standard-setting responsibilities for the Foundation. The IASB develops IFRS, and follows a rigorous process. It is "committed to developing, in the public interest, a single set of high quality, understandable and enforceable global accounting standards," and "co-operates with national accounting standard-setters to achieve convergence in accounting standards around the world."[4]

Other agents for reporting standards include the Standards Advisory Council (SAC), a forum for organizations and individuals with an interest in international financial reporting. Its main function is to give advice and to represent to the IASB the views of those organizations and individuals involved in standard-setting projects. The International Financial Reporting Interpretations Committee (IFRIC) works closely with national bodies on accounting issues. It interprets actions with reference to the IFRS framework, and generally makes technical decisions on reporting issues not dealt with by an IFRS.

Until 2001, the Board of ISAC referred to Statements of International Accounting Standards as International Accounting Standards (IAS). In 2001, the IASB announced the standards would be called International Financial Reporting Standards (IFRS). These IFRS "summaries" cover IFRS, IAS, and interpretations issued on or before March 31, 2004, and are published by the IASB, which also publishes the interpretations of the IFRIC.

Preparation and presentation of financial statements

The Framework for the Preparation and Presentation of Financial Statements supports the financial reporting standards and interpretations of the IASB. It involves:

- developing and reviewing future standards
- promoting the harmonization of standards and rationalizing the options currently available
- assisting those who wish to adhere to the standards by providing information.

This body consults with:

- national standard-setting bodies
- auditors who need help in forming an opinion on conformance to the standards
- users of financial statements in interpreting whether financial statements conform to IFRS
- parties interested in the work of the IASB.

The Framework is not an IFRS, nor does it define standards, but it provides guidance on the preparation and presentation of financial statements.[5]

TRANSACTION STANDARDS: SWIFT

The SWIFT transaction standards may be appropriate for transactions and for reporting on audit trails and the like. In the financial services sector, speed of information transfer, privacy, and standards are all generally wrapped up as one issue. The organization that is responsible for maintaining the standards of messaging (and therefore reporting) is the Society for Worldwide Interbank Telecommunications (SWIFT), which is appointed by the International Standards Organization (ISO).

SWIFT also manages its own network, being a cooperative of over 8,000 financial institutions. SWIFT is by no means the only network messaging provider, but it is the most dominant. Until relatively recently, the cooperative concentrated on issuing annual standards (standards releases or SRs), and establishing messages that its members could use between themselves to create a straight through processing (STP) environment as the key way to reduce costs for everyone. The internet began to be a threat to this situation, since it offered an easy alternative way for institutions to transfer data, with security provided by digital certification. The data standards could be replaced with simple file transfers, which at that time SWIFT could not support. This has created a revolution not only in what SWIFT provides to its cooperative members, but also in the data transfer methods it provides and the communities to which it can reach out.

SWIFT now operates two networks. FIN connects institutions, and allows messages to ISO standards to be moved between nodes: that is, data packets to a predefined format and business purpose. General messages can be sent between any two or more points in the network. These could concern payment instructions, for example, or announcements of corporate actions such as cash dividends and so on. Messages with a more restricted use can also be sent between parties which agree to the common use of such messages in either closed user groups (CUGs) or message user groups (MUGs). Overall, SWIFT also manages market practice groups (MPGs), whose role is, as the name suggests, to analyze messages and establish what the accepted market practice should be for the use of such messages.

In answer to the internet threat and also to the need of some financial institutions to send data quickly that did not easily fit one of the FIN message types, the cooperative launched SWIFTNet, the main feature of this being a product called FileAct which enables firms to send any type of file across the SWIFT network with the benefit of consistency. It is easier to control data traffic when it all goes across one network provider, and the other benefits of SWIFT, and other network providers in this space, are non-repudiation and guaranteed delivery.

Apart from its role in standardization, SWIFT's network is a private network. The importance of the messages sent cannot be overestimated. Information about individuals, their investments, and their income (as well as the money itself) move around the network every day. At the macro level, the financial statements of the banks themselves and other financial institutions, being public companies and thus subject to the Act, are reliant on a data transfer method that assures security and privacy. A bank's share price could be substantially damaged if it allowed such information to be transported across an insecure network. This became clear in 2006:

- UK and US individuals found the headlines in newspapers reporting that their details might have been sold on the open market in India, as a result of outsourcing of account management in call centers, with a consequent effect on their confidence in the institutions concerned.
- The US government admitted that post 9/11 it had accessed SWIFT messages across the network in an effort to combat international terrorism. This is currently under investigation by the Belgian government. SWIFT is incorporated in Belgium.

There are two key aspects to transporting data over the SWIFT network, guaranteed delivery and non-repudiation. The first is based on SWIFT's five-nines availability (that is, its up-time), and the second ensures that once sent between two BIC addressees on the network, if the option is selected, the receiver cannot repudiate the message (that is, say it never arrived). In terms of the Act, these features are fundamental. For those designing systems to deal with the Act in the corporate world, such features are relatively rare.

So in respect of the Sarbanes-Oxley requirements, SWIFT itself provides an excellent model for others to follow in terms of methods to assure privacy and guarantee delivery of data. Such guarantees of course create traceability, which is critical to the identification of exceptional items. Some of SWIFT's messages also pass through validation gates on their way through the network. They are often more aimed at making sure that data formatting rules are followed, but the principle however is that SWIFT is a network capable of standardizing data, thus creating traceability and validation options in addition to non-repudiation and guaranteed delivery. This then is a system inherently consistent with the Act.

TECHNICAL STANDARDS: XBRL

As there are financial standards for reporting, such as GAAP, and regulatory standards on transparency in reporting, such as the Act, eXtensible Business Reporting (XBRL) brings technical standards to financial regulatory reporting. How does XBRL contribute to reporting in general and compliance in particular? Generally, XBRL is a move to benefit capital market participants. XBRL uses the accessibility and the protocols of the internet through the World Wide Web to move financial, and financial-related, information. XBRL "tags" enable data processing of business information by computer software solutions. XBRL means there is no need to enter data manually. Companies can preselect and analyze data for storage; they can select, consolidate, and exchange this data as part of automated processes. XBRL is an enabling technology for business intelligence for layered data selection. In principle this use of XBRL:

- reduces the cost of producing information
- reduces the cost of sharing information
- allows better access to data
- provides consistent financial statements shared among permitted users.

This is advantageous in that comparisons of data are much easier and more consistent, and compliance process controls are easier to monitor. XBRL has also been positioned for any size of company; it draws from a common and well-understood pool of web protocols, which include HTML and XML. This greatly eases acceptance and use by smaller companies. The overall value is that it allows the critical process of automating data interchange, and reinforces the transparency of information for financial markets. Electronic certification is now receiving backing from a number of sources. The US Securities Industry Association has for some time been pushing the SEC to allow the delivery of listed securities to investors and eliminate physical certificates. Their proposal envisages a direct registration system (DRS) operated by a securities depository.

That XBRL has generated a lot of interest among regulators is widely acknowledged. There are some reservations, based on practical issues of implementation and cost. However, because of the longer-term cost bene-fits noted above and the way it can improve efficiency and accuracy, it is, for many, such as the Financial Service Authority (FSA) in the United Kingdom, and tentatively the SEC, a protocol with considerable potential. The FSA is developing a mandatory electronic returns program based on XBRL standards. As with most innovations, it will be tried on new arrivals first; in the case of the financially regulated community in the United King-dom, mortgage and general insurance intermediaries. The descriptive title of "protocol" implies that it is a language for defining and delivering infor-mation for business reports. The information with which it works is typical of that found in financial reporting and includes a range of material that contributes to regulatory requirements:

- financial statements on matters such as such as:
  - balance sheets
  - cash flow
  - income
  - shareholder equity
- non-financial documents on:
  - performance measurements
  - regulatory reporting
  - loan applications
  - statistics.

Advantages for reporting

XBRL also offers not just raw data, but data wrapped in context to trans-form it into viable financial "information." It also enables such information to be assembled at layered points within the business, fitting into business intelligence schema for consolidation and publication in a totally auto-mated manner. It can be exchanged with external bodies such as regulators, bringing the value to the business that automation generally conveys:

- reducing complexity, by breaking difficult processes into stepped and simpler processes

- a one-off entry of information for multiple reuse
- reducing the overhead of importing data, by providing a common taxonomy for disparate sources
- eliminating errors from operator input and translation.

The prime value of XBRL is that it provides information and context in a format that can be managed electronically and communicated across a network to other machines. XBRL includes definitions, relationships, calculations, presentation and reference information, collecting material in a taxonomy as it defines and structures all the data for a particular type of report.

For users who use this information as financial information, such as investors, regulators, stock brokers, financial analysts and auditors, the benefits are considerable. This information is:

- consistent
- formatted in a predictable way
- well defined
- accurate within reasonable limits
- able to be processed electronically.

To gain common acceptance among financial institutions, XBRL must be seen to have benefits that are not just for external regulators but offer something that internal reporting does not already provide.

XBRL: internal reporting and barriers to adoption

Automation of processes through XBRL may smooth the path and help deliver benefits internally to the organization by reducing the effort to produce and process information internally, and improving reporting transparency for internal auditors and those, such as senior executives, who need to comply with the Act. The perspective of medium and longer-term time and effort will help companies decide. As the compliance effort unfolds, it is likely that XBRL will be part of the tool set that helps the organization simplify and manage its compliance process. Yet it is these technical demands that may hold back adoption. In the United Kingdom it was anticipated that it would be compulsory by now for such reports to be exchanged using XBRL. However, delays in implementation have been caused by technical challenges and rising implementation costs.

The SEC's rule on its voluntary XBRL filing program went into effect recently, and it accepts filings tagged in XBRL,[6] although it has indicated that XBRL filings do not replace traditional flat text-based versions of financial reports. Nevertheless it is an attractive option for ensuring compliance to the Act in this area.

For regulators there is a real attraction in the widespread use of XBRL. Much of their time is occupied in validating and collating the information delivered to them in a great variety of formats. Anything that can speed this up and free time for analysis and review on a more structured basis is welcomed. Costs are real, and the investment costs incurred will be passed on to regulated organizations; nevertheless, from the point of view of practical compliance, the implementation of XBRL is an idea that has to come. As compliance is a long-term project, so too are repeated reports in the context of regulation. The efficient thing to do appears to be to automate as much as possible, and XBRL does just that.

IMPROVING REPORTING

In the general life of a business, activity will occur based on a need to improve the reporting process. This may happen independently of any legislative requirement. At one level, there is an obvious advantage in producing a report that is comprehensive, accurate and promotes the company. Any ongoing assessment of the reporting process should measure it against recognized standards, such as GAAP. An assessment should identify issues that need to be addressed, and prioritize them for action. If deficiencies are identified, they must be analyzed as being specific to a technology or the process as a whole. Projects should be initiated with budgets, resources, and solutions, developed or acquired.

A background of process knowledge, financial closing expertise, specific skills, and relationships both internal and external, provides a basis on which to build the compliance effort. Most of the activities indicated above are relevant to the practicalities of becoming compliant to the Act. Supported by internal IT function expertise, they provide a key contribution to the compliance process and act as the bedrock for a company-wide response.

PRACTICAL COMPLIANCE SUMMARY

Checklists of activities are routinely adopted:

- Examine or audit the process and ensure it is effective and timely.
- Take an overall view of the value of the existing process.
- Consider external resources and expertise for remediation, and use internal or external knowledge of best practice as a basis for action.
- Consider software solutions from known vendors.

To do this, staff will most likely have experience of managing projects and have developed skills in:

- Gathering relevant data and understanding the data
- Managing the financial closing process.
- Using spreadsheets, databases and other sources of data.
- Defining and implementing policies and procedures for these activities.
- Using auditable processes that allow audit trails.
- Making the most of the financial report.
- Publicizing the compliance process and providing details of spend on compliance and governance, stressing the ongoing nature of the program to protect investors in the longer term.

NOTES

1. COSO and COBIT are discussed in greater length in Chapter 23.
2. The PCAOB was mandated by the Act to draw up guidelines on auditing. These were published as the Auditing Standard No. 2 (AS2).
3. Differences between the US GAAP and UK GAAP, for example, are enough to mark differences in the way pensions, intangible assets, taxation, dividends, employee share schemes, cost structuring, and so on are reported.
4. The Federal Accounting Standards Board (FASB) in the United States has joined this movement to converge US GAAP and IFRS.
5. The Framework for the Preparation and Presentation of Financial Statements was approved and published by the IASC in 1989. In 2001 it was adopted by the IASB. It is a guide for the IASB in developing accounting standards and for resolving accounting issues that are not addressed directly in an International Accounting Standard or International Financial Reporting Standard or Interpretation.
6. The SEC voluntary program has some qualifications. The SEC rule requires volunteers to provide the XBRL documents as an addition to the filing from which they were derived, while originals must be submitted along with legacy ASCII and HTML formatted filings.

CHAPTER 7

The Impact of Cost

THE COST OF COMPLIANCE

Whenever any project is implemented in any organization, the cost of the activity is a primary consideration. All financial organizations exist to make a profit. Certainly listed companies have this as a core objective. Given this and the way risk is interpreted as financial loss, any legislation that implies risk has to be considered as a cost issue.

The Sarbanes-Oxley Act has distinguished itself as having especially expensive consequences compared with other recent legislation. The burden of complaint about the Act from the perspective of organizations affected is that it is costly to respond to. This cost is generally not budgeted for, nor is it often seen as part of an investment strategy. It is more akin to contingency funding than strategic spending to grow and develop the business. In this context it is not surprising that any spend in this arena is likely to be faced with considerable scrutiny. Yet so significant is the overall impact of the Act that budgets have been found and costs accepted. Some significant aspects of a mixed picture are emerging:

■ IT is the key to cutting compliance costs.
■ Compliance is an incomplete project.

Much of the onus for dealing with the quick response and the longer-term response to the Act has fallen on IT. IT projects have long been regarded as "costs" rather than "investments." In a "cost center versus profit center" world this is more than semantics, since it represents another facet of the long-standing division and lack of understanding between IT and the business functions. IT functions are frequently viewed as a treadmill of cost, of unpredictable return based on constantly changing technologies, challenging and expensive to staff, involving often disruptive upgrades with disappointing results. This view has been reinforced by the many spectacular project failures, and constant struggles to match the hype of new technology with the reality of everyday business. This disparity between promise and delivery has led to much resentment at board level, and a "necessary evil" acceptance.

However, there is a wide acceptance that IT is essential for business. The business case for effective systems in an information economy is unarguable, and good IT systems built on the needs of the business and tightly coupled with organization strategies can deliver real differentiation in the market and huge business benefits. Without IT, compliance with the Act would be impossible. More fundamentally, at a practical level compliance with the Act is about IT. So what is the cost of such compliance, and how does it affect the way an organization sees itself?

The Act is a driver for spending on IT. An analyst's report in 2005 talked of IT investment being driven up by governance and compliance laws. It anticipated increased budgets of up to 15 percent. As a result, in 2006 reserve and discretionary resources are being channeled into ensuring compliance by companies in the United States and Western Europe. As ever, these budgets had to come from somewhere, and they often left other projects exposed. As the importance of compliance has been established, there is now a willingness to allocate fresh budgets to corporate governance efforts. The costs are focused on:

- consulting services
- audits
- process management
- workflow
- documentation
- planning
- security.

Software solution spending is reflected as support for these areas. Overall there was an awareness of investing in solutions for multiple compliance efforts to make the most of the economies of scale and reuse.

COST–BENEFIT ANALYSIS

While there is a substantial debate about the increase in costs generated by the Act, it does not follow that this necessarily means these costs are too high. This is a cost–benefit position. If the benefits are great enough, then the cost is justifiable and cannot be classified as "too high." If a high-cost option defers great risk and heavy non-compliance costs, it is justifiable from a cost–benefit perspective. Any debate on costs must go beyond expenses and spend alone, and include the benefits. This moves the debate from considering the effectiveness of a system of internal control, to considering the efficiency of the system being controlled. There is a case for the argument that the Act is a mechanism for making your organization more efficient.

Benefits of the investment approach

As well as consuming resources, IT is now so embedded and essential to business processes that any improvements here can lead to cost savings. Practically all IT systems, applications, and platforms are under-used. There is a great deal of redundancy in implemented systems. For example, when buying mission-critical applications software suppliers often mandate that a dedicated system—such as a UNIX new platform—is allocated to their application alone. Software has traditionally been the driver for capital expenditure on platforms, from stand-alone PCs to complex mainframe environments, involving new infrastructure costs such as dedicated and specialist rooms, even buildings and ancillary staff and systems. Yet these systems have considerable slack built in. The potential for reuse and maximization of existing assets to support new processes or controls is considerable.

A number of CIOs have endorsed the value of compliance activities for the wider business benefits such projects have brought. This return on investment (ROI) is not generally part of the overall compliance assessment picture, unless it has been introduced as a decision criterion at the beginning of the compliance process. There will be piecemeal ROI assessments, such as with the procurement of software and externally sourced integration efforts. These will contribute to the bigger benefits picture, but compliance is largely reactive, unless it is truly married to active projects to improve processes and business activities to make them more efficient as well as effective. The argument for compliance spend is stronger if it can be shown to generate substantial business efficiencies. It is likely to do this only if it is planned and implemented with efficiency in mind, and with a more proactive approach to the value to the business, typical of a mature model. CIOs have cited a range of benefits resulting from compliance work, including better IT governance of projects which results in cost reductions and improved products, and long-term benefits as corporate customers demand proof that a supplier is a compliant operation.

COST AND COMPLEXITY

Given the breadth of the Act's implications it is inevitable that the business processes affected and the IT systems that support them are bound to be considerable in terms of both scope and cost. The equation between cost and complexity sees a compliance cost point located at the cross-over point between the increasing complexity of the organization and its processes, and the drive to push down costs. Figure 7.1 represents a simple linear relationship between the reality of increasing complexity and the drive to reduce costs. Over time, costs are assumed to fall, and the cost of controls is directly related to this balance, and is a function of the risk tolerance of the organization. The lower the risk tolerance, the higher the factor affecting the cost of compliance. It is here that the benefit of automated systems can make a difference, significantly reducing time and error in the processes driving cost; and accommodating complexity while achieving cost reduction. Without automation this ideal is impossible, since staff costs are also reduced.

When performance management is factored into the equation, additional costs begin to make an impact longer term. These are often poorly understood and rarely fully accounted for in the overall cost of ownership, and include especially recovery procedures, security systems, user access and authentication, and data integrity and life cycles.

ONGOING COSTS

As the compliance effort unfurls and the ongoing nature of the process carries it forward, a bigger cost begins to emerge. Some industry estimates use a simple equation to predict compliance costs based on the activities of the business. Viewed from a point of view of turnover, rough costings equate the cost of compliance to the Act as $1 million to every $1 billion of revenue.[1] This is a yearly cost. The assumption is that costs are high in the first year of implementing a compliance framework, and thereafter the costs fall, by as much as 35 or 40 percent. This also assumes that:

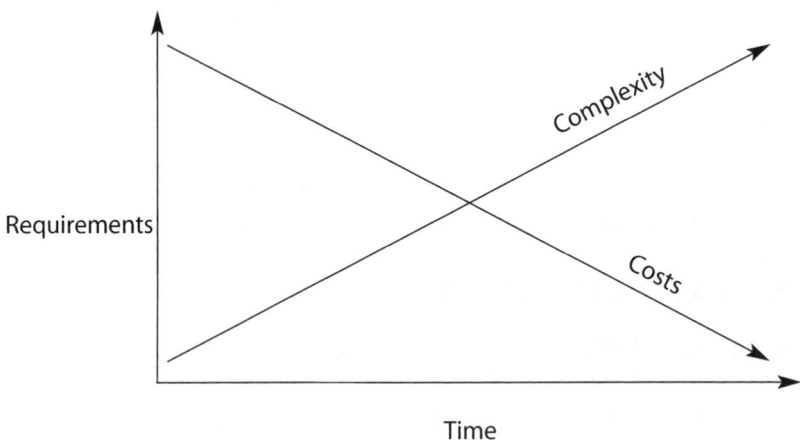

Figure 7.1 Cost versus complexity

- there is a consistent and well-conceived compliance process
- compliance efforts are broadly on track in the first year
- much of the work farmed out to consultants is handled in-house in subsequent years
- the skills developed are retained within the organization
- controls operate effectively
- the remediation efforts of following years are able to significantly reduce the risks
- these controls are subject to proper review by an experienced and skilled internal auditing function
- board-level commitment to the process is sustained.

However, as we shall see when looking at the COBIT model (which refers to company maturity; it is detailed in Chapter 23), the compliance "maturity" of the organization will also influence the approach to compliance in the first place. If that maturity level is relatively low and the organization has concentrated on quick fixes and manual solutions to deal with individual audit hurdles, some of the above assumptions will not hold true, and the ongoing costs in subsequent years may well be up to 10 percent higher.

Other hidden costs include those of maintaining skills:

- training for auditing and compliance staff, in familiarization with the Act and tools needed to manage the system of internal control.
- external training for IT staff tasked with managing and running software tools
- external training for auditing and management staff in current requirements
- internal training for all affected staff on policies and behavioral practice.

Cost and control objectives

However we look at the cost of compliance, we recognize the importance of time and the significance of the degradation of any cost effort. In Figure 7.2 the axis of "effectiveness" (e) is pitted against "time" (t). While the "expedient" phase sees a ramp up in value to a period of effectiveness, after a time this begins to degrade and sustainability becomes a challenge. Maintaining the cost of ongoing compliance here is a function of the effectiveness, expedience, and sustainability of a control or controls within a control objective.

Much of this translates into hours of human effort. The SEC, when assessing the costs to companies of becoming compliant, estimated that meeting the requirements of Section 404 would entail around 400 person

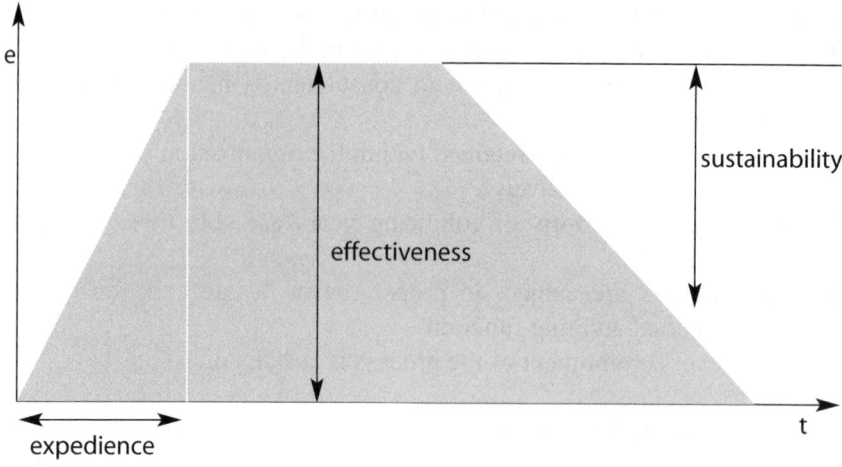

Figure 7.2 Maintaining the cost of ongoing compliance

hours of effort. However, industry surveys of actual efforts by affected companies indicate that for larger firms the effort is likely to total nearly 100 times the SEC's initial estimate. Estimates also project spending on external resources, such as consultants and software tools, to be an average of $1.3 million. The anticipated spend on audit fees is to top $1.5 million.

THE TRUE COST OF COMPLIANCE

Internationally there has been concern about the perceived cost burden of the Act. The Confederation of British Industry (CBI) called for changes to the Act, claiming that it is too onerous and costly,[2] reflecting views by non-US companies that have experience of existing legislative frameworks that implement Act-like measures without what they see as undue financial overheads. The CBI has a history of supporting corporate governance and transparency in disclosure, and has expressed its belief that the Act has improved US corporate governance and transparency. However, there are many caveats. In a response to the SEC's request for written comments on section 404, the CBI surveyed its members. They noted a number of concerns with the Act; among which were the costs of implementing compliance measures and the way the Act affects them. They believed costs:

> are not felt to be proportional to the risk. Companies have already invested significant amounts of money in complying with section 404 requirements but do not feel that the current level of cost or resource is sustainable.

The CBI survey makes a central point, which is critical to the experience of its members, about the cultural diversity of true international companies:

> There are practical difficulties, which make the current system unsustainable—e.g. there are simply not enough English speakers within the foreign subsidiaries of multinational companies to document all the risks to the degree necessary for compliance with the current PCAOB rules.

The debate has spilled across from the United States, and although there is recognition of the heavier balance of cost in early years, the CBI verdict was that "our members do not believe that these costs will decrease significantly." In the general course of planning making changes, implementing new systems and generally carrying out business, "Each of these activities will require internal controls to be modified and retested. The costs will continue to be huge and disproportionate to the benefits, unless changes are made" ("Costs," CBI 2005).

Visible and invisible costs

The real cost may not be easily measured. A cost that companies should also focus on is the potential cost of not being compliant. Fines and other penalties have built into substantial funds that could have been spent on the organization. Intangibles, such as loss of reputation and market presence, are almost incalculable, but still very real. In the case of Arthur Andersen, the cost amounted to a total loss. This is an extreme example, but it sets a final boundary that encompasses the whole organization as a potential loss of non-compliance. Clearly no risk profile can respond to that. However, there is still a correlation between the risk profile, losses that the organization is willing to suffer, and the amount an organization is willing to spend on becoming compliant. This is a discussion that has to occur early on in the compliance process, at the strategic level (see Chapter 12). As with all such initiatives, they are at heart insurance policies, and carry a premium. It is a question of how big a premium the business is worth. For financial services this invariably is a large figure, and the debate tends to be less about the total cost than about the timescale within which it has to be paid.

Costs can be categorized as visible and invisible:

- Visible costs reflect the budgets that have been discussed and agreed, and are signed off and/or declared in departmental accounts and reports.
- Invisible costs are those that are borne by the organization but not factored into the compliance effort. In effect these are the "hidden" costs of compliance.

Invisible costs

Because of the lack of visibility, these costs are not easy to quantify. Nevertheless they exist, and time and effort should be spent on identifying and valuing them. They may well be linked to risks associated with other activities, such as those identified in a comprehensive information security management system. This underlines the importance of scoping the compliance process as widely as possible at the outset.

An example of an invisible cost is listed in Table 7.1. This scenario can be multiplied many times. If it can be defined in terms of staff roles and time involved, a value can be assigned. This example touches on change control in support operations. In some instances the consequences of the Act can have an extraordinary effect.

DIVERTED COSTS

A further cost consideration is the way unexpected compliance funding diverts spending from other projects areas, such as treating security threats. The international security association Information Security Forum (ISF)

Table 7.1 Invisible costs of compliance

Scenario 1	IT support staff, such as application and database administrators, maintain a large installed base of applications and servers. Staff churn, internal movement and rotation, and application upgrading can lead to many changes being made, almost continuously.
Before the Act	Generally administrators and IT staff made noted changes according to "work queued."
Act Requirement	Internal controls are introduced to maintain responsibility, accountability, and traceability.
Actions as a result of the Act	Each change now has a control process that ensures all activities follow an approvals procedure that requires that any changes have to be "signed off" by appropriate managers.
Cost Implications	This greatly increases the time taken to make a change, translating into less efficiency, greater operational costs and staff dissatisfaction. This cost can be calculated as increased person hours, sometimes doubling or trebling the real cost of the change. The visible cost to implement the change is one-off, with additional costs at review points. The invisible costs are ongoing and cumulative. All costs are generally passed through to the consumer, leading to a less competitive product set.

has calculated that many members expect to spend double-digit millions of US dollars on information security controls for the Act.

Information security specialists also claim it has proved difficult to interpret the meaning of the Act. A lack of detail in the text of the Act on this subject means each company has to reinterpret the Act from its own perspective. This has advantages in that it focuses effort on really understanding the Act and shaping a response unique to the organization, but it is not good for consistency of response, something the PCAOB would encourage. Critical issues such as business continuity and disaster recovery are addressed directly. For financial services this is not such an acute concern, since in information economy institutions, information security and compliance can be integrated.

COST EXAMPLES

Two examples demonstrate how cost estimates vary and tend to push companies into following a compliance rather than risk-based approach.

BOC Group plc

In the non-financial sector in 2005, the global industrial gases company BOC, operating in 50 countries and employing 30,000 people, said that it expected its bill for complying with the Act to be higher than estimated, at around £20 million over the period to early 2007. It anticipated spending £10 million in 2005 and another £10 million in 2006. BOC states its total revenues as £4.5 billion in 2006. The company publicly stated that one of the drivers for its increasing corporate costs was the Act. The Annual Report and Accounts for 2005 (BOC 2005), directed at investors, states, "We estimate that meeting the requirements of Sarbanes-Oxley cost your company some £10 million this year. We are likely to spend the same next year before the costs reduce somewhat."

The report highlights a situation common to a number of large international companies with a US listing: "BOC has to comply with these provisions because we are registered in the US, but being a complex and diverse business working globally means that the cost of such compliance is very high" (BOC 2005). Note that our simple cost equation given earlier does not reflect the reality of the BOC Group's experience. A billion (turnover) to million (cost) should translate as £4.5 billion turnover to £4.5 million compliance spend; whereas BOC's spend was nearly double that in both the first and second years.

Dresdner Kleinwort Wasserstein

Anticipating similarities in demands from disparate regulations is another approach to compliance. The appropriate systems must be in place for investment bank Dresdner Kleinwort Wasserstein (DrKW). As an investment bank with international reach, DrKW offers a range of capital markets and advisory services. It is the investment bank of Dresdner Bank AG, and a member of the Allianz Group, with headquarters in London and Frankfurt, and offices in financial centers such as New York and Tokyo. In the "Corporate governance statement" in Dresdner Bank's Corporate Profile (2005), it reported:

> As a German corporation whose stock is listed at the New York Stock Exchange, the Allianz AG is subject to the more restrictive U.S. Corporate Governance regulations. The "Sarbanes-Oxley Act," in force since 2002, includes requirements of information disclosure, the installation of internal monitoring systems and regulations on increased reliability of company reporting. Additionally, it includes detailed regulations for an examination board. These regulations ... are already widely implemented within the Allianz AG.

DrKW's IT function claimed that nearly 15 per cent of its back-office staff were focused on compliance and regulation implementations. This represented a considerable cost which was expected to continue. The message from DrKW is that a greater awareness of how back-office systems support financial data processing is critical to developing the correct IT governance solutions. The organization also notes that the only way these costs can be reduced is through embedding automated processes in everyday business activities. Part of the problem is getting a full view of the overall process and understanding where the links and dependencies lie to ensure the system is complete.

Because of the way legislation is moving, there are likely to be substantial efforts in other areas such as the EU Markets in Financial Instruments Directive (MiFID),[3] which could reuse the control systems established for the Sarbanes-Oxley Act. Getting the control environment right is doubly important. In the case of DrKW, ITIL and COBIT have been used as frameworks to shape the company's response to the Act.

Allianz notes, in its Corporate Governance Report 2005, that "the Sarbanes-Oxley Act (SOA) of 2002 in particular has a significant effect on our corporate governance." A great deal of effort has gone into complying with Section 404 in particular.

On the positive side, such intensive investigations into the way the company operates and the documentation of control systems have led to the identification and remediation of weak points. The company had already made amendments on internal rules for the audit committee, and procedures for handling complaints, and for ensuring the independence of auditors.

AUDITOR COSTS

In the United Kingdom, the CBI has warned that the Companies Bill may create a criminal offence of "knowingly or recklessly" allowing material that is "misleading, false or deceptive" into an audit report.[4] This Act-like measure could lead to legal constraints on the way auditors operate, and could be reflected on their clients as a £250 million per year cost, replicating some of the perceived mistakes of the Act. The CBI believes that the consequences could make auditors more defensive, more cautious in their approach to clients, and more sensitive to risk. These are all behavioral observations made in the United States since the inception of the Act.

Over recent years in the United Kingdom, driven by the new regulatory climate, the accountancy profession has lost self-regulatory powers and been subject to tougher auditing and accounting standards, as well as inspections by an independent regulator. Under this legislation the UK government allows audit firms to agree with clients limits on liability from damages claims. The intention is to make auditors think hard about signing off a report they know to be wrong. This increased risk aversion translates into higher fees. There is also a likely tendency to err on the side of caution and pessimism in evaluating clients, and auditors are more likely to publicly disclose information that calls into doubt a company's ability to stay in existence. This might also affect the ability of a company to get additional funding and affect mergers and acquisitions.

PRACTICAL COMPLIANCE SUMMARY

- Adopt solutions that support multiple regulations to gain the most from investment.
- Ensure solutions support as much of the business as possible.
- Widen the scope of the compliance process to include cost assessments of other initiatives: on security, legislation, internal policies and business-driven IT projects.
- Use automation to trim costs, especially for controls where possible.
- Turn exception reports into work programs.
- Centralize on enterprise resource planning (ERP) or other central storage to consolidate and centralize support costs.
- Reuse system assets and make use of "spare" capacity in the existing infrastructure.
- Ensure the skills required to maintain compliance are retained. These are the real longer-term investment.

NOTES

1. For a fuller discussion of this relationship see Curtis and Stone (2006).
2. In "Comments on Sarbanes-Oxley Act," April 2005, the Confederation of British Industry (CBI) canvassed the views of members in its response to the SEC's call for comments on Section 404. The response was a representative cross-section of UK businesses, many of which were listed in the United States, and so affected by the Act. The companies included 80 of the FTSE 100, 50 US listed companies, major UK investors, and some 200,000 small and medium-sized firms and more than 20,000 manufacturers.
3. The Markets in Financial Instruments Directive (MiFID), part of the European Union's Financial Services Action Plan (FSAP), replaces the Investment Services Directive (ISD), legislation for investment intermediaries and financial markets. MiFID supplements the ISD regime and introduces new and more extensive requirements to which firms will have to adapt, in particular in relation to their conduct of business and internal organization.
4. Source: CBI (2005). The CBI has warned the UK and US governments of the potential cost of a crackdown on auditors. The CBI speaks on behalf of 240,000 businesses in the United Kingdom which together employ around a third of the UK's private sector workforce, and coordinates British business representation around the world. Although not all CBI members are US-listed or SEC registered, nevertheless Sarbanes-Oxley has affected a wider group of companies because of their relationship with those that are directly affected by the Act. The CBI notes the example of linkages, for example where a bank that is a US-listed company has private equity in a non-listed company. In this instance the bank might have to report this investment and request Sarbanes-Oxley style information from the unlisted company.

CHAPTER 8

Responsibility

INTRODUCTION

Initially the Enron scandal was about a lack of clarity and accuracy in the financial statements on the organization. Investigations looked at the activities of the company as a whole, and its officers were deemed part of this. As the investigation moved forward, more and more emphasis was placed on the roles and responsibilities of the company's senior executives. The investigators found that although the company was at fault, with apparent systemic weaknesses in transparency, it was the specific personal misdeeds of individuals in positions which gave them power and control over the resources of the organization that were doing the most damage. From this has developed a sharp focus within the Sarbanes-Oxley Act on specific roles within the organization, notable the CEO, the chief financial officer (CFO), and others whose roles approximate to these functions. The novelty in this legislation is its insistence on the culpability of these individuals and the responsibility they bear for a publicly listed company. This responsibility translates, in the worst case, to heavy fines and long periods of imprisonment. Here, if ever there was, are instances of incentive to ensure the compliance process works. To spell out this incentive, if it can be called such, is the purpose of much of the Act.

SUMMARY OF KEY ISSUES FOR SENIOR EXECUTIVES

The Act places the CEO and the CFO at the center of the compliance process. Ultimately they have the responsibility for its success or failure and they are the primary victims of any such failure. Table 8.1 is a summary of their relationship with the Act. However, as we shall see, responsibility by no means stops at board level. In fact, responsibility for compliance is shared among everyone involved in the company.

Table 8.1 Impact on senior executives of the Sarbanes–Oxley Act

Requirements	Impact on senior executives
Disclosure controls and procedures	The CEO and CFO are specifically responsible for establishing controls over financial reporting. These controls ensure that all relevant information is available for reporting.
Certification of the effectiveness (quality in operation) of disclosure controls	The CEO and CFO must certify that they have evaluated the internal control system, and by their assessment (through an internal control report) found it does provide them with all material information and that they need.
Filing the internal control report	The internal control report must accompany the company's annual 10-K SEC filing. This report contains details of the assessment. This assessment must be reported on by the organization's statutory auditors (who attest to its veracity).
Penalties for non-compliance	The CEO and CFO, as signatories to the reports, are subject to fines and criminal penalties, including imprisonment, for violation of the provisions of the Securities Exchange Act, amended by the Sarbanes–Oxley Act.
Real-time disclosures	Any change to a company's financial condition, operations, and general state, if relevant to investors, must be disclosed on a real time basis.
Responsibilities of audit committee	The audit committee is now responsible for appointing and overseeing the work of the internal auditor. An external auditor is required to report directly to the audit committee.

EXECUTIVE RESPONSIBILITY

The system of internal control

Section 302 specifies that the "signing officers" have overall responsibility for the system of internal control and its documentation and disclosure. Traditionally, senior executives point to IT management for systems controls, procurement decisions, and effective control over internal communications. The selection of internal processes and their management may also be a function of IT, but this can be shared with other departments, such as sales, administration, finance, or customer relations, depending on the culture of the organization. Traditionally the board reviews and passes on requests for expenditure, but it largely only reacts to a prominent failure of an internal control: responsibility for the operational effectiveness of the control system lies elsewhere. It is also worth noting that the status of the IT function varies according to company and country. The head of IT and communications might not be a member of the board of directors, and this lack of status can have a debilitating effect on prioritizing systems of control.

Under the Act, the signing officers are publicly accountable for any failure in internal control that leads to non-compliance with the Act. This implies a greater personal involvement of the board in the selection and funding of projects to initiate effective internal controls, and for ongoing maintenance and support of these controls.

Design and construction of internal controls

These senior executives are also responsible for the construction of effective controls. This responsibility links to others detailed in Section 404: Management assessment of internal controls. This specific follow-up to the generality of responsibility for internal controls places a deadline for action on this evaluation, which is rolled into financial reporting to ensure it is published, verified, and tested.

EVALUATION AND ASSESSMENT

The officers are also responsible for an evaluation of the present state of affairs on internal controls. This is no passive "awareness": the requirements insist on an active evaluation of the systems for which they are responsible, and for this evaluation to be included in an annual report. The evaluation, moreover, is a detailed assessment, which should include weaknesses and deficiencies in the system, and comment on the effectiveness of the system.

Executive responsibility under the Act is, then, more than an officer's duty to do his or her best. It is a compulsion to perform well a number of activities and demonstrate personal competence through published disclosure. For investors this is a powerful measure to focus involvement in the compliance process where it is most effective—at the very top of the organization. Investors and the general public have been spectators to the practice of departing executives who have conspicuously failed to deliver value to their investors, being rewarded with bonuses and golden handshakes. It seemed as if non-performance was being rewarded. The Act completely changes this, since non-performance in this area can lead to large fines and imprisonment. Any such contribution to corporate best practice is generally welcomed. This may have gone some way to taking the edge off of investor activism. In financial services, for confidence to be high, the custodial expert who decides what to do and what not to do with securities on behalf of the client must be seen to be competent and honest. Anything less than the highest of standards is damaging. How do executives demonstrate that they are worthy of respect and their companies are worth investing in?

ETHICAL BEHAVIOR

One way is to demonstrate that the behavior of the company is subject to best practice; or to be more precise, the behavior of those targeted by the Act—senior executives—is of the very best. By "behavior" we mean activities governed by adherence to rules and regulations that protect the interests of investors. This is what lies behind Section 406, the Code of Ethics, a requirement for the public company to disclose that it has adopted a code of ethics for senior financial officers (see Table 8.2). Through this the company is mandated to publicly demonstrate that it has a set of guiding principles, and that these principles are ethically in keeping with good industry practice. The SEC is to revise its regulations to require the immediate disclosure of "any change in, or waiver of" a company's code of ethics.

But what is this "code of ethics"? Broadly, this is a code of behavior subscribing to standards necessary to promote "honest and ethical conduct" in the handling of conflicts of interests between personal and professional relationships. The Act talks of "the full, fair, accurate, timely and understandable disclosure in the periodic reports required to be filed by the issuer"; and "compliance with applicable government rules and regulations." Having defined the requirement for an ethical framework, the Act assumes this will encourage, even force, companies to change their behavior where necessary, and rebuild a reputation for corporate good practice across the securities and allied industries.

The publication of a code of ethics is not onerous in itself. However, adherence to it might be. The power of compulsion through penalties and similar threats, might induce a degree of compliance, but what really generates compliance is a true interest in abiding by behavior which benefits individuals and the company, and is seen and believed to generate such benefits. These benefits are always financial. Proof of delivery of such benefits is the strongest suite in the hands of regulators. It leads senior executives towards the true goal of cooperation.

THE ROLE OF NON-EXECUTIVE DIRECTORS

One study the SEC was tasked to perform when the Act was first passed was to track back and investigate why senior executives and boards of directors were able to subvert what was thought to be good business practice. Evidence emerged of a number of failings. One of these was the failure of non-executive directors to perform as expected. These roles were assumed to address a number of vital functions for the boards of large corporates. Two of these were of special importance:

■ Introduce needed expertise on reporting, general financial skills, and experience of markets for the company.

Table 8.2 Requirements for a code of ethics for senior executives

Section of Act	Requirement	Practical compliance
Section 406 (a) and (b)	"Prompt" disclosure on Form 8-K (or any successor thereto).	Define and agree a code of ethics for board level behavior and senior executive behavior. Amend any relevant documentation to include a code of ethics section.
Section 406 (c) The term "code of ethics" is defined by standards that promote: (1) honest and ethical conduct (2) full, fair, accurate and timely disclosure (3) compliance with regulations	The management of conflicts on interest between personal and professional relationships, in an ethical manner.	Ensure periodic reports (such as 10-K and 8-K) contain a reference to the code of ethics. Establish specific rules to manage conflicts of interest in the company's handbook on ethical conduct. Make this information available to all staff. Ensure there is a board review at least once per year and that an ethical section appears on the regular company board agenda.

- Act as overseers of the behavior of the officers of the board, to ensure ethical behavior was being observed.

It was clear, from investigations and research, that non-executive directors were not delivering on at least one if not both counts. The role of these appointees, and succession planning around the absence of such board members, has been the subject of legislation in the United Kingdom as well as the United States.[1]

THE RESPONSIBILITY CASCADE

It is not just executives who have to be aware of the ramifications of the Act at a personal level. The Act addresses staff throughout the organization. When, in Section 802, the Act says, "Whoever knowingly alters, destroys, mutilates, conceals, covers up, falsifies, or makes a false entry in any record, document, or tangible object with the intent to impede, obstruct, or influence the investigation … shall be fined under this title, imprisoned not more than 20 years, or both," almost anyone can be culpable. The reality is that direct responsibility is focused at the top of the organization. However, those who have access to and control the materials under discussion are most likely to be in a senior position. When we come to consider the separation of responsibilities, or separation of duties, as a factor in the compliance process, liability may not track to the level of customer interfaces, but responsibility for ensuring a compliant organization does. As the process unfolds, it becomes clear that responsibilities accrue to a number of key staff other than senior executives. Certainly it will appear that way to those executives who are going to suffer the consequences of events that trigger non-compliance at lower levels.

From a practical point of view we need to consider how responsibility for compliance "cascades" down the organization, and what this means for staff at all levels. This is built into our review of compliance as a system of internal control. Within this there are two parameters that identify the degree of responsibility and the active level of participation required:

- Control and process ownership identifies responsibilities.
- The process itself activates these responsibilities as positive actions.

Figure 8.1 indicates how responsibility cascades down the organization, taking in and touching all staff. The internal control system, which we examine in detail, helps flesh this out. Most functions are clarified throughout this process. However, some functions have a special significance under the Act for good reason. These are dealt with and allocated specific requirements:

- the responsibilities of auditors, both internal and external
- the responsibilities of attorneys.

AUDIT COMMITTEE

The audit committee plays a central role in overseeing compliance activities within the company. Its importance to the realization of the objectives of the Act is visible in the number of references made to it. In Section 204 the issuer audit committee, as a committee of the board of directors, is responsible for appointing, paying, and managing external auditors, and the external auditors must report directly to the audit committee.

This section places responsibility on the auditing firm to disclose practices in the relationship between client and auditor. The audit committee must manage complaints on all aspects of financial reporting, as well "confidential, anonymous submission" of concerns on "questionable

Responsibility cascade

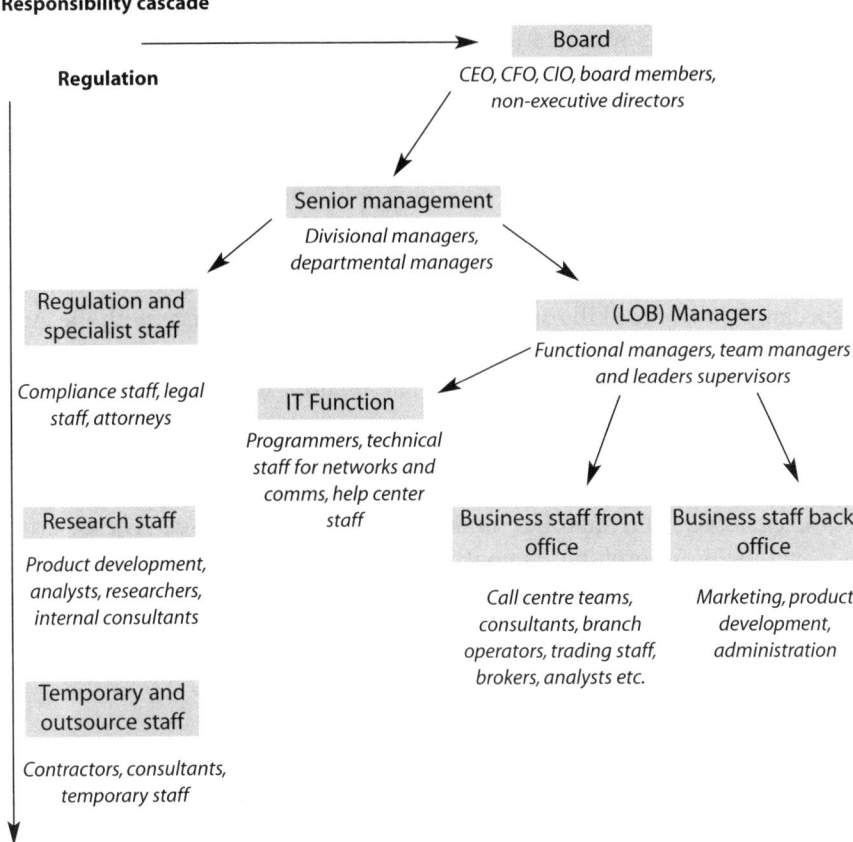

Figure 8.1 The responsibility cascade

accounting or auditing matters." This responsibility as the receiver of whistleblowing contacts is particularly important. Under Section 307, an attorney has to report in a similar manner. If there is no appropriate response, then the attorney must report this to the audit committee or to the board of directors By implication, if the whistleblower cannot get a response from the audit committee, the next option is to report to the regulator, so any response to such a complaint must be measured. Section 302(a)(5)(A) notes that there is a requirement to disclose to the audit committee all "significant deficiencies" in the design or operation of internal controls and any "material weaknesses" in these controls. All these activities must be covered by appropriate funding.

Generally the audit committee consists of representatives of the board of directors. Under Section 407, at least one member of the committee must be a financial expert, acknowledged as such through certified qualifications.

This is a common expectation since the NYSE and other stock exchanges require an audit committee to have financial expertise. The SEC sees a financial expert as someone with expertise in:

- Generally Accepted Accounting Principles (GAAP)
- audit procedures
- internal controls.

There may be an issue finding someone who is suitably qualified. This is especially so of the skills specific to overseeing compliance with the Act. Boards of directors do not always have auditing, banking, or general financial expertise and experience of sufficient quality. In these situations there are two options available to organizations:

- Recruit a director or non-executive director with suitable skills and experience who qualifies under the terms of the Act. These terms include those prohibiting conflicts of interest with external auditors.
- Hire financial expertise for the duration of the compliance process. The Act specifically condones the use of external financial expertise. Given that the compliance process should be ongoing, these will be almost a permanent posting.

As well as managing the relationship with external auditors, the audit committee is responsible for appointing and overseeing the work of the internal auditor. The relationship extends, under the compliance process explored later, to include the compliance task force (CTF). As the representative body for the board in the compliance process, the audit committee acts as an ultimate authority in the organization. The Federal Reserve Bank of New York details the remit of its Audit Committee through a charter (Section 4 of its Audit Committee Charter: www.ny.frb.org/aboutthefed/audit.html). The responsibilities and authority cover reviewing the financial statement and disclosures made by the organization, oversight of the relationship with the external auditor, oversight of its internal audit activities, and responsibility for compliance with regulations and operational risk. This scope and responsibility underpins the role of auditing in general, but has special significance for internal auditing. It is here that the audit committee engages directly with the practical work of compliance.

PRACTICAL COMPLIANCE SUMMARY

- Ensure the audit committee is suitably staffed with financial expertise.
- Ensure the audit committee and the board of directors are educated to an appropriate level on their responsibilities under the Act.
- Ensure key operations and support staff are made aware of their responsibilities under the Act.
- Set up a compliance dashboard as an early warning system for senior executives.
- Introduce a "financial monitor" to detect significant qualifying changes on the state of the company that need to be reported on.
- Educate senior executives on the evaluation for the assessment process.
- Institute and publish a code of ethics for the board and senior executives.
- Define a responsibility cascade for the organization.
- Review the skills and responsibilities of non-executive directors, and recruit or hire necessary skills.

NOTES

1. The role of non-executive directors has been stressed in a number of national directives and legislation, notably the Combined Code and the Turnbull Report in the United Kingdom. The Combined Code recommends that non-executive directors should play an important role in guiding the remuneration of directors, and in audit committees. The Turnbull Report reinforced these recommendations by offering additional guidance to directors.

CHAPTER 9

Internal Auditing

INTERNAL AUDITING

Internal auditing is an activity that examines and reviews the reliability and integrity of financial and operational information, and compares compliance with company policies and procedures as well as external regulations. The Sarbanes-Oxley Act is about risk management and the processes within an organization that shape its governance. Internal auditing is in a position to provide objective assurance for management responsible for developing the processes essential for compliance with the Act. The internal auditing role should ideally be one of support through consultation and assurance. Internal audit is the eyes and ears of senior management, who want to know, in a formal and verifiable way, the operational state of play for their organization. As such it assists financial and operational management and highlights weaknesses, the potential for loss and business irregularities, and provides, as part of its function, practical guidance on remediation.

The importance of effective internal auditing is fundamental when a company is going through a compliance process. The success of this function, probably more than any other, makes or breaks the company's response. Yet it is not always the case that the audit function is listened to with as much attention as it should be. Traditionally, auditing has been seen as a burden on the business, an imposed and necessary evil rather than an asset. The Institute of Internal Auditors has invested time and energy in correcting this view, and reinforced the professionalism of this function through certification and standards setting.[1] The Act has played its part in raising the profile of internal auditing; it is now seen as a fundamental necessity for the future health of the organization. At a SEC round table on the implementation of reporting requirements of Section 404 (SEC 2005), those present, including regulators, CEOs, CFOs, board and audit committee members, recognized this by agreeing that internal auditors were now fundamental to effective corporate governance, critical to efficient business operations, and essential to systems of internal control. Ideally effective internal controls nullify the need for more legislation and onerous regulation. If companies can get their internal auditing to a sufficient standard, regulation is an unnecessary extra layer of business administration.

EXECUTIVE ACTION

Quality systems have established themselves in the corporate psyche. The time is ripe for regulatory specialists to have their contribution recognized. This is especially so for company directors and senior executives who have direct responsibilities under the Act. The National Association of Corporate Directors (NACD) has urged its members to understand how internal auditors add value to their activities (Bookal 2003). From a practical perspective there are a number of recommendations for senior executives to follow:

■ **Communicate with internal auditors about the problems they face.** Internal auditors operate on behalf of the company and have its best interests at heart. As the Act bites and forces external auditors to review their own risk profiles and begin to distance themselves from their clients, internal auditors are the closest that companies have to a true audit adviser. It makes sense to ensure they can do a good job. As a priority:
   – ensure they are managing well with the resources available
   – consider them as real allies
   – train them to make the best possible contribution.
   Invest for the future as well as the present. One of the industry trends we noted earlier is to ease reliance on external consultants. While external auditors are necessary, internal auditors represent a flexible and valuable pool of expertise for now and the future.
■ **Coordinate activities with compliance staff.** Ensure that the internal auditors understand the purpose of the Act and what it is intended to achieve. Link them with compliance staff, and involve the chief compliance officer (CCO) in planning internal audits, if he or she is not already involved. An ideal forum for this cooperation and exchange of ideas is the compliance task force.
■ **Coordinate the work of the audit committee with internal audits.** Ensure both sides reflect the business objectives, and that internal auditing has a clear, supported mandate for action.
■ **Join up the codes of practice and conduct.** This is needed to ensure a consistent code of behavior for everyone involved in the audit process. In particular use the executive code of ethics mandated by the Act as a basis for promoting the company's good corporate governance, and make internal auditing part of that published picture.

- **Involve staff in the audit process.** Adopt CSA methods[2] to involve operations staff in decision making and feedback on practical measures. Rotate board-level member involvement to spread the understanding of responsibility and accountability.
- **Offer advice and input to the internal audit process.** The perspectives of a director brings a unique perspective to the internal audit process, especially from a strategic angle. Directors:
  - can help prioritize and shape direction based on high-level objectives
  - can indicate key control objectives for limited resources to focus on, and help in defining some of the vaguer terms of the Act
  - can spell out responsibilities and concepts such as deficiencies and weaknesses
  - operate with authority and simplify decision making.
- **Encourage and involve fellow directors.** Generate interest in the internal auditing process by championing the activity; ensure fellow directors are educated about the Act and the necessity for effective auditing by bringing in experts for seminars and involving their own internal audit specialists; support the audit committee.

For those engaged in internal auditing, the Act has brought a number of challenges. These challenges spring directly from the specifics of the Act and the primacy of the system of internal control. The finance sector, along with the manufacturing world, has long understood the importance of maintaining quality standards. The maturity of their systems plays a great part in the perception of the integrity of operations, but the failures in corporate controls that led to the Act suggest a re-examination of internal controls.

Auditing activities tend to fall into two areas, financial auditing and IT auditing. These areas are often managed by the same audit function, but the skills and domain knowledge are separable. They might also require a difference in emphasis. The IT function sees a great deal of specific auditing activities, and its planning process offers insights which marry well with the compliance process.

IT AUDIT PLANNING

There are many risks in the IT arena. They stretch across the functional areas of:

- internal networking—LANs, intranets
- external communications systems—wide area networks (WANs), metropolitan area networks (MANs), virtual private networks (VPNs), leased line systems, email systems, and unstructured communications

- back-office support systems—clustered servers, centralized data storage, data hosting, server farms, core applications, and websites
- front-office systems—desktop PCs, mobile PCs, mobile PDAs, front-end applications, application tools (such as Microsoft Office™), browser applications, and dispersed data storage.

This is an immense area to cover, and can generally only be managed through intense prioritization of resources. Information security and formal IT management frameworks such as ISO 17799 and ITIL are models for managing the many processes that have their origins in, and flow through, this environment.

Best practice dictates that to adopt a strategic approach, auditors need to work with management to establish a framework for audit activities. Many IT auditors are responsible for reviewing the technical and operational aspects of existing and planned systems, and assessing the risks they pose. This generates an audit plan which pools the experience of management and audit staff. Married to a familiarity with known risks, this produces an initial plan on how these issues should be approached, and determines the level of priority to assign to each process area.

The initial plan focuses on:

- The scope of activity and responsibilities and roles. Initial planning explores expectations and builds responsibilities around these.
- Prioritization within the overall internal audit subject area. Audits happen over timed periods; these periods can be months, years, or cycles of three years and so on. There are a number of factors that influence the way processes and activities are selected for first, second, and third period audits:
  - the culture of the organization and the way it sets priorities
  - the experience of auditors within the company and other companies
  - the strategic direction of the organization: this is the business direction for IT derived from the overall organizational strategic plan
  - the effect of new projects in a constantly changing technology world.

The planning structure will look something like this, in terms of the key elements to be addressed for IT audits:

- business strategy and auditing strategy
- the scope within the business
- risk analysis
- resource management
- approvals process
- implementation planning.

One challenge faced by the compliance process is that there is often no a coherent strategic plan for IT itself. Rather there is a set of tactical plans as it struggles to meet the demands of business in the context of limited budgets and constantly shifting capabilities within IT technology. New business directives also drive the generation of new risks and unanticipated consequences. Plans to expand into overseas markets can introduce huge volumes of work not captured in the original business plan. Assumptions about business conditions, cultural behavior, and communications capacity may be well off target. This tends to put more emphasis on IT operations and systems as a way forward. IT auditing must somehow accommodate this to ensure it offers the kind of assurance that management expects.

The scoping exercise has to cover a great deal, and do so thoroughly. It covers:

- people
- policies
- processes
- communications
- hardware and software

IT audit management must be able to assess the key risks that the business strategy encompasses.

Risk register

The IT audit manager should evaluate risks relating to these activities, but should also have access to the organization's risk register. This register is generally the result of an exercise that examines the business functions and documents the risks identified. Each risk is owned by the relevant manager, who should work on ways to mitigate, eliminate, or work around it. IT auditors can help analyze and define the risks.

A risk register can help speed up the audit process, depending on the quality of its construction and thoroughness of its assembly. It should include a review of the risks, based on the risk strategy of the organization. At a strategic level it is also dependent on a strategic risk analysis, which priorities audit activities.

IT audit staff and managers will decide on what risks to review based on their resources and the priorities assigned. Audit plans from the past will also be an important input to this process, and will have made their contributions to the risk register, but because of the wide remit of the Act they are likely to be dated and in need of review anyway.

Risk analysis

Within a risk analysis process there are several methods to determine the nature of IT risks. One approach is to assign a monetary value to the impact of each identified risk, then determine the probability of that risk occurring. This is an approach seen in ISO 17799.[3] The risk value is then equal to the cost of the risk multiplied by the probability of the risk occurring. In the case of an IT audit on security and security controls, this probability is subject to the vulnerability of an asset covered by the risk, and the likelihood of an attack on that asset being successful.

Very quickly, using an effective risk register and good auditing tools, risks can be reviewed and evaluated as inputs to the compliance process. They should be graded, and documented as high, medium, and low. From this, prioritized treatment can be planned.

If the organization has not implemented a risk register or something close to it, IT audit leaders may need to undertake the full risk assessment themselves by developing a risk register, or by working in an ad hoc fashion based on a set of priorities set by business functions independently of a systematic risk register.

Resources

The whole audit activity is very much dependent on available resources. As with most areas that require skilled resources, extra resources must be found by:

- training internal staff in audit skills
- recruiting skilled audit staff
- hiring consultant auditors for the duration of audits.

A further alternative is to delay specific auditing activities and adjust the auditing "period" associated with that area. This may not be an option for the activities linked to the Act. As with all compliance process activities, the longer-term view dictates that a permanent capability should be developed that matches the needs of the organization, or at least a core of staff established that can be supplemented from time to time with hired consultants. Much depends on the costs the organization is prepared to carry to achieve its auditing targets.

Senior management approval

Nearly all formal frameworks include an approvals process, stressing the importance of having senior management consent to the activities to be undertaken, as well senior management recognition that tasks have been satisfactorily completed. In particular the audit committee will need to approve the plan and the proposed schedule of work. Audit plans will be subject to last-minute changes at this stage because of unknowns such as sudden projects and periods when no activities can be carried out "parallel running" of new solutions, and classic instances such as month-end accounting.

The IT plan: timescale

The plan is to carry out auditing within a time frame. Resource restrictions normally require auditing to be staggered. This is desirable anyway, since auditing is a time-bound monitoring process. Ideally it might be automated continuous self-monitoring, but that is for the future in an ideal world with the "perfect" organization, an unrealistic and unlikely concept.

The frequency of auditing for any department or function is generally from one to three years. The department will be placed on a rota and audited accordingly. However, some sections of the Act, such as Sections 302 and 404, imply an auditing frequency of once a quarter. The reality will see departments monitored according to internally set priorities. In this case the prioritization would be set by organizational, not regulatory, requirements. This can sometimes be a contradiction and decisions may need to be made at the strategic level (within the strategic part of the compliance process). Inputs to these decisions will include new risks to the business, reprioritization of audit activities, and external factors such as updates to regulations.

By exploiting feedback from the process and moving closer to continuous monitoring of these factors, IT audit can continue to refine and improve the plan to ensure that the organization gains the reassurance it needs, and that management continue to place their trust and reliance in their IT audit department.

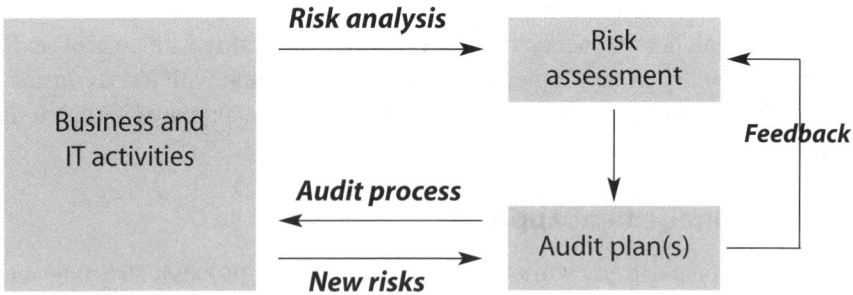

Figure 9.1 IT audit feedback to risk assessment

Implementing the IT audit plan

Once the plan is approved, the next step is to make everyone involved in the audit process aware of its scope, terms of reference, dates of implementation, auditing staff, and expectations of departments affected. The most efficient method is to publish the plan. For many financial organizations this now means publishing through a company intranet. The feedback loop illustrated in Figure 9.1 should be accounted for, and a process put in place, again using a collaborative intranet forum or similar mechanism to capture risks and comments for the register and future audits.

The IT audit provides a number of useful modeling activities for internal auditing. However, there are other, more generalized models that are common in the industry and particularly suited to the mature compliance process.

AUDITING MODELS: CONTROL SELF-ASSESSMENT

Control self-assessment (CSA) is an internal audit methodology that enables an organization to assess the effectiveness of its controls as well as support the audit of business processes. It emerged as a means of involving staff other than audit professionals in the audit process, dealing with "soft," or informal, opinion-based controls, as well as "hard," quantitative controls, and has gained acceptance across many industry sectors. The IIA definition (IIA 1998) sees CSA as a process for examining and assessing internal control effectiveness to provide assurance that business objectives are being met. It broadens the scope of staff involvement by allowing management and those engaged in the work processes to:

- actively engage in the assessment process for internal controls
- contribute to the evaluation of risk
- be part of the solution for identified weaknesses
- assist in achieving business objectives.

CSA as a technique is anchored in standards and linked to the internal auditing profession. The approach of CSA greatly helps the design phase of generating controls, as well as helping to assess operational effectiveness by increasing an operating unit's involvement. The scope of internal auditing concerns the evaluation of the adequacy and effectiveness of an organization's system of internal control, and the ability to carry out responsibilities.

As well as supporting the evaluation of effectiveness, the CSA process supports performance reviews of management's self-assessment activities. The practical mechanism developed for CSA is based on one of three approaches, or combinations of them:

- facilitated team meetings (also referred to as workshops)
- questionnaires
- management-produced analysis.

This practical scheme is very aware of the organization within which it is operating, and is responsive to the company culture, which often thwarts a well-established process. It is recommended that the organization understands its own culture and selects an approach accordingly. Participation by staff at all levels is critical to the success of the process. Those who can accommodate facilitated team meetings gain the most. Others can combine questionnaires with other formal analyses.

CSA offers four basic facilitated meeting formats:

- A control-based format, focused on how well the controls in place are actually working. Specialists with input from upper management define objectives and control techniques. This results in a gap analysis on control operations.
- A process-based format, which focuses on activities performed within selected processes to update or streamline them. It leads to breadth of analysis.
- A risk-based format, which focuses on identifying and managing risk.
- An objective-based format, which determines the best way to accomplish an objective.

CSA and compliance

CSA adds significantly to the compliance process for the Act. These formats act as supplements to standard internal auditing, and enable staff from many disciplines to collaborate in larger entity-wide efforts. CSA can be used to increase a sense of ownership and responsibility, increasing the effectiveness of corrective action by transferring ownership to operating employees.

When it comes to implementing CSA practically, there are a number of issues that the organization must consider:

- The scope of the compliance process measured against the CSA process. The organization must decide what section will use CSA, in terms of functions, geographies, and detail.
- The impact of the organization's culture, placing compliance within the cultural characteristics of the organization.
- The use of results. The results of risk assessment can be used to tailor, or validate, internal auditing work. This is especially useful for pragmatic compliance work.

■ CSA process enhancements. Tools, techniques, frameworks and documentation are decided on for gathering and reporting CSA information.
■ Internal auditing involvement. The issue here is, who is to drive the process: internal auditing or operational management? It is an issue for the compliance task force when allocating responsibilities. This introduces the question of how far auditing professionals should get involved in the facilitated process, and what their involvement entails.

Ultimately, how the CSA process is used is very dependent not only on the corporate culture and the balance struck between auditing professionals and actual user involvement, but on the nature of the frameworks chosen. The Act anticipates that COSO and a COBIT or COBIT-like framework will be the backbone. Resolving how to use self-assessments or audits so as to conform to these reference models or fit in with their processes is part of the strategic phase of the compliance process.

The IIA indicate that the preferred approach is to use a control framework with both self-assessments and formal audits. The power of frameworks lies in the way they can cross functional boundaries and consolidate information, providing a "completeness of control."

AUDITING TOOLS

Behind every successful internal auditing team sits a toolbox that is tailored to meet the requirement of the company. The evolution of computer-assisted audit techniques (CAAT) based on sophisticated software products has mirrored the growth of other business software. There have been a fair amount of hype, great expense, difficult implementations, and considerable disappointment at the point of delivery. However, the tool box is getting fuller, and current internal audit teams have a number of products to select from. The complex of software solutions can be visited separately. What does hold true are common-sense steps to ensure the tool is a worthwhile investment:

■ Check that it does what it claims to do.
■ Check that it does what you want it to do.
■ Test and evaluate it before use, ideally using a proof of concept (POC) project, with data and processes from the organization.
■ Choose from a selection of solutions, not just one tool.
■ If the tool is part of an integrated package, carefully weight up the trade-off between the loss in functionality against a better stand-alone tool, and the costs of integrating the tool with other, often existing, tools. For example, in many instances a relatively small loss in functionality is greatly outweighed by ease of integration. Apply the 80:20 rule here, as elsewhere.

CAAT

CAAT generally involves using software applications to gather and analyze data, perform trend analysis, and manage activities that would otherwise be overly time-consuming and which need a degree of automation. The types of CAAT available vary from specialized languages for constructing tailored solutions to out-of-the-box applications for quick implementation. Time, as ever, is a critical decision criterion. There are claims in the market that astute choice of software tools can reduce compliance costs by as much as 25 percent. With a trend towards automation and the simplification of processes, software offers enormous rewards longer-term if the choice is correct and the implementation successful.

CAAT tools have evolved from solutions that traditionally supplied technologies for data analysis to support auditors in their role of repetitive controls testing. Some claim to offer continuous monitoring, handling very large volumes of data, filtered for anomalies and exceptions. Some are specialist or specific to types of legislation, such as supporting sustainable Sarbanes-Oxley Section 404 compliance. They are characterized by:

- applying automated, predefined analytics mapped to a framework
- independently testing controls against large volumes of transactions
- alerting and highlighting exceptions for fast remedial action.

Many of these solutions also apply automated analytics to test the effectiveness of controls against control objectives; many CAAT tools use the web and browser technologies. This kind of product begins to highlight the advantages over manual data testing. Handling large volumes of data in the modern financial systems enterprise is critical. CAAT tools can manage a range of activities such as:

- balance checks
- test for compliance with standards
- aging analysis of receivables and payables
- identify and highlight internal control issues
- test for duplicates
- apply tests to invoice numbers.

CAAT enhances the productivity of auditors, enabling them to make informed decisions and assessments of errors with confidence and evidence. At a higher level, senior management tend to be more comfortable with data tested in this way, as a quality basis for their own assessments.

PRACTICAL COMPLIANCE SUMMARY

As well as the object of auditing—the systems and internal controls active in IT and the business—a financial services company can use the audit process to maintain a constant review of the audit activity itself, its methodology, the way it is executed, and the performance of its practitioners. If these are examined, any review will have definite practical outcomes that will support the compliance process.

- To ensure maximum efficiency for maintaining compliance with the Act, the audit function must focus on some key activities:
- Make knowledge accessible and shareable across the organization. This is partly education and partly internal marketing to ensure the company accepts and then acquires the knowledge to make sure the internal auditing part of the compliance processes is successful. This can be delivered through:
  - training sessions, such as lunchtime meetings and sessions
  - internal bulletins
  - effective intranet availability
  - the use of learning management systems (LMS) and e-learning to "push" knowledge to the reluctant desktop.
- Develop an auditor assessment scheme. Such a scheme can be common to all the functions represented by the CTF. The auditor scheme should have clearly defined measurement criteria related to the activity being undertaken.
- Create a pilot project that brings all the elements together and enables the audit department to thoroughly test its assumptions. This can include recently acquired or adapted tools as well as methodologies.
- Invest some effort in determining what best practice means for the organization and its compliance efforts, especially the internal audit function. There are many tools available, such as CSA. What is needed is a methodology that reflects the organization's interest as much as it reflects the interests of regulators and investors.

NOTES

1. The Institute of Internal Auditors has produced a range of publications to support and guide internal auditors in general, and on the Act in particular. It stresses the value of internal auditing as a foundation for corporate governance, and positions it favorably in comparison with the board of directors, senior

management, and external auditing, because of its contribution to assurance about corporate governance, and its objectivity on risk management.

2. Control Self Assessment, discussed later in this chapter, is an effective model for building compliance awareness in staff involved in the responsibility cascade and involvement in the compliance process.

3. ISO 17799 is examined in Chapter 24.

CHAPTER 10

External Auditing

External auditing is crunch time for the organization. The compliance audit is likely to be a "special" audit variant on the routine audits that lead to financial reports. The Sarbanes-Oxley Act has put an edge on the process. The assessment of internal controls, processes, and documentation is oriented more to a certification process than a standard audit. This is all the more reason to ensure that the organization is fully prepared for the auditing experience, and that the compliance process works well and is successful. The external auditor, under the terms of the Act, has a place of importance marginally behind that of the executive management of a listed company. The obligations and requirements are considerable, though not tightly defined in the Act.

WHO IS TO DO THE AUDIT

External auditing is now generally performed through public accounting firms. They vary in size from relatively small practices to the "Big four." The advent of the Act has offered many an opportunity to expand and deepen client relationships, despite the frostier climate engendered by the Act. The selection of an auditor should be treated with the same thoroughness and due diligence used to select any other vendor. It is likely to be a well-known firm, used by the company for some time. The advantages of this are that the management know the players involved. However, there is greater potential for a conflict of interest.

If the organization has selection criteria, use them as a basis for auditor selection. Research the market for a suitable match, and ask especially whether there is there a good "cultural" fit between the auditor and the organization:

■ Does the auditor understand the business, and any specific financial specialization?

- Does the auditor understand the "extended" business, including its supply chain dependencies?
- Is the auditor equipped to deal with the organization's international dimension?
- Within the constraints of the Act, has the auditor worked with or supplied services to the organization before?
- Can the auditor offer an ongoing service, in view of likely repeated audit requirements?

In spring 2006, the SEC's Division of Enforcement[1] noted that the role of lawyers and directors as gatekeepers in the audit process was to be reviewed, with possible increases in penalties. Part of their remit and those of audit committees is to examine the auditors on how well they have been remedying deficiencies found. Size is no indicator of probity: there have been marked procedural shortfalls among the larger auditors.

TYPES OF AUDIT: CERTIFICATION AUDIT

A certification audit, such as a periodic audit for ISO 9001 or ISO 17799, uses "negative" reporting, in that it looks for and notes weaknesses and inadequacies or non-conformances in a system being audited, rather than its adequacies or conformances. It assesses the systems to ensure the documentation, procedures and processes, and the records of implementation of stated scoped compliance programs meet the requirements of a definition of "certification." Almost inevitably there will be some non-conformances, and perhaps non-compliances. These will be noted in a written compliance report together with observations on the whole level of compliance. The report will include suggested corrective actions to be taken to address the non-compliances, and these will have associated agreed timescales for remediation.

ENSURING THE ORGANIZATION MEETS THE AUDIT REQUIREMENTS

If the organization is to pass through the external audit, in the sense of meeting its aims, there are some points to be observed:

- Preparation before the audit is critical:
  - identify the individuals most involved in the audit
  - test thoroughly or in a prioritized manner
  - plan time for interviewing.
- Behavior and control during the audit maintain the compliance process.
- Post-audit reviews and assessments are essential in an ongoing system relying on effective feedback for continuous improvement.

- Maintain the impetus of the audit for the next audit.
- Resources are important: ensure there are enough staff and external consultants assigned.
- Also regarding resources, ensure there is enough budget and there are sufficient quality tools.
- Base auditor selection on experience and on market research.

THE ROLE OF THE CPA IN AUDITING FOR THE ACT

Certified Public Accountants (CPAs) have come to play a major role in compliance. Although IT and financial internal auditors are significant, the CPAs in an organization have a special status. Their presence should be exploited to the full in the compliance process, and they should be co-opted to bring the benefit of their insights into the fundamentals of auditing, and their likely understanding of the language and the requirements of the SEC and the PCOAB. Their contribution should be examined for their experience in:

- financial reporting processes and assertions
- documentation of internal controls
- identifying and testing for internal control deficiencies and weaknesses
- COSO exposure.

CPAs have the advantage of performing financial audits for their clients, and add value through knowledge of the financial positioning of their customer, market presence, and knowledge of financial management benchmarking.

PREPARING FOR AN AUDIT

It is likely there will be at least two auditors with complementary expertise. One will be the lead or principal auditor, responsible for the overall audit. In effect, he or she will act as the project leader.

Non-conformances will be major or minor, or detailed deficiencies or weaknesses within the meaning of the Act. It might be that on the discovery of a major non-compliance/conformance, the audit is suspended until this non-compliance is fixed. In such an event, the organization has to act carefully to ensure morale and confidence are not affected. It also has to consider this as confidential information lest it has an adverse affect on its market position or share value. It might be that the way an auditor manages this kind of information should be part of the selection criteria in choosing a suitable auditor.

As a general comment, there are two critical successful factors (CSFs) that are highlighted at this stage: the state of compliance of the organization to the

Act in general, and the state of preparation by staff of the organization in the face of an audit. An internal review of the state of compliance is a first major objective of the compliance team. The compliance officer or other appointed individual should lead this activity, with coordination with existing quality functions and review by the management compliance forum. Preparation is implied through timelines referenced in the Act. A review before the main compliance effort has been started will naturally overlook some issues. But by the time an audit is due, the compliance process should be complete and a subsequent review of any additional identified tasks or areas of weaknesses can be made. These reviews will add credence to the compliance effort and give confidence in facing the audit.

Logistics

The organization is expected to offer full and open liaison through the compliance team with the auditors and individuals appointed. Resources within the organization, such as intranet access, are expected to be made available. The daily brief, with perhaps the work team, will consolidate the day's findings. The auditors will often require a separate secure room for the length of their stay, and communications resources such as network points and telephone points.

AUDIT PROCESS

The process of external auditing will vary according to auditor practice. Ultimately all auditing achieves the same set of objectives, which in this case is the preparation of audited financial reports with an additional component of the external auditor's attestation to the management's assessment of internal controls over financial reporting. We can identify at least two stages.

Stage One

This is the pre-certification process, which allows auditors to:

- familiarize themselves with the organization, its business, and key contacts
- carry out a document review
- check that there are no major obvious areas of non-compliance (which might limit the value of doing an audit at that stage)
- gather enough material and information to plan the audit.

Generally this process will not take long, but the time needed depends on the size of the organization and the scope of the audit.

Stage Two

This is the formal audit stage. It consists of a number of tasks:

- Establish that the organization has determined to comply with the Act.
- Test actual compliance through assessment of effectiveness of internal controls and according to Public Company Accounting Oversight Board (PCAOB) Standard 2, and test the documented processes against requirements of the Act.

Resources involved

Appropriate individuals will have been identified, and time set aside for assessment, interviews, and testing. The auditors may use their own testing tools or adopt some of the organization's where appropriate.

The auditing process is similar to a project, in that it has a beginning, middle, and end, is time-bounded, and starts and finished with a management/ stakeholder meeting.

STEPS IN THE AUDITING PROCESS

Compliance process

1. The compliance task force (CTF) conducts comprehensive assessment and gap analysis.
2. This assessment leads to a compliance implementation plan.
3. The plan is phased, resourced, and implemented (this includes staff preparation for an audit).
4. Implementation is internally audited and reviewed (with a statement of applicability).

Audit process

5. There is a pre-certification visit from the external auditors.
6. The external audit is carried out, including a review of control objectives, management assessment (based on statement of applicability), and testing of internal controls.
7. Non-conformances and non-compliances are highlighted and detailed for remediation.
8. A management forum reviews non-compliances and identifies remediation action.
9. The external auditors' "attestation" of management's assessment is included in a financial report.

ONGOING AUDITING

Very often auditors will establish a baseline and look for improvement from that line. This is typically done over a series of periodic audits. However, there must be at least a full cycle of assessment of all relevant processes and internal controls at some stage. The compliance process and the compliance cycle are well matched to this ongoing baseline. Because audits are run on an exception basis, it is possible to minimize the effort over time, as all risks and non-compliances are addressed. Generally, audits only occur after an implementation project has been completed, and given the repeated nature of ongoing compliance, further audits will look for indications of improvement over time. The statement (statement of applicability) that defines the status of the organization's compliance:

- is a starting point for ongoing reviews
- contains detail, which is critical to ensuring that the audit process determines compliance
- provides detailed evidence, which is particularly significant under the Act
- offers an opportunity to review why certain controls were or were not implemented.

The compliance process cycle itself should include continuous monitoring. An illustration of the audit process is given in Figure 10.1. It summarizes the overall process and the obligations of the auditors.

STATEMENT OF APPLICABILITY FOR THE ACT

This statement, or one similar to it, consists of the control objectives and controls selected to ensure the system of internal control is effective under the terms of the Act. Its value is both in the compliance process and as a summary of internal control effectiveness for management's assessment. It includes:

- control objectives
- selected controls to achieve these objectives
- reasons for the choice of controls
- a summary of the risk treatment to ensure compliance.

The decisions made on which control objectives and controls to implement comprise the risk treatment process. The statement here forms the basis for management's statement of the effectiveness of the system of internal control. It is both a collection of the departmental and functional detail on

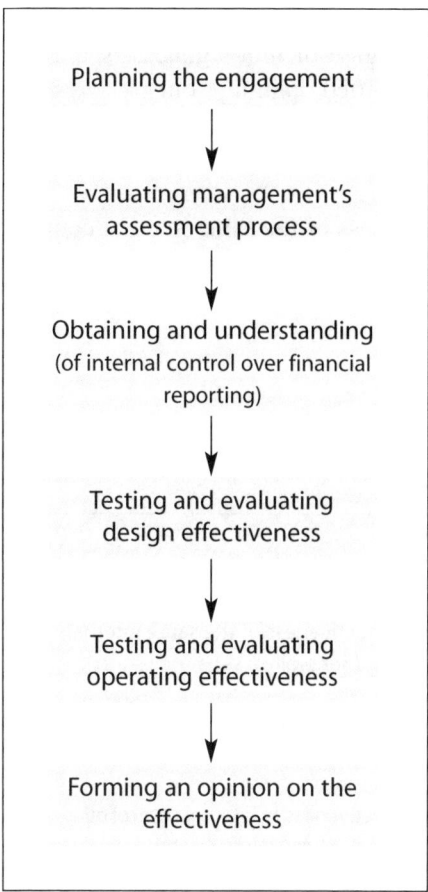

Auditor obligations
• Generally accepted
  auditing standards
• Technical training and
  proficiency
• Independence
• Due professional care
• Fieldwork and reporting
  standards

Figure 10.1 The audit process

internal control, and a consolidated statement of the overall organization's system of internal control. It provides auditors with a statement that they can then assess, under the terms of the Act, so they can attest to whether the system of internal control meets the statement made by management.

EXTERNAL AUDIT REPORTING

Thanks to the PCAOB's standard we have a clearer picture of the auditing process. In Appendix A2 it notes that "Paragraphs 167 through 199 of this standard provide direction on the auditor's report on management's assessment of internal control over financial reporting." This Appendix also provides illustrative reports of the type expected by the PCAOB and hence the Commission. There are several reports, described as "Illustrative reports on internal control over financial reporting," which indicate the structure of the final result. There are seven examples provided for guidance, which attempt to provide a degree of thoroughness (see Table 10.1). They are all expressions of "unqualified opinions" on:

- management's assessments of the effectiveness of their systems of internal control over financial reporting
- the auditor's opinion on the effectiveness of the same internal controls over financial reporting; which is generally provided as a separate report.

Table 10.1 Example reports in the PCAOB standard

Example	Comments
Example A-1	Reports on a) management's assessments of the effectiveness of the systems of internal control over financial reporting b) the auditor's opinion on the effectiveness of the same internal control over financial reporting (generally a separate report).
Example A-2	Reports on a) management's assessments of the effectiveness of the systems of internal control over financial reporting b) an "adverse opinion" on the effectiveness of internal control over financial reporting because of the existence of a "material weakness."
Example A-3	Reports on a) management's assessments of the effectiveness of the systems of internal control over financial reporting b) a "qualified opinion" on the effectivness of internal control because of a "limitation on the scope of the audit."
Example A-4	Presents a "disclaiming" opinion on a) (above) and "disclaiming opinion" on b) "because of a limitation on the scope of the audit."
Example A-5	A report "that refers to the report of other auditors as a basis, in part, for the auditor's opinion" on a) and is an "unqualified opinion" on b).
Example A-6	This report is "an adverse opinion" on a) and an "adverse opinion" on b) "because of the existence of a material weakness."
Example A-7	Reports the following as a "combined report:" • an unqualified opinion on financial statements • an unqualified opinion on a) • an unqualified opinion on b).

Report structure

The PCAOB provides a report structure as a reference. It is the same for all these examples, and follows the outline:

- Introduction
- Definition
- Inherent limitations
- Opinions
- Explanations
- Confirmation.

Report of independent registered public accounting firm

Introductory paragraph

This paragraph states the action—of auditing management's assessment of effectiveness—with an audit date, and references the control criteria (such as that established in the COSO "Integrated framework"). It notes the responsibilities of the management of the audited company in maintaining the systems of internal control and for making an assessment of its effectiveness. It notes that "Our [the auditor's] responsibility is to express an opinion on management's assessment and an opinion on the effectiveness of the company's internal control over financial reporting based on our audit."

Scope paragraph

It then establishes the standards used to conduct the audit. These are "the standards of the Public Company Accounting Oversight Board (United States)." It outlines the broad aim of these standards: to "plan and perform the audit to obtain reasonable assurance about whether effective internal control over financial reporting was maintained in all material respects."
   The audit is stated to include:

- understanding the systems of internal control
- evaluating management's assessment
- testing and evaluating the design and operating effectiveness of the system of internal control
- carrying out other necessary tasks.

Based on these, the audit is attested as being "a reasonable basis for our opinion."
   The PCAOB standard also notes that if there are separate reports involved (such as the audit of financial statements), then both reports

should include a statement that the audit was conducted in accordance with standards of the PCAOB.

Definition paragraph

This paragraph is a summary of the key objectives of the Act so as to put the auditing activity in context. The company's internal control over financial reporting is defined as "a process designed to provide reasonable assurance regarding the reliability of financial reporting." The significant recognition of internal control compliance as a process is fleshed out in the rest of the paragraph. It notes that a company's internal control includes policies and procedures that:

1) "Pertain to the maintenance of records." These must be of sufficient detail that they can be judged to "accurately and fairly reflect the transactions and dispositions of the assets of the company."
2) "Provide reasonable assurance" that all relevant transactions are part of the company's archive or live, stored environment so that financial statements can be prepared in line with Generally Accepted Accounting Principles (GAAP). This reasonable assurance must extend to the receipts and expenditures of the company so that they are subject to "authorizations of management and directors of the company."
3) "Provide reasonable assurance" on the security of company assets, through preventative measures or detective controls to avoid their unauthorized use or misuse, especially if this misuse has a "material effect" on financial statements.

Inherent limitations paragraph

As no organization is perfect, so no system is perfect. The limitations of a system of internal control are qualified here, since it might not prevent or even detect all misstatements. This also points up the time-bound nature of an evaluation. A system of internal control that is effective at the date of evaluation might no longer be as effective shortly afterwards. Projections are prone to second-guess a future status. A number of factors can affect this. Controls might become inadequate because of changes in conditions, or compliance with the policies or procedures might degrade.

Opinion paragraph

The purpose of this report is for the auditor to give an opinion. This is either qualified or unqualified depending on the findings of the audit. The core aspect of the process, and perhaps the Act's ultimate deliverable, is this opinion. There are two expressed opinions required:

1. Opinion on management assessment

   "In our opinion, management's assessment that [the company being audited] maintained effective internal control over financial reporting as of [month, day and year], is fairly stated, in all material respects, based on..." and here follows the critical internal control framework reference. The PCAOB example report uses the "criteria established in Internal Control-Integrated Framework issued by the Committee of Sponsoring Organizations of the Treadway Commission (COSO)." Other qualifying frameworks would apply. But again the significance of COSO as the reference framework is underlined.

2. Opinion on system of internal control

   In the auditor's opinion, the company being audited maintained, in all material respects, effective internal control over financial reporting [dated]. The reference is again to a suitable framework. The PCAOB example again cites "criteria established in Internal Control-Integrated Framework issued by the Committee of Sponsoring Organizations of the Treadway Commission (COSO)."

Explanatory paragraph

This paragraph refers to the standard by which the auditing process has taken place. The example references "the standards of the Public Company Accounting Oversight Board (United States)." The financial statements of the audited company are identified and the report dated (same date as above for the effectiveness of internal control over financial reporting). The auditor's opinion is then detailed.

Signature

This section signs off and dates the report, with:

- auditor signature
- city and state or country
- identification of the location
- date.

PCAOB SUMMARY

Because of the importance of the PCAOB's guidelines on auditing as the basic reference for auditors working on compliance with the Act, the following looks briefly at some useful aspects of the standard as inputs to the compliance effort. It contains concepts and definitions that occur throughout the discussion of auditing and internal controls. The document *Auditing Standard No. 2: An audit of internal control over financial reporting performed in conjunction with an audit of financial statements* (PCAOB 2004) is the standard guide. This document is divided into paragraphs, and the references are to "paras."

Applicability of standard

Para 1 is quotable as a definition of what the document is about:

> This standard establishes requirements and provides directions that apply when an auditor is engaged to audit both a company's financial statements and management's assessment of the effectiveness of internal control over financial reporting.

Note that the standard states requirements and gives directions for auditor activities in pursuit of the Act. The auditor here "includes both public accounting firms registered with the Public Company Accounting Oversight Board... and associated persons thereof."

Para 2 turns to the company, or "issuer," and notes its requirements, specifically under Section 404 of the Act. Section 404 is dealt with separately, but in summary the issuer management is required to:

- include in its annual report a management report on the company's internal control over financial reporting
- include management's assessment of the effectiveness of the company's internal control over financial reporting
- include in the report a statement as to whether the company's internal control over financial reporting is effective
- file the attestation of the auditor auditing the company's financial statements as part of the annual report.

Para 3 notes that this standard, AS2, is one referred to in the standard on attestation engagements referred to in Sections 404(b) and 103(a)(2)(A)(iii) of the Act. It also notes that the auditor's attestation of management's assessment, which we will refer to simply as the attestation, is the "audit of internal control over financial reporting." For clarity, both the audit of internal control over financial reporting (the process) and an attestation of management's assessment of the effectiveness of internal control over financial reporting (outcome of the process) comprise the same professional service.

Auditor's objective in an audit of internal control

Para 4 examines the auditor's objective in an audit, which is to:

- express an opinion on management's assessment

- build a case for an opinion
- plan and perform the audit to obtain "reasonable assurance" as to whether the company maintained an effective internal control
- audit the company's financial statements as of the date specified in management's assessment
- note that the information the auditor obtains during a financial statement audit is relevant to a conclusion about this effectiveness.

Effective internal control over financial reporting means, in this instance, that no material weaknesses exist. Consequently if the auditor can obtain "reasonable assurance" that no such weaknesses exist, the assessment can be verified "as of the date specified in management's assessment."

Auditor and client relationships

For the auditor, an opinion expressed on management's assessment must be very soundly based. This is different in spirit from previous types of opinion, in that the legislation of the Act is more censorious; there is a greater expectation about the neutrality of the auditor. **Para 5** notes that to obtain "reasonable assurance" the auditor:

- evaluates the performance of management's assessment
- gets and analyzes evidence about the design and operation of the system of internal control to evaluate its effectiveness. This evidence is the result of the auditor's efforts and those of others.

As a final comment the PCAOB reminds auditors in **Para 6** of the reason for this activity. Those who rely on the information such as the assessment and attestation are:

- investors
- creditors
- the board of directors
- the audit committee
- regulators in specialized industries (such as the finance sector).

External consumers of these reports are also interested because of the way such information on internal controls "enhances the quality of financial reporting" and increases confidence in financial reporting, including all periodic reporting.

Significantly such information also serves as an early warning mechanism for those responsible for implementing checks, controls, and remediation of weaknesses in affected companies, such as the audit committee and specialized regulators. The PCAOB also refers to Section 302, and the responsibility of senior executives in this task.

Para 7 concerns the definitions the PCAOB uses to identify internal control over financial reporting. The standard details these, and we can summarize them as follows:

- Internal control is a process.
- It is designed by, or under the supervision of, the company's principal executive and principal financial officers, or persons performing similar functions.
- It is necessary for the company's board of directors, management, and other personnel to provide reasonable assurance regarding the reliability of financial reporting.
- There is a similar responsibility in the preparation of financial statements for external purposes.
- These must be prepared in accordance with GAAP.

The policies and procedures affected are those that:

- Cover the maintenance of records that "accurately and fairly reflect the transactions and dispositions" of the company assets.
- Provide "reasonable assurance" that transactions are recorded for the preparation of financial statements in line with GAAP, and that all receipts and expenditures are authorized appropriately.
- Provide assurance that "unauthorized acquisition, use or disposition of the company's assets" is either prevented or spotted in time to avoid "a material effect on the financial statements."

This definition is the same one used by the SEC in its rules requiring management to report on internal control over financial reporting, except the word "registrant" has been changed to "company" to conform with the wording in this standard.[2] Note that throughout this standard, internal control over financial reporting (singular) refers to the process described in this paragraph. Individual controls or subsets of controls are referred to as controls or controls over financial reporting.

Para 8 discusses the concept of a "control deficiency" in some depth. This is explored further when considering internal controls. In summary, a control deficiency exists when the design or application of a control does not allow management or employees to prevent or detect misstatements. There are further useful definitions of language such as "remote likelihood" as used in the definitions of significant deficiency and material weakness (**Para 10**), and explanations of the use of the words "probable," "reasonably possible," and "remote," relating to events occurring. It also covers "misstatement" and "material weakness."

The standard has become something of a main reference for auditors working on audits for Sections 302 and 404. However, it is one of many inputs to compliance planning for external auditors, and not the whole picture. At all times, the objectives of the organization should be pressed in dealing with external auditors; management should maintain an approach that effectively combines regulatory requirements with the compelling needs of the organization. For this there is a need for a process that reflects the realities of complying with the Act. Within this the external auditing activity plays a part, but it is not the dominant driver. There must be a review of compliance in a practical context, and a process that reflects the ongoing nature of the implications of the Act, and how it can be turned to good account on behalf of the organization.

PRACTICAL COMPLIANCE SUMMARY

■ Be aware of the risks faced by external auditors, and work with them to ensure a mutually beneficial relationship.

■ Ensure documentation is accurate.

■ Prepare all relevant staff for the external audit.

■ Maintain the impetus of the audit by using continuous monitoring throughout the compliance process.

■ Review the use of auditors and institute a review as part of the compliance process (at a strategic level).

■ Hire expertise on external auditing to educate the CTF.

■ Allocate enough resources—staff, time, location, systems—for the audit.

■ Use an internal audit as an opportunity to prototype auditing (testing the overall process).

■ Be aware of audit deadlines under the Act.

■ Ensure the statement of applicability has external auditors as a potential audience and prepare it accordingly.

NOTES

1. Created in 1972, the Division of Enforcement conducts investigations into possible violations of the Federal securities laws, and is the prosecuting arm for the Commission's civil suits in the federal courts.

2. See Securities Exchange Act Rules 13a-15(f) and 15d-15(f).2.

PART III

Practical Compliance

CHAPTER 11

Building the Strategy

THE STRATEGIC NATURE OF COMPLIANCE

Before we do anything else we need to establish that compliance is a strategic concern with considerable tactical implications. By this we mean that decisions about compliance are made at the highest level, the responsibility of the success of the compliance effort rests at the highest level, and the interests of the organization are affected directly by the outcome of the compliance process. In that all these considerations shape the direction and future of the organization, the compliance process can be seen to be strategic. Much of what follows addresses tactical mechanisms that deliver the strategic objectives.

So what does practical compliance look like? How do we achieve it? What is the process that leads to renewable confidence in a solution that delivers compliance? According to the *Collins English Dictionary* (2003, p.347), compliance is "an act of complying; acquiescence," or "a disposition to yield to or comply with others." Most dictionaries follow a similar track; they stress the passive, reactive nature of compliance as subservience of some kind. We need to develop this into a positive, proactive concept in practice.

Another presentation sees compliance as a state of being in accordance with guidelines, specifications, or legislation, or a process of "becoming" or moving towards this state. Our response to the Act is centered on this idea of becoming compliant as a process; one that is not a one-off project that delivers us to a state, but constantly seeks that state. This is a strategic business concern, and these ideas should be reflected in the approach we take to becoming compliant with the Act.

Within the meaning of compliance is another concept that can appear contradictory: the implication of effectiveness. From the regulatory perspective, simply having controls in place is not enough: the emphasis is on monitoring for effectiveness. The demand is for an effective compliant solution. From the point of view of the company, effective controls are not

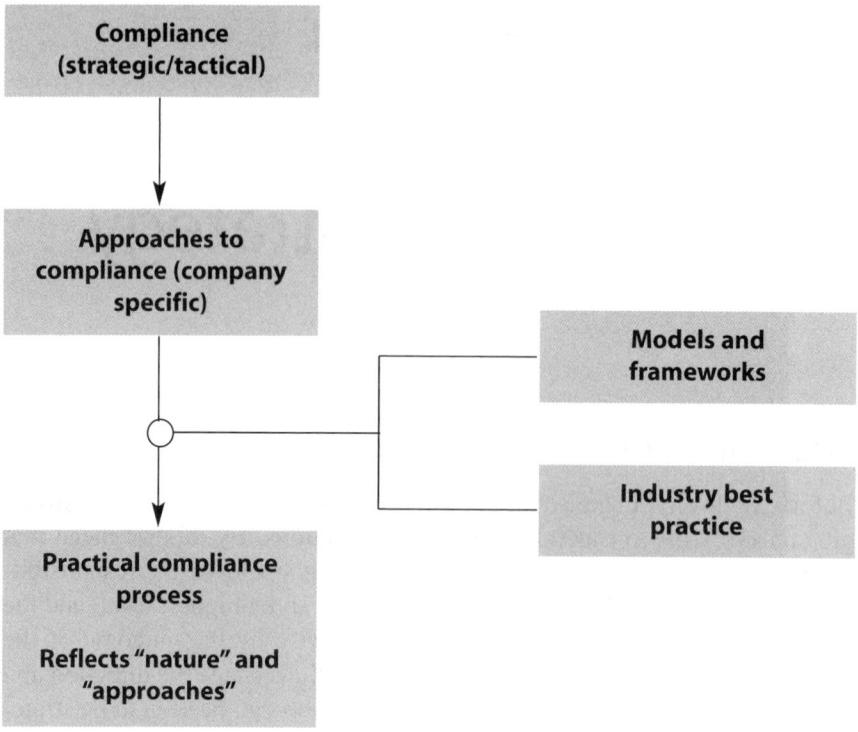

Figure 11.1 The strategic compliance process

enough: they may be too costly to sustain. There are dangers in internal controls that are claimed to be in use but which are found not to be operational (Gorrod, 2004, p.15). Therefore it is important that they are efficient. For both considerations there must be an approach that allows periodic validation coupled with internal auditing.

APPROACHES TO COMPLIANCE

The compliance iceberg

One of the striking aspects of the compliance process is the "iceberg" realization. By this we mean that superficially, the focus of the Act is on a qualifying company's periodic financial reports. However, it quickly becomes clear that the real effort is in the systems and processes within a company that provide the information from which these consolidated reports are generated. The emphasis on internal control is to ensure that this broad base of process and activity is effectively monitored, measured, and evaluated. This is the base of the iceberg (see Figure 11.2). The tip, the financial report, is the visible portion that carries the market image of the company.

But it cannot exist alone, and is shaped by the hidden mass of everyday company activity.

There are several challenges for the company in this. Complying at the level of generating a financial report appears to be a limited and achievable task. It does not, in itself, add a great deal in terms of resource and financial expenditure to an existing process. It appears to be a "quality" rather than a "quantity" issue. However, the more daunting task is to ensure that the information inputs to this report, which originate from across the functions of the company, are of the right quality. This is the area addressed by internal control. The resource and budgeting overhead for this part of the compliance process is the stuff of headlines. Cost appears to scale with the size of the iceberg. The sums are large and the effort is not one-off, or simply periodic, but ongoing. How then do we approach this major task of compliance?

Once the iceberg is understood and measured, we can grapple with the scale. This is also affected by time as a resource. Compliance is a function of time, in that all legislation has a deadline or deadlines. This has a real impact on compliance at a practical level, and affects our selected approach. Broadly there are two practical approaches to compliance, the systematic and the pragmatic.

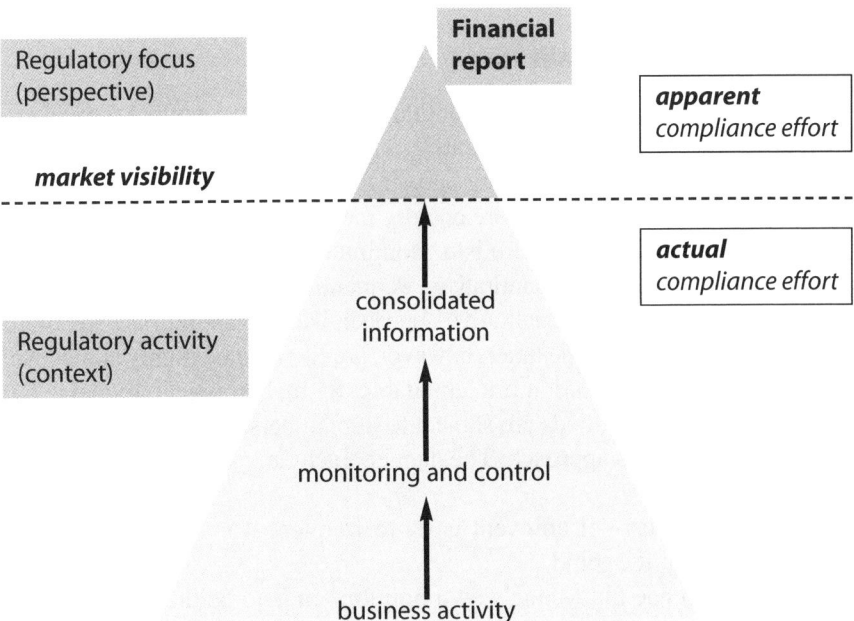

Figure 11.2 The compliance iceberg

Systematic approach

This approach is characterized by being thorough and comprehensive. It is generally typified by frameworks and references, such as standards, that "model" systems. This is of particular value to companies that need a reference model as a guide to an unfamiliar subject, or that work in an area of such complexity that a highly structured approach is needed. The thoroughness ensures all possible compliance issues within a function or area of interest are addressed, and being comprehensive means that all possible functions and operational areas are investigated thoroughly.

Pragmatic approach

This approach is driven by the need to gain the most from the least effort, using past experience and elements of generally perceived best practice as guidelines. It is "pragmatic" in that the approach is constrained by the resource and financial realities of the business.

To gain the most from the least effort, using known examples and best practice, is a very common response to problem solving. It is often driven by considerations of cost, and guided by references such the company's risk profile—its definitions of acceptable and unacceptable risk. Best practice provides reliable references based on the experience of others.

These approaches are balanced with two further concepts, quantitative and qualitative.

Quantitative and qualitative

The focus of the Act appears to be qualitative, but once we explore the iceberg we can see that equally it is quantitative. These factors are constant guides in the compliance process, balancing and shifting the emphasis of activities to ensure that scale and direction are equally met. When discussing risk identification and measurement, there is a "continuum of possible approaches ... from the qualitative to the quantitative." A quantitative approach uses data for precise modeling, but the qualitative approach is more appropriate for "hard to categorize" systems. The latter, however, are likely to be highly subjective. Quantitative methods are more amenable to mathematical models, but because qualitative methods are subject to human perspectives we can detect a range of bias in this approach: The dangers include:

- availability bias—if an event is more frequent it is likely to be more prominent in the mind
- overconfidence bias—one's own opinion tends to be the correct one
- confirmation bias—we stick to the first impression and overlook conflicting information

■ hindsight bias—we tend to be more certain in retrospect than we actually were.

However, quantitative approaches tend to be predictive, focused on probabilities rather than experience. For the compliance process, where statistical modeling is relatively unusual territory, this translates into a pragmatic approach that mixes modeling and experience. The focus of the Act, we noted, appears to be qualitative, but the quantitative dimension is revealed in the compliance iceberg.

STATE OF COMPLIANCE

In the preparation for compliance many assumptions are made. One of these is that the company can become compliant. Achieving a "state of compliance" is similar to the concept of the "ideal state." Once in this state, any investigation will find the company compliant, its activities in accordance with the requirements of the Act, and good governance and transparency will prevail. As a description of what is desirable this might work. Certainly at board level, strategically the aim is to ensure that the company complies with the requirements of the Act. However, as a basis for creating a realistic practical program it is too simplistic. We can make a number of observations:

■ The state of compliance is hard to define comprehensively.
■ There are many requirements stemming from the Act, non-compliance to any of which can render the company non-compliant.
■ The active areas, or units, of a company are various. Some units might be in a state of compliance while others are not. The non-compliance of one area might render the whole organization non-compliant.

Passive linear compliance

The state of compliance can be seen as a passive state, with the implication that once it is in that state, the activity or process will tend to rest in that state. The hard work is in getting a process into a state of compliance, and once it is there the job is largely done. From then on it needs the occasional monitoring or review. This tends to be a linear approach, project-driven, easy to measure in terms of the resources needed, and predictable in its behavior. There is a path towards compliance that can be determined, with achievable milestones. The project ends in the desired state. (See Figure 11.3.)

Active linear compliance

Another form of representation sees the state of compliance as an active state. In this scenario, compliance is an unstable state, where a process is

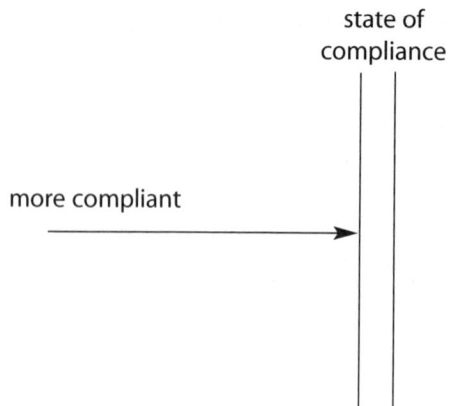

state of
compliance

more compliant

Figure 11.3 Passive linear compliance

brought into a state of compliance but forces at work pull it away from such a state. Once we have got the process into a state of compliance the job is not over. There is a need for constant monitoring and testing to ensure it is still in the desired state. (See Figure 11.4.) Because of the pull away from the state, some of the process has to be undertaken again, perhaps on a regular basis.

This is also a linear approach, project-driven, relatively easy to measure in terms of the resources needed, though less predictable in its behavior. The challenge is to have a clear idea of the state of compliance. The path towards compliance can be determined, with achievable milestones. The project, does not necessarily end in the desired state, however, and rework might be constant in the form of sub-projects.

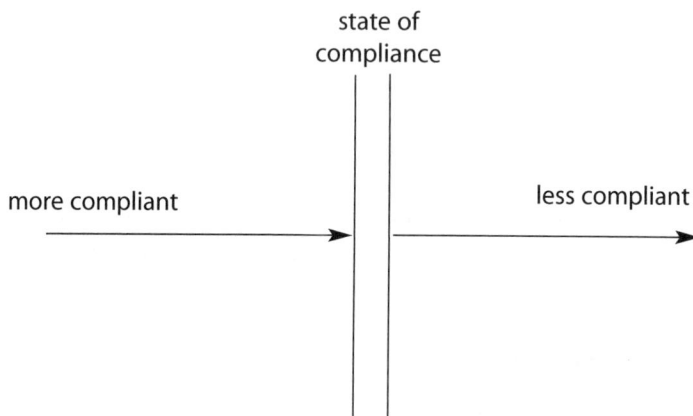

state of
compliance

more compliant   less compliant

Figure 11.4 Active linear compliance

Cyclical compliance

A third perspective is to see the state of compliance as part of a cyclical process. In this picture, the state of compliance is reached, but as in the active linear compliance process, it is very unstable. However, instead of initiating projects to maintain the state, cyclical compliance assumes insta-bility and builds a feedback process into the effort to achieve the state so that the project is, in effect, endless—a cycle. Reviewing and testing is part of the cycle.

These models can be applied at the macro or micro level. At the macro level we can see the company as in a state of compliance, or not in a state of compliance. At a realistic level, it is impossible to define a company this way, yet we do talk in this binary manner. Are we compliant? The answer tends to be either "Yes" or "No." After all, decision making is based on this assumption that we can resolve a question with a binary yes/no. So how do we become compliant? We initiate a company-wide project to make it compliant.

The micro level can also be binary: a process is either compliant or not. The overall company state of compliance is then a totality of all processes being compliant, or not. These considerations apply to both the passive and active linear compliance models.

Because we do not really see the situation in such stark binary terms, we are aware of the concept of almost being compliant, since most of the processes being worked on can have a binary "Yes" against them. Or rather,

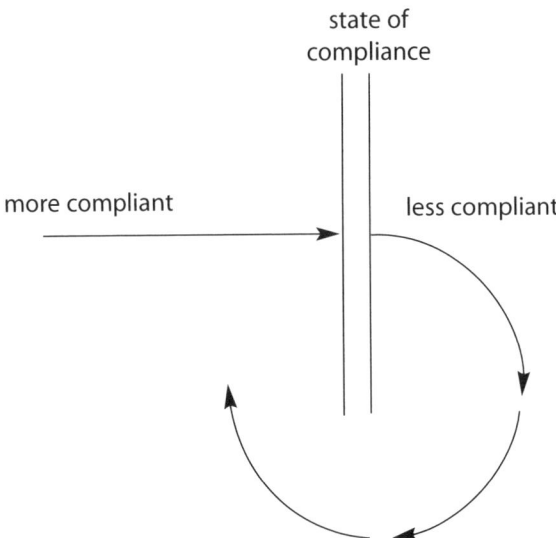

Figure 11.5 Cyclical compliance

they are in a state of compliance for a period of time; if enough are coincidentally in this state at once, we can claim to be largely compliant. From this we see that it is not a simple yes or no for the company as a whole; rather it is undergoing a process of transformation that delivers a degree of compliance.

The granularity of compliance: degrees of compliance

There is a certain granularity to compliance. It may be that at the micro level some processes can work with a passive or active linear compliance model. Fully automated processes may well be in or out of a state of compliance. But larger, more complex processes work best with a model, such as the cyclical model, which allows for a degree of compliance, because reaching and falling away from compliance is a series of granular steps, and there is the possibility of regaining compliance quickly through a cycle. There is a tension in the state of compliance because of the possibility of non-compliance. To hold something in this state calls for an active process.

The cyclical compliance model in action

An advantage of the cyclical model is that it assumes feedback, and assumes change in the state of compliance. It also assumes repetition, albeit through a loop, in a closed and controlled system. The controls can be few or many, operating for maximum efficiency over and over again. The closed system is also more predictable, and it is largely effective. It is suitable for the largest macro compliance activity—a corporate-wide compliance process—or for micro activities. It works with linear models as well as other circular models. As we look for practical approaches to delivering compliance, we see that the "cycle" view is very versatile and consistent with the vital compliance cycle, a major component of the tactical response to developing a compliance process.

Completeness and the perfect organization

Another term we can use to describe the state of compliance is "completeness." We see processes not in the state of compliance as incomplete. As they move away from the state they become more incomplete. As they move towards the state they become less incomplete. This is a distinguishing aspect of the Act. Unlike other legislation, it assumes a degree of perfection on behalf of the organization. By this we see perfection as a sense of completeness. It assumes that all operational systems that support the business and communications functions operate fully and perfectly, exactly as specified. Any events, activities, or transactions that result from operations are viewed as exceptions. The completeness of any process is broken by exceptions. The systems of internal control imposed are to ensure that exceptions and anomalies in behavior are quickly addressed and remedied.

This terminology marries with some of the confusion about the perception of the Act and some of its more "intolerable" features. This stems from the assumption that a state of compliance can be reached for the whole organization, and that there is such a thing as the "perfect" organization. This perfection is almost moral, in that the ethical organization, with full, demonstrable adherence to a set of regulations, behaves perfectly.

This perspective does not assume that the intent of the systems is to provide a best effort to deliver working solutions which do not fail in this sense, and generate exceptions. It assumes systems operate beyond intent at the level of exact match to regulatory requirements. This approach is reflected in the system of internal control, which is an observational and interventionist model, event-driven and reactive. The systems under observation are assumed, at best, to be in an ideal state and complete, and ideally not in need of intervention or remediation.

Part of the idea of competitive advantage is flexibility—so constant change redefines "completeness," which becomes a shifting concept and is subject to a "sliding window." Completeness exists only at a moment in time as a temporary state. To an extent this is reflected in financial reports, which are acknowledged to be periodic, time-bound, and specific. Section 409 emphasizes this by mandating ad hoc updates, in near real time, on significant events that occur in between periodic reports. Such an assumption is a considerable issue for most organizations that have "incomplete" systems, and specifically assume that exceptions might occur and not be addressed because of their view of risk, as reflected in their risk profile and risk related to business opportunity. The reluctance to implement a system of internal control that ensures completeness may be a function of:

- cost: the sheer cost of implementing and delivering and maintaining a control system
- organization: the way the company is structured, functionally, geographically, or legally, might not easily lend itself to completeness
- marketing responses: the way the company reacts to changes in the market may require a degree of flexibility in the face of constant change, and this flexibility may require incompleteness.

Given the way organizations are subject to constant change, as a result of both internal developments and external factors such as shifting market conditions, and political and social conditions, the one ideal instance of completeness may be an unreasonable assumption. The Act itself is part of

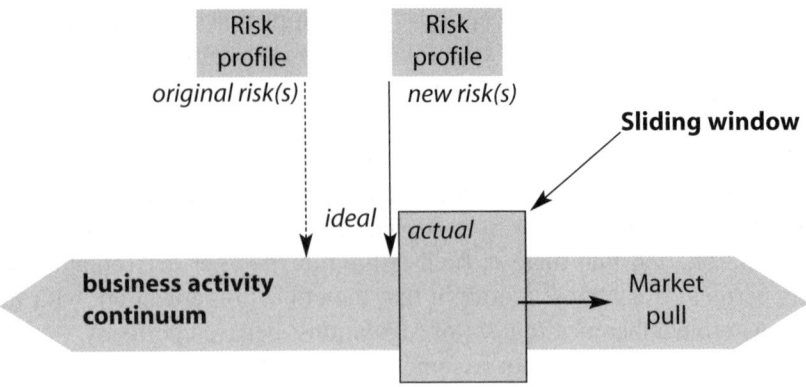

Figure 11.6 The sliding window

a continuing process of regulatory change which forces a degree of incompleteness on affected organizations. With this in mind we can take a pragmatic view of compliance as being an ideal response and a specific response:

- An ideal response assumes completeness and perfection, and is a reference model; in effect, an aspiration.
- A specific response is the way a company in a business sector with a certain risk profile responds to the Act.

The compliance process, as we discuss it, is an ideal response in real time, as a specific response.

COMPLIANCE AND RISK

A recent research report (Rasmussen et al. 2004) noted that organizations faced by the need to comply with regulation are often confused by the meaning of compliance, especially when discussing risk. It is recognized that the notions of compliance and risk overlap. The ongoing nature of the compliance process is in the continual monitoring of processes and activities because of the risks they pose to the organization through non-compliance. Incidents are noted and events assessed as to how they affect this compliance. Although we talk of models and the perfect organization, we also recognize that, in reality, every organization is different and has by necessity a unique risk profile. The correlation between compliance and risk is mirrored in the practical, process-intensive nature of both compliance and risk monitoring. Compliance does not exist in a vacuum. Its activities are often governed by risk assessments, however formal or informal. Compliance is often measured against the risk profile of the organization, and these requirements are frequently assessed as threats, and then subject to processes that identify vulnerabilities and remedial action. In this way the two areas of risk and compliance are entwined. It is no wonder there may be some confusion over how the organization should allocate resources and practically implement response processes to both disciplines. It may well be that in order to meet their regulatory requirements and ensure their internal risk profiles are met, organizations should address both as part of the same strategy.

Types of risk

When discussing risk in the context of the Act we talk of systemic concerns, which affect large numbers of clients and extensive parts of the organization's operations. We can also refer to a variation on this: systematic risk and unsystematic risk.

- Systematic risk is a risk that affects large numbers of assets. This tends to engulf the organization. Typically examples are ecological events like weather disasters, and power failures.
- Unsystematic risk is really any other risk. This implies that the risk has its origins within the activities of the organization, in the context of a market or political environment. By implication the scale is less than systematic, and this implies that this type of risk can be controlled.

Systematic risk largely falls outside this discussion, except in as far as it might be addressed through "disaster recovery" planning. It is not relevant to the Act. However, unsystematic risk is central to business life, and companies use many standard techniques to deal with these risks. We revisit this when discussing an internal security management system (ISMS) later. A common approach is to minimize a type of risk by spreading its impact. This is done through componentizing the overall risk and then diversifying the way the discrete risks are dealt with. This implies analysis and understanding of risks to the extent that decisions can be made based on their impact on the business and how easily they can be dealt with. In the financial services sector there are a number of specific risk areas such as:

- Credit: where a company or individual investor cannot pay the interest or the principal on a debt. This risk varies according to the underwritten security of the risk: for example government bonds are inherently less risky than new and emerging market securities.
- Foreign exchange: where currency exchange rates fluctuate, affecting all financial instruments.

- Interest rates: fluctuations in the interest rate, often specific to countries, affect the performance of stocks and bonds, and investment in general.
- Market risk: or the everyday volatility of the market.

As players in the market, financial service institutions suffer from and cause others to suffer these risks. However, although these types of risk are significant for the organization, and they are a vital part of the risk profile, they are largely external risks. These risks are not directly controllable within the organization; they are influential for making investment decisions, but they are not internal to the organization. They cannot be directly controlled.

The development of a risk-averse attitude by the auditor, and the application of punitive regulations, have complicated the response of some finance executives. Faced with a mass of detail, they look for a mechanism that enable them to make decisions that are less risky and yet relevant for the business. To manage this they can adopt a "risk-based" strategy that is more pragmatic, where working through exhaustive programs of analysis under tight time constraints is replaced by an initial prioritization and a strict focus on the most serious and best-understood risks.

Risk-based strategy: prioritize around risk

Although we are looking for a strategic prioritization, this is really a version of the "pragmatic" approach. Rather than explore every avenue exhaustively, by using a risk analysis the overall compliance effort can be prioritized:

- Wherever we start, the compliance iceberg offers many directions in which to go. Using a systematic approach, however, the prioritization can be based on business imperatives rather than an externally suggested set of regulatory objectives, which form the regulatory perspective (see Figure 11.1).
- This approach introduces a high degree of flexibility and a high level of control, while major risks are addressed within reasonable timescales.
- We can submit compliance to the risk strategy and its assessment process, and measure it for a "fit" to the risk profile. The essence is to ask "Can we afford not to comply and in what areas?" and "How much will this cost and can we afford to do it?" Establish a benchmark for compliance.
- Existing control architectures and frameworks already in use can be employed for this strategy. If these are not sufficient to deliver against

the benchmark, introduce appropriate models, such as those of COSO, COBIT, and ISO 17799. These will flesh out and detail the controls necessary to deliver effective monitoring of policy making and implementation, operational activity, and controls specific to the technologies used. This could mean that all areas of the business are monitored to a lesser or greater extent. The actual extent will depend on the risk profile.

The organization perspective and the compliance chain

For the company best suited to the pragmatic approach, management is not forced into responding to the Act. Nor is the response based on the auditor's response to PCAOB Accounting Standard No 2. By establishing internal, organizational priorities first and then accommodating external priorities such as those of the Act and the external auditor, the compliance process builds an extended set of priorities. A carefully managed extension of priorities, through awareness of the variables of conflicting interests, can ease the pressures that build up in the "compliance chain" (see Figure 11.7).

Through this approach organizations, and particularly the CFO, must anticipate "external" priorities in their assumptions about good governance. This is especially true of auditors, who have their own agenda and have a financial incentive to be as thorough as possible, since this means more fees. They are supported by the PCAOB instructions on this. The CFO must ensure that auditors recognize their organization's specific risk profile and balance their efforts towards "internal" priorities. Managing the compliance chain and its pressures is part of the compliance challenge that senior executives must somehow address in their planning.

PREPARING FOR COMPLIANCE

Having a good grasp of the requirements of the Act is an important first step, and provides an awareness of factors that influence the approach an

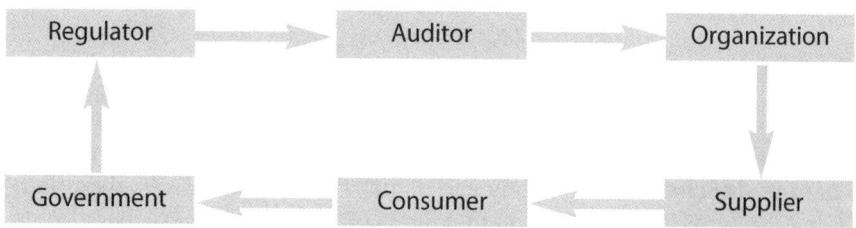

Figure 11.7 The compliance chain

organization might take. How might we prepare the organization to meet these requirements?

Much of the information for formulating these questions will come from existing risk assessments, security assessments, and assessments made as part of other compliance projects. If the organization has a compliance office or legal team with regulatory expertise, there may be sufficient in-house expertise to get the compliance project moving. If not, a gap analysis can identify the areas that need more in-depth work and resources.

It is likely that as a financial institution, the organization will already have implemented compliance processes. There may be a degree of reuse in the processes, systems, and in-house knowledge of how best to tackle compliance. Nevertheless, an initial assessment should be undertaken to ensure that the specifics of the Act, not just compliance in general, are being addressed directly.

Initial gap analysis

A useful tool for an initial gap analysis is a questionnaire similar to that shown as Table 11.1, a preparatory assessment checklist. This touches on the key players and issues. Its use offers a number of real advantages before the compliance process is started:

- It can help establish how well a company is prepared for the compliance project. The detail in the answers will quickly establish just how well prepared the organization is for the compliance effort.
- It is a valuable input to the strategic phase of the compliance process.
- It is especially valuable if a selection of critical stakeholders, such as the members of the CTF, each complete it. A consolidated version of the questionnaire will provide a broad and representative view of the state of preparedness, and identify some critical issues that are likely to arise later. This can be published in advance of the creation of the CTF.

The preparatory assessment

Since the preparatory assessment checklist is a useful formative tool, we should clarify the significance of each of its main sub-sections.

Board members

Since the Act is unambiguous about where responsibility lies for failures in the financial reporting process, and sees accountability residing with the board of directors of a company and its most senior executives, these individuals must be involved in, and take responsibility for the success of, the process from the outset. It may be possible to introduce non-executive

Inputs

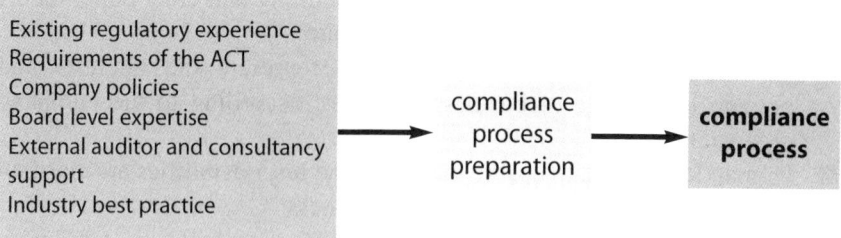

Figure 11.8 Inputs to preparation for the compliance process

directors with experience of a compliance effort with a similar company to strengthen board-level expertise. The responsibility cascade discussed earlier means the rest of the board must also be included, by association and function. It is vital that they buy in to the compliance effort and are aware of what it means.

Compliance task force

This is variously referred to as a compliance committee, a steering group, a compliance forum, and so on, but its operational nature should be consistent, with a set of tasks and responsibilities that relate to the needs of the compliance process. While many organizations set up a CTF on a project basis, we emphasize the ongoing nature of the compliance effort and the need to ensure this is reflected in its mandate. Using the Act's title in the task force title might also be useful, since it emphasizes the importance of a specific set of requirements. We use the term "compliance task force" to generalize the compliance effort as well as emphasize the cross-functional aspect of its activities. The structure of such a task force will depend on the organization. The suggested membership is a reflection of recommendations and best practice:

- board-level members, such as the CIO or CFO (several CFOs if necessary)
- a project manager (who might be the senior compliance officer or a senior project manager) who implements a project-oriented methodology in a cyclical manner, and manages the activities of compliance as well as the budget
- legal representation, to add expertise on any legal issues
- a financial expert, with experience with interim and annual company financial reports
- an IT manager; preferably the most senior IT manager (CIO or IT director or deputy) to ensure IT responsibilities are fulfilled

- a chief compliance officer, who will be responsible for overseeing the cross-functional links between internal auditing and other departments through an internal controls working group
- business function managers, who can represent the interests and domain knowledge of business activities, according to the company organization
- Human Resources, to ensure that roles and responsibilities are clarified and recruiting is part of the resource process
- optional representation and co-option of permanent or temporary members depending on need: for example, if a supplier is important to the process, procurement might have a contribution to make and a senior procurement manager should be co-opted.

The CTF is the organization's internal oversight body for the Act, and reports to the audit committee and through this to the board. The aim of the task force is to see that a compliance program to meet the requirements of the Act is implemented throughout the organization. If it is a multinational organization, it will have replicated sub-task forces in national entities.

Business function owners

IT DEPARTMENT AND IT MANAGEMENT

The role of IT in realizing compliance is paramount. As such the responsibilities of the IT representative are critical. Many organizations have invested considerably over the years in centralized IT functions to gain the benefits of centralized administration and control. In a multi-national company, this centralization enables central control, but local IT departments will have to implement their part of the program. There is likely to be a range of local and different applications operating in the business, and these must be considered as part of the overall process of internal control. If subject to other compliance programs, IT will have varying degrees of experience of implementing compliance processes. It will also have staff familiar with introducing and managing controls for these processes.

EXISTING COMPLIANCE ACTIVITIES

A compliance office or department might already exist. Its staff will have experience of implementing regulatory standards, and experience of working directly with regulators. It will also have knowledge and experience of other regulatory bodies, and have worked with IT and business functions to achieve compliance. This could also mean that an existing program is available to act as a skeleton for the specifics of the compliance process. Many companies have instituted a compliance department, or recruited staff in legal or financial departments with compliance expertise. They will bring with them previous experience. This experience should be captured at this stage and used as an input to the compliance process.

The role of external auditors has changed as a result of the Act. However, they do represent a body of knowledge and experience that should be used where appropriate. They could offer valuable insights into the way the company can move this effort forward.

A further resource is the expertise in sector consultancies with experience of helping companies respond to the Act. Consultants could even be co-opted into the CTF as long as there is no conflict of interest.

Company policies

Published company policies are the way an organization manages the behavior of its members and defines a quality system, for example for the control of business processes. If there is no existing model, such as ISO 9001 for process quality, then a review of common practices needs to be made and formulated at this stage. This may represent a considerable amount of work, but is a practical aspect as a beneficial spin-off from the preparation phase. ISO 9001 or a similar certification process provides a very practical model for documenting compliance processes, and falls within the exploration of "existing compliance activities."

Budget and project creep

A budget is critical to the success of the compliance effort. It is perhaps the most discussed and most pressing concern of the compliance effort at board level, mainly because the compliance process is perceived to be an expensive undertaking. It will be the subject of many reports and external conference discussions, and tends to dominate user groups, special interest groups, and web-based forums on the subject of compliance to the Act.

If Sarbanes-Oxley requirements have been in place for several years, it is less likely that they will not have been budgeted for. However, special pleading may gain a reserved budget. Often budgets have to be shared with other projects, such as IT projects. Control over budgets may be especially sensitive; "shared" budgets may well fall under the control of a specific department, such as the IT function.

Assuming that the board has bought into the whole exercise, any budget must be guarded against encroachment, and attempts at project creep, which might eat away at its focus, should be highlighted. This is a common temptation since so many sub-projects are likely to be suggested as the inadequacies of systems and processes are uncovered, and attempts made to bring them into the remit of the CTF. However, any such efforts should be measured against the objectives of the CTF. If the initiatives are not strictly in line with these objectives, they should be resourced and budgeted for separately. The involvement of board-level executives on the CTF may help keep the budget separate and focused.

Table 11.1 A preparatory assessment checklist

0	Board members (CIO, CFO, and CIO)
0.1	Are they aware of the implications of the Act?
0.2	Are they aware of the importance of establishing controls?
0.3	Have they provided sufficient authorization for the CTF for it to carry out its activities?
1	**Compliance Task Force**
1.1	Has it made an initial risk assessment of the Act and its overall impact on the company?
1.2	Has it identified the way the Act affects IT systems?
1.3	Has it identified compliance responsibilities?
1.4	Has it assigned roles to individuals?
1.5	Has it identified any skills shortfalls in those assigned to roles?
1.6	Has it identified any specific skills needs for carrying out compliance activities on internal controls (e.g. in IT, legal, project management, internal consultancy)?
2	**Owners of business functions**
2.1	Have they identified the areas that have operational input to financial reporting?
2.2	Have they identified processes with existing controls?
2.3	Have they established which processes require controls?
3	**IT department and IT management**
3.1	Has it a demonstrable grasp of business requirements?
3.2	Has it implemented controls for IT systems and applications to meet these business requirements?
3.3	Is its risk assessment process fully integrated with the CTF risk assessment for financial reporting and the company's risk assessment process?
3.4	Does it routinely document, evaluate, and remediate IT controls?
3.5	Is there an IT function process for responding to IT control deficiencies?
3.6	Are any such controls tested and monitored?
4	**Existing compliance activities or processes**
4.1	Have these been identified and noted?
4.2	Are any such processes of value for the compliance project?

Table 11.1 continued

5	**Company policies**
5.1	Do they cover security, expected behavior and general business integrity?
5.2	Are they properly documented (to match external standards and regulations)?
5.3	Are they routinely made available to all staff?
5.4	Are they effectively implemented through IT support systems and applications?
6	**Budget**
6.1	Has a suitable budget been allocated to a body, such as the CTF, for the purposes of implementing compliance projects?

INDUSTRY BEST PRACTICE

A primary input to the preparation of a successful strategy is an assessment of common industry best practice, modified by the experience of other financial institutions in the market since the inauguration of the Act. Broadly these bodies of best practice fall into a number of categories: IT governance, corporate governance, and internal controls. The best elements of these are subsumed under the compliance process. As a general comment, best practice is a reference model rather than exact prescription. It requires modification to "fit" the organization.

IT governance

- IT governance is covered in detail by a number of frameworks such as ITIL and ISO 17799. Practice is not just about tools and software solutions, but also about the re-examination of company culture and behavioral change among end-user communities.
- Staff should have accessible, accurate, up-to-date information on policies and procedures. which must be clearly communicated; tools should be provided to facilitate this access.
- Change management should operate effectively at the management and the end-user level to allow efficient adoption of change across the organization. This is especially relevant to procedural changes resulting from the compliance cycle.
- Compliance should be capable of being demonstrated through internal and external auditing as a matter of practice.
- Reuse as much as possible to allow for sustainable solutions and minimize costs and effort.

Corporate governance

- Institute a formal corporate governance framework. This should include a code of ethics for senior executives, and in line with the Act, these should be published. Behavioral codes of conduct should also be produced.
- Public regulatory requirements should be translated into practical and observable internal policies.
- Clearly define roles and responsibilities to avoid ambiguity and confusion over ownership and accountability.
- Develop effective internal communications to ensure all staff know exactly what they have to do to achieve objectives. Publish this using mechanisms such as intranets.
- Embed corporate governance in frameworks for meeting regulatory obligations.
- Set up a permanent watching brief on compliance integrated with an ongoing compliance forum. This is often managed by the compliance function if there is one.

Internal controls

As controls underline all efforts to maintain a compliant system, all efforts should be made to embed best practice in the company's response.

- Automate the use of controls as much as possible.
- Ensure monitoring solutions assist end-users in observing codes of conduct and conforming to internal policies.
- Use a compliance architecture to rationalize the number of controls and their costs.
- Determine how far controls reflect the risks to the business and develop a coherent plan to minimize these risks through the realistic application of controls.
- Assess and identify the "gaps" in controls systems; use comprehensive frameworks, such as COBIT, to help guide this task.

The strategic nature of compliance, once accepted, with its tactical implications for implementation, generally reflects the approach taken to compliance. The compliance iceberg is really a recognition that the Act, despite its overt simplicity, actually covers a huge area. The state of compliance is somewhat deceptive since the perfect organization is unobtainable and to an extent any compliance effort is a compromise. Basing such a compromise on a risk-oriented approach is a practical response, and making the case for the organization's interests in the compliance chain is vital. Preparing for compliance through a thorough review can be a very useful first step, and the incorporation of recognized industry best practice should be an assumed objective. With this preparation in mind we can look at the compliance process itself in more detail.

PRACTICAL COMPLIANCE SUMMARY

> ■ As a point of best practice, any pre-work should be made available to key stakeholders in the project to raise awareness of issues and stimulate discussion on what are perceived to be the real issues to be addressed.
> ■ Involve senior management in strategic assessment of compliance.
> ■ Ensure the "actual" and "apparent" compliance effort are compared and understood.
> ■ Make the case for a systematic approach to compliance and modify this with pragmatic considerations.
> ■ Decide on how best to approach a cyclical process for the organization.
> ■ Prioritize efforts around risk—risk specific to the company.
> ■ Use a preparatory assessment checklist to assess the overall readiness for compliance.

NOTES

1. Through Auditing Standard 2, the PCAOB instructs auditors on how to check their clients' internal control assessment. The PCAOB, however, is moving towards a more flexible way of regulating auditor attestations. In November 2005, through a report on the initial implementation of AS2, the board criticized auditors who "did not alter the nature, timing, and extent of their testing to reflect the level of risk."

CHAPTER 12

The Compliance Process

THE COMPLIANCE PROCESS

To become compliant, an organization must undergo a process. This process might be fairly simple and familiar, or represent a range of challenges based on a lack of familiarity. It will involve varying levels of cost and resources. However well prepared an organization is, it is more than likely to prove a challenge that involves time and resources and the uncovering of unforeseen weaknesses in the way the organization operates. Such a process can be viewed as a business overhead, an unnecessary endangerment of vital interests, or a beneficial opportunity to improve business activities.

Responses to the Act vary. From a practical point of view we can adopt a number of approaches:

- Respond to the Act section by section over time, where each response is a separate project, with separate budgets, resources and scope.
- Assume a risk profile and measure the requirements of the Act against the profile to produce a "measured" response.
- Plan for an ongoing process rather than one-off project that assumes year-on-year compliance.
- Combine all these responses in a strategic plan which assumes that compliance is an ongoing set of activities.

Each organization will respond uniquely to the requirements of the Act, and in doing so will establish its own benchmark for best practice. To cover all these responses we envisage a process representing best practice, which is outlined in Figure 12.1. It consists of a number of stages, each dependent on the previous stage, and each of value to the successful completion of a planned response to the Act:

- Establish awareness of the Act and its relevance.

- Assess the readiness of the organization to respond.
- Establish control guidelines for compliance.
- Build a road map for compliance.

These stages constitute a process that is ongoing, subject to changes in the organization and external regulation.

THE COMPLIANCE PROCESS: STRATEGIC AND TACTICAL

The compliance process is a two-part endeavor. While the process is not a simple project, in a sense it is a project in that the strategic phase has a start and an end point, but the tactical phase is really a cycle, the compliance cycle. This is an engine for continuous assessment, change, and quality review to ensure the enterprise stays up to date and fully compliant on a year-on-year basis. Without such a mechanism the compliance effort will become fragmented. The advantages of such a process are many:

- It ensures the compliance activity is planned, tailored to the overall aim of the compliance effort, and driven by the objectives established at a strategic level.
- In this sense, there is a clear strategy at work. This strategy is demonstrable, and acts as an input to generating public confidence in the good governance of the company.
- The cycle ensures that a consistent approach is maintained. This has the advantage of maximizing the investment in skills and resources made during the planning and implementation.
- Feedback is critical to the practical success of compliance. The cycle has a natural feedback structure which underpins its value.
- A comprehensive sequence of events involving as many relevant departments as possible is another factor for the continuing success of compliance.
- The compliance cycle is a model for sub-cycles, which can be applied as necessary to specific activities within the overall chain.
- Existing models for planning, problem solving, and decision making are natural complements to the cycle and its applicability.

The compliance process: outline

The compliance process is captured in Figure 12.1. This indicates both the strategic and tactical dimensions of the process, defining activity stages and grouping them according to function.

Strategic dimensions

A: AWARENESS OF THE ACT

An understanding the Act, who it affects, why they are affected, and its significance for the organization establishes its importance. This phase is especially valuable for involving the board of directors and gaining their support. The preparatory phase ensures that key management and functional leaders are made aware of the implications of the Act for them and their company, through the use of a preparatory assessment questionnaire or a similar means. This initial process provides a strategic overview of:

■ the nature of the Act
■ its overall likely impact on the organization and departments, as a set of risks, as well as costs
■ the basic inputs needed to be made to ensure compliance.

B: ASSESS READINESS TO RESPOND

Once the significance of the Act is established and the board have decided on a general response by allocating resources for a compliance effort, some work has to be done to see just how much effort is required, and enough resources must be assigned over an appropriate period of time. From the initial assessment a picture emerges of the state of the company in relation to the compliance process. It illustrates how well the company can respond in terms of:

■ the ability of the culture of the company to manage compliance
■ the state of preparation of the IT function and business functions, their tool sets, and staff needs
■ any existing experience of the company with regulation and compliance planning
■ the weaknesses and strengths of the organization from a SWOT or similar analysis
■ the priorities to assume, from a gap analysis
■ training and education needs of specialist and general staff, and a review of skills audits.

C: ESTABLISH CONTROL GUIDELINES

Based on the readiness to respond to assessment, the next step is to identify the way the organization can best utilize its existing resources in responding to specific sections of the Act, such as 302 and 404. As a consequence of this review, an overall aim and set of objectives must be defined,

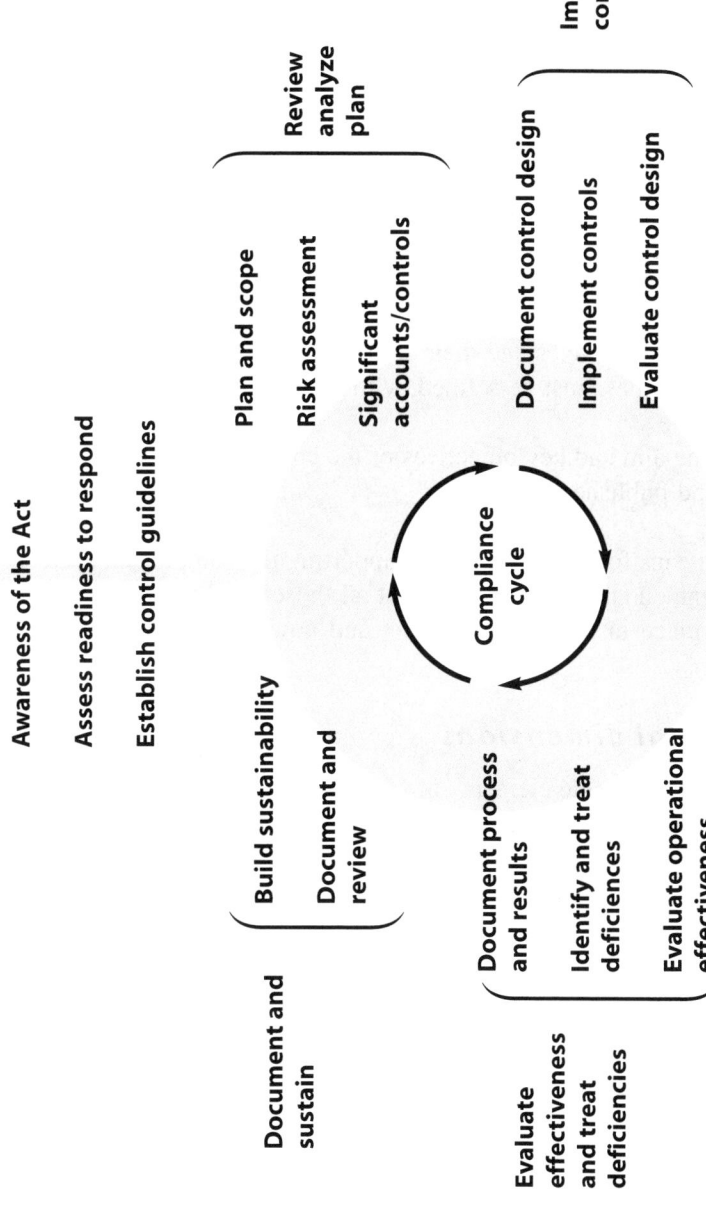

Figure 12.1 The compliance process

and a set of guidelines drawn up or adopted as the basis for all further compliance work. Building on this foundation, practical measures need to be put in place to deliver verifiable compliance:

- The cross-functional team must be set up, as the compliance task force (CTF).
- The relationship with the audit committee must be defined.
- Roles and responsibilities must be defined and allocated.
- A procedure for staff to be able to communicate non-compliance issues must be set up and published (commonly referred to as "whistleblowing").
- The responsibilities of the company attorney under the Act must be formalized, including the reporting escalation procedure.
- The code of ethics for senior management must be established and published as a requirement of the Act.
- Internal communications must be established as part of a review of internal policies and their effective distribution and awareness.
- Timelines must be defined, with review milestones agreed for an initial cycle.
- The aim and key objectives of the compliance process must be agreed and published.

The means for controlling and supporting the compliance cycle need to be recognized and resourced, so that all those involved understand their role, their place in the bigger picture, and how they are accountable for their actions.

Tactical dimensions

With the strategic elements of compliance in place, further work can now take place on those areas that relate directly to implementing the objectives. Generally the CTF is empowered to get on with meeting the requirements of the first annual assessment, using the next periodic report, either quarterly or annual, as a key milestone.

D: COMPLIANCE CYCLE

Review–analyze–plan
1. Plan and scope.
2. Perform a risk assessment.
3. Identify significant accounts/controls.

Implement controls
1. Document the control design.

2. Implement the controls.
3. Evaluate the control design.

Evaluate effectiveness and treat deficiencies
1. Evaluate operational effectiveness.
2 Identify and remediate deficiencies.
3. Document the process and results.

Document and sustain
1. Document and review.
2. Build sustainability.

Repeat cycle

The activities represented by this part of the process are the efforts to specifically respond to the Act in detail. They consist of implementing a model or models of control, and a process of evaluation.

Review–analyze–plan

■ **Plan and scope**
Produce an applicability statement, of a scope derived from the work of the previous stages.

■ **Perform risk assessment**
Expand the existing risk assessment to identify assets and processes in need of further assessment and identification of types of risk.

■ **Identify significant accounts and controls**
List and qualify the areas that need attention—accounts, transaction processes and workflows that require internal controls and types of internal control.

Implement controls

■ **Design controls and document the control design**
Design the controls that have been identified and that are needed.
Adopt a model for documenting the internal control system.

■ **Implement the internal controls (new or modified existing)**
Purchase systems, applications, or resources to implement controls where necessary.
Establish a go-live point and test period (with parallel running).
Roll forward the planned use of internal controls in line with established rollout procedures.

■ **Evaluate the control design**
Test and evaluate the controls for effectiveness in design: are they the right control type(s) for a given process?

Evaluate effectiveness and treat deficiencies

- **Evaluate operational effectiveness**
  Test and evaluate the controls in operation by generating exceptions and events. Assess how well exceptions are captured and dealt with.
- **Identify and remediate deficiencies**
  Report on the weaknesses in the control system, in design and operation.
- Change, modify, or replace deficient controls.

Document and sustain

- **Document processes and results**
  Ensure that all activities (design, operational testing, and so on) are documented in parallel according to the accepted documentation model for review and auditing purposes.
- **Build sustainability**
  Establish periodic reviews of the systems' design and operational effectiveness.
  Review the resources needed to maintain the system of internal control and other compliance requirements.
  Provide a report as an input to manage the assessment.

Review and assess for change

Following the initial iteration of the road map consider two further steps:

- Lessons learnt.
- Process review.

This will be part of the ongoing remit of the CTF. Since compliance is not a one-off activity (although it will be treated as a project, it is an open-ended project), there is no formal end-point or date. The objectives are largely unrealized except as ongoing aspirations. If it does not produce exceptions the organization is maintaining compliance with the intention of the Act.

THE COMPLIANCE PROCESS: SYSTEMATIC AND PRAGMATIC

In the previous chapter we discussed the approaches the organization might adopt in responding to the Act. Based on a risk-oriented view which reflected the interests of the organization itself, we noted the options to be systematic or pragmatic, where systematic is an approach characterized as thorough and comprehensive, and pragmatic is an approach driven by the need to gain the most from the least effort. Ideally these approaches can be combined to exploit their benefits and deliver maximum flexibility in implementation.

Systematic approach

This is generally typified by frameworks and references, such as standards, that "model" systems. This is of particular value to companies that need a reference model as a guide to an unfamiliar subject, or that work in an area of such complexity that a highly structured approach is needed. Its thoroughness ensures all possible compliance issues within a function or area of interest are addressed, and because it is comprehensive, all possible functions and operational areas are investigated thoroughly.

Pragmatic approach

This approach is driven by the need to gain the most from the least effort, using past experience and elements of generally perceived best practice as guidelines. It is "pragmatic" in that the approach is constrained by the resource and financial realities of the business. The aim is to gain the most from the least effort, using known examples and best practice. It is a very common response to problem solving. It is often driven by considerations of cost, and guided by references such the company's risk profile: its definitions of acceptable and unacceptable risk. The best practice provides reliable references based on the experience of others.

These approaches are balanced with two further concepts, quantitative and qualitative.

Plan-Do-Check-Act (PDCA)

A method that has proven itself in work to comply with a number of standards, such as ISO 17799, and is recommended by practitioners, is plan–do–check–act (PDCA). This is an improvement process for solving quality and other issues, and implementing long-term solutions. It also an effective short-term problem-solving model which is characterized by:

- fast response
- use of minimum resources
- maximum usage of available time
- a highly reactive feedback system
- its cyclical nature.

This combination of a systematic approach and pragmatism is a well-known business tool. It is a cyclical process that assumes that an analytical and remedial task has to be done in a short time frame with limited resources.

Combining this process with business and analytical tools, and applying them to specific activities within the compliance cycle, ensures a highly practical, relatively low-cost, and efficient approach to managing compliance. Broadly the PDCA process breaks down into a number of tasks, which are well documented across the industry. Tables 12.1 and 12.2 are examples of mapping the PDCA generic approach to process development and policy implementation.

If you prepare and use this combination of practical measures, the compliance cycle can move forward based on a systematic approach that can also accommodate a degree of qualitative and quantitative measures, depending on the resources and tools available. The generic PDCA process is a cycle that includes a number of standard activities. The flexibility of this process is that these activities can vary and still provide a firm framework for a fast response.

Plan

1. Identify the activity.
2. Define the problem through an aim and objectives.

Table 12.1 The PDCA method

PDCA steps	Process development activities	Typical business tools used
Plan	Define the process	Brainstorming
	Collect performance data	Process mapping
	Analyze the process	Cause and effect analysis
	Identify improvements	Benchmarking
	Evaluate options (alternatives etc)	Cost–benefit analysis
	Rework the process	Process mapping
	Develop an implementation plan	Gantt chart, planning tools
Do	Carry out the plan	Project management toolsets
Check	Monitor against the plan	Project planning tools
	Analyze variations against plan	Decision charting, checklists
Act	Correct variations	Brainstorming
	Standardize the changes (absorb solution into process)	Formal control management tools
	Review	Cost–benefit analysis, planning tools

3. Research and collect data around the objectives.
4. Analyze to determine the cause of the problem (using root cause analysis, RCA).
5. Identify the solution (or solutions).
6. Plan to apply the solution (or solutions).

Do

1. Implement the solution.

Check

1. Monitor the activities of the applied solution.
2. Evaluate the monitored results against the aim and objectives.
3. Carry out a gap analysis to compare the results and plan, and identify deficiencies.

Table 12.2 Applying PDCA to the compliance process

PDCA steps	Policy implementation activities	Typical business tools used
Plan	Define the corporate governance scope	Brainstorming
	Define the threats and potential of the policy implementation	SWOT analysis
	Identify critical success factors (CSFs) for the policy implementation	Priority planning
	Define measures for identifying success	Cause and effect analysis, Pareto analysis
Do	Carry out the plan	Project management toolsets
Check	Monitor against the planned implementation	Gantt chart
Act	Review policy results	Brainstorming, cause and effect analysis
	Report on status of implementation (for another iteration if necessary)	Internal reporting framework tools

Act

1. Treat the variations and differences from the gap analysis.
2. Incorporate any new processes, changes, or amendments into the overall process.
3. Produce recommendations for actions to review.
4. Repeat the PDCA cycle through periodic reviews.

MAPPING THE COMPLIANCE CYCLE TO BUSINESS

The compliance process as a system for delivering compliance requires an assumption for its success: that it consists of an integrated mix of skills, knowledge, and authority from across the organization. Without this cross-functional dimension, the results are likely to be limited, with a greater risk of non-compliances surfacing to damage the interests of the whole. With a cross-functional team and sufficient support for the internal auditing function in place, the compliance process can be applied to all the functions of the organization that have been identified at a strategic level as presenting risks under the Act. The organizational functions, represented at a high level by IT, and the business activity functions, together with the board, are the internal entities that require specific (and generally differing) attention. IT activities are separable from the business activities for the purposes of internal controls, although they support the latter and make them possible. However, the compliance process is

Practical compliance

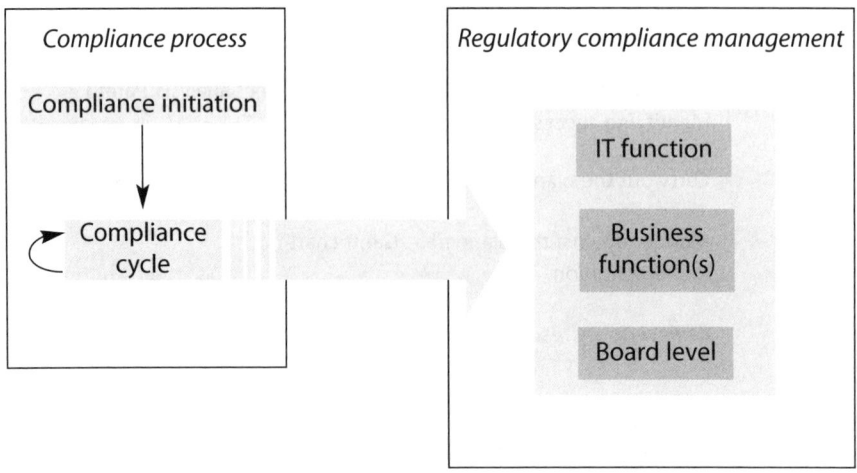

Figure 12.2 The compliance process and management

structurally equipped to manage all these internal entities and integrate them within a dynamic cycle of improvement.

APPLYING THE COMPLIANCE CYCLE TO PROCESSES

One way of looking at the compliance process is to view it as a "machine" or "engine" that can be introduced into a process, fired up, and used to resolve issues. This is a simplistic view but it captures the flexibility of a process that contains its own feedback mechanisms. Figure 12.3 illustrates how a consolidation process for generating financial reports can be addressed through the compliance process. It enables the skills, tools, and best-practice elements of the compliance cycle, for example, to be concentrated on a process in a structured and consistent manner. An advantage of the compliance process is that for external auditors, once the compliance process is understood and validated as an effective mechanism, there can be a high level of confidence in its use, whatever the process or system of control.

THE COMPLIANCE PROCESS IN CONTEXT

In effect, the compliance cycle engine can be dropped into any process, control, or group of processes or controls, and operate predictably in line with the control guidelines established at the start of the compliance process. Reporting lines stay consistent and accountability is transparent. As a mechanism for delivering compliance, the compliance process is applicable to not only internal entities and functions, but also external elements that affect the overall ability of the organization to stay compliant. Figure 12.4 places the compliance process in context.

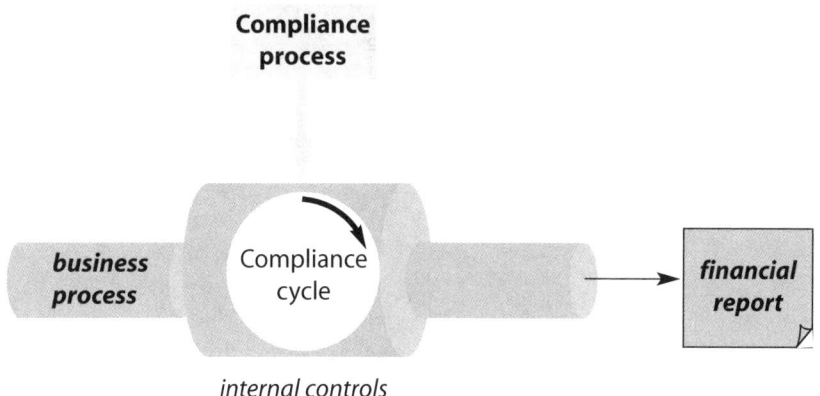

Figure 12.3 The compliance engine

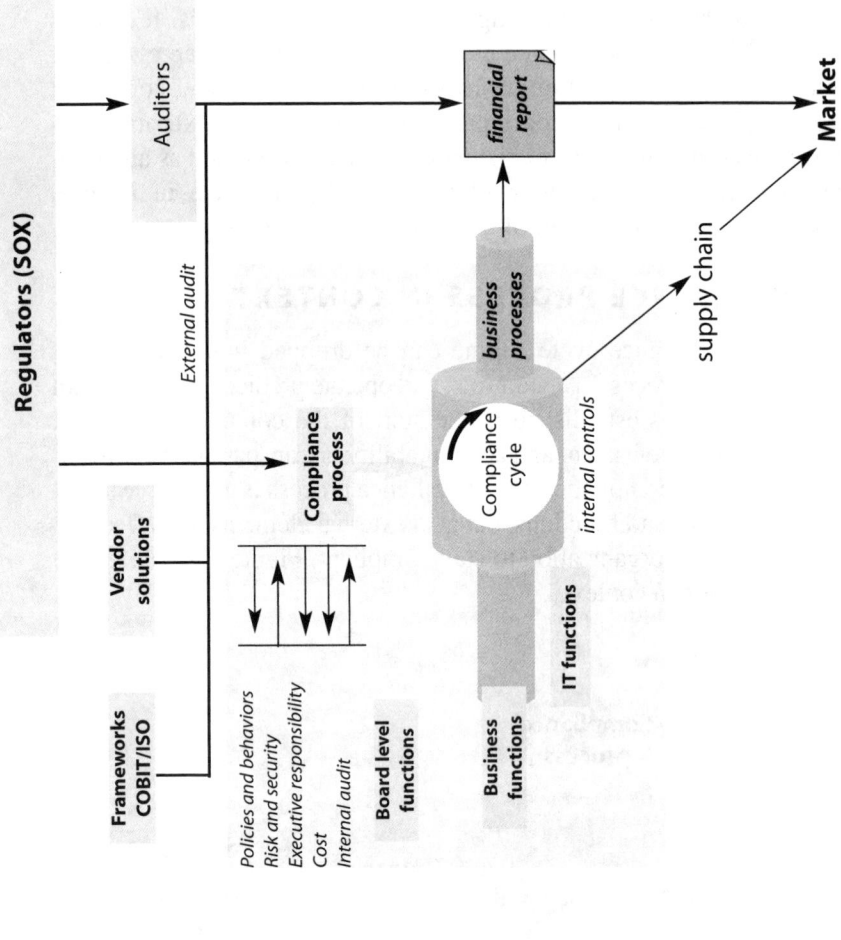

Figure 12.4 The compliance process in context

Strategic phase

During the initiation, or strategic, phase the process takes into account:

- the pressure from external regulation, in this case the Act and its requirements
- the interaction with policies, risk assessments, cost considerations, and internal auditing requirements
- the internal pressures of business and board-level market considerations
- the interaction with vendors and their specific tools for delivering compliance
- the interaction with external auditors and their requirements and constraints
- the frameworks that need to be assessed for relevance and as working models.

Tactical phase

The compliance cycle is then applied specifically to areas of interest:

- IT functions and activities
- business functions and activities
- supply chain compliance issues
- processes in general that lead to financial reporting
- the system of internal control that leads to financial reporting.

This larger context illustrates the power of an approach focused on practical application, and the value of having a diversity of support from tools, skills, management oversight, and business relevance. With this structured approach available, the specific sections of the Act can be directly addressed.

PRACTICAL COMPLIANCE SUMMARY

- The COO gets advice from the legal function on the penalties of the Act.
- The COO or other(s) draw up a summary report on why the Act should be examined in detail, and a process is initiated to deal with it.
- Those involved attend seminars, receive training, seek industry information, and talk to consultants who can advise on the significance and implications.

- The board members are educated on their responsibilities and roles in ensuring compliance.
- A task force or sub-committee is created, reporting to the audit committee, and representing major interested parties.
- Responsibilities are assigned for managing this part of the process.

Focus at this stage on:

- Examining existing compliance processes and programs for their suitability as potential models for a response.
- Reviewing past experience of compliance, non-compliances, and risk events.
- Estimating resource needs for the IT and Communications functions to undertake a more thorough study.
- Examining the state of play with the success of rolling out internal policies, and the effect on staff behavior.
- Assessing existing workflows and control systems as the basis for management assessment reporting.
- Pursuing a gap analysis of what must be done as an input to the compliance road map activities.
- Assigning responsibilities to manage this part of the process.
- Creating a set of guidelines for compliance activity based on the company risk profile (if any) and the nature of the company's business.

CHAPTER 13

Compliance with Section 302

Section 302, more than any other, sets the bar for regulatory response for affected companies. It was the first point of focus for these companies, and the area where the first substantial efforts were made to ensure compliance. Section 302 became effective on August 29, 2002. It establishes the accountability of senior executives (for most companies these are the CEO and CFO) for the certification of financial reports, and the system of internal controls over the process that supports those reports. This section applies to companies filing quarterly and annual reports with the SEC under Section 13(a) or 15(d) of the Securities Exchange Act. It has two main requirements:

- Senior officers must certify financial reports.
- The companies must make a set of disclosures that are not misleading and are timely.

The introduction of "internal controls" as an area of scrutiny, and the depth of investigation that this implies for the public company, have ramifications beyond the original intention of this section of the Act. The nature of these controls and how they can be assessed in practice is the substance of much compliance work. The responsibilities of senior executives are brought into sharp focus by penalties introduced by the Act. This section, like so many others, points up again the relationship with the SEC 1934 Act. Table 13.1 summarizes the section, requirements, scope, and practical compliance activities.

DOCUMENTATION FOR DEMONSTRATING COMPLIANCE

Information is central to an information economy player such as the financial sector. As it is a heavily regulated sector, there will most likely already be systems for generating and managing documentation. The requirements

Table 13.1 Section 302 and practical compliance activities

Description	Compliance scope	Compliance activity
The Section mandates that the "principal executive officer or officers and the principal financial officer or officers, or persons performing similar functions" certify in periodic reports that they have reviewed the report. *302(a)(1)*	Executive officers (CEO and CFO) (issuer)	In the document control of the financial report introduce a review option and sign it. This might already be part of the report; if not, introduce it.
The report must not contain any "untrue statement of a material fact or omit to state a material fact" which is "misleading." *In 302(a)(2)*	Executive officers (CEO and CFO) (issuer)	This status for the financial report is the result of a series of control measures which are addressed by the compliance effort in general, and the compliance process in particular. A statement to this effect can be introduced and signed.
The financial statements, along with financial information included in the report, "fairly present in all material respects" the financial status of the issuer for the period of the report. *302(a)(3)*	Executive officers (CEO and CFO) (issuer)	This is part of the standard signing process for reports. An additional paragraph can make this clear if necessary.
The signing officers are held responsible for "establishing and maintaining" internal controls. *302(a)(4)(A)*	Executive officers (CEO and CFO) (issuer)	The establishment of internal controls is part of the compliance process (CP). (See Chapter 12 for more detail.) Critical to this is thorough documentation of the controls for external auditing (CP). Responsibility can be indicated in an appendix or sub-section within the report on the systems of internal controls (derived from the CP). These can be sourced from the Statement of Applicability.

Table 13.1 continued

Description	Compliance scope	Compliance activity
The signers must ensure they have designed internal controls to ensure that the company and its subsidiaries provide suitable "material information." *302(a)(4)(B)*	Executive officers (CEO and CFO) (issuer)	The system of internal controls review document should include some details on how internal controls provide "material information" (CP). It should refer to the design and selection of internal controls (CP).
The signers must have "evaluated" the effectiveness of the issuer"s internal controls 90 days prior to the report" Section 302(a)(4)(C). They must also include their "conclusions about the effectiveness of their internal controls" based on their evaluation. *Section 302(a)(4)(D). This responsibility links to Section 404, "Management Assessment of Internal Controls."*	Executive officers (CEO and CFO) (issuer)	An internal audit on internal controls should be conducted before the report (CP). The selection of what part of the business is audited depends on the risk assessment and internal priorities (CP). The audit must evaluate and demonstrate the effectiveness of the controls in place—the metrics involved are part of the design of the controls themselves (CP). The signers must indicate that they have considered how effective these controls are (derived from the CP).
There is also a requirement to disclose to auditors and the audit committee all "significant deficiencies" in the design or operation of internal controls. This is especially so if these deficiencies could affect the issuer's ability to record, process, summarize, and report financial data. They must also identify to the auditors any "material weaknesses" in these controls. *302(a)(5)(A).*	Executive officers (CEO and CFO) (issuer)	Significant deficiencies will be identified and categorized for impact on financial data (CP). Material weaknesses will also be identified and categorized (CP). Significant deficiencies and material weaknesses must be identified for remediation (CP). (See Chapter 17 on internal controls.)

Table 13.1 continued

Description	Compliance scope	Compliance activity
Similarly, they must disclose any fraud, "whether or not material", that involves management or other employees who have a significant role in the issuer's internal controls." *Section 302(a)(5)(B)*.	Executive officers (CEO and CFO) (issuer) Staff involved in internal control compliance	Internal audit(s) must identify instances of fraud uncovered; they must also detail how this fraud occurred and how it is being redressed, and its likely impact. The extent of disclosure is not detailed but it must be sufficient to eliminate ambiguity as to its nature as fraud (CP).
The signing officers must also detail any important changes to internal controls, or highlight factors related to internal controls that could affect them after the evaluation has taken place. They should provide information on how such "significant deficiencies" and "material weaknesses" have been treated. *Section 302(a)(6)*.	Executive officers (CEO and CFO) (issuer)	Change management over internal control is part of the compliance cycle (CP). It is also an aspect of effective IT and other frameworks such as ITIL. Identify changes to internal controls (these are likely to be continuous in response to business development) (CP). Treatment of deficiencies and weaknesses is part of the compliance cycle (CP).
The comprehensive international scope of the Act is reinforced since "Foreign re-incorporations have no effect." The requirements of the Act cannot be avoided by moving the corporate HQ, typically to a country external to US legislation. *302(b)*.	Affected company executives	This is normally detailed in non-financial information included in the financial report.

of Section 302 specifically place an onus on senior management to ensure that the organization effectively demonstrates a system of internal control for the processes that generate the information that goes into the periodic financial reports. If this system of control exists, senior managers might be led to believe that everything is already covered. However, as part of the compliance process we need to examine how far existing systems cover the obvious requirements of the Act, and also how far less obvious aspects of the Act are addressed.

Reuse of existing tools

Reuse has a number of benefits that appeal to the budget-conscious. However, there are some issues that could have a considerable effect on the prospect of reuse. Table 13.2 summarizes the advantages and disadvantages of reuse as a cornerstone of the compliance strategy.

For an existing system to be able to meet the challenge of Section 302 it must have certain characteristics. It must be:

- flexible: the design must able to be modified quickly
- to scale: able to encompass the whole of the organization and hold large amounts of formatted data
- accessible: most likely a web or intranet-based solution with universal access
- secure: for controlled access to change management
- integrated: with features that enable it to be integrated to other systems if necessary, such as policy distribution and information management
- structured: typically modular in structure to allow for segregation of access and ease of build and modification.

The system must also ideally expand beyond simple document management to include:

Table 13.2 Advantages and disadvantages of reuse

Advantages	Disadvantages
The system tools have already been developed or purchased	The system tools may well be dated and inadequate to meet the challenges
Skills in their use have been invested in	Skills are already obsolete or do not or no longer exist
Users have passed through an acceptance barrier and the systems are probably productive	Staff churn may mean the user population needs retraining

■ **An effective search engine.** A search capability will allow process owners and others to access any relevant documentation, as either structured or unstructured data.

■ **Help desk support.** An interactive capability to allow users to provide feedback on system use, internal control issues, and generally maintain familiarity with tools.

■ **An automatic audit trail capability**, for change management and user tracking.

■ **Some project control capability**, for compliance process management, to allow compliance teams to coordinate and document their activities. As compliance is a cross-functional activity the system must support some collaborative working.

■ **Publishing capability**, to issue alerts and updates on use and policies.

For managing documentation there are a number of ideal components for the document and information management suite:

■ **Audit trail**: a management module that enables activities to be logged, tracked, and progressed through workflows, and inbuilt reporting capability and email alerting.

■ **A document library**: built around libraries and taxonomies that simplify and automate the process of managing documents across a large organization. (Consider integrating this with automated solutions that centralize storage, such as ERM, or automated document transfer solutions such as XBRL.)

■ **Publishing support**: authorization, publishing, version control, and document distribution.

■ **Scanning and storage**: the ability to scan hard-copy documents and link these to storage to enable searching.

■ **Workflow processing**: extend and develop existing workflows and process map events specific to compliance.

■ **Archive management**: for archiving documents in a managed way, with effective retrieval for compliance demands.

PRACTICAL COMPLIANCE SUMMARY

■ Include clear signing options in quarterly and annual reports to signal compliance with certification.

■ Ensure attention to detail in the form of the certification prescribed by the SEC.

■ Beware of timescales for evaluating the internal control certification.

- Ensure all known significant deficiencies are identified and included.
- Ensure all known events that qualify as fraud are identified and included.
- Indicate any post-evaluation major changes to internal controls.
- If the company is foreign to the United States, be aware of the obligations if it is listed in the United States.
- Examine reuse of tools and systems to maximize the confidence in existing solutions.
- Exploit the investment in training in existing tools, and focus on developing these.
- Develop a flexible document management system that is detailed and comprehensive enough to manage compliance.
- Review all documented systems to ensure they are comprehensively covered. Prioritize around Section 302 to cover any exposure.

CHAPTER 14

Compliance with Section 404

THE SPECIAL CHALLENGES OF SECTION 404

Section 404 of the Act is a challenge for any organization. It centers on the importance of senior management attesting to the accuracy and reliability of systems that produce the information for the financial reports. Not surprisingly, the Act provides a number of specific compliancy requirements, and these have been analyzed for implementation by affected organizations, agencies, consultancies, and any body responsible for assisting in the process of ensuring that financial reports are up to scratch. Section 404 is a driver for much of the work that deals with the practicalities of compliance. Table 14.1 is a summary of the section and its associated activities.

Who is affected by Section 404

Section 404 applies to companies, or "issuers," filing reports under Section 13 (a) or 15 (d) of the Securities Exchange Act of 1934. The Sarbanes-Oxley Act defines an issuer as an entity "that has a class of Securities registered under Section 12 of the Exchange Act" and is "required to file reports under Section 15 (d) of the Securities and Exchange Act of 1934." The requirements also apply to a non-public subsidiary of a public company. The parent public company needs to evaluate the controls of such non-public subsidiaries.

SECTION 404: MANAGEMENT ASSESSMENT OF INTERNAL CONTROLS

Section 404 is a key to shaping the way the Act is perceived. It is a driver for the way the financial industry is responding to compliance with the Act, greatly influencing the way compliance projects are being introduced and financed. The principle is that management has to provide assurance, in the annual report, that the company's system of generating information for the financial report is adequately monitored through a system of internal controls. This assessment is examined by the auditors who prepare the annual report, and they must "attest to, and report on" this assessment. The rules and guidelines that govern this process are to be provided by the PCAOB. The conditions of this section are evaluated quarterly, with an annual internal control report.

How can management be confident that the system of internal control over financial reporting is effective for their organization? The Act presents a definition of that confidence: management can reach this conclusion when there are no material weaknesses in internal controls. The controls must be effective in design and in operation throughout the period of audit to satisfy the Act.

CONTENT OF MANAGEMENT'S INTERNAL CONTROL REPORT

The content of the internal control report attached to periodic reports must include the following:

- A statement of management's responsibility for establishing and maintaining the systems of internal control over financial reporting. This must be expressed clearly using terminology that indicates management responsibility.
- Management's assessment on the effectiveness of internal controls.
- A statement which identifies the internal control framework used by the management to evaluate the effectiveness of internal controls. This is generally COSO or an equivalent.

In addition to the management internal control report, the auditor must include a statement attesting to the statement made by management, offering an opinion on management's assessment of the effectiveness of its system of internal controls.

CRITICAL SUCCESS FACTORS (CSFS) FOR SECTION 404

- **Tone at the top**: this is part of the COSO environment for compliance. The company attitude to compliance activities is conditioned by the commitment of top-level executives and the audit committee. This is a strategic phase issue but informs all aspects of the compliance cycle.
- **Realistic timelines**: in planning Section 404 work, define realistic timelines. Allow for extra resources and project drift. In fact, standard project time planning is fundamental, since the deadlines are partly external, although they are controlled by quarterly and annual deadlines: in particular, Form 10-K financial year filing dates.

Table 14.1 Summary of Section 404 requirements

Description	Compliance scope	Compliance activity
This section tasks the SEC with prescribing rules for annual reports to include an "internal control report."	SEC, PCAOB	
Management is responsible for "establishing and maintaining" an "adequate internal control structure" and "procedures for financial reporting."	Management (issuer)	This is the bulk of the activity associated with this section—building or monitoring a system of internal control and developing procedures (CP). Specifically ensure the responsibility cascade operates well, so that all involved know their place in the compliance hierarchy.
The report must include "an assessment" of the "effectiveness" of the "internal control structure and procedures of the issuer for financial reporting."	Management (issuer)	An in-depth assessment by management can only be realistically achieved if the internal control system is effective in demonstrating a thorough coverage of all eventualities. This has to be part of cyclical activity (CP—compliance cycle).
For "internal control evaluation and reporting," the registered public accounting firm that prepares or issues the audit report for the issuer must "attest to, and report on," the internal control assessment made by the management of the issuer. This attestation is subject to the standards for attestation engagements issued or adopted by the Board.	External, public auditor	The external auditor's attestation report. This is likely to use the PCAOB's AS2 guide. Testing of internal controls may be carried out cooperatively or separately depending on the degree of independence and objectivity the auditor wants to demonstrate (the auditor's risk profile will define this). Be aware of these factors when drawing up the internal control report.

- ■ **Regular reporting**: report progress at observed milestones to the audit committee and board of directors. Keep external auditors informed on a regular basis. Regular reporting avoids surprises later on.
- ■ **Focus on risk management.** Ensure the focus stays on a risk-

oriented approach to compliance and on keeping to deadlines through streamlining.

Taking the point of view of the auditor, which is a useful perspective for management in their process of assessment, the evaluation process must be based on evidence. The auditor must obtain evidence for the effectiveness of internal controls and cannot rely solely on the process controls. It is not easy to demonstrate that the system is in a "state of grace"—that is, without fault, a passive dimension. The auditor's opinion must have some corroboration—a positive dimension. This is essential to demonstrate the auditor's high level of assurance that management's assessment is correct. The compliance process, especially the compliance cycle, generates evidence through its activities. The assessment undertaken, which the auditor must review thoroughly, should provide as many pointers to necessary evidence as possible.

PROJECT MANAGEMENT LIFECYCLE

Implementing Section 404 of the Act is a major activity. Rather than deal with it as simple stand-alone project, we suggest applying the compliance process and its internal compliance cycle. However, the process can operate as a series of cyclical projects that have closure but loop back according to the overall compliance monitoring process. In this way the Section 404 work operates within its own cycle:

- Initiation: identifying the initial steps of the project, and creating specific objectives for this project, resourcing the activities and sub-activities and integrating with the compliance process.
- Scoping: identifying what is included in the project and what is excluded. Scoping the Section 404 project has special considerations. This includes identifying:
  - documentation required
  - criteria for testing such as the timing and extent
  - significant accounts
  - business processes and sub-processes, and mapping the same to significant accounts
  - relevant financial statement assertions for each and every significant account.
- Planning: developing working solutions to meet the project objectives, generally within the context of a project plan.
- Implementation: coordinating people and resources to carry out the plan.
- Monitoring: project slippage occurs even with good oversight; monitoring allows corrective action.

■ Project close: once all activities in a project are complete, the project needs to be closed formally by appropriate sign-offs. Normally, a 404 implementation project is closed after sign-off is received from the CEO, CFO, and above all, the statutory auditor.

■ Review and reflection: consider the results of the planned process, how it can be improved, the impact in general, and the cost overall. Complete closure does not occur in this context, since the process cycles back into a fresh timed initiation phase.

IMPLEMENTING A SECTION 404 PROJECT

The overall project timescale is illustrated in Figure 14.1. It consists of a financial year and its quarterly reporting periods. Since the financial year will vary from company to company there are no absolute dates; rather this is a timeline template.

■ **Walkthrough of significant processes**: this is an example of how the Section 404 work is part of the compliance process. Significant accounts or lines of business and their processes will have been identified within the compliance process. Walkthroughs are familiar

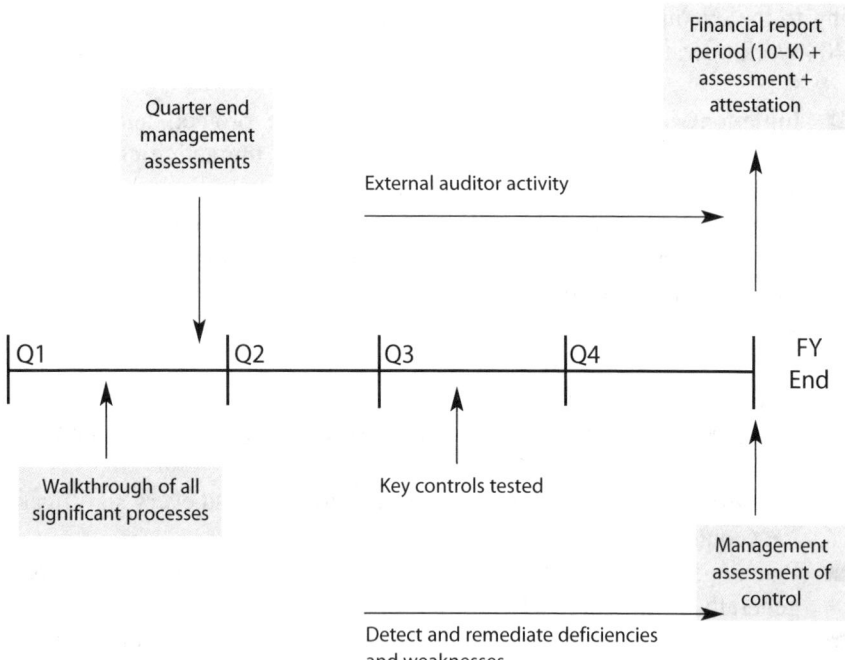

Figure 14.1 Planning the compliance timetable

to external and internal auditors, and give appropriate staff a good feel for the status of this process and the way the controls are operating. This work forms a basis for the testing of controls and the remediation work carried out up to the financial year-end.

■ **Key controls tested**: allows important controls to be tested thoroughly just after half-way through the year. Depending on timescales agreed, this allows external auditors to make an early start on their testing.

■ **External auditor activity**: auditors should be invited to begin work in good time to measure the system on internal control, form an opinion, and make an assessment on management assessments.

■ **Detect and remediate deficiencies and weaknesses**: this is a process of amendment, redesign, and process review.

■ **Quarter end management assessments**: these are regular assessments made by senior managers as part of the ongoing compliance process. These cumulative assessments together with the internally audited key controls, testing, and remediation, put management in a position to make an informed and reasonable year-end assessment as the internal control report.

■ **Financial report**: this is the outcome of all the previous activities. In this the Section 404 requirements will be met for financial reporting. It includes the standard financial and non-financial information; the internal control report, management's assessment of the effectiveness of the system of internal control; and the auditor's attestation and opinion on the internal control report.

Since we recommend that Section 404 compliance activity should be treated as a project, a number of project-specific tasks also need to be scheduled:

■ Review the quality of internal project management capabilities: does the company use a methodology such as PRINCE2™?

■ Performance management: have project metrics been defined and key performance indicators been established?

■ Future planning: has a lifecycle project management methodology been implemented and enforced for continuous improvement?

■ Sources of information: have company information assets such as SAS 70 Type I and Type II reports[1] been examined as useful inputs for Section 404 compliance?

Complying with Section 404 calls on the features of the compliance process. Its requirements broaden the scope of Section 302 and anticipate the demands of Section 409. But by adopting an approach that is characterized by ongoing compliance and continuous monitoring, the demands of management assessment can be met in a way that maximizes the benefits to the organization and reduces the risk of non-compliance.

PRACTICAL COMPLIANCE SUMMARY

- Define how Section 404 work fits into the company-specific compliance cycle. In reality is it is likely to drive much of the compliance work.
- Use the resources of the CTF to work on management's assessment (internal control report).
- Focus on CSFs for Section 404, especially risk management and regular reporting.
- Properly resource Section 404 project activities with strong project management skills.
- Use "walkthroughs" on a regular basis.
- Decide on test methods for Section 404.
- Recruit and hire expertise if necessary.
- Research industry best practice on Section 404 experience.

NOTE

1. Enforcement of the Act is dependent on a number of operational aspects such as logs and audits, as well as network security reports and incident response metrics. These security processes and control frameworks tend to be drawn from standards such as ISO 17799, based on the British Standard 7799, the National Institute of Standards process definitions (NIST) and SAS 70.

CHAPTER 15

Compliance with Other Relevant Sections

The Sarbanes-Oxley Act consists of a number of sections which have specific compliance requirements. Sections 302 and 304 have received most of the effort from companies. However, there are a number of other sections that require a practical response to ensure the overall compliance process achieves its objectives. This chapter does not detail the activities of the PCAOB except where they are strictly relevant.

SECTIONS 802 AND 1102

Documentation

The context for these sections is examined in Chapter 18 on documentation, testing, and evaluation. Sarbanes-Oxley document record retention requirements are covered in two sections of the Act, 802 and Section 1102. Documents are the raw material of auditing. The accuracy and the conformity or lack of conformity to accepted presentation of documents can make a difference to whether a company passes or fails its audit. In this sense, the formalities of documentation are not trivial.

Section 802: Criminal penalties for altering documents

CSFs for Section 802

- **Regular review of retention policies.** Report archiving and storage events in summary to the audit committee and/or board of directors. Keep external auditors informed on a regular basis as part of larger reports.
- **Effective policy education of staff.** Staff must be made aware of the importance of managing their documentation and storing it centrally. The organization should have a policy on document destruction: whether it is handled centrally, or users are allowed to delete their own work, or a combination of both depending on the nature of the documentation.

Table 15.1 Section 802

Description	Compliance scope	Compliance activity
This section highlights the value the SEC places on its sources of information. In Federal investigations those who deliberately alter, destroy, change, conceal, or falsify, any "record, document, or tangible object" with the intent to "impede, obstruct, or influence" the investigation can be fined, imprisoned for up to 20 years, or both.	Staff of company under investigation (issuers)	Documentation must be monitored for amendment, through change management, and an audit trail created on its use.
All audit records and review work papers must be retained or for at least five years from the end of the fiscal period in which the audit or review was concluded.	Auditors	Hard copies where they are not available electronically must be stored in a safe environment. Soft copies should be identified and stored appropriately through storage systems. These should be part of a larger information life cycle (perhaps based on information life cycle management, ILM) and part of an ERP solution.
The SEC must expand the rules and regulations relating to the retention of relevant records that form the basis of an audit or review.	Auditors, SEC	The compliance process can accommodate changes to the requirements in its iterative reviews.
Willful violation of any rule or regulation under this section will lead to fines and up to ten years imprisonment, or both.	Affected company staff (issuer), auditors, SEC	Controlled access to documentation through an effective information security management system (ISMS) and through segregation of duties (SOD) measures and ID control will reduce this risk considerably.

- **An information security management system (ISMS).** There should be strategic program for managing the security of information within the organization. This should extend to covering documentation vital to the compliance process.
- **An effective information life cycle management (ILM) system.** A working system should underpin the create–store–archive–retrieve–delete life cycle process for all created data.

Controlled documentation is the basis of many certified programs. An important example is ISO 9001. By using these standards as guidelines, or in-house policies of a similar kind, the organization ensures a high degree of compliance to this section.

Section 1102: Tampering with a record or otherwise impeding an official proceeding

Table 15.2 Section 1102

Description	Compliance scope	Compliance activity
Anyone who intends to reduce the value of or make unavailable by altering, destroying, mutilating, or concealing "a record, document, or other object," or obstructing an official proceeding, can be fined or imprisoned for up to 20 years, or both	Company staff (issuer)	Access to stored and active documents based on ID controls and SOD criteria will reduce this risk. The compliance process should control this and institute protective controls in line with an ISMS, if available.

CSFs for Section 1102

- **An ISMS**: there should be a strategic program for managing the security of information within the organization. This should extend to covering documentation vital to the compliance process.
- **An effective ILM**: a working system should underpin the create–store–archive–retrieve–delete life cycle process for all created data.
- **Regular reporting**: report archiving and storage events in summary to the audit committee and/or board of directors. Keep external auditors informed on a regular basis as part of larger reports.

SECTION 103: AUDITING, QUALITY CONTROL, AND INDEPENDENCE STANDARDS AND RULES

Table 15.3 Section 103

Description	Compliance scope	Compliance activity
The board can carry out inspections of accounting firms and impose disciplinary measures and penalties.	Auditors	The need for auditors to have their own internal compliance process is stated here. It does not have to be the same as for financial organizations but it must address the relevant sections of the Act.
Public accounting firms are expected to include in their document and records management the maintenance of auditing records "for a period of not less than 7 years."	Auditors	The document controls discussed under Section 802 should help auditors. Many will have these measures in place, but they need to be updated to reflect the requirements of the Act.
The Board is expected to cooperate with professional and advisory groups for standards setting. It can adopt existing or new standards and take them as models for modification if necessary and report on this annually to the Commission (SEC).	PCAOB	This measure is directed at the PCAOB and falls outside our discussion.
The Board requires a partner review for approval of audit reports.	Auditors	The partner review is best practice in most consultancies and should be part of a controlled process for auditors. The process might already exist and need only to be formalized.

CSFs for Section 103

■ **A compliance process for auditors**: there should be a strategic program for managing the compliance process within an accountant or auditing firm.

■ **A system of peer review**: such a system should be instituted if it is not already in place. This could be extended to the financial organization as a good working practice for internal auditors working through the compliance process.

■ **A quality system for client auditing**: to realize the needs of the Act in "auditing, quality control, ethics, independence, and other standards relating to the preparation of audit reports for issuers." To manage an overall standard of quality control for the auditing process, that matches that required by Section 404(b).

SECTION 201: SERVICES OUTSIDE THE SCOPE OF PRACTICE OF AUDITORS; PROHIBITED ACTIVITIES

The importance of the independence of the auditing firm is significant for the organization, especially in its choice of an auditor. A firm at fault here will entail risk for its client or customer base. The organization must ensure there are no conflicts of interests within its organization. This might not be easy. For example a large, multi-national financial organization may be using a firm in a European operation to implement new financial processes, and at the same time, in the United States, it may be using the same firm to audit periodic reports under the Act. These activities might happen simultaneously and independently, with neither operation knowing of the other's contracted work. How far has the organization strayed into non-compliance?

CSFs for Section 201

■ **A log of auditor and accountant activity**: this will raise the awareness of a firm's involvement in prohibited simultaneous project work.
■ **Internationalize the compliance process**: to ensure overseas operations and subsidiaries communicate through the CTF and the compliance process, using its mechanisms to extend best practice.
■ **Provide internal education on prohibited activities**: by publishing this on an intranet, and providing internal briefings and management training.
■ **Explore the potential for exemptions under this section**: an audit firm can provide non-audit services provided they have been expressly permitted by the audit committee. Tax services have been allowed under the Act.

SECTION 409: REAL-TIME ISSUER DISCLOSURES

Introducing real-time disclosure into the compliance process means operating disclosures at a tactical level, whereas under Section 302 and 404 they are at the strategic level. The issue for financial organizations is how they detect an event, action, or condition that constitutes a "material change," and report it through the internal chain of command for qualification before it is reported externally.

Table 15.4 Section 201

Description	Compliance scope	Compliance activity
A public accounting firm cannot simultaneously provide auditing and other services to the same public company. Such "prohibited activities" or kinds of activities constitute a breach. They include: • bookkeeping or operational accounting activities • designing and implementing information systems for financial operations • valuation or assessment of financial options and actuarial services • performing or assisting in internal audit services. Other prohibited parallel activities include: • performing management activities functions on behalf of the client company • providing broker, dealer, legal and investment services.	Auditors, the client (issuer)	Ensure that all audit firm activities are centrally controlled and the CTF is aware of them through regular briefings or updates. Conflicts of interest should be reported to the audit committee.

Table 15.5 Section 409

Description	Compliance scope	Compliance activity
The affected company, or issuer, must disclose to the public "on a rapid and current basis" any extra information about "material changes" in the financial condition or operations of the company. This must be "in plain English." The information may include trend and qualitative information, and graphic presenta-	Affected company (issuer)	Amend the compliance process to include near real-time reporting. Ensure controls, especially automated controls, can generate events in real time and these can generate alerts electronically to the relevant CTF members. Establish the timescales for reporting events (within days).

CSFs for Section 409

- **Add ad hoc reporting to the compliance cycle**: this will ensure that the changes in the financial condition of the company will be trapped by the compliance cycle. A process for reporting these, through the audit committee should be introduced.
- **Use the compliance process for external reporting**: for the internal reporting chain, representatives of the board and senior executives are in the process and are members of the CTF. They can qualify the event or condition and recommend external reporting.
- **Provide or develop real-time IT systems:** include solution (software) reviews in the compliance process to ensure systems are increasingly automated to make ongoing compliance with Section 409 a reality.
- **Implement an early-warning system**: based on controls implemented as alerts in systems.

PRACTICAL COMPLIANCE SUMMARY

- List, assess, and prioritize vulnerabilities around the other sections of the Act.
- Review the CSFs for each section.
- Start to anticipate issues around Section 409 reporting.
- Put in place a warning system to detect issues that might need near real-time reporting.
- Ensure provision is made in the strategic guidelines for Sections 802 and 1102.
- Put in place retention plans and staff training.
- Institute an effective ILM, if necessary.
- Use peer review whenever possible.
- Research and clarify the use of external auditors and consultants to prevent Section 201 breaches.

CHAPTER 16

Compliance in the Supply Chain

The nature of financial services is that any organization is positioned in a complex supply chain. By this we mean there are a set of dependencies and obligations built into any transaction that extends beyond one company or entity to others, equally linked and dependent on the actions of others. This chain of dependency and obligation extends from the end-user or customer through a service chain to an end-point where the objective of the transaction or activity is satisfied. An example is the chain considered earlier, based on broker exchanges across borders. How far does compliance extend through the chain? This is akin to the responsibility cascade, in that, although it is the senior executives who are ultimately responsible, accountability does extend throughout the organization.

Risk in chains is often considered as stemming from isolated business units. When a risk analysis is carried out this appears to be the case. However, there are a number of aspects which ensure that risks within the chain that appear unrelated are connected and can have a cumulative impact.

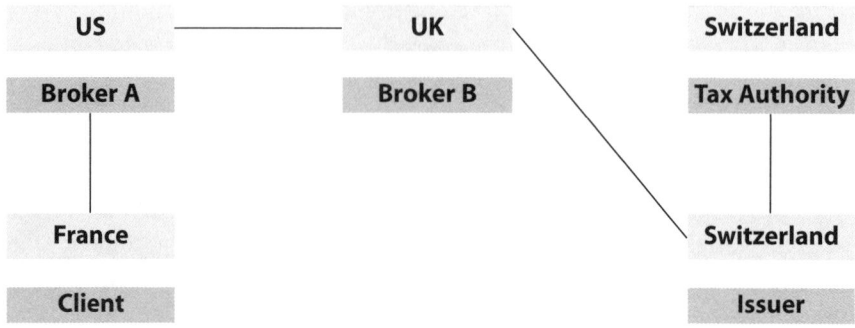

Figure 16.1 A financial services supply chain

- **Quality**: where the service being provided to an organization by other organizations needs to meet certain standards. SAS 70 is an example of service provider measurement based around a service level agreement (SLA). The IT function in particular might have considerable dependencies based on quality of service relations with external suppliers. This has been an issue with entities that have followed an ISO 9001 certification path and then insisted on suppliers being similarly certified to ensure the integrity of their compliance. For financial services the relationships are even closer.
- **Product supply**: a classical issue for organizations is the supply of discrete elements of the end product sold to consumers. As financial services organizations increasingly productize their offerings and translate financial instruments into marketable packages for the larger market, the dependency on other entities for components, in the form of either partial packages or the skills that make them work, is an ongoing concern.
- **Delivery processes**: this is addressed directly at the business processes that realize financial solutions for customers. The delivery process may have many dependencies as a generalized workflow. For example, credit agencies are specialized instances of activities in a workflow. Each instance is a process that needs to be part of the system of internal control. Extending the control so that it includes the external supplier is a challenge that is generally met with internal resources. However, the size and significance of the process may be too much for the resources of the organization. If the supplier has an effective system of internal controls, certified or demonstrably effective, this can be introduced as evidence. Without such measures there may be compliance "holes" in the delivery process, which may be audited as deficiencies and are difficult to remediate.

Contingency planning and what-if scenario planning are part of the response to these challenges. However, in order to comply with the Sarbanes-Oxley Act, these challenges must be treated as more than optional risks for the organization. Once identified they must be addressed as an integral part of the overall business activity. This might come down to the balance of risks, which affects all compliance planning. Nevertheless it should be accounted for within the compliance process.

COMPLIANCE IN THE EXTENDED ENTERPRISE

One aspect of supply chain risk is that it points up the importance of the company-oriented view of compliance. These risks are unique to the company and its business hinterland. How it tackles these risks will also be unique, within the generalized context of compliance to the Act. The "extended enterprise" has been a common theme. This implies a link between companies in the dependency chain that goes beyond simple supplier relationships. It is implies tighter integration of procurement, supply, and delivery systems. Straight-through processing (STP) is characteristic of this. The common element here is technology. IT and communications technology enable companies to react to each other almost instantly, and exchange information in an "intimate" way. This intimacy is a result of:

- communications capability: through the internet, linking the internal intranets of chained companies, through specialized web portals
- secure access: enabled access to company systems, controlled through controlled internal information management security systems (ISMSs)
- IT infrastructures and applications: the desktop-to-server relationships across internal and external networks with identity control and roaming access to information systems.

This aspect of the extended enterprise includes "co-opetition," where competitors combine and cooperate to gain mutual advantage in the marketplace. This mix of relationships also extends the nature of corporate governance, widening the web of relationships, and deepening the potential for ambiguity in financial reporting by obscuring transparency.

THE SIGNIFICANCE FOR INTERMEDIARIES, UNDERWRITERS, AND OTHERS IN THE CHAIN

What does this mean for financial organizations? They all operate in markets within exchanges and regulatory bodies, generating pressure for conformity in a fluid and complex environment. The supply chain has a number of elements which include:

- intermediaries, which by definition are in a chain of activity
- regulators, overseeing and inputting to supply chains along their length
- brokers, operating off the back of supply chains
- financial institutions of all kinds, which are involved in many chains; for large organizations these might be international internal chains, from front office to back office to external agencies, such as credit assessment agencies
- investors small and large.

SAS 70 IN THE SUPPLY CHAIN

The Statement of Auditing Standards (SAS 70 was developed by the American Institute of Certified Public Accountants (AICPA). SAS 70 is a standard that relates to the credibility of a service provider's services since it has undergone a thorough audit of its control activities. The value of this kind of audit sits well within the supply chain. Although SAS 70 audits are thorough in a different context, they need to be enhanced if they are to help a company in its efforts to be compliant with the Act.

The SAS 70 audit is a general-purpose audit of a service provider to which an organization has outsourced some of its support functions, such as IT. As an audit on the outsourced function, it is sent to all the customers of the service provider. There are a number of issues with using these audits as part of the organization's management assessment of the effectiveness of these outsourced functions:

- The timing of these audits might not be aligned with the fiscal year of the client. Some service providers do run rolling audits on a quarterly basis to cover this, and some companies have negotiated more frequent reports.
- The SAS 70 reports on the degree to which the outsourced function is under control; there is a lack of detail on what exactly is audited.

For those companies that outsource everything and rely on the service provider's processes for their financial reporting, these processes and controls must, at some point be tested by the customer. The SAS 70 dilemma poses a mixture of issues around security, risk, and the assessment of internal controls, which it is not yet clear how the Act will address. Companies relying on third-party SAS 70 reports should expect:

- the service provider to have fully documented their systems, and make this available as well as share information on their policies
- to negotiate on the timing of reports
- service providers to let customers have access to information on the types of control being used and the results of tests.

All these might be very problematic, and they are most likely to involve extra costs that might not have been budgeted for.

Any financial organization in this position needs to understand just what the provider can do to help manage the compliance issues and how far contracts can be renegotiated. It is likely that financial organizations will want to introduce their own auditors in an SAS 70 audit. This might not currently be allowed in the contract. The benefit of experienced external auditors here is that they can offer opinions on whether the company's own audits or SAS 70 audits have primacy when it comes to compliance. Much of this is yet to be tested in practice. However it operates, as an internal or outsourced service, as far as the Act is concerned responsibility for the audits and control assessment rests with the organization and its signing officers, the CEO and CFO. The onus is on them to find a solution with the external provider if necessary.

OUTSOURCING FUNCTIONS IN THE SUPPLY CHAIN

An option that has been widely adopted throughout the sector and across geographies is outsourcing, especially using call centers and for some back-office work. This has been regarded as a competitive step, offering significant growth options and cost reductions. However two problems with cost reduction through outsourcing are that it has created significant risk, and complicates control issues. For example, India has no formal data protection legislation.

As a supply-chain issue this illustrates a number of issues:

- There is no consistent and transparent regulatory control over the life cycle of a transaction.
- Regional jurisdictions are not necessarily mutually supportive. In other words, countries in Europe, the United States, and Asia might not have mutually reinforcing regulations. The absence of a key piece of legislation in one jurisdiction might jeopardize the larger process.
- Regional policing regimes might not be equally effective. Personal data disclosed through a call center in one region might contradict data integrity legislation in another. What is the position of confidence for the consumer? In India, it was recently shown to be possible to buy the UK customer list of a major retail bank on floppy disk from the employees of the bank's call center.

Labor costs in emergent markets might be low, but so are compliance costs—they have nothing to comply with.

PRACTICAL COMPLIANCE SUMMARY

- Review the supply chain, noting all consultants and contractors as well.
- Review outsourced IT activities and functions.
- Review major software, vendor, and systems integrators.
- Review SLAs to include compliance as a risk factor.
- Review supplier delivery processes and assess whether they need internal controls.
- Review SAS 70 reporting. Negotiate additional clauses for documentation and appropriate timing of supplier reports.
- Examine leasing and outsourcing arrangements for compliance issues.

CHAPTER 17

Internal Controls

INTRODUCTION

What are the "internal controls over financial reporting" that Section 404 of the Sarbanes-Oxley Act talks of? It is worth noting that there is a distinction between the *disclosure controls and procedures* referred to in Section 302 and the *internal controls over financial reporting* specifically addressed in Section 404. The management responsibility mapping varies from section to section, although all sections relate to public, periodic financial reporting. (See Figure 17.1.)

The Section 302 remit is broader, and the Section 404 internal controls are a subset of the Section 302 disclosure controls and procedures (see Figure 17.2). This emphasizes the breadth of the Act's implications for general controls. It is part of the reason that the PCAOB adopted a broadly

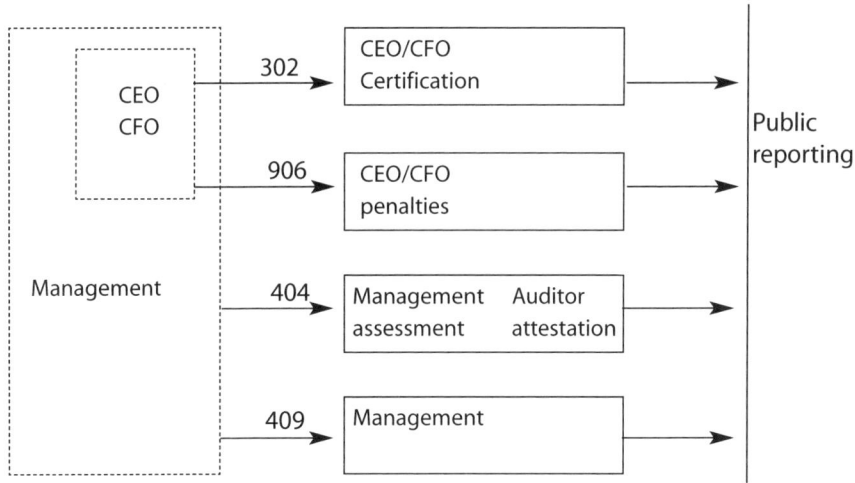

Figure 17.1 Management mapped to compliance responsibilities

based framework (COSO) as a useful reference model for audit preparations, and as a guide to what should be expected for external auditing. Internal controls should be understood in this context.

The PCAOB, through its standard (AS2), cites the Codification of Statements on Auditing Standards.[1] This defines "internal controls" as a process under the control of the board of directors, management, and relevant personnel. This process is assumed to provide a high degree of assurance on:

■ the reliability of the information found in financial reports
■ the effective operation of the systems and processes that underpin this information
■ compliance of the systems and information to regulations and legal requirements that affect the organization.

Specifically the reference is to five elements or areas of focus for internal controls. These are the five components of the COSO Integrated Framework:[2]

■ control environment
■ risk assessment
■ control activities
■ information and communication
■ monitoring.

DISCLOSURE CONTROLS AND PROCEDURES

The concept of disclosure controls and procedures was introduced by the SEC to describe the controls to which the information required under the

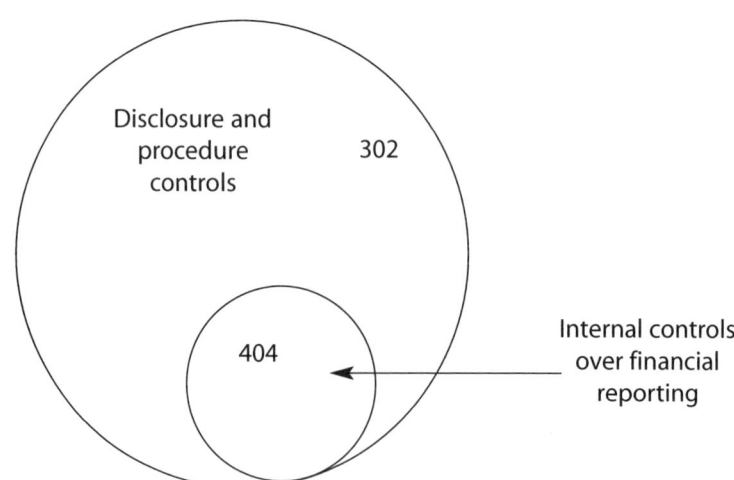

Figure 17.2 Section 404 as a subset of disclosure controls

SEC Exchange Act should be subject, in order to ensure it is properly recorded, processed, and reported. The remit of these controls and procedures is potentially very extensive. They are to ensure that all relevant information that contributes to the report is made available for periodic reporting and disclosure by the company's senior management, whether it is financial or non-financial in nature, provided it relates to the state of the business. The Act inherits this sentiment, and underlines the role of internal controls.

The SEC envisaged that the information disclosed would be a reasonable reflection, and fair estimation, of:

- an issuer's financial state
- the results of all operations
- the results of cash flows
- details on accounting policies and methods
- additional disclosures on material issues that might affect investors, including anything that can shed additional light on any of the above.

A principle at work is that disclosure controls and procedures operate to ensure that a reasonably accurate picture of the financial and non-financial activities and information of the business has been identified and made available to management for appropriate disclosure, as in Figure 17.3. This places disclosure controls in a larger context, but one that forms the basis for internal controls.

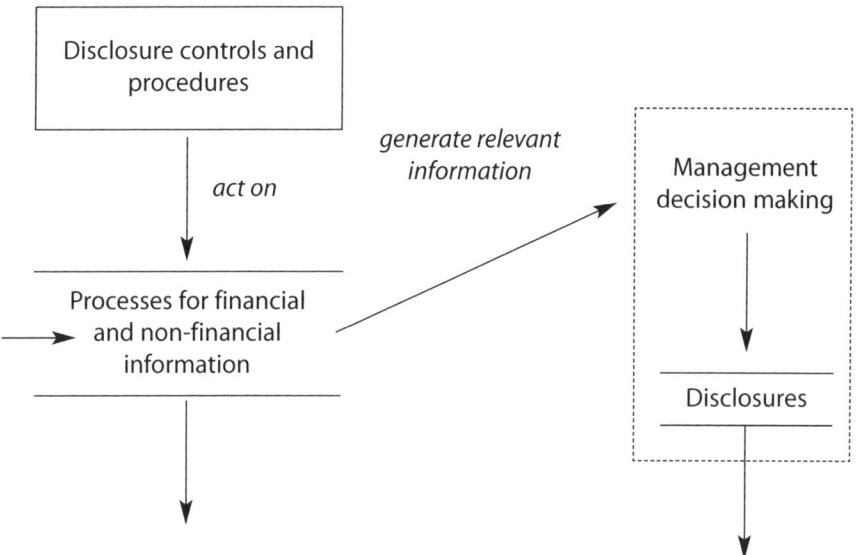

Figure 17.3 Management decisions on disclosure

SCOPING INTERNAL CONTROLS

The Act is specific about controls, in that its concern is with the effectiveness of the system of internal control and its demonstrable compliance with the spirit and letter of the Act. It implies that such a system should help produce reliable information and a quality product in the periodic financial report.

The process of identifying internal controls as a subset of disclosure controls is focused on the financial reporting process. In practice many of the same controls apply to both internal and disclosure controls. This serves to point up the wider aspect of the Act and its broader implications for those who focus solely on a narrower concept of financial reporting processes. One suggestion is that a possible exception might occur for "immaterial accounts and balances." Internal controls on these would most likely fall outside of the concern of disclosure controls and procedures, since the latter has a focus on "material" information. By and large the best approach is to take the bigger set of controls as the base, then work through the controls necessary to remediate the system, following a thorough risk assessment and analysis, and provide systems and applications that can address these issues. From the perspective of auditors, the focus will be on all controls relevant to the process, and the system of internal control that addresses them.

A further approach is to take the two sections and summarize their scope, bearing in mind that both must be addressed over time in order to be compliant with the Act. Table 17.1 lists the comparative components of Sections 302 and 404 as applied to the business processes of a typical organization.

Table 17.1 A comparison of sections 302 and 404

Activities	Section 302	Section 404
Apply, document, evalu-ate, test, and remediate	Disclosure controls and procedures	Internal control over financial reporting
Monitor and assess	All information that is rele-vant to a periodic public report	Financial statements
Frequency	Periodic	Periodic
Review points as part of compliance process	Filing date plus regulated period	At financial year end
Auditor attestation		At financial year end as part of financial report

INTERNAL CONTROLS

Quick compliance

"Quick compliance" might be conceived as of a short-cut version of the compliance process, heavily dependent on the PDCA cycle, and a version of the pragmatic approach. Since it limits compliance efforts solely to specific internal controls, there is an apparent saving in time and effort.

Systematic compliance

However, it is more likely that the larger control picture will be addressed so as to include the full subset of internal controls and disclosure controls. In either case an understanding of internal controls as understood in practice is essential for building an effective compliance process. Perhaps the central reference for any discussion on internal controls regarding the Act is that of the PCAOB in its "Auditing standard no. 2: An audit of internal control over financial reporting performed in conjunction with an audit of financial statements."

This document is in effect the working reference for the Act, and as such it is central to our evaluation of how to devise a working solution for responding to the Act. It carries the authority of the PCAOB, and many of its references are themselves restatements or modifications of SEC definitions and rulings. It is written as a guide for auditors and those concerned with managing the area of internal controls. Since much of our discussion centers on the nature of internal controls, it is important that we understand what is meant by the concept from the perspective of the Act.

Definitions

In the section on "Definitions related to internal control over financial reporting," the PCAOB establishes a basic definition "For purposes of management's assessment and the audit of internal control over financial reporting in this standard." This narrows the scope to the specific interests of the Act; the industry-wide view of internal controls, and even that of the COSO model, is wider in scope. The definition is established and extended as discussed below.

Process

The most important initial definition is of internal control as a process. The nature of internal control as a cross-functional activity or series of activities is declared at the outset, whether it be one-off or continuous.

Accountability and responsibility

The declaration then states responsibilities and who is accountable for the process. This is a process "designed by, or under the supervision of, the company's principal executive and principal financial officers, or persons performing similar functions and effected by the company's board of directors, management, and other personnel... ."

Purpose

The purpose of the internal control process is then established: "to provide reasonable assurance regarding the reliability of financial reporting and the preparation of financial statements for external purposes... ." Here the two central themes that underlie the purpose of the Act are stated: for investors and the world at large. Companies must produce reliable financial reports; and the activities and processes that prepare these reports must be seen to be reliable.

Reference standard

The definition also includes a standard as a reference to ensure that the context of financial reporting is understood "in accordance with generally accepted accounting principles."

Policies and procedures

These are established for the maintenance of records that provide reasonable assurance that transactions are recorded as necessary to permit preparation of financial statements in accordance with GAAP. This definition is derived from that used by the SEC in its rules. A change is that "registrant" has been changed to "company." The process is referred to as *internal control* over *financial reporting*, in the singular. Individual controls are referred to as controls, or controls over financial reporting.

The standard goes on to define control deficiencies and other concepts essential to controls. These are examined as part of a summary of the PCAOB standard.

As we have seen, the PCAOB standard is divided into paragraphs, and the references are to "paras."

The standard as a whole states that it:

... provides directions that apply when an auditor is engaged to audit both a company's financial statements and management's assessment of the effectiveness of internal control over financial reporting.

The focus on internal control is central. The issuer management is required to include:

- a management report on the company's internal control over financial reporting
- an assessment of the effectiveness of the company's internal control over financial reporting
- a statement on this assesment
- it must also file the attestation of the auditor auditing the company's financial statements.

Para 4 states the auditor's objective in an audit, which is to:

- express an opinion
- build a case for an opinion
- plan and perform the audit
- audit the company's financial statements

The definition of effective internal control over financial reporting means that no material weaknesses exist. Because of the Act an auditor needs to be confident of obtaining "reasonable assurance" that no such weaknesses exist.

The spirit of the Act had a greater expectation about the neutrality of the auditor. In fact the Act had had a considerable effect on the auditor–client relationship.

Consumers of these reports are also interested because of the way such information on internal controls "enhances the quality of financial reporting" and increases confidence in financial reporting, including all periodic reporting. Significantly such information also serves as an early warning mechanism for those responsible for implementing checks, controls, and remediation of weaknesses in affected companies, such as the audit committee and specialized regulators. The PCAOB also refers to Section 302 and the responsibility of senior executives in this task.

Company-level controls

Controls that operate on the control environment at corporate level are referred to as company-level controls. Thus company-level controls are used to monitor functional operations, and ownership is at a senior level in a department or division. Company level controls include:

- the high-level risk assessment process
- central processing through centralized systems
- performance of operations
- the financial reporting process
- "the tone at the top," the control environment in place at a senior level
- internal policies and procedures
- management practices over business processes
- company-specific controls to manage change and strategy
- board-level executive and non-executive director management (succession management and so on).

IT controls operate within the entity, generally at user level or at the level of the network and infrastructure functions. IT controls can be subdivided into:

- general controls, such as those covered by frameworks like ITIL, including system management, change management, access and authorization controls within security management, computer operations, and software development
- application and process controls: authorized access, permissions, ID controls, configuration control, and interface management.

Para 7 concerns the definitions the PCAOB uses to identify internal control over financial reporting. The standard details these, and they are summarized in Table 17.2.

From the point of view of the Act, the PCAOB identifies the system of internal control as consisting of certain policies and procedures: see Table 17.3.

The PCAOB has broadly followed the existing SEC definition. The use of the singular "control" refers to internal control as a process.

Para 8: Control deficiency

We have noted that "effective" internal control is the result of no identified material weaknesses existing. The PCAOB talks of a "control deficiency." This is specific to the control itself and its operation. It is the consequence of a design or operational flaw in a control so that it does not "allow management or employees, in the normal course of performing their assigned functions, to prevent or detect misstatements on a timely basis." Further notes are summarized in Table 17.4.

Significant control deficiency

In para 9, moving up the scale, the PCAOB identifies a more severe form

Table 17.2 Summary of PCAOB internal controls

PCAOB definition—internal control	Compliance issue
Internal control is a process	A key point since compliance is seen as a process rather than a project
It is designed by, or under the supervision of, the company's principal executive and principal financial officers, or persons performing similar functions	The key reference to the Act—reminding us of the responsibility of senior executives
It is necessary for the company's board of directors, management, and other personnel, to provide reasonable assurance regarding the reliability of financial reporting	The criterion underpinning management's assessment: "reasonable assurance" on the "reliability" of reporting
There is a similar responsibility in the preparation of financial statements for external purposes	Extends the responsibility in principle to the financial statements themselves
These must be prepared in accordance with GAAP	GAAP is one of the few references directly cited in the Act

of deficiency in internal controls as a "significant" deficiency. This is a control deficiency or a combination of control deficiencies that adversely affects the company's ability to initiate, authorize, record, process, or report on external financial data reliably. The major concern is that there is "more than a remote likelihood" that a misrepresentation or "misstatement" of the company's annual or periodic financial statements may lead to a reporting problem. The importance of such a problem may then be "more than inconsequential," especially since this misstatement will not be prevented from being included, and might not even be detected by the system of internal control. This relationship between a control deficiency and its consequences is illustrated in Figure 17.4.

MEASUREMENT CRITERIA

In discussing measurement criteria, the PCAOB references the definitions established by the Financial Accounting Standards Board in its Statement No. 5, Accounting for Contingencies (FAS No. 5). In particular it highlights the standard's use of the critical term "remote likelihood" in the context of a significant deficiency. This usage reappears when discussing

Table 17.3 Summary of PCAOB policies and procedures

PCAOB definition—internal control	Compliance issue
(1) Pertain to the maintenance of records that, in reasonable detail, accurately and fairly reflect the transactions and dispositions of the assets of the company	This focus is on the extent to which documented records accurately detail the transactions and movements of information assets of the company.
(2) Provide reasonable assurance that transactions are recorded as necessary to permit preparation of financial statements in accordance with generally accepted accounting principles, and that receipts and expenditures of the company are being made only in accordance with authorizations of management and directors of the company	Again, the PCAOB seeks reasonable assurance that transactions are properly recorded (according to GAAP) so that their contribution to financial statements is appropriate. This also applies to "receipts and expenditures," which must be properly authorized. A key consideration of the Act, resulting from the misuse of corporate assets in the scandals that led up to the Act, where senior executives had access to funds and misused them, often clouding the misuse through creative accounting measures.
(3) Provide reasonable assurance regarding prevention or timely detection of unauthorized acquisition, use, or disposition of the company's assets that could have a material effect on the financial statements	Following on from this misuse, the system of oversight or internal control must be able to provide "reasonable assurance" that such misuse can be trapped and appropriate levels of responsibilities alerted should such misuses be undertaken. The intention is to: • prevent unauthorized acquisition • promptly detect unauthorized acquisition • prevent use of assets that have a material effect • promptly detect use of assets that have a material effect.

Table 17.4 A control deficiency

A deficiency in design exists when	Issue	Action
(a) a control necessary to meet the control objective is missing or	There is no control (or control objective)	Follow compliance process to introduce a control
(b) an existing control is not properly designed so that, even if the control operates as designed, the control objective is not always met	The existing control is inadequate	Review control and remediate
A properly designed control does not operate as designed, or	Operational environment is inadequate	Review context for control
when the person performing the control does not possess the necessary authority or qualifications to perform the control effective	Improper authorization for use of the control	Review allocation of responsibilities

material weakness (Standard para 10). It is noted that it has the same meaning as "remote" in the FAS reference. This reference, when talking of the loss or impairment of an asset, uses a range of criteria to identify three areas from a range of possibilities:

■ probable: a future event or events is likely to occur
■ reasonably possible: the chance of the future event or events occurring is more than remote but less than likely
■ remote: the chance of the future event or events occurring is slight.

In this context, the likelihood of an event is "more than remote" when it is either reasonably possible or probable. The usage of "inconsequential" is important here. The standard claims that a misstatement is inconsequential if a "reasonable person" has a considered opinion that this misstatement

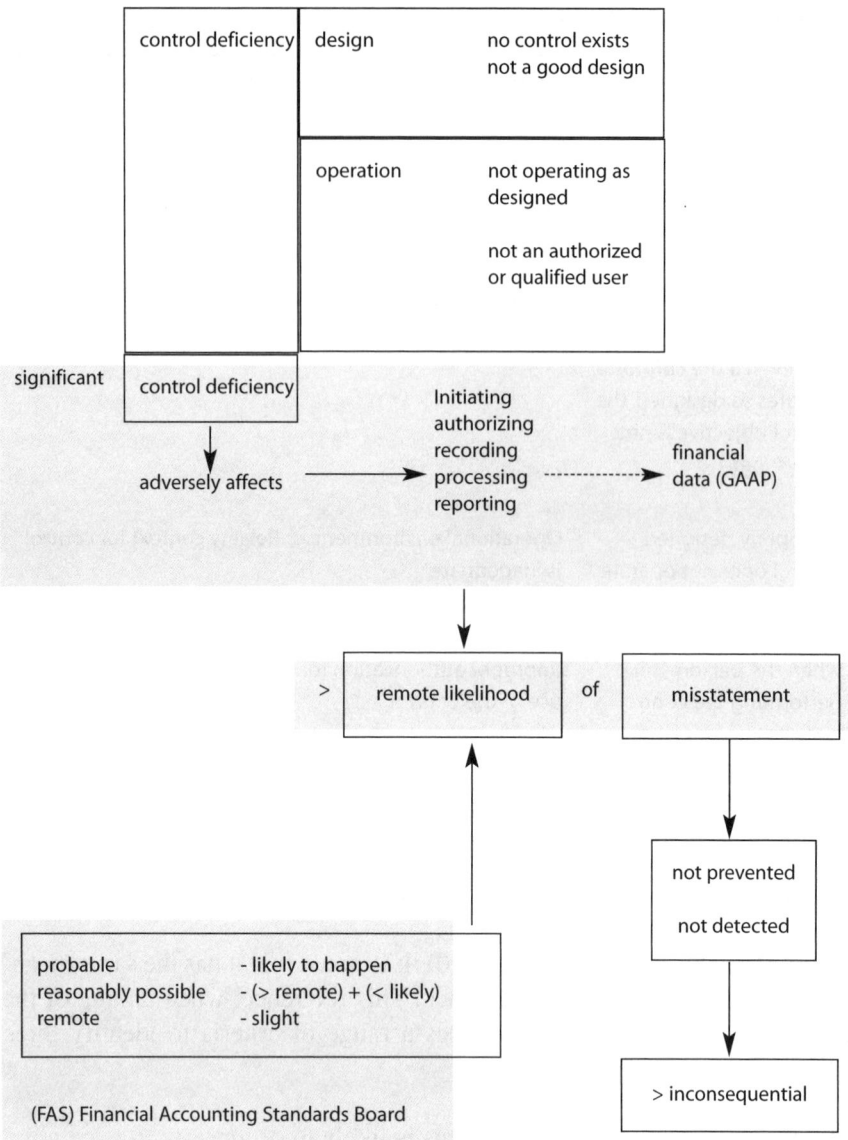

Figure 17.4 Control deficiencies

and maybe others of a similar nature would not materially affect the financial statement. However, if the same "reasonable person" could not reach that conclusion, the misstatement is "more than consequential." In other words, where there is substantial doubt or confusion about the impact of a misstatement, the misstatement is not inconsequential.

Material weakness

In para 10, and in a similar manner to that of a control deficiency, a material weakness is defined as "a significant deficiency, or combination of significant deficiencies, that results in more than a remote likelihood that a material misstatement of the annual or interim financial statements will not be prevented or detected."

Evaluating deficiencies

The evaluation of deficiencies, critical to the way an auditor is to approach an assessment, requires a good grasp of how far a flaw is a deficiency or a weakness. This should include the definitions outlined above—control deficiency, significant control deficiency, and material weakness—and the specific guidance given as part of the forming of an opinion on the effectiveness of internal control (paras 130–137).

Quantitative and qualitative considerations

The standard notes that any evaluation of the materiality of a control deficiency should involve both quantitative and qualitative considerations. Guidance on this is provided (para 23). Qualitative factors include:

- the way the financial statement accounts have been collated and consolidated and presented
- assertions involved in their presentation
- possible future consequences of the deficiency considered reasonable.

Key to the way a control deficiency, or a combination of such deficiencies, is deemed to be a significant deficiency or a material weakness are the effect of compensating controls, and whether compensating controls are effective.

Preventive and detective controls

The standard states that controls over financial reporting may be "preventive" controls or "detective" controls. According to the standard, "preventive controls" prevent errors or fraud that could result in a misstatement of the financial statements from occurring in the first place. We can use a richer set of preventive controls from information security, which take a number of forms:

- relative prevention: making it difficult for a mistake to be made
- partial prevention: which slows down or restricts the mistake
- technical prevention: the application of automation to avoid mistakes
- procedural prevention: which establishes a human dimension by using procedures.

There is also

- intensive prevention: which makes it as hard as possible to make a mistake
- confrontation prevention: which confronts a potential mistake (maker) with the consequences of the mistake
- little prevention: which disallows the mistake by removing the option to make it.

"Detective controls" often work alongside preventive controls, detecting errors and triggering preventive controls. According to the standard, detective controls detect errors or instances of fraud that have already occurred, and that could result in a misstatement of the financial statements.

Using an information security model we identify several types of detective controls:

- technical detection: relying heavily on automation in processes to avoid errors
- procedural detection: using human intervention to review, spot check, and so on.

Detection in controls must be:

- timely: early detection of an error that has a knock-on effect is critical
- appropriate: since some events may be too sudden for standard detection.

This combination of preventive and detective measures is a potent option for detecting and preventing misstatements. The standard acknowledges that "effective internal control over financial reporting often includes a combination of preventive and detective controls to achieve a specific control objective."

Further controls

Further controls that we can consider in this context are:

- deterrent controls: these reduce the likelihood of mistakes by making them expensive for the offender
- corrective controls: these reduce the effect of a mistake, and include recovery controls.

A fuller examination of these control types is seen later when we consider ISO 17799 control types as a potential compliance process model.

Auditor procedures

When discussing the design of controls, the standard notes that the procedures used by an auditor as part of the audits of internal control or financial statements are not to be considered part of the company's overall system of internal control. There is an assumption that the auditor's procedures are also effectively controlled.

Key controls

The IIA has introduced a generally acknowledged definition of a "key control" as "a control that, if it fails, means there is at least a reasonable likelihood that a material error in the financial statements would not be prevented or detected on a timely basis."

The complexity of internal controls is something that several frameworks have tried to simplify. Once it has broadly defined controls, within the scope of the Act, the organization needs to document them, as for Section 302, then work on the requirements of Section 404 by testing and then evaluating their effectiveness as a system for financial reporting.

PRACTICAL COMPLIANCE SUMMARY

- ■ Understand the responsibilities around internal controls.
- ■ Define and document controls (as part of Section 302 and 404 compliance).
- ■ At the strategic level, assess controls in general, using CTF resources and regular reporting.
- ■ Ensure any company competences are "published" to promote the company.
- ■ Identify key controls: those with the greatest impact on the business and financial reporting.
- ■ Prioritize for "quick" and "systematic" compliance within an overall compliance process.
- ■ Ensure the AS2 is understood and information on PCAOB decisions is kept up to date. Make this available on an CTF intranet site.
- ■ Have a clear understanding of deficiencies and weaknesses.
- ■ Establish criteria for measuring these.
- ■ Define and use control types suitable for the organization according to other criteria (such as the supply chain and so on).

NOTES

1. Codified AICPA Professional Standards. These statements constitute the SAS series (including SAS 70—Service organizations) of guidance for auditors.
2. The COSO framework is discussed in detail in Chapter 23.

CHAPTER 18

Documentation, Testing, and Evaluation

DOCUMENTATION FOR DEMONSTRATING COMPLIANCE

The emphasis placed on documentation by the Act and allied legislation is not surprising, since it is the formal expression of business activity. The flow of information throughout the enterprise is an electronic form of documentation. Text and graphics are the primary exhibits. Documentation exists in a number of forms, and all should be considered and addressed as part of the compliance process.

As a functional business discipline, managing documentation is part of many common methodologies:

- document management systems
- information management systems
- information life cycle management
- information security management systems
- quality systems.

Traditionally document management has been a kind of workflow across many areas of the business. Business process management (BPM), enterprise resource planning (ERP), and other frameworks insist on the importance of documenting their elements. "Control" is also a feature of these schemes, primarily through audit trails.

Documentation as evidence

Close to the value of the definition of a document is the emphasis on it being "proof" or "evidence" as a recording of ideas, facts, transactions, or images. This is its meaning from the perspective of the regulators; the emphasis is on providing of proof or evidence through recording. There is a sense in which the material becomes authoritative and reliable once officially recorded; this is reflected in the idea that you get at the truth by going to the archives and searching through documents for evidence. Documents carry their meaning as a summary of the context in which they were devised. It is the product of a process of creating, distributing, and retaining management or business information. Document management as a business discipline has its adherents, specialist skills and knowledge, and software tools. The nuances of the traditional definitions of "document" and "content" lean on this view of the document as "proof."

REGULATORY REQUIREMENTS FOR DOCUMENTATION

The sections of the Securities Exchange Act of 1934, and therefore the Sarbanes-Oxley Act, that exercise the minds of senior executives in this area are SEC Rules 17(a)-3 and 4, and NASD 3010 and 3110. These define the need for technical and procedural controls to ensure the authenticity, accuracy, and accessibility of stored electronic records for review and audit. In 1997, the 17a-4 rule allowed broker-dealers to store records electronically, including electronic messaging. Those organizations affected by the Act, such as traders in securities, brokers, banks, securities firms, and financial institutions trading in securities, must observe the rules on retention, non-rewritable storage, and ease of retrieval. Among these rules are requirements to create policies and maintain management of customer records and transactions. The perspective is a regulatory one, and focuses strongly on access. The SEC has made clear that "records are the primary means of monitoring compliance," and recent cases involving the deletion of emails and other electronic records "have affirmed the need to have measures in place to protect record integrity."

Organizations respond through a combined strategy: leveraging existing in-house IT systems, and outsourcing certain IT functions. For some it is mandatory to use external agencies. For example, for brokers and dealers subject to the legislation, 17a-4 requires "every member, broker, or dealer exclusively using electronic media for some or all of its record preservation" to have an arrangement with a designated third party (D3P) which enables the SEC regulators to arrange access through the D3P to the organization's stored information. The aim is to ensure access to archives in the event of an uncooperative violator or a business that has folded. The very public nature of misdemeanors and the effect on investment confidence have meant that the criteria for compliance are strict and penalties severe. Major dealerships, brokers, and securities organizations have all fallen foul of inadequate email retention procedures. To be compliant organizations must have:

- written and enforceable retention policies
- the capability to store data on non-rewritable media
- data formatted for retrieval, with searchable indexes
- data stored offsite.

The SEC and NASD regulations have been in effect from May 2003, and throughout the period since; meanwhile regulators constantly reassess what they require to be stored.

Of course, despite its use as evidence, a document does not have to be "truthful" or represent the facts. It might be selective about what is included, inserting some facts and omitting others. However, the risks of not documenting effectively or truthfully are now considerable, thanks to the Act. Yet there are a number of issues inherent in relying on this evidentiary base. Looking at Section 802 of the Act, how do we prove "intent" to falsify through change? Change control is a necessary discipline, but for general documentation it is difficult to enforce. How do we detect document changes?

Retention

When it comes to keeping evidence, there are considerable cost implications. There is a tremendous emphasis on managing storage costs, an area that requires its own body of expertise. In the United States alone, there are over a thousand retention requirements set out under federal laws, and many more under state laws. Internationally there are many more. There are three practical areas of activity in the retention of documentation:

- the defining and documentation of business processes
- the retention of the evidence
- the need to enforce these processes.

These activities are in line with the emerging industry framework model that defines how the burden of managing company documentation is handled end-to-end: information life cycle management (ILM). This model has been adopted and developed by a number of vendors, and recognizes the challenges of regulation by providing a framework that assumes a mix of core competencies.

A question that arises in this context is, when is a document a document and not a change or an amendment to a document? Is there a specific legal definition? This is important legally. Consider the following distinctions:

- A document is proof of evidence relating to a material event, but an amendment might not offer proof.

- A new document is potentially a new piece of evidence, and an amended document is in all probability an amendment to existing evidence.

We must be aware of managing implicit risk through an audit trail for all amendments and changes. Another sense of the definition in this context is that a document covers what you do, as normal practice. It does not mean a last-minute change or remediation, such as to a financial report. It tends to mean business practice on an ongoing basis. This is important for a discussion on reporting. There are parallels between the Act and quality frameworks, such as ISO 9001, in that the organization documents what it does and then proves that it does it.

In considering jurisdictions and conflicts of interest between sets of rules we need to consider whether local rules take priority over the Act for a non-US based subsidiary of a US-listed enterprise. Part of the answer lies in the "type" of documentation. Much of the legislation in place from the 1930s onwards has been based on paper documentation, or what we now call hard copy. But as we have already noted, even company reports are now registered electronically. In the age of electronic information and the era of soft documentation, the media that deliver this type of evidence are thoroughly electronic, soft, and malleable.

DOCUMENTATION, EMAIL, AND COMPLIANCE

The global economy has electronic messaging as its lifeblood, and of all messaging systems, email has come to be the defining edge for a successful business. Yet for major corporations, uncontrolled email and its flow of information presents a threat that few are equipped to deal with, and many are only just beginning to fully understand. The Act heightens this awareness. The threat is often buried deep in the company memory. Billion-dollar settlements with the SEC highlight the potential of email to seriously impact reputation, brand, and ultimately shareholder value. Now that compliance is shaping many aspects of everyday business, it forces organizations to monitor their communications and preserve activities for legal retrieval. Most importantly, it stores the bad with the good.

The significance of email

Electronic documents are no longer static entities. They move around an organization in a flow of information. Certain technologies are establishing themselves as the arbiters of new types of information flow. A recent concept neatly sums it up: "email is workflow." Over the last decade, email has become the primary means of doing business for huge sectors of nearly every vertical market. The communication culture of many organizations is characterized by a voice or text bias, leaning towards either telephony or email. Although email is one of many communication media, increasingly it is the dominant one. This is reflected in the transformation of service provider business from voice to data. Even mobile communications, where voice has been a dominant driver for growth, is seeing a huge increase in "texting" and multimedia messaging, including email, for generating new markets. The significance of this transformation of business communications is enormous.

Organizations vary in their response to email as documentation, especially for legislation such as the Act. It is good business practice to preserve transactions; well-archived business data is a rich source for marketing, strategic business planning, and general monitoring. Some organizations leave it to users to store and delete their own messages, while other organizations implement centralized control based on internal policies.

The financial impact of lost emails and deletions based on personal rather than company policy is difficult to gauge. Yet it was the deletion of an email by Andersens that was pivotal in the Enron scandal, and in 2002 five financial companies in the United States were tracked and fined more than US$8 million by regulators for improper email management. We cannot doubt the importance of email control when there are examples of major litigation cases having been won or lost on the strength of a found or lost email.

The statistics of email documentation

As well as the significance of a single transmission, there is the impact of scale. The statistics are daunting. In 2003 it was estimated that email traffic would reach 36 billion messages per day. It is estimated that the average corporate user transmits and receives more than 70 messages per day. In IT departments focused on handling and storing this volume of data, the average user sends and receives 7 MB per day. Projecting forward from past trends, this doubles every four years and could soon reach 14.7 MB. Scaling up, for 1,000 employees this would represent 1,680 GB of storage requirement per year. Since few IT departments are equipped to handle this growth, this is good news for the storage industry, but a huge challenge at a time when investment in IT is under tight scrutiny. Less than half of Global 1000 companies have reported having a formal email archiving policy in place, yet all recognize that the obvious challenges of managing email are growing,

The challenges of email management

Not surprisingly, the management of email has evolved as a discipline in its own right, sometimes dominating IT strategies. The two issues dominating management of email are email storage and regulatory compliance. These issues force email data to be stored in specific ways, with an emphasis on fast search and retrieval. Aided and abetted by internal and other legal policy compliance issues, the strategic interest touches on other document management systems, involving:

- human resource restrictions
- access for users
- privacy
- data protection rights.

These factors have driven a market and forced solutions from vendors. However, most surveys report that it is still the case that very few organizations are using a commercial solution that specifically addressed the issues of interactive email archiving.

RISK MANAGEMENT: DOCUMENTING CONTROLS WITH A CONTROL MATRIX

Documentation as evidence and proof has implications for risk management. Documentation has many forms. Broadly most organizational documents consist of:

- text documents (plain, rich, or application-specific formatted text)
- graphics and bitmap images
- flowcharts and process maps
- audio-visual recording and presentations
- email.

One practical approach to ensure that these issues are visible is to manage documentation through a control matrix. This enables the compliance process to track documentation and risk at the same time. Ideally, a control matrix should include:

- key controls for the item
- definition of the relationship between the risk and its controls
- control type (such as manual or automated)
- frequency of action: daily, monthly, weekly, yearly
- objective and significance of document control.

Part of the process of making things visible ensures that documents without controls are quickly identified as well, as are their risks. These can be investigated further to establish the level and probability of risk, and whether there is a need for treatment as part of the compliance process.

EVALUATION AND TESTING

Selecting internal controls and their effectiveness

One way of addressing how we decide on which control to adopt following documentation is to define some principles for selection and evaluation. The objective of introducing a control is the reduction or elimination of an information security risk by remediation of vulnerabilities.

Primary and secondary control risks

A consideration here is the way in which controls affect one another. A significant factor is the way in which primary and secondary risks interact. In this formula we can tackle the risk to an item through a control. However, there are often subsidiary risks that result from this action. The introduction of a secondary control might introduce a level of risk that in some way negates the effectiveness of the primary control. The "total" risk is the balance of primary and secondary controls. Sometimes it is impossible to assess in advance the impact of secondary controls, and these might only be known at a much later stage. It is this total risk that determines the effectiveness of the controls applied.

Cost–benefit analysis

A further common approach is based on cost–benefit analysis. In this the cost of fixing a vulnerability is weighed against any resultant risk and the overall benefit to the company. This is a useful method for deciding between two possible controls. A further consideration is to localize and build in some depth to the system of defense for document storage. This helps address deliberate or "rational" attacks as well as "accidental" attacks.

A great deal can also be done at the level of personnel, for example to ensure the separation of roles is effective. This can be achieved through staff education to improve tolerance for what might be seen as intrusive or difficult controls. The most serious threat is accidental action by staff, especially with commonly shared document structures that could be modified or destroyed, or simply moved so that they are "lost." Attempts to manage this are currently haphazard, based on common sense: for example, informally limiting access to material by not telling employees about a subdirectory, or discouraging their use of it.

TESTING CONTROLS

Management's periodic assessment of internal controls is coupled with a review of the effectiveness of controls through testing. The organization must develop a strategy for testing internal controls, as part of the compliance process. There are a number of questions for management to answer in developing a testing strategy:

- How complex is the control, in terms of resources (staff, time, and materials) required to test it?
- Is the control automated or manual?
- Have there been any changes in the design of the control since the last test or review?
- Have the operational staff performing or monitoring the control changed or been trained?
- How well does the control meet the control objective?
- What effect do significant changes in the volume or type of business have on the design or effectiveness of the control?
- How reliant is the control on IT systems or other support systems, such as external suppliers, contractors, or outsourced elements?

Armed with answers to such questions, management can move on the testing and evaluation of the control to determine its effectiveness for the assessment.

When an auditor begins an audit, an early question that has to be answered is how to scale the audit. This will depend on the size of the company. Absolute thoroughness is impossible, but the audit must be thorough enough to capture any deficiencies. This is a question that management will also ask. Internal audits will have stepped through the organization on a regular basis, so there is more confidence in having been thorough. However, being comprehensive in the period running up to a report, on a quarterly basis, and even annually, is still a major activity for the larger organization. The sample size is a matter of best practice, based on experience and best-guessing the state of compliance in the first place. This is where an effective compliance process, generating regular reviews, reports, and risk analysis with actions and remediation, builds a favorable picture of the organization. In these circumstances, auditor resources can be focused and there can be a high confidence that samples are a true reflection of the state of the system of internal control. The sample rate is a product of a number of factors:

- the type of control being tested
- the anticipated rate of error in the control domain
- previous results from internal audits
- the way internal compliance is approached by the company, based on a structured system
- the frequency of previous testing and the regularity of reviews and remediation.

Automated controls and the extent to which the organization has invested in continuous monitoring can make a big difference. Control types and frequency are the major parameters. Table 18.1 indicates some metrics. The sample size grows with the granularity of the frequency, and frequency suggests a more limited control domain or set of controls. Where controls are grouped, they might be tested individually but aggregate to a group number.

Automated controls

These controls should be assumed to be tested by auditors, though the "black box" nature of most automated systems will ensure a high degree of integrity in the operation of the process. Generally these processes are only visible when exceptions occur, and events notify operations staff of such exceptions. In these systems a representative range of deliberate errors should be introduced to test their effectiveness. Frequency will depend on the significance of the control. Managers, through the CTF, should work to similar criteria.

Deficiencies and material weakness

Auditors reporting material weaknesses in the financial report is something to be avoided. Deficiencies and material weaknesses (for more detail on these see Chapter 17) must be registered as part of management's assessment. However, there are some steps management can take to deal with this. If an issue is uncovered, the auditor evaluates whether management have taken adequate steps to remediate the material weaknesses. If the financial statement is fairly stated, with no intention to mislead or misrepresent the situation, the auditor may issue an unqualified report. This process can benefit from a number of actions:

■ Expand the scope of testing, to understand the context in which the issue has arisen.

Table 18.1 Controls: frequency of application

Control Type: Manual	
Frequency of performance	**Minimum sample size**
Annually	1
Quarterly	3
Monthly	5
Weekly	7
Daily	15
More than once per day	30

- The process of focusing on the weakness and documenting it means that it is being recognized and earmarked for treatment.
- The testing might be approached in a different way. By using other metrics, it might be possible to rework the assumptions behind the conclusion.

Whatever the approach, it must not appear to avoid the issue. The real benefit of a compliance process is that no issue remains isolated; it is part of a larger process of improvement, and with proper documentation it is seen to be so. The way deficiencies and weaknesses are handled by the audit committee and board of directors is a good indicator of the seriousness with which the system of internal control is approached. This, as much as the way staff are managed, is an indicator of the COSO quality, "tone at the top."

Fraud management has been a reflection of this in the past. It is likely that uncorrected significant deficiencies in internal controls will have been reported to the audit committee or senior management, and they are a strong pointer to the potential for material weaknesses in processes. By dealing with all reported issues, management can meet this concern head on in its assessment. A proper follow-up should be organized through the audit committee. The assessment is an opportunity to repeatedly make strong statements about the probity and transparency of the organization, independently of ensuring compliance and good business practice.

MANAGEMENT ASSESSMENT

Management's assessment of the effectiveness of the system of internal control is a critical activity under the Act, and is referenced within the PCAOB's AS2. It benefits from the creation of the compliance process, since management can:

- call on the resources and work of the CTF
- be assured by the thoroughness and transparency of the compliance process
- see practical implementation of assessment techniques and activities in the compliance cycle.

There are guidelines for management, notably in the PCAOB's AS2, which requires management to:

- acknowledge ownership of the system of internal control over financial reporting
- evaluate the internal controls using criteria defined under the Act and the AS2

- draw up documentation and gather evidence in support of the evaluation of internal controls
- present an assessment of the effectiveness of the company's system of internal control at financial year-end.

Timing

Management's assessment of internal control is an assessment that occurs at a specific point in time. Under the Act this is at the end of the fiscal period. The process may cover an extended time period, but the assessment itself is made at a single point in time. The implication is that all the controls referred to in the assessment are in place and operational at the end of the financial period. However, there must be evidence that these controls have been operating effectively over the entire period of time covered by the periodic report.

Evidence and documentation

Under the Act, in their assessment management must evaluate the design of controls as well as their operating effectiveness. For all activities, for management to present their assessment there has to be evidence of the activity and the status of the system of internal control. Primary evidence is the documentation, as direct evidence that management's findings are reasonable, reliable, and from the point of view of auditors, verifiable. A sample list of such documentation should demonstrate:

- the way controls are designed
- how significant transactions are initiated, authorized, recorded, processed, and reported
- the application of the COSO structure, or other framework, as necessary
- fraud controls active over the period
- preventive, detective, and other control types
- any further evidence that corroborates management's testing process, for example from external consultants
- any material weaknesses and significant deficiencies identified.

Significant processes

Identifying significant processes linked to internal controls is part of the compliance process, and the combined knowledge and expertise of the CTF can make a valuable contribution to this activity. Once management have identified significant accounts and the related financial assertions, they can then select significant processes. These are processes that affect major classes of transactions, and directly address accounting, disclosures, and assertions. To detail these processes, certain aspects of the context in which they occur must be documented, including an understanding of transactions:

- how they originate: the originating point in the process
- how are they recorded: which might be manually, automatically, at the creation point, during the workflow; storage, and access
- how they are processed: the transaction flow or workflow itself, and the dependencies and interactions with other processes and operators
- how they are reported: ownership, recipients, reporting formats
- how they are controlled: the nature of their internal control(s).

This builds a picture of the context within which the transaction takes place. It adds information important for the selection process by assessing:

- its importance, or significance
- its complexity, or resource requirements
- its priority rating.

Based on this background knowledge and an understanding of the relevant internal control, management can begin to identify areas where a misstatement on a financial assertion might occur. Allied to this is the need to introduce or develop key controls, where a key control provides assurance that material errors will be spotted in a timely manner. Because of the work done on identifying controls or lack of them, management can indicate whether:

- the existing internal control is sufficient and effective enough to address a potential misstatement
- the existing control needs to be modified, through a documented change management process
- a new control needs to be introduced, through a documented change management process.

Finally, management can then, through the CTF and the compliance cycle:

- implement any control changes necessary
- update the documentation
- ensure that the response to the risk level associated with the process is appropriate
- indicate the potential cost in terms of resource allocation to the modification or new control.

Equipped with documentation that is generated by this activity and the structured approach of the compliance cycle, management have the necessary ingredients to make their assessment of the system of internal control over financial reporting.

PRACTICAL COMPLIANCE SUMMARY

- Initiate a document management system, or adapt an existing one for compliance purposes.
- Manage document retention.
- Determine an effective strategy for email and unstructured communications (see Appendix B).
- Devise testing methods: adapt existing control tests and introduce new ones, as needed.
- The CTF should identify significant processes.
- The CTF should help management detect deficiencies and material weaknesses for remediation (using "quick" compliance).

CHAPTER 19

Process and the Organization: Policies and Behavior

THE IDEA OF A PROCESS

For financial services, perhaps more than any other industry, the concept of a "process" is essential to defining its value to itself and to the world. It is used in a general sense, as a way of loosely grouping or referring to activities that have some kind of connection in a sequence; it is also used in a specific way by analysts and traders who link lender and borrower in a web of processes that crosses companies, markets, and borders. The threads of processes are the stuff of financial activities, especially in the electronic world of the information economy, where transactions rarely become "physical" and usually remain abstract.

WHAT CONSTITUTES A PROCESS?

One simple definition of a process is as a sequence of operations or functions, which result in something of value. The emphasis on the process being of value is critical; it is important to identify that value before a process is developed. Processes can originate in an organization in a number of ways:

- created as part of a planned piece of work
- introduced as change to existing functional activities
- evolved over time from ad hoc working practices.

There is a sense in which processes are proactively introduced or reactively arise as a result of existing practice. The value of the process is not always explicitly stated, but it is there, whether stated or not, as an assumption. However, it is only when a process is documented that the value is uncovered.

It is then that the process is scrutinized to see if it delivers that value. Often it does so inefficiently or ineffectually. In these instances the process needs to be reviewed, redesigned, or even collapsed into another, perhaps external process, that carries the value more usefully. Cost and value are not necessarily the same thing here. The value of the process might be clear and the process may deliver that value, but the cost of doing so might be very high. Then the value objective has to be reconsidered. Because of this, and the significance of processes in general for compliance, we need tools that can help determine answers to question like:

- What does the process consist of?
- What is its value to the organization?
- What are its risks?
- What are its controls?
- How effective are these controls at reducing risk and maintaining its operational effectiveness?

One way of approaching these questions is to develop processes using process maps, a variation on flowcharting. This tool makes it easier to document controls.

PROCESS MAPPING AND FLOWCHARTING

A process map is a graphical illustration of the functions or activities performed by a process. The power of the map is the way it uses an image to convey a sometimes complex sequence in an easy-to-grasp manner. It has the ability to:

- indicate the use of computer systems
- convey a common image of the process to all members of a team
- illustrate the risks and controls involved in the function
- help make decisions for change.

In addition, process maps as well as flowcharts can:

- help scope audits
- document controls
- increase efficiency in control design
- provide a reference for ad hoc training
- indicate risks in a process
- provide a method for a thorough analysis of an activity
- resolve muddled thinking around processes
- separate past practice from best practice, and introduce the latter.

This means that process mapping is a very effective tool for understanding and developing processes from the perspective of the compliance process. Process mapping is especially useful for providing a meta-model of the organization, since its logic cuts across departmental activities and follows the flow of the activity wherever it leads. It is also manageable, in that it has a start and an end point. For financial services these processes can be very specific and functional, or all-embracing. They can cover activities such as:

- issuing policies
- making loans
- taking deposits
- selling instruments as products, such as mutual funds, mortgages, and annuities, and developing new products and services
- installing new service support systems.

Any of these processes and many like them, must add value to the organization. They represent a financial cost, in terms of resources and budgets, carry risk, and have implications for compliance under the Act.

The process itself may consist of separate components, or tasks and activities, that perform a function and contribute to the overall process. The difference is between whole and part, between ends and means. Tasks or activities include:

- underwriting
- credit checking
- reviewing, creating, and closing loans
- managing mortgage applications.

Such activities are sub-sets of the main process, and can be considerable sub-processes in their own right. For the internal auditor the granularity of inspection, documentation, and testing becomes a matter of expertise and judgment. The allocation of controls, and the analysis required to understand which controls, by type, should be applied, can be complex. Much of this work is difficult to carry out without tools such as process mapping and flowcharting. This is especially so for undocumented processes which operate without any formal control or definition; untangling these can be very time-consuming. This process can also be very painful for the staff involved, since any rework represents change, and change is a source of another, potent risk: fear.

COMPLIANCE AND PROCESS

In fact, the process concept has a precise and simple definition: a process is end-to-end work, in contrast to piecemeal work. It focuses on the totality of work, on whole sequences of tasks rather than on the individual tasks themselves. It concentrates on how these tasks fit together into a whole, rather than on how they are individually performed. Process focuses on the outcome of work and on its customers, rather than on the work as an end in itself.

Process and workflow

We talk a great deal about business processes and IT processes. Business process management is a discipline in its own right dedicated to this area. We also talk of business activities being part of a workflow. Often the terms are used interchangeably, and this may be acceptable for many circumstances. However, it would be useful to have a clearer, more succinct definition that we can use within the context of compliance. Specifically, such definitions should be related directly to the Act. There are many specific contexts in which we use the word "process" in business and IT. Earlier we saw COBIT define a process as a series of joined activities. However, we use concepts interchangeably. Another term that is often used in the context of process is "workflow."

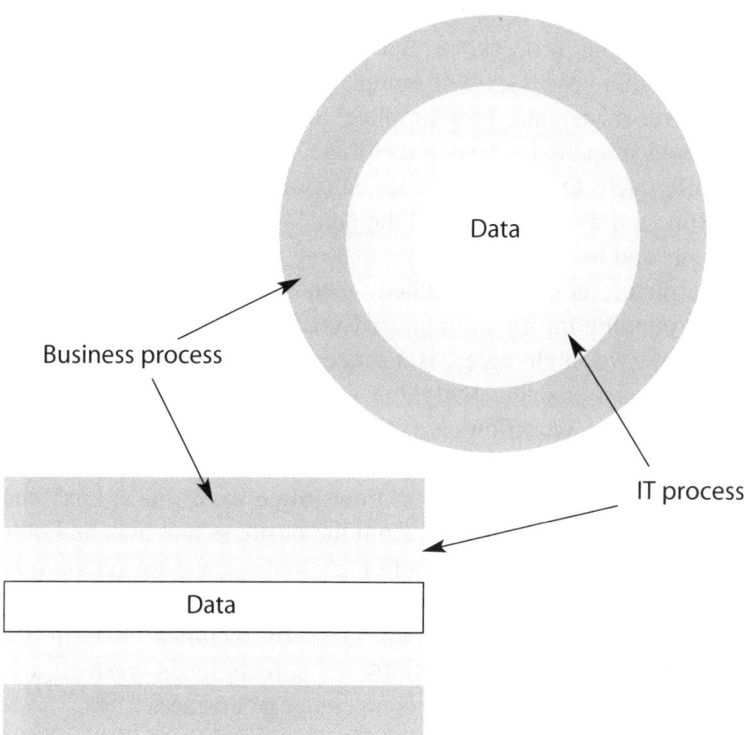

Figure 19.1 Process and layers of control

We speak of a business process or workflow as if the words were synonymous. In some context they are. The above definition works for "workflow" as well as process. However, there is some value in teasing out a fuller definition, since workflow is a major software sub-industry, and can mean a short activity with only local relevance, or a sequence of activities that span a larger enterprise.

The Act looks to senior management as the responsible agents of action in response to its requirements, but senior managers naturally look to their own hierarchy of responsibility when it comes to achieving compliance. In particular they look to their own cascade of responsibility. The organization might have a very clear idea of what department, and who within that department, is responsible for each activity or process. In the COBIT model and others, there is an emphasis on assigning responsibility for monitoring, reviewing, responding to, and remediating, processes and their controls. Without this level of responsibility and accountability, the integrity of any system fails.

Figure 19.1 touches on some of the issues around this definition, and specifically the separation of responsibility between the business and the IT function. Who in effect owns the process? If the process is decomposed, we might indicate an IT layer and a business layer. The data that are carried through a series of transactions or activities constitute the value to the business, yet the IT function actually delivers the data through the system. This might be a simple process, or a complex workflow including many handovers to other processes. The complexity of this processing can lead to confusion over ownership. In a simple example, the IT function supports the data, looks after its passage and storage, and is clearly responsible for it in this life cycle to the point of its deletion years hence. However, the business function will have created the data, and the business function has requirements and uses the IT system, making decisions about creation and usage. The picture is further muddied when we introduce security and the criteria surrounding information under COBIT.

A workflow, we might agree, is a sequence of processes. Some of them might only consist of one activity, but generally the workflow amounts to many discrete tasks. Workflows are often broken down into work queues for manual processing. A great virtue of workflows is the way they are amenable to automation. Fully automated workflows often have "black box" characteristics. They have inputs, usually from the business function, and outputs, for further use by the business function. Actual manual intercession in the internal processes might only occur when "exceptions" occur. Event-driven and reactive, these interventions might be by technical staff in a troubleshooting role, since the exceptions are defects in the system, and the nature of the system is beyond the competence of business users.

The assignment of responsibility for the workflow, the process or processes, and the discrete tasks and their controls, might be problematic.

It might also be the case that automation simplifies a previously intractable problem, and this is one of its beneficial side-effects.

There is a more technical definition of process in IT programming, when we talk of several instances of a process running. Here a process is a defined set of instructions. These are launched, and either run once and terminate, or are continually alive in the background, checking or waiting to react to another process. When we have such dependencies for action on other processes, we have a complex of processes which we might call a workflow.

Workflow

There are many example of "workflow" in contemporary financial business. A term that is constructed from several words has a meaning suggested by its constituent words. So in this case "work—that is, tasks or activities—forms part of a "flow." There is a sense in which there is a path along which tasks occur, and there is a link between them, which might involve an exchange of information. One definition of workflow talks of routing information, usually in the form of documents, between users who then carry out an activity on them before passing them on. This workflow can be automated or manual, or most likely in contemporary financial business a mixture of both. This view of workflow is the one most closely aligned to our interests. "Users" may be skilled or semi-skilled individuals with accumulated knowledge, who "process" information as defined above, by transforming it in some way. Generally we see each activity step of the workflow as being a point at which any such transformation "adds value," or improves its value to the organization.

A business cycle may consist of a workflow, where information is passed through a number of steps which process the information to complete the cycle. The flow itself may be abstract since the data might not move from central database, but simply be accessed and worked upon by a series of users. However, there is always a sense of movement, or progression through a series of tasks. The advent of IT has enabled the automation of many repetitive tasks where the processing can be abstracted and become rule-bound. Decision points may require skilled human intervention, but an objective for many organizations is to automate their common business tasks as far as possible. This is looked at wherever we consider automation in the overall compliance process.

The overlap between process and workflow is reflected in another use of the word "process." In business we often talk of the overall process, which may contain many linked or separate workflows, each containing task-oriented processes. Strategically we may discuss the process of introducing and implementing new technologies or a new business process. The way we use the word in the phrase "compliance process" is one such usage. Workflow as a part of business process management or compliance solutions is discussed later. For now, we can understand workflow in the context discussed above, and a process as a task-oriented activity.

The compliance process as workflow

Workflow links discrete processes and tasks in a "flow" in which "work" is allocated to either manual or automated "work queues." When considering internal controls, auditors often work at the task level. Once control objectives have been determined, specific controls are discrete, quantifiable—that is, measurable—and able to be modified if necessary. The compliance process, especially in its cyclical phase, can be represented as a number of processes operating simultaneously, subject to their dependencies and the critical path of an activity. Various members of the CTF will be active, and the tasks will accumulate according to workloads and capabilities. In all, we have a workflow. This means that common workflow tools should manage the overall compliance process. These can be:

- commercial off-the-shelf (COTS) software
- consultancy built
- developed in-house.

The choice is governed by relationships with vendors, systems integrators, and in-house software capability. A range of methodologies can be focused on this process:

- ITIL has a process-aware structure, centered on the service desk as a model for the support structure for the CTF.
- Six Sigma, with its focus on quality in processes, through measurement.
- COBIT, as a process and control reference model.

BUSINESS PROCESSES IN FINANCIAL SERVICES

The breadth of the subject of business processes in financial services is considerable. Technology is a specific driver with two major contributions to the sector: it is an enabler of change in business processes, and it introduces business concepts and techniques, making previously impractical options possible.

The end-to-end functionality of many technology driven processes is a relatively new thing. It enables the seamless delivery of products and services. It drives broader access to services. It also serves to drive the acceptance of the discipline of business process management (BPM). These processes are now core to business in every sector, and are generating value generators for whole industries. This is especially so for financial services.

BPM has become embedded in management practice. The compliance process is a form of BPM, in that it subscribes to:

- process redesign
- process improvement
- process management.

The processes of setting up an account, servicing it with products, maintaining an ongoing relationship, up-selling and building the relationship, and stripping down the account, are fundamental to the way financial services operate whatever their sector focus. Process management helps deliver improvements in the business through better results and enhancing customer satisfaction, since it is goal-directed and outcome-focused. In another way the compliance process assists process improvement. For many organizations processes are characterized as:

- fragmented: implemented piecemeal and fractured across departments
- invisible: having evolved as business practice without official review or documentation
- unmeasured: not subject to controls or metrics
- unmanaged: lacking ownership and accountability.

The compliance cycle uncovers all these aspects as it evaluates design and tests processes. Financial services companies have typically not had the focus on processes that is key for engineering companies and those companies managing complex product on environments with raw materials and finished goods. There are parallels, but the physical nature of manufactured goods highlights good and bad processing in a spectacular manner. The reject bins are an ultimate metric, along with returned goods. However, the nature of modern call centers and workflow systems has changed that.

Processes and errors

Errors proliferate in this environment, both as the result of inevitable misunderstandings and because different departments are working with different and inconsistent information. Inadequate information, poor communication in the process, assumptions about common language, and varying interpretations of common facts and figures lead to mistakes. These are the errors that can lead to non-deliberate misrepresentation in financial reporting. The consolidation process is prone to this. High error rates can result from a missing field that makes interpreting an invoice difficult, or a lack of information about the sales terms.

Reviewing process through compliance

By dealing with processes in a systematic way, organizations can uncover failing processes, or mechanisms for improving existing processes, and introduce new processes to make dramatic improvements in their performance. In this way, as a by-product of reviewing an entire process, end-to-end, an organization can eliminate non-value-adding work.

The benefits here derive not just from looking at tasks to see how they can be improved, but from redesigning processes as a whole. This involves reconsidering:

- who should perform a task
- when a task should be performed
- where (in a process) it should be performed
- how it should be performed (operator behavior in line with company policies and ethics, or interplay with a customer)
- how tasks should be interconnected (the interfaces can be bottlenecks and the source of errors)
- what information is necessary to eliminate ambiguity.

The cross-functional benefits are also made clearer through process redesign. A specific improvement in a task in one department might not have any benefit in the overall process because it does not address issues in a dependent task in another department. If the whole process is reviewed, both tasks are accounted for. For some activities there might be no overall process, or at best a segmented process unattached to the main business process, with poor links to other processes. These will be highlighted through a compliance audit, and control testing of the whole process is kept in mind. Remediation immediately delivers real benefit to the company. A process that can be performed reliably and consistently dramatically improves performance. It can also be measured, tested, and approved.

Companies can also suffer from too many processes. A multi-national might find that it has too many procurement processes, or localized versions of a process that is efficient at the HQ but grossly inefficient in a subsidiary located in a country with a different economic infrastructure and terms of business. Sometimes introducing a standard process generates benefit; sometimes a process has to be varied to suit local conditions. Simplification, though, is generally a sound approach. One of the major benefits of the compliance activity is the establishment of processes, documenting them with an eye on the chance to improve them at some stage. To derive this benefit, all compliance activity should look to the opportunity to measure, through controls, and mark for change where appropriate. This activity is also a very valuable input to business intelligence, providing real, quantifiable insights into the way the business operates for further analysis. Thus we should consider the performance of the process for the company as a whole, as well as its status in the compliance process.

CORPORATE GOVERNANCE

The Act is a response not only to specific misdemeanors but also to a perception about the current state of corporate governance. The International Chamber of Commerce defines corporate governance as "the relationship between corporate managers, directors and the providers of equity, people and institutions who save and invest their capital to earn a return."[1] The "corporate" nature of the definition focuses on specific organizational responsibilities: "It ensures that the board of directors is accountable for the pursuit of corporate objectives and that the corporation itself conforms to the law and regulations."

The concept of "governance" itself varies, but the corporate perspective defines it as the relationship that links those who invest and those who generate a return on the investment, succeeding or failing on the notion of "trust." Legislation such as the Act ensures that corporate enterprises manage and return that trust. There are new directions for governance as a whole, and as ever, technology has a hand in this. The spread of e-commerce has meant that business timescales have collapsed to "real time." Transactions occur simultaneously, and the "governance" of an organization cannot escape this, being placed in jeopardy in a time frame that is very difficult to "govern."

The relationship model

This view of governance as a web of relationships linked by the common interest of investment and return, held together by trust value, is central to the human dimension of business. The Act moves to realize and enforce transparency in corporate life as an attempt to reveal a very human interaction—exchange based on trust and assumed value. Business activity, as an expression of activity focused on profit and shareholder return, is subject to responsibilities to external agencies and individuals who place a trust in that activity, and who believe those organizations act in their interests. The driver of self-interest is translated, at an organizational level, into a matrix of dependent relationships: organizations and agencies acting on behalf of either themselves or others in pursuit of the financial interests of all.

The key words of "trust" and "relationship" are crucial; the significant failure of either places the enterprise in danger. The governance dimension addresses the requirement for someone or something to be accountable for the setting of organizational objectives and their implementation. In this way governance both examines the objectives and the way they are set, and ensures that measures are in place to make relationships operate in a way that conforms to expected behavior.

Governance does not define what this behavior is exactly, but seeks to ensure that it does not put at risk the greater good. In this moral view, the relationship web extends beyond establishing the responsibilities of organizations. The statutory Acts that define regulation and prescribe penalties set up agencies to monitor and administer this framework for behavior, and define the responsibility of other players in the web. For example, the activities of accountants and auditors, whether internal or external, are detailed to ensure perceived "fairness" in the relationships. A prime objective of corporate governance is to ensure that all the relationships are characterized by transparency and minimize the risk to relationships within corporate entities.

The ambition behind much process improvement is transformational, with some kind of state change occurring. Generally this concerns the process itself, but governance emphasizes the staff who operate processes, and it is in their behavior and the policies that govern their behavior that the compliance process offers additional value.

BEHAVIOR

Behavior is about staff working according to the policies of the organization. Many policies are developed in response to regulation, so regulation such as the Act has a direct bearing on the behavior of organizations. Indeed the Act was a response to the behavior of organizations, through their senior members and auditors as advisors. Although good behavior is assumed, it is rarely defined. It is regulated because it is also assumed that codes of conduct will be breached. The code of ethics mandated by the Act for senior executives falls into this area. Regulation elsewhere, such as the Combined Code in the UK,[2] and many other voluntary codes and business contractual codes, addresses the same area. In effect, these are all mechanisms introduced to reduce risk—the risk to the organization of staff who behave in a way that jeopardizes the value of the business. The Act has moved the reference to now include senior executives and their misuse of company assets.

We saw that the compliance process is a "transformational" process. Not only does it change and improve the processes through analysis and control, it also seeks to change the behavior of staff so that they do not put at risk these processes, and ultimately the organization. With this emphasis come other considerations:

■ awareness training: staff must be made aware of the value to them and the business of the compliance process

- skills training: specified staff are identified for specific skills training, through a training needs analysis
- information alerts: through the intranet and other internal systems, staff are updated on changes to the policies that govern their activities
- behavioral training: interpersonal skills training, customer care, diversity and other regulatory training must be implemented to ensure that staff maintain levels of probity and transparency in their interactions with customers.

These are all aspects of the transformational capability of the compliance process. Throughout the cycle, at every stage, behavioral change must be a factor influencing remediation.

- **Review–analyze–plan.** Behavioral change should be included in the scope. It should be assessed as a risk or set of risks, and allocated appropriate controls.
- **Implement controls.** Document behavioral controls; acquire solutions that reinforce behavior, such as desk-top systems, voice monitors and email prompters; ensure controls are designed to address behavioral objectives.
- **Evaluate effectiveness and treat.** Test behavioral responses to issues; identify key issues; test controls for correct behavior, and treat those that are failing.
- **Document and sustain.** Capture as much information as possible for the next cycle review, and review governance at all level. This ensures compliance into the next cycle for new regulation.

INTERNAL POLICIES

Policies are pervasive within any organization. Financial services are particularly rich in internal policies, since it is an information economy sector. Policies and guidelines are distinct from behavioral models in that they are documented, maintained, and central to many standards and certified standards-awarding bodies. ISO 9001 has a model for managing policy documentation. The behavioral activities around this are more to do with the use of processes than with soft skills or ethical conduct. So it is with policies: they generally instruct and advise on the use of tools and procedures.

Managing internal policies and guidelines

The information economy is now dependent on the web. The internet and especially email have transformed business activity. This is a prime example of a technology that can transform core business activity, subject to a raft of policies. It also illustrates how external regulation is expressed internally through policies. For a company engaged in e-business, policy statements may consists of:

- high-level statements about the aims of e-business
- the overall approach that the business is taking to e-commerce
- specific guidance on subjects such as e-commerce regulations and the way they affect the organization.

There would then be a considerable number of specific policy documents on the detail of working through e-commerce within the company, touching on:

- aspects of the business: such as management, website content, staff use of email, information management, security
- business specific policy: integration of departments, outcomes to policies, quality expectations, definitions
- practical guidelines for staff: on ownership, budgeting, time frames, scope, quality control, prohibitions and restrictions, storage, office and home use.

The compliance process will help the organization:

- to determine what aspects of the business (or e-business in this instance) require a policy statement and guidelines or procedures
- through the CTF owning the drafting of policies and documenting them as part of the process
- since interactive consultation with staff can be integrated into compliance process activities and models such as CSA
- because the CTF will have an increasing knowledge and early warning alerts on government and other regulation that will generate policies.

PRACTICAL COMPLIANCE SUMMARY

- Incorporate the compliance process and cycle into the company policy management system. This may be ISO 9001 or a variant.
- Identify working definitions relevant to the organization for workflow, process, and tasks.
- Document the main business workflows for CTF reference.
- Ensure sufficient systems are in place to assist staff behavior from policies.
- Provide desktop solutions at the customer interface.
- Provide training on policies and systems where necessary.

NOTES

1. The International Chamber of Commerce has acted as an advisory body to encourage corporate governance among its members.
2. The Combined Code in the UK emphasizes the responsibilities and ethical standards expected of directors.

PART IV

Securing the Organization for Compliance

CHAPTER 20

Risk Management

RISK ASSESSMENT

Risk management has always been a fundamental aspect of financial services, and the minimization of risk is an ongoing goal which involves more than just the preservation of the assets of the company. Security and the trust engendered by security are critical to the willingness to take a risk through an investment. It is this fundamental trust that was so undermined by the misdemeanors that led to the Sarbanes-Oxley Act. Keeping the organization secure, and the activities of financial services secure, are objectives that are of paramount importance.

Managing risk is a business discipline in its own right. A company's "risk profile" is a carefully considered reference for making business decisions on a daily basis. This profile is derived from the mission of the company and the business objectives that realize this mission. Every entity exhibits many vulnerabilities which might turn into threats, major or minor. The Act introduces compliance requirements as potential threats to this already full mix. Each organization will decide how it responds to a threat, based on its risk profile and the degree to which it believes a vulnerability will become a threat. The Act, more than most legislation, takes a vulnerability and emphasizes it as a threat. Because of this, the process of risk analysis is all the more significant.

However the assessment is carried out, it must be thorough and realistic. When we look at the Committee of Sponsoring Organizations of the Treadway Commission (COSO) reference framework, one of the five "components" is "risk assessment." In this review of risk we must assess:

- company-level risk: organizational, board-level, strategic
- activity-level risk: departmental, process, or transaction
- external risk: malicious disruptive activity, market volatility, non-compliance, acts of God
- internal risk: malicious or accidental staff activities, systemic failures, poor systems and processes.

TREATING RISK

For COSO, risk is treated through a system of internal control. Other reference models offer an approach based on information, and model risk assessment on the preservation of "information assets" as the means of maintaining an organization. A good example of this is ISO 17799. This is examined in depth when we look at information security and how an information security management system (ISMS) can contribute to the compliance process.

Since risk is a fundamental component of decision making, business decisions are largely guided by the concerns of generating profit and reducing business risk. If these twin aspects of business life are ignored, the business will fail. This is especially so for the financial sector. The rationale of the markets and institutions that represent investors or act as intermediaries in the capital acquisition process is about mitigating, spreading, or eliminating risk. In a competitive market this is a key differentiator, since reducing risk is fundamental to survival and growth.

The interplay of relationships that make up business activity represents a series of opportunities and risks. While opportunity defines the positive side of change and growth, risk appears as the negative side. The Act intends to reinforce the broader, positive aspects of the business relationships through good governance, while simultaneously it is perceived as a negative force, compelling extra cost and introducing extra threats. One job for the compliance effort is to unify these apparently conflicting aspects of business by:

- focusing on the potential benefits of the compliance process
- demonstrating the benefits of being in a state of compliance, or having good governance
- delivering improvements to the practical business processes of the organization.

RISK AND THE ACT

The Act signals to the business community that the risks of operating in the modern economy are increasing. As a backdrop to the Act, though not consciously part of the legislation itself, risk constitutes a way of seeing; it is a cultural base in which certain actions not only can take place, but in retrospect seem inevitable. Action and consequence, cause and effect, are now, more than ever, constantly reviewed and balanced for advantage and disadvantage. All business activity has a risk assessment attached.

Sometimes the risks are obvious—not to invest, or "risk," investor funds is not a valid option—and there is no choice but to take them. In other circumstances the risk is based on a complex calculation involving likely market forces, company objectives, and personal gain. In such a scenario the potential for realizing the worst aspects of the risk increases. Enron and other scandals were essentially calculated choices where the risk was perceived to be outweighed by the benefits of an opportunity. The probability is that the calculation was too complex: that is, there were too many factors involved in too many relationships, so the calculation was poorly founded.

No longer can we simply balance risk against benefit in a limited way, focusing simply on a department or program with recourse to the greater impact on the organization. Any risk is recognized as being part of an entity-wide risk strategy. The complexity of governance and its manifestation in risk analysis greatly influence the way organizations are beginning to think about how they implement key objectives. Enterprise risk management (ERM) is now a major business discipline, largely driven by legislation, including the Act.

Business risk has been a background noise for some time. Those businesses that see advantage in developing programs that positively promote their operation in the community, fronting their PR with socially acceptable messages about the environment, biodiversity, and relieving social injustice through agencies such as charities, are using a trend to advantage. However, very often these measures do not affect the way the organization works, or intrude upon its objectives and means of making a profit. If there is a conflict of interest, the program might soon be diluted or dropped. This is not a cynical view, more a view based on the assumption that a cost–benefit analysis will be made. Certainly without regulators and enforcement agencies, the perceived risk of business misdemeanor, however it is defined, increases dramatically.

BUSINESS RISK

There are also substantial and real risks as defined by the business, by itself for its own interests. These are wide-ranging, and some of them can be insured against, but others cannot.

Global warming and climate change have huge and largely unpredictable implications for many organizations. Insurance premiums are climbing, and insurance companies face a very difficult future. Some are withdrawing from sectors long seen as bread-and-butter activities because of the costs of underwriting.

Corporations have had to manage operational risk from elements they cannot control for centuries. But the nature of global activity, and its transnational scope with multiple zones of regulation and censure, require full-time resources to manage. The board, focused on key decision making based on the simplicities of the bottom-line spreadsheet, now look over their shoulder at increasing investor scrutiny, state-sponsored regulation, and economic conditions.

Risk is everywhere, in many guises, and the costs are almost incalculable. The Act caps this by mandating that the existence of the business no longer depends just on the final balance sheet, but on the perception of how that balance sheet has been arrived at.

IMPLICATIONS OF THE ACT

In a sense, the Act is all about risk. The business is at risk from non-compliance: the implications of prosecution by the SEC are considerable for share value alone. The key players in the business are at risk, from very punitive measures that include imprisonment. If both the business as a whole and the key players fail, so too does the business. The Enron debacle has shown how risk spreads across the organization, forcing lay-offs, and hugely damages investors. One of the ironies of this process is that if the Act is diligently enforced with the aim of protecting investors, a prosecution under it could damage the organization so severely that the investors suffer more.

However, we have seen that the overt aim of the Act is the establishment and preservation of good governance, and specifically good business practice in financial reporting. For the company, this can translate into many things, including continuous business practice improvement. Section 302 of the Act lays the foundations for monitoring financial processes. Its objective is accuracy in reporting, and the effectiveness of internal controls to achieve this accuracy. Section 409 is essentially about timing; it takes the work of Section 302 and assumes accurate reporting is in place, then ensures this is coupled with timing to guarantee an up-to-date picture of the state of the business.

RISK FACTORS

Section 409 and risk

The risk factors inherent in the implementation of these sections are not necessarily new. It is the exacting nature of the Act and the insistence on timely reporting that stretches the capability to respond. However, many risk factors are "traditional" in nature and well understood, and a well-defined risk strategy, with effective monitoring and control, makes tasks associated with Section 409 easier to quantify, cost, and tackle.

For the financial process there are many factors that affect the business as a whole and have an impact on the reporting process. These tend to be among the most well known in general business practice, and cover activities initiated by the business and those that originate outside the business.

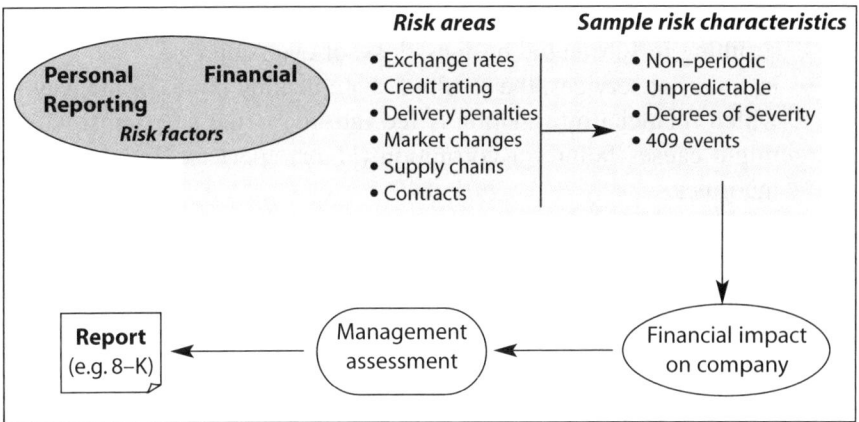

Figure 20.1 Risk areas and characteristics

They have at least one thing in common: they all have attendant risks. They include:

■ Exposure to the volatility of currency exchange rates for those organizations that trade internationally. Most US-listed companies carry this risk, which is often substantial.
■ The sometimes arbitrary nature of credit rating and the effect this can have on borrowing.
■ Everyday business penalties associated with delivery deadlines and so on.
■ The vagaries of demand, including unexpected increases in demand and market changes that reduce demand.

Many of these risks will be reflected in 10-K and 10-Q SEC listings (see Figure 20.1). However, others might or might not be included here, and might form part of an 8-K listing. Equally they are the sorts of activity that could interpret as being addressed under Section 409 of the Act. Section 409 is somewhat general and vague about what it considers to be relevant events that need to be reported in a timely or real-time context. Such events might include:

■ Sudden changes to circumstances relating from supply chain impact. This could include:
   – unexpected power shortages that have an effect on production processes, storage facilities (for food, for example), distribution networks and so on
   – an internet virus not properly anticipated, which could bring down

IT systems vital to business, such as an airport booking system, resulting in substantial business loss, or even collapse

- in financial services, the result of share dealing issues or the way in which financial information is fed into the issuer's systems, which might causes failure or corruption (IT or otherwise), or simply be incorrect
- "acts" of either humankind or nature, such as extreme weather. These events are not "periodic" as understood under the Act for the purposes of financial reporting. They are often unpredictable, sudden, and significant, with unpredictable severity of risk. But they do affect the business, and according to the Act, investors must know about their impact.

■ Changes to any significant agreements the organization has with customers, partners, or creditors. The termination of partner agreements can have a big impact on a product company that relies on indirect sales. For international companies this is particularly significant: a loss of a key partner in a different country or region might have big implications for the profit forecast. In a similar manner the addition or loss of a major customer might warrant a special report.

■ Debt management, including restructuring and write-offs, and changes in investment practices are potential events of this kind.

■ Any significant change to the financial health of the company is an all-encompassing rider to this. This would includes most of the above events as well as many more unspecified ones.

Generally Section 409 events are part of the ongoing history of the company, and should have an impact on the business. They might not be financial in nature but include all events that could make a difference, such as a change in the political structure of a country which adversely affects all US-listed companies. Many of these assessments are subjective, and they must be made in the light of current circumstances. While this reflects the current openness of the Act in Section 409, it also highlights how the Act is concerned with how well the business is understood, and how well senior management can articulate and present ongoing issues. Naturally they will strive to convey the best impression, but bad news is part of the feedback mechanism, and best results are obtained with full company involvement.

Personal risk factors

The risk factors for senior management are perhaps those articulated most clearly within the text of the Act. In particular the "signing officers," such as the CEO and CFO, are affected by the requirements of the Act. Their duties and the attendant risks have been listed. In summary they are:

- The duty to sign off periodic financial reports as accurate statements on the financial state of the company. The risk of false or misleading information makes them liable to fines and imprisonment. It is this personal risk that is shaping the urgency of the response within many organizations, and creating the willingness to assign resources to compliance programs. There is also the requirement of Section 409 to sign off non-periodic reports with similar mandates and penalties.
- The duty to include an assessment of the state of internal controls that monitor and assure the efficacy of the processes producing the financial reports.

By implication there are other risk factors in the duties of senior managers, such as:

- The whole exercise of mitigating risk, especially on an entity-wide basis. If this is left unattended the non-compliance of one part might be multiplied across the organization, and subject it to a systemic investigation by regulators. This would involve greater cost and greater exposure of the workings of the organization to external agencies for comment.
- Internal structures of accountability down to departmental level, holding individual line managers accountable for their area. The risk of the Act not being enforced at this level has a knock-on effect all the way up the reporting chain.
- The control of information exchange within the organization and between the organization and the other players in governance. This is a massive area of risk, and deserves to be examined on its own. In the end, the Act is about the right kind of information being produced through correct channels for the right audience.

Reporting

The very visible result of activity in the organization, in the form of a financial report, as detailed within the context of internal controls, makes explicit the importance of external and internal disclosures. Failure at this point is also a pivot point for assessing risk. It is here that all other risks are concentrated. A weakness here potentially exposes the whole organization. Financial reporting lies at the intersection of the management of risk, functional business processes, documentation, and controls. Hence we place financial reporting at the point where risk management, document and records management, and process management overlap.

RISK MANAGEMENT

Best practice

Best practice is really an operational interest. At the highest level we can say that it is best practice to devise a strategy with the common elements of involving senior management, allocating sufficient budget and resources, and so on. But thereafter, it is an organization-wide issue. Every department and every individual should pursue best practice. After all, one definition of a company is a group of individuals working towards a common aim, whether they are the shareholders or the employees. The implication of the Act is that the organization is a chain, and a break in any link can have serious consequences. This involves starting small with prioritized events, using the best people within the business, and IT divisions obtaining external help from the right specialists.

Risk tolerance

A sub-text of the Act is a set of requirements which can be couched as questions or challenges that need to be addressed in parallel with its more overt requirements. Risks are not new, on the whole; many of them are standard for all businesses. The task is to identify them, define, and categorize them. Naturally the definitions will vary from industry to industry, company to company, and even within the company depending on size and geography. They help establish a reference for further decisions and prioritization. The establishment of "risk tolerance" levels is something that is even more specific to the organization, and the subject of detailed analysis by risk management. These tolerances should be calculated and established up front, not at the end of the process. This is a guide to decision making and prioritization. Since time is now so important, triggers for action must be in place, and very clearly so, in order that early warning systems can work. When selecting triggers, it is as well to establish cause and effect as far as possible. When we talk of the impact of risk, we examine and quantify these necessary twins. Section 409 of the Act all but demands that this is given more attention.

For handling traditional risk factors there are already a number of tools in place across many industries. If it is in a heavily regulated sector, the organization might have a wealth of such resources available. However, the organization still has to answer the questions what information needs to be captured in the first place, and whether this process needs to be automated through the triggering of events for near real-time reporting. The activity of defining, automating, and producing fast-response reporting is a substantial challenge. This might call for a stronger architecture than that used traditionally.

So for risk management we add further necessary investigative steps in building a strategy: assess and measure the magnitude of any impact. For entity-wide risk management we must also know whether the event is a one-off or one of a series of events. The probability of an event and its frequency, along with the need to report it in the first place, build the profile of each risk factor. If the event is likely to happen often but have a minimal impact, how much effort should be expended on tracking and reporting it? When we look at expectations and estimations, there are mathematical models that can be used. Statistical analysis and risk assessment often go hand in hand to try to give an objective edge to what is really a very subjective response.

Forecasting and scenario modeling is a sub-discipline within risk management that has an even greater reliance on statistical tools. It requires access to internal and external data feeds of as high a quality as can be generated, from sources based in data warehousing and analytics. There are so many factors involved in forecasting that the tool sets are potentially endless, each adding their incremental refinement to the risk assessment. Scenario generators and simulators are reliant on perceived best practice, which may or may not be current, and the output of other tools and testing systems. Much of this work has to be done either using systems honed in practice or using "best guess" assessment.

When risk assessment and implementation is time-critical, the stakes tend to rise proportionately. For compliance with the Act, at some stage in this process the significance for financial performance has to be factored into the plan. Although "events" that have a "material" effect have been positioned as the guiding factors for assessing risk by the PCAOB, the ultimate impact to be considered is still on the earnings and share price indicators.

Enterprise risk

The uncertainty of events that face us every day as individuals, and our very human reaction to this unpredictability, underlie the significance of risk in daily life. This is equally true for business enterprises. This uncertainty is further refined by the notions of opportunity or threat, according to the perspective of the user. Managing this uncertainty is found in the emerging concept of enterprise risk management. This offers a framework for effectively managing uncertainty, responding to risk, and exploiting opportunities as they arise.

COSO, the private-sector group dedicated to improving financial management through effective risk management, internal control, and corporate governance, launched a landmark initiative in 2001: to build a commonly agreed-upon framework for enterprise risk management. The

COSO framework has been valued by the PCAOB and placed at the center of its compliance efforts on internal controls for financial reporting. This exploration of how the framework can be expanded to provide comprehensive risk management aligns well with the interests of the Act. PricewaterhouseCoopers was asked to lead COSO's project to research and develop this comprehensive enterprise risk-management framework. This defines enterprise risk management as "a process ... applied in strategy setting and across the enterprise, designed to identify potential events that may affect the entity, and manage risk to be within its risk appetite, to provide reasonable assurance regarding the achievement of entity objectives" (originally published in Steinberg et al 2004).

The significant aspect of this approach from the perspective of the Act is that managing risk through such a framework enables organizations to achieve their performance and profitability targets, prevent the loss of resources, and ensure effective reporting and, critically, compliance. The benefits of managing risk are almost self-evident. The framework, by linking "risk appetite," or acceptable levels of uncertainty, to the process of defining business strategies, enables goals to be set more effectively in the context of the overall corporate strategy. Further, linking growth, risk, and returns develops a capacity to identify, assess, and set risk tolerances consistent with growth and return objectives.

Anything that can aid decision making in this context has enormous value, especially when the organization is faced with multiple risks that affect different functions and operations. In particular:

- Recognizing potentially adverse events is difficult when they are isolated and not cross-referenced their cumulative impact.
- It is imperative that the organization can respond quickly and take advantage of any opportunities that result.
- Accuracy of information enables the deployment of resources more effectively, reducing overall capital requirements and allocations.
- Ideally, ERM is a framework consisting of dynamic processes that permeate every aspect of an organization's resources and operations.

Since risk is ubiquitous, ERM involves staff at every level, and applies a portfolio view of risk across an entire enterprise. This comprehensive measurement and application of risk has to be well thought out and previously defined. Given this, by embedding the framework in day-to-day operations, an enterprise can monitor the success of its own risk planning.

COSO has grasped the essential nature of risk management and extended its previous framework to encompass eight interrelated components categorized as:

- internal environment
- objective setting
- event identification
- risk assessment
- risk response
- control activities
- information and communication
- monitoring.

These topics are covered later. However, the briefest overview shows the significance of the thought behind this initiative and its relevance to the Act.

Since risk is a constant but unpredictable feature of business life, ERM must be a dynamic process; and for it to be effective, all eight of the components must function. While it does not guarantee results, such a framework can greatly increase the board's confidence that they are not missing critical issues for the business, and that they have a mechanism in place that will trap events that can threaten the corporate well-being. To understand the basis for this assumption we need to briefly consider each of the categories.

Internal environment

Essentially, an enterprise's internal environment influences how strategies and goals are set. It is characterized by many aspects of the organization, such as ethical values, personnel qualities, the senior and line-level management operating style, and the management philosophy on risk and how it fits into the company culture. From this comes the key concept of "risk appetite." A sales-driven environment sees risk as an everyday fact of life full of opportunity, whereas a financial services company does its best to monitor and eliminate risk. This process is the foundation for setting objectives on risk management. The organization's response to the Act is to see it as having a direct bearing on the company culture, if it accepts the argument that the Act is about behavioral change. In reality, because of the implications for high-level management, the "risk appetite" for the Act is likely to be very low.

Objective setting

The framework provides the opportunity to explore the alignment of objectives with strategic company goals, and a mechanism for setting these objectives and ensuring that they are consistent with the defined "risk appetite." These objectives can be seen from four perspectives:

- strategic: or high-level goals and mission statement
- operational: in terms of efficiency, performance, and profitability

- reporting: for internal and external reporting
- compliance: relating to internal policies, laws, and regulations.

Once the objectives are in place, anything that affects them can be identified. This fits well with our discussion of the implications of the Act. In every arena we have highlighted how the Act influences objective setting by infiltrating the cultural view of the organization, through governance and risk awareness.

Event identification

Through the framework, management can identify those events, internal and external, that affect its strategy and achievement of objectives. These events will be categorized and cross-linked to give a bigger view of their impact on the company as a whole. They provide the raw material on which risk assessment is carried out. The assessment of events is very much part of the Act's set of requirements. This is all the more so when it comes to that broad selection of events that fall under Section 409.

Risk assessment

The application of analytics and qualitative assessments is a process that reveals the potential of events and the nature of their impact. For example, it determines whether an event is internal or external, and assesses its degree of severity. The risk assessment is extended in the case of the Act to the assessments made by senior management for periodic reporting on the effectiveness of internal controls. It also extends to the attestation made by external auditors, who typically use a form of analytics or qualitative assessments as part of their process.

Risk response

Once the risks have been assessed, options are examined, and responses decided upon, depending on the company policy on risk tolerance. Generally, risks are categorized for some kind of action, for example to be avoided, shared, reduced, or accepted. The response is an implementation plan. The feedback mechanisms assumed to be in place by the Act from the risk assessment phase provide the basis for planning responses, building an architecture of assessment and response.

Control activities

It is critical that responses are carried out efficiently. Each company is unique, and control activities will vary, reflecting the internal environment and industry conditions. Heavily regulated industries will have very different controls in place from those in industries based entirely on self-regulation and voluntary regulation. These controls are focused on business tools, the IT infrastructure, and security management. For the Act, the discussion on internal controls is fundamental and now seen to be closely tied to risk management.

Information and communication

Information from both internal and external sources underlies the value of this whole exercise. It must be captured and shared in a timely manner. We see how important this is for the present and the future requirements of the Act. Inevitably, good information is the content of effective communications. These channels can involve external parties, such as customers, vendors, regulators, and shareholders. It is a major challenge in itself to manage information that is both historical and current. The management of this conforms to other frameworks, such as information life cycle management (ILM), and touches on the complexity of overlapping but mutually supportive frameworks. The way information management and the Act are linked is discussed further when we look at solutions.

Monitoring

For any activity to be successful, it must be monitored effectively. In the context of risk, this ensures that the framework is operational at all levels of the organization. The monitoring can use one-off tests and audits, or be an ongoing process. This is typified by the many software solutions that are introduced to oversee unstructured communications, which monitor them constantly in real time and produce risk alerts for defined events. Events and activities then have to be reported, either as part of a formal periodic process or in the form of reactive one-off reports on process exceptions. The important thing is for the information to be presented to those charged with ownership of risk management, for timely action or escalation. The overlap here is with the security framework, with the separation of roles and responsibilities clearly defined. For the Act, the true aim of all controls is to produce long-term monitored processes rather than one-off periodic responses. It is critical to ensure that both discrete components of the reporting process and the best-practice behavior of its users are monitored.

EXTENDING THE SCOPE OF THE ACT

It seems that the COSO ERM framework might be a valuable extension of traditional risk management for compliance with the Act. Most companies are demonstrating compliance with Sections 302 and 404. Extending compliance efforts to other risk areas of the business might be a useful next step. It is certainly something advocated by many consultancies, albeit they have a vested interest in extending the scope of compliance as widely as possible. Nevertheless, the investment is being made, the tools are being purchased, and the skills introduced to internal divisions. Why not maximize this effort?

If we look at examples of risk beyond the categories outlined earlier, we see ready opportunities to extend the cultural impact of the Act. Anything that increases the efficiency of the organization is of value, usually with a rapid return on investment. In like manner, anything that seeks to differentiate the organization in a competitive marketplace will catch the interest of the board. The failure to attend to these issues is, conversely, a risk. Exposure to acts of God and humanity across many geographies is a becoming more of an obsession in an era of overt terrorism. Risk mitigation through a well-aligned, compact, and compliant organization reduces this exposure to international events. It is arguable that markets are more sensitive to such events. As business models and technologies become obsolete, technology investments are ever more costly, necessary, and prone to risk; company infrastructures can be undermined very quickly if the technology base of interlocked supply chains running through whole markets begins to shift. The example we examined in some depth, of corporate governance and behavioral change, is forcing public companies to review disclosure practices and internal controls through the lens of risk.

Addressing these risks as part of a broad-based strategy is a beneficial spin on the value of the Act. It assists, in this instance, in the process of establishing ERM for the whole organization, and discovering something that might have gone unnoticed. However, ERM is not a panacea in itself, but a part of the overall response to the Act. When we come to look at information as a source of value to the organization in its own right, we can recognize that the organization cannot manage its risks when it suppresses or distorts information about the reality of its business processes. Auditor attestations alone will see to that.

Executive confidence

Senior executives need confidence that their systems are effectively monitoring and capturing a true picture of the business, and that this picture is a compliant one, with all significant risks identified. But mere compliance is clearly insufficient to generate and maintain this confidence, for without this assurance, attestation to internal control effectiveness and transparent reporting is an illusion. Clear accountability, in a defined process-based chain that involves unit managers and process owners, can be exploited to address risks of all kinds, across the spectrum beyond just financial reporting.

Benchmarking and best practice

We come now to the specific area in which real progress can be made with specific targeted spending. The organization can improve risk management, its processes, internal controls, and performance metrics to reap the real rewards of managing risk.

Most companies would benefit considerably from the exercise of benchmarking their processes against industry best practice. Processes can be compared and redesigned to reduce costs and improve controls. This exercise is the best opportunity to develop a practical approach to compliance and risk management. The industry has a widely referenced model in the COSO framework. The PCAOB practically endorses it as the mandated reference for companies being audited for compliance. The framework extends beyond the Act and encompasses all risk.

CHANGING BEHAVIOR

At the junction of the twentieth and twenty-first centuries, it is clear that the business world, its markets, the mechanisms of value creation, and its technologies, never stand still for long. In the context of this continual transition, risk transforms itself, appearing in many new guises. Existing risk management will not meet these changes unless it is robust enough. An ever-present danger is that in the face of change and the suddenness and severity of new risks, risk-averse behavior will start to drive the business, with the strong prospect of stagnation and failure.

The potential for change in organizational attitude and behavior is significant. This is a process which is inclusive in its overall approach, in contrast to the traditional siloed exclusive approach. It builds awareness, and helps foster commitment from the affected departments to encourage acceptance of responsibility as part of the corporate responsibility and ownership tree. This ability to transform an organization should be considered at an early stage. It aligns well with the Act and its effort to change behavior, and helps change staff values on risk and their attitude to corporate responsibility. It in effect "sensitizes" the organization to risk and the dangers of non-compliance.

Implementing ERM

Moving from a perspective that silos risk, isolates departments, and separates a much needed integration of function driven by the board, ERM differs from current risk management approaches in terms of focus, objective, scope, emphasis, and application. In common with the logic of compliance to the Act, ERM places an emphasis on preserving as well as creating business value. Yet it is not limited to a single function, in the way that the Act at first appears to be. ERM is truly a strategic exercise. It aligns strategy, people, processes, technology, and knowledge, in managing risk strategically across the enterprise. The Act contributes to this strategy by revealing risks for resolution. Within this process, disclosure complements transparency.

Implementing ERM falls into standard project management processing, with a number of best-practice guides to shape the overall planning. Risk management objectives should be agreed by all interested parties at the outset. Ensure too that the risk assessment process is enterprise-wide and is well integrated with normal business process planning, with ownership and accountability separated and clearly defined.

At the core of this process is information, and its quality determines the success of the decision-making process. Circling around this are the functional processes, outlined below, which are subject to an ongoing review. Risk appetite, risk tolerance, risk threshold, are phrases used synonymously to identify the risk thought appropriate for the entity as a whole and a department in particular, giving a considered assessment of a "risk and reward" balance.

Functional activities

Functionally we can list the risk-related activities for implementing the compliance process:

- Establish risk management objectives, tolerance, and limits for all the entity's significant risks.
- Assess risks in the context of these tolerances.
- Develop strategies and processes.
- Implement processes.
- Monitor and report on the performance of processes.
- Review and improve continuously.
- Communicate information relevant to risk decision making.

Again we see a real overlap between the Act, risk management, and governance, where the Act hits well above its apparent weight. If the organization has effective systems and good reporting practices, the ability to produce timely reports that reflect well on it is a real business benefit. The lack of this ability can, conversely, result in severe exposure and loss of reputation. With continuous improvement comes a kind of maturity. Ultimately the question is how to change the company culture through training and enforcement of policies. Key to this is effective dissemination of information. Full internal disclosure is part of the bigger picture, so that everyone knows how the company is doing.

THE FINANCIAL FUNCTION AND RISK MANAGEMENT

There is a need to assess and prioritize risk. At that point, compromises are made based on "best effort" judgments. As with all assessments, we return to the qualitative versus quantitative question: is it an assessment based on figures, or is it about value judgments based on intangibles?

Perception is a powerful instrument in determining an investor's approach to a potential target. That perception is only partly based on the figures. It is also dependent on qualitative "guesses" and predictions about the target's potential in the market. It is also a reflection of the past experience of the investor. The same is true for executives. If, for example, they are to grade the significance of the financial function within their organization and try to value it—a qualitative call—so they can prioritize risks for treatment, how do they do this? What are the measures?

A recent survey of CFOs of global non-financial companies (Servaes and Tufano 2006) asked them to measure this. A general consensus emerged that the finance function contributed close to 10 percent of the market value of the company. This function is the one that ultimately generates the inputs to the financial report. The survey found little variation in this figure in different countries. It explored sub-functions such as capital structure, liability management, liquidity management, distribution policy on dividends and shares, and risk management. The value of risk management was ranked in the upper half of the finance functions; it was seen, generally and regardless of region, as a key contributor to corporate value. It also figured as one of the functions most in need of extra resources. Essentially, risk management was valued as an opportunity, creating value for the organization, and seen as contributing a risk in itself through under-resourcing. This risk is a result of the importance risk management plays in making effective business decisions.

In this context the Act could be seen as not another risk in itself, but a driver for risk mitigation in general, through its emphasis on tackling risk through controls. One strong view that emerged from the survey was that the central benefit of risk management perceived by CFOs was that it enabled them, and the business, to make better decisions. This was in contrast to the traditional view of its focus on optimizing programs and investments. For the financial sector which has to take risks, often substantial ones, on a daily basis, good decision making is crucial.

Getting the most from risk management is a challenge to all organizations. Understanding risk and measuring its effects on the business are hurdles for any resource-stretched program. One aspect that has been emphasized is the importance of broadening an understanding of risk throughout the organization. If we apply this to the impact of the Act, then it falls within the important activity of ensuring all staff are aware of policies and policy changes, and the risk their activities might pose for the organization, not just as everyday business risks, but through non-compliant activities or actions.

PRACTICAL COMPLIANCE SUMMARY

- Use risk assessment as a reference model for ensuring the compliance effort is specific to the company.
- Adapt the existing risk management system.
- Determine the organization's risk profile.
- Use the risk profile as input to the strategic compliance process.
- Use this profile as a guide for all risk assessments in the compliance cycle.
- Clarify risks for the organization as a whole.
- Clarify risks at a personal level: senior executives, attorneys, and staff in general.
- Approach the Act as an opportunity for a risk mitigation and as an enabler for more effective risk management.

CHAPTER 21

Intellectual Capital

INTELLECTUAL PROPERTY

Information is, without a doubt, the new "capital" of business. It is not an exaggeration to state that without reliable, accurate, and up-to-date information, the organization cannot operate. However, the deliberate sharing of information exposes enterprises to the risk of intellectual property (IP) loss. To protect this and gain the most from its potential, the complexity of intellectual capital must be acknowledged and its "life cycle" managed. When the Sarbanes-Oxley Act talks of documents, records, and reports, it is really referencing the information that is placed in the public domain to enable investors to make decisions. The assumption is that the better the quality of information, the more able the investor is to make a truly informed decision. This is a critical consideration.

Faced with costs and the risks from regulatory controls, such as the Act, the preservation and protection of business value warrants a strategic response. Such a strategy has emerged in the form of information life cycle management (ILM). It provides a way of easing the concerns now experienced by accountable CEOs and CFOs about the existence of so much stored non-compliant and potentially damaging information. More importantly it provides the basis for building solid cost control, and a platform to demonstrate a way to mitigate risk.

When we talk of "intellectual capital" we are referencing the reality that all business discourse is about the exchange of information. However, there is often confusion about the distinction between data and information. After all, it seems, it is data that the organization generates, consumes, and relies upon. If we consider information as transformed data, we understand it as having a context and a meaning dependent on this context. It is this data, as "information," that is used by the business to make its fundamental business decisions. Redefine the key activity of business as decision making and we begin to see its value emerge. Operational decisions are often driven by many factors, but they are above all dependent on the quality and integrity of the information available.

Herein lies the value of that data, a value defined partly by usage and partly by its meaning to everyone involved. However, determining such value is not always easy, and value comes in many guises: client lists, sales contracts, financial statements, competitive analyses, product materials, and pricing information. The link between information value and business benefit is paramount. It is the key for unlocking the sources of value all organizations seek when addressing business efficiency: the mitigation of risk, the containment of capital expenditure, and the reduction of operational costs. These three concepts are the mantra of the value-based business. They appear under many forms, and are implemented through many solutions, but are constants whatever the area of business under scrutiny Ultimately they influence every business decision. From the point of view of the Act we see them come together in the financial report: the summary, as it were, of the decisions made, and a product of the quality of information available.

IT AND THE BUSINESS: THE VALUE OF INFORMATION

At origin, a business unit creates intellectual property, but it relies on the IT function for it to survive. That the modern business is so reliant on such systems is a dilemma that generates a tension between technical operation and business aspiration. We can distinguish between business processes that generate huge volumes of information, and IT processes that archive, store, and migrate it. However there is no common understanding of the value of the information. To the IT function, focused on the cost of storing data and its technical mechanisms, all information is data and all data is created equal. To the business units focused on inherent meaning and usage, all information is charged with business value. As a consequence, as information passes through the IT function, the visibility of its value is lost. To lose the value of information is to potentially lose the business. In short, IT processes do not fully understand the risk that IP loss poses to the modern enterprise. The links between value, business benefit, and the sources of value are severed.

When we look at these issues operationally, we see how this balance of cost and value in the life cycle of information preoccupies organizations. The Act directs them on what information must be saved and for how long. As we have seen, risk can be mitigated by the application of "risk tolerant" controls in ERM, or some other strategic approach. Balancing the cost of applying a strategy with the peace of mind that results from the knowledge that business information is compliant is of tremendous value to management. However, the sheer quantity of this stored data is increasing. Controlling and predicting capital expenditure on storage and retention is fundamental. Closely aligned with this is a dramatic increase in archiving costs, and a universal effort to manage retrieval and review to deliver operational cost savings.

The traditional approach to rising storage requirements compounds the problem rather than alleviates it. Simply adding more of the same cheap storage does little to improve retrieval times when the business is under pressure to operate in real time. When premium storage is used there is little awareness of prioritization based on the "value" of the information and content being stored. What is worse, the overall lack of visibility of these processes makes it almost impossible to effectively identify and deal with operational costs. Since relevance and value based on the originator and destination are not reflected in this regime, there is a further risk of IP loss through internal boundary breaches. The result is that current storage solutions deliver an unacceptable retrieval performance.

This is a vital ingredient in the mixed response to the Act at an operational level. Approaches that characterize IP protection from the perspective of storage have emerged. One is to save and store everything; another stores information according to the role of the originator, based on the status of the originator or originating department. Hence the CEO will have a higher storage priority and status than the receptionist; finance will have a higher status than facilities management. Other approaches are to store information according to its defined value, based on the originator, or to select and store according to company policies enforced through a form of life cycle management.

There are many questions that are uncomfortable for IT departments and difficult to quantify. How much of the content of email and instant messaging (IM) sessions should be stored? How are business and personal sessions identified and separated? How much of the stored data in high-cost systems consists of personal, non-business traffic? How can we be sure that the data stored is compliant with internal and external policies? What are the criteria of business protection, and how do they marry with the greater entity-wide issue of risk management?

These approaches assume a coincidence between actual customer requirements and archive and storage strategies. The response of vendors does not always reflect real market drivers. Organizations are now looking for archive solutions that "understand" electronic communications such as an email or instant messages based on their content, so they can make decisions such as where to store it and how long to store it for. As we have seen, this requirement is based on an understanding of its value. Organizations are also looking beyond rigid solutions to flexible and highly configurable packages that allow them to significantly reduce implementation and maintenance costs. The Act places a burden on the organization which exacerbates the overall tension between business and IT functions, and increases the size of the problem facing storage strategies.

How do we simultaneously meet the policy requirements of the Act, protect and preserve this vital business capital, and yet minimize the capital and operational costs associated with managing the risks? We need a solution that bridges the interests of business units and the IT function, founded on the value of information. The Act makes it clear that a rapid, responsive, and accurate retrieval system is not an optional luxury but a required business function. For the enterprise, its absence can be life-threatening. The ability to make intelligent business decisions predicated on an understood context is also critical; the capability to allow retrieved results, such as emails, to be isolated and reviewed by regulators while the business is fully aware of their context can make a great difference to the outcome of a punitive investigation.

Whatever this solution looks like, it must deliver proven financial benefits. It must be scrutinized for relevance to every area of IP protection; each must be identified, qualified, and quantified. Vendors and suppliers have responded to this approach by evolving frameworks that look at information as an end-to-end process. From this have emerged solutions such as ILM, based on understanding and acting on the sources of value to gain the maximum business benefit. ILM is explored further in our examination of solutions.

DOCUMENTS AND RECORDS: THE RISK OF INTELLECTUAL PROPERTY LOSS

Overwhelmingly, information and intellectual capital are captured in documentation. Even here we see another tension between IT and the dependent business. This is centered on the regulator's need for reliable evidence. It is something of a paradox. Generally the SEC and its regulators see documents and records as proof of intention or action, and they are viewed as "evidence." As a document is transformed into a record under standard IT practice, its meaning and context change. The evolution of records management as a separate discipline within IT is an acknowledgement of the importance of records as the collective intellectual capital of the business. However, for the Act, records management is the more important since the focus is generally on the fiscal and regulatory aspects of keeping records of a certain type for mandated periods of time. For the organization, there is also a parallel world of content management, with its focus on the value and meaning of the record for the business. But however they are defined, electronic documents are "soft" and malleable, and lawyers need evidence that does not change.

Generally the risk of IP loss is typified as the absence of information. To lose information is to be unable to locate and therefore use it. The severity of the loss is reflected in the degree to which the organization is incapacitated. IT might cover its responsibility to limit risk by providing back-ups, redundant fail-over systems, and disaster recovery. However, the act of storage does not in itself eliminate the strategic risk of IP loss. Vital information can be "lost" in a huge data store, since the business not being able to find and access information is equivalent to losing it! If it has not been identified as having a particular value, it could be anywhere on a series of back-up tapes. The cumulative operational costs of this "lost" information can cripple a service. Regulators see the inability to access data in a similar manner to data that is lost. It is simply not available to satisfy the enquiry.

A potent further source of IP loss is the "leakage" of value. Effective risk management can mark the "leakage" points, the points where information traverses a boundary or is lost. Tracking this process is a source of value in itself. Sharing information, intentionally or otherwise, is a risk-prone activity. The result is that much unfiltered information leaves the organization unsupervised. Webmail is used to avoid formal systems. Such external sharing of sensitive information means that information moves into a larger, almost public, domain, and is no longer under the company's control. Very often the absence of internal policies and tools forces an "all or nothing" approach to the release of business capital, resulting in extreme cases in a degrading of the business effectiveness of the organization. Emails are sent to the wrong recipients, often accidentally.

Although unstructured communications presents the greatest risk to many organizations, the fragility of electronic media also presents problems for storage and retention. Reliability is measured in years before degradation begins to have an impact. The problem is critically affected by bad storage conditions and procedures. Being "soft," electronic records are easily manipulated and overwritten. Because of this, regulations such as the Act tend to be specific in their storage and retention requirements, generally falling back on regulatory practice. Yet as we have established, even when successfully retrieved, electronic records are dependent on contextual information to establish their nature and purpose.

The loss of IP value to business can also occur at the heart of the IT organization. Often overlooked is the threat of poor accountability: records will be lost unless the right people protect them. Despite the best efforts of organizations to centralize information through systems such as enterprise resource planning (ERP), the tendency has long been towards a diversity of storage sites, from main system servers to individual desk-top hard drives. Departmental independence in choosing solutions exacerbates the problem, along with the consolidations, separations, mergers and acquisitions that typify corporate life. The wastage in storage systems outlined here concerns the lost value of information, and is generally caused by storage decisions being made from an IT perspective, where the cost of storage is dominant, as against the business perspective based on the value of what is being stored.

If information is the new currency of business and its possession represents wealth, then the contemporary organization must make every effort to acquire and protect it. This is more than a market trend. The recognition of the significance of intellectual property as the key company asset, on a par with its human resources, has placed a spotlight on the nature of stored capital. If valuable information is distinguished from mere data, and the meaning of this value in a business context is appreciated, decision making is enhanced by the ability to call upon this rich store. Protecting IP is not just another function of IT, but a collaborative exercise by all interested parties, including business units and the expertise of the legal arm. If it closes off the leakage of information, appreciates potential value, and develops a life cycle approach to the bearer of this value, the organization can respond to its potential, and adjust its behavior to manage the risks inherent in change. As the IT function works more closely with business units, the management of this information no longer merely responds to the short-term demands of regulation, but builds a deeper level of protection for the business. In effect, it is preparing the organization for ongoing compliance. The real benefit, aside from mitigating the risk of non-compliance with the Act, is that by preserving its intellectual capital and fostering its thought leadership the organization becomes truly intelligent, adding an edge to its decision making that transforms its competitiveness and takes it ahead of its rivals.

PRACTICAL COMPLIANCE SUMMARY

- As an information economy player, financial services must move information security to the center of the compliance effort.
- Secure effective financial reporting inputs through a secure system.
- Controls derived from security systems are appropriate (see Chapter 22).
- Clarify and quantify the value of the company's intellectual capital.

CHAPTER 22

Information Security

USING ISO 17799 AS A FRAMEWORK FOR COMPLIANCE

There are many approaches to building a satisfactory reference framework when considering how best to manage compliance. A framework that is gaining wide acceptance is the ISO 17799 standard.[1] Although its focus is on information security, it has a number of synergies with the concerns raised by the Sarbanes-Oxley Act:

- It stresses the importance of documenting compliance activities.
- It has an emphasis on the confidentiality, integrity, and availability of information.
- It stresses a structured approach to compliance, based on senior management authorization and a comprehensive acceptance of the need for all staff to be aware of and involved in the compliance effort.

A meta-framework could be reproduced by simply aping the steps and processes of the standard. Indeed, its similarities with other standards has been recognized. We might adapt the standard to suit our interests in the Act and examine and highlight best practice in the context of maintaining the security of the organization's information and intellectual capital.

The standard suggests a staged approach to readying the organization for compliance to the Act's requirements. Because it concerns building and maintaining an information security management system (ISMS), it has a natural interest in the detail of:

- asset identification
- risk assessment
- risk treatment.

The parallel metaprocess for the Act can use the risk assessment and treatment characteristics, and adapt the "asset" stages for identifying and evaluating risk, by substituting for assets business processes, or business objectives and needs.

DOCUMENTATION

In parallel with these steps is an ongoing task of documentation. This delivers demonstrable proof of the activities that are critical to the compliance process. The documentation itself follows a staged process. Table 22.1 illustrates a formal process, as recommended by the standard, and a parallel meta-process that might be applied to compliance. SMP is the abbreviation for a Sarbanes-Oxley metaprocess.

STATEMENT OF APPLICABILITY

The statement of applicability under the standard is a valuable tool in the strategic phase of the compliance process. Extended to the compliance process it is a statement that details the decisions made by the CTF on its choice of controls, as well as summarizing the compliance process itself. Formal versions of the statement are suggested by the standard, but under the Act there is no formal requirement or standard. Adopting an ISO 17799 version is an option. It constitutes an important part of the overall documentation, and one of its intended audiences is the external auditor, for whom this statement might be a first introduction to the compliance activities of the organization, and a positioning of those activities as part of the auditable scope.[2] A statement can be drafted once the work is under way, and its structure and intent could be adopted by the CTF for regular review. The time frame will depend on significant non-compliance incidents, but should be at least annually.

This is the formal document that makes the case for the CTF approach policy, and prepares the process for gaining approval from senior management. The wording of the controls will follow best practice, including:

- a description of the control requirement
- details sufficient for a third-party auditor to understand the reasons for the choice of this control
- any references to underlying documentation, where necessary.

ISO 17799 CONTROLS FOR COMPLIANCE

Types of control

Controls are a subset of control objectives; this is also paralleled in the COBIT approach. In this a "control objective" is a statement of an organization's intent to control some part of its processes or assets. It is a

Table 22.1 A comparison of ISO 17799 and the compliance process

Stage	ISO standard (ISMS)	Compliance (SMP)
1	Define the scope: Context and scope of the ISMS approach to information security. Consists of five stages: three initiate the planning process and two that finalize it.	Define the scope: Context and scope of the compliance regime.
2	Define a policy: Defines the process and establishes how it might be repeated. Sets up criteria for risk evaluation.	Define a compliance policy: Defines the compliance process and establishes how it might be repeated. Sets up criteria for risk evaluation.
3	Define a systematic approach to risk assessment: Includes a process for evaluating the likelihood of a risk to an asset, the impact of a breach of an asset's security requirements, and a definition of what is an acceptable risk.	Define a systematic approach to risk assessment: Includes a process for evaluating the likelihood of specific risks, the impact of a threat being realized, and a definition of what is an acceptable risk. (Using information security language, such as threat and vulnerability, might be useful in certain contexts.)
4 (ISMS Stage 8)	Statement of applicability: This is completed based on ISMS stage 7 (risk treatment) material. It is a formal document that reflects the risk assessment, the selection of controls, and the reasons for selecting or not selecting recommended controls (ISO 17799 controls).	Statement of applicability: This is a formal document that reflects the risk assessment, the selection of controls, and the reasons for selecting or not selecting recommended controls (these may be ISO 17799 controls or others such as COBIT).
5 (ISMS Stage 9)	Management approval: Completed documentation is submitted to senior management for approval.	Management approval: Completed documentation is submitted to senior management for approval, and where needed, budgetary sign-off.

strategic activity in that control objectives reflect the interests of the organization as a whole. They are tactical in their implementation through selected "controls" as processes and procedures. Selecting controls is part of the design process. In this design process a number of factors should be considered that shape the decision on a control:

■ It should be able to demonstrate its effectiveness, that it has been implemented and working.
■ It should reduce a risk to an acceptable level.
■ Failure in the control should be detectable.
■ It should be amenable to prompt remediation, if necessary.

The ISO 17799 standard has 12 major clauses, and there are 127 sub-clauses with associated controls. This body of controls is a resource for selecting and designing controls that fit the financial services company, and build the structure of compliance. Each selected control, from whatever source, will need to be documented, as above, and available for testing by internal and external auditors.

Control type and risk treatment

One of the common aims of an ISMS and the compliance process is to address identified vulnerabilities in the organization. To that end the standard suggests developing a treatment process. This is achieved by selecting and implementing a set of controls, which are characterized as policies, practices, procedures, organizational structures, and software functions, manual and automated. The compliance process can expand the normal controls, adopting security system controls. For "attack" in the following we can substitute "misuse." These controls are categorized as:

■ **Deterrent controls**. These discourage attack on the basis of the undesirable action to be taken from the point of view of the attacker. The consequences of an attack are made clear through this control.
■ **Preventive controls**. Although complete prevention is impossible, various levels of prevention can greatly limit an attack.
  – "Relative" prevention makes a successful attack difficult to realize.
  – "Partial" prevention slows down an attack.
  – "Technical" prevention adds software automation.
  – "Procedural" prevention is the most common, using manual procedures to stop human action or trap human misuse.
■ **Detective controls**. These are event driven, working closely with preventive controls to detect attacks and trigger responsive action. They can be technical or procedural.
■ **Corrective controls**. These are fallback controls, often occurring after the event as a recovery control, designed to fix problems, or as a contingency control on the failure of other controls.

Options for treatment

As controls operate they will detect risks. When a risk has been identified there are a number of options on how to treat it. The main alternatives are to:

- accept it
- avoid it
- transfer it
- control it.

The choice made will depend on how we prioritize risks according to the risk profile of the organization. This is founded on a good understanding of what are acceptable and unacceptable risks. If the organization has a risk-oriented approach, controls that are specific to managing and treating risk will be central. Risk factors are guiding principles for these controls. Categories used in tabulating risk include:

- **Critical process**: the process at risk that most requires treating through a control.
- **Risk**: the nature of the risk.
- **Risk level**: the current risk level before the application of a success control or controls. Determined in the risk assessment of information assets, it reflects the impact on the organization. (It is usually measured as high, medium, or low.)
- **Acceptable risk level**: the level of risk that the organization is happy to accept, which is the result of successful treatment through the application of a control or controls. (It is usually measured as high, medium, or low.)
- **Controls**: references to the defined controls to be applied, or those of a standard such as ISO 17799.
- **Comments**: information on the controls that will help in understanding their purpose for treating this risk, especially for reviewers and auditors.

Incident management

When a risk, misuse, security breach, or event that generates a compliance reaction is detected, a planned response is needed. Incident management is critical to the compliance cycle, to ensure the problem is not repeated or escalates to a weakness, and is conceptually part of the iterative process of continuous improvement. There needs to be a procedure or system for addressing the incident, which involves:

- a review of controls for effectiveness
- feedback into the compliance process, through the mechanisms of the compliance cycle

- review through techniques such as scenario modeling
- sufficient information on what to do in the event of a specific incident.

The nature of these incidents is that they are largely unpredicted and various. The need for a flexible response is paramount. An iterative approach that follows a PDCA cycle is of value here, especially coupled with the experience of internal auditing staff as a distillation of active best practice.

Since events have causes, root cause analysis (RCA) is a viable approach.[3] A sample incident illustrates the approach. A set of policy documents was published, through the intranet and through email, instructing staff on the advice to be given to customers. Unfortunately it specified the wrong advice. The discovery of this error was triggered by an internal audit of the call center, consisting of a walkthrough, using a cross-section of typical calls and cross-referencing them to recoded live calls to determine current practice. This created a need for clarification, since the call center staff were confused about which set of advice policies to use. The incident history and remediation process is as follows:

1. Material is posted out, and noticed to be different from what is expected by call center staff receiving enquiries on a new financial product.
2. Contact is made with management for guidance, and ad hoc discussions take place in which all involved try to understand the policy documentation. Effective change controls and versioning should ensure that a comparison can be made between live materials and stored materials.
3. There is an immediate review internally by staff responsible for policy materials, leading to a request for change control authorization to clarify the document. Exchange control is refined to avoid future incidents.
4. A revised, controlled version is published, relying on change controls to ensure integrity.
5. The CTF updates the information policy and statement of applicability at the next cyclical review.

Note the reliance on existing effective controls in steps 2 and 3, and modification of change controls in step 3. Incident management overlaps with contingency management, and controls relating to business continuity may be affected as part of the CTF review. This documented approach also adds to the compliance process audit trail, for input to a strategic review of the whole system of internal control. The above process, an incident response procedure, ensures that actions taken are controlled, appropriate, and careful. A sample documented version is given in Table 22.2. It follows a sequence that represents a sample rather than an exhaustive list of phases:

- **incident**: a brief description of the incident
- **phase live incident**: description of the symptoms
- **phase recovery**: description of circumstances of recovery and any sub-phases
- **activation criteria**: assessment criteria and countermeasures employed

Table 22.2 Sample incident management process

Incident	Phase		
A policy bulletin is incorrect	Live incident: The policy documents instruct staff to give the wrong advice to calling customers.	Activation criteria	The immediate countermeasure was to put a hold on this product, and take customer details for recontact. Notify process owners of the issue for correction.
		Strategy	The detail of the internal auditor's report is forwarded to the process owners and the CTF for action. Call center staff to be updated ASAP.
		Personnel	Call center staff, process owner, internal auditor, departmental manager.
	Recovery: Correct version is identified and versioned, then published through the intranet and by email to relevant staff.	Activation criteria	Review of controls and remediation, and versioning and control of managed updates.
		Strategy	The process is documented and incorporated into business policies, with a review of controls and compliance process documentation.
		Personnel	Internal auditor, senior manager, process owner, CTF authorizer to sign-off latest version as current version.

- **strategy**: a record of the planned responses
- **personnel**: staff responsible for dealing with incidents and those who have relevant expertise.

Management of incidents and improvements

The above incident illustrates the response to an incident and the way it can be captured in a formal way. There clearly needs to be a control objective and set of controls that deal with this. A sample expression of this is contained in Table 22.3, where it appears as a sample entry in a statement of applicability. This identifies the risk, its probability of occurring, the acceptable level of risk for the company, and appropriate controls applied to treat the risk, with comments. The control objective is to ensure that a consistent and effective approach is applied to the management of such incidents.

Table 22.3 Incident management and the statement of applicability

Critical asset	Risk	Risk level	Acceptable risk level	Control	Comments
Internal policies	A slow response by call center staff with poor or misleading information on a financial product risks repetition of business opportunity loss or customer dissatisfaction and action because of misleading information.	Medium	Low	(Numerical reference to specific control)	Establish management responsibilities and procedures for a quick response to incidents.
	Lack of measurement exposes the company to recurrent costs and product degradation.	High	Low	(Numerical reference to specific control)	The company, through the CTF, needs to learn from and address poorly defined policies, and quantify the costs.

Control objectives and controls

Under the standard, control objectives are defined and then detailed. The following tables indicate how these might be designed as actual controls. Control Objective A.5 Information Security Policy is expanded to indicate how the control can be defined and designed. Any of the ISO 17799 control objectives and controls can act as useful inputs to a set of controls for the compliance process (see Table 22.4).

Table 22.5 lists the main controls objectives for a number of categories, including: the organization of information security, asset management, human resources security, physical environment security, communications and operations management, access control, and business continuity management.

Reviewing controls is an important activity in between audits. This can be done ad hoc by control owners, and updates made at any time as long as they are approved and documented as part of the compliance process. We can further our understanding of potential controls by looking at some of the ISO 17799 controls is a little more detail.

Controls on organizational motivation

These controls are focused on management setting a clear policy direction and demonstrating support for the maintenance of a compliance and security system across the organization. They focus on providing management with support for direction and support for information security as a whole. Sample controls are expanded, and for others indication

Table 22.4 Control objective: information security policy

	Control	Detail	SOX relevance
A.5.1.1	Information security policy document	An information security policy document shall be approved by management, and published and communicated to all employees and relevant external parties	As a vital part of the controls systems, this can be incorporated into the compliance process
A.5.1.2	Review of the information security policy	The information security policy shall be reviewed at planned intervals, or if significant changes occur, to ensure its continuing suitability, adequacy, and effectiveness	Reviewed as part of the compliance process update and feedback reviews

Table 22.5 Sample control objectives and controls

Control objective	Control	Objective
A.6 Organization of information security	A.6.1 Internal organization	To manage information security within the organization
	A.6.2 External parties	To maintain the security of the organization's information and information processing facilities that are accessed, processed, communicated to, or managed by external parties
A.7 Asset management	A.7.1 Responsibility for assets	To achieve and maintain appropriate protection of organizational assets
	A.7.2 Information classification	To ensure that information receives an appropriate level of protection
A.8 Human resources security	A.8.1 Prior to employment	To ensure that employees, contractors, and third party users understand their responsibilities, and are suitable for the roles they are considered for, and to reduce the risk of theft, fraud, or misuse of facilities.
	A.8.2 During employment	To ensure that all employees, contractors and third party users are aware of information security threats and concerns, their responsibilities and liabilities, and are equipped to support organizational security policy in the course of their normal work, and to reduce the risk of human error
	A.8.3 Termination or change of employment	To ensure that employees, contractors, and third party users exit an organization or change employment in an orderly manner.
A.9 Physical and environmental security	A.9.1 Secure areas	To prevent unauthorized physical access, damage, and interference to the organization's premises and information
	A.9.2 Equipment security	To prevent loss, damage, theft, or compromise of assets and interruption to the organization's activities

Table 22.5 continued

Control objective	Control	Objective
A.10 Communications and operations management	A.10.1 Operational procedures and responsibilities	To ensure the correct and secure operation of information processing facilities
	A.10.2 Third party service delivery management	To implement and maintain the appropriate level of information security and service delivery in line with third party service delivery agreements
	A.10.3 System planning and acceptance	To minimize the risk of systems failures
	A.10.4 Protection against malicious and mobile code	To protect the integrity of software and information
	A.10.5 Back-up	To maintain the integrity and availability of information and information processing facilities
	A.10.6 Network security management	To ensure the protection of information in networks and the protection of the supporting infrastructure
	A.10.7 Media handling	To prevent unauthorized disclosure, modification, removal or destruction of assets, and interruption to business activities
	A.10.8 Exchange of information	To maintain the security of information and software exchanged within an organization and with any external entity
	A.10.9 Electronic commerce services	To ensure the security of electronic commerce services, and their secure use
	A.10.10 Monitoring	To detect unauthorized information processing activities

Table 22.5 continued

Control objective	Control	Objective
A.11 Access control	A.11.1 Business requirement for access control	To control access to information
	A.11.2 User access management	To ensure authorized user access and to prevent unauthorized access to information systems
	A.11.3 User responsibilities	To prevent unauthorized user access, and compromise or theft of information and information processing facilities
	A.11.4 Network access control	To prevent unauthorized access to networked services
	A.11.5 Operating system access control	To prevent unauthorized access to operating systems
	A.11.6 Application and information access control	To prevent unauthorized access to information held in application systems
	A.11.7 Mobile computing and teleworking	To ensure information security when using mobile computing and teleworking facilities
A.12 Information systems acquisition, development and maintenance	A.12.1 Security requirements of information systems	To ensure that security is an integral part of information systems
	A.12.2 Correct processing in applications	To prevent errors, loss, unauthorized modification, or misuse of information in applications
	A.12.3 Cryptographic controls	To protect the confidentiality, authenticity, or integrity of information by cryptographic means

Table 22.5 continued

Control objective	Control	Objective
	A.12.4 Security of system files	To ensure the security of system files
	A.12.5 Security in development and support processes	To maintain the security of application system software and information
	A.12.6 Technical vulnerability management	To reduce risks resulting from exploitation of published technical vulnerabilities
A.13 Information security incident management	A.13.1 Reporting information security events and weaknesses	To ensure information security events and weaknesses associated with information systems are communicated in a manner allowing timely corrective action to be taken
	A.13.2 Management of information security incidents and improvements	To ensure a consistent and effective approach is applied to the management of information security incidents
A.14 Business continuity management	A.14.1 Information security aspects of business continuity management	To counteract interruptions to business activities and to protect critical business processes from the effects of major failures of information systems or disasters and to ensure their timely resumption
	A.12.2 Correct processing in applications	To prevent errors, loss, unauthorized modification or misuse of information in applications

is given whether they form part of the statement of applicability or not. The control numbering is accordance with references to the standard, and they can be renumbered as necessary for the compliance control program. The comments are for a hypothetical company that has implemented controls. They indicate how far a control has been implemented; some controls are partially implemented for reasons of practicality or policy.

Controls that continue the responsibility of the organization to commit to the policy and compliance to the standard are also included. They

Table 22.6 Sample implementation of controls

Control	Entry Template	Comments
A.3.1.1 Information security policy document	The board and management of a financial services company, which operates in the financial services sector, and is located in New York, is committed to preserving the confidentiality, integrity, and availability of all the information assets throughout the organization in order to maintain the competitiveness, profitability, and image of the organization. These commitments are documented in detail as an information security policy, to which all employees and relevant third parties are required to comply. The board has documented, approved, published, and communicated this information security policy through the internal intranet to all relevant employees and third parties.	This control will be fully implemented throughout the organization and with third party partners and suppliers. The policy is available, read-only, for reference or inspection on the intranet.
A 3.1.2 Review and Evaluation	This control relates to the owner of the information security policy, the information security manager. It indicates when, and with what frequency the policy will be reviewed.	This control is fully implemented. More detail will be provided in the full statement of applicability.
A6.2.1	Identification of risks related to external parties.	This control is fully implemented. The company has many third-party partners.
A6.2.3	Addressing security in third-party agreements.	Agreements with third party trainers involve contractual discussions on IPR. As critical assets these must be controlled.

address the management of the compliance and security infrastructure in the organization, detailing other controlled areas such as:

- the remit of the CTF and the management information security forum contribution to the CTF
- a cross-functional forum to involve all functions within the organization
- specific roles and responsibilities within the CTF
- a management authorization process
- how and when specialist advice should be sought
- relevant contacts that will assist the organization in understanding and complying with legislation
- the nature of independent reviews of the compliance process in action.

These are not detailed here but would form part of the full statement of applicability.

Access control

Controlled access to information is vital for effective compliance, and is manifest as "physical" and "logical" control. Physical is strictly relevant when physical access to an area should be limited, and is typified by preventive controls, perhaps with additional detective controls. For financial services, logical control is often more broadly based, centered on restricted access to applications. In our instance of a misleading policy, restricted access should be only for those staff, mostly call-center staff, who have a real need for access. Even then, it would only be for a sub-set of call center staff, with limited access to this policy through a controlled email group, and to a controlled intranet area for that group.

In the compliance process there is a case for implementing all the access controls listed under the ISO 17799 standard. Some sample controls that may be included in a statement of applicability or equivalent are listed below.

Business requirement for access control

Objective: to control access to information.

Table 22.7 Controls and risk

Critical asset	Risk	Risk level	Acceptable risk level	Control(s)	Comments
Product sales policies	Poor access control might lead to materials being lost	Medium	Low	(numeric reference)	The current company access control policy is inadequate and needs review

User access management

Objective: to ensure authorized user access and to prevent unauthorized access to information systems.

Table 22.8 Controls and user access

Critical asset	Risk	Risk level	Acceptable risk level	Control(s)	Comments
Policy documen- tation	Weak user registration can lead to a range of risks to the assets, from modifica- tion to destruction, especially for versioning	Medium	Low	(numeric reference)	User registration needs an overhaul and a new policy instituted
	Lack of password control allows potentially unlimited access, especially from exter- nal hackers and other malicious sources	High	Low	(numeric reference)	Password schemes are ad hoc and not centrally controlled

Other controls from this section are relevant and might be implemented but are not detailed here.

User responsibilities

Objective: to prevent unauthorized user access, and compromise or theft of information and information processing facilities.

Other controls from this section are relevant and might be implemented,

Table 22.9 User responsibilities

Critical asset	Risk	Risk level	Acceptable risk level	Control(s)	Comments
Training materials	Poor user use of passwords exposes assets to loss and modification	Medium	Low	(numeric reference)	The company needs to establish best practice use of passwords

but they are not detailed here. The company might consider a single sign-on (SSO) approach for all relevant staff, including externally based consultants. Traditionally SSO has proved hard to implement. It should also be reviewed as a potential weakening of defense in depth for security, and undermines localization and departmentalization of information assets.

Correct processing in applications

Objective: to prevent errors, loss, unauthorized modification or misuse of information in applications. The example here is the use of training materials, either on compliance or compliance-related issues, or in general.

Business continuity

A framework for business continuity management is essential for ongoing security. For the integrity of the company and its business, and hence compliance, it is essential that provision has been made for this. This should pull together departmental and functional controls and strategic controls to shape the business. The compliance process requires any plan or set of processes to be tested regularly. Table 22.11 lists a number of testing options.

Information security aspects of business continuity management

Objective: to counteract interruptions to business activities, to protect critical business processes from the effects of major failures of information systems, or disasters, and to ensure their timely resumption.

MANAGEMENT APPROVAL

The ISO 17799 standard is keen to ensure not only that senior management are directly involved in the security process, which is very much in line

Table 22.10 Correct processing

Critical asset	Risk	Risk level	Acceptable risk level	Control(s)	Comments
Training materials	Invalid data can lead to risk from copyright infringement and misquotation as well as offensive material (dated material can have "dated" references)	High	Low	(numeric reference)	This control is vital for the integrity of the materials. Validation is especially needed.
	Unvalidated data can lead to misstatement and inaccurate data, risking libel and disclosure	Medium	Low	(numeric reference)	If possible, control of internal processing and validation should be incorporated into applications such as MS Word. This may not be a full implementation because of skills shortages.

with the compliance process, but also that management approval for all important activities is present and consistent. This also marries well with our ideal of the responsibility cascade, so that ownership is pushed down through the organization, and managers and owners at all levels are accountable for their contribution to the compliance process. When the CTF has defined the compliance cycle objectives, set measurements and controls in place against these objectives, and assigned responsibilities for monitoring the policy in action, senior management should sign off the compliance process. Ultimately this is part of their assessment of internal controls and their sign-off in line with Sections 302 and 404. However, this approval cannot be assumed without accountability throughout the process.

Table 22.11 Testing options

Business continuity test	Example description (staff training)
Table-top testing	of failures in training aids for customer-facing staff in the training environment through non-delivery, loss, or corruption of material
Simulations	of course preparation in production; these could be used for internal awareness training depending on who is involved in the simulation
recovery to an alternative site	where a course is diverted along with its support materials and equipment; or standard system operations, such as networking, moved to an alternative site

Table 22.12 Business continuity

Critical asset	Risk	Risk level	Acceptable risk level	Control(s)	Comments
Policy materials	Without a managed process these assets are at risk of loss and modification	Medium	Low	(numeric reference)	Information security must be included in the business continuity management process
	A lack of consistency in planning or prioritization leads to asset risks through loss and destruction	High	Low	(numeric reference)	A business continuity planning framework needs to be implemented

For a financial services company it may be prudent to introduce some additional management approval steps.

Throughout the stages of the implementation of the ISMS there can be sign-off steps for:

- documentation (common to all): management could sign off at every milestone
- risk identification: sign off when assets have been identified and classified
- risk assessment: sign off on completion of this phase
- risk treatment: sign off when controls have been established and the Statement of Applicability is complete and approved.

In this way senior management involvement is maintained to ensure they are aware of this overall process. Care must be taken to prevent any sign-off point from becoming an opportunity to stall progress, either deliberately or unintentionally.

PRACTICAL COMPLIANCE SUMMARY

- Adapt ISO 17799 risk assessment process and controls to broaden the types of control available beyond preventative and detective controls.
- Use a staged sign-off in the compliance cycle. Maintain senior management involvement through this continuous sign-off.
- Adapt options for treatment.
- Use a statement of applicability to summarize the compliance process, and a system of internal controls for internal and external use.
- Utilize incident management processes.
- Build ISMS relevance through examples of incident scenarios. Mount an internal competition for realistic company scenarios.
- Use scenarios in training awareness. Involve senior managers as sponsors and maintain their involvement in training awareness programs.

NOTES

1. The ISO17799 standard is based on the BS 7799 model. It has been through a number of iterations and has been tested in a wide range of organizations.
2. This is the statement of applicability, as specified in clause 4.2.1.h of BS 7799-2 2002.
3. Root cause analysis (RCA) is also known as cause and effect analysis.

PART V

Solutions for Compliance: Joining the Dots

CHAPTER 23

Frameworks for Compliance: COSO and COBIT

COSO: AN INTRODUCTION

Although each organization is unique, culturally and operationally, and the financial sector has a great variety in the way its organizations operate and do business, nevertheless there are fundamental features that can be abstracted and considered to be common to all. The Act refers to organizations that are publicly listed on the US stock exchange. Our interest here is in financial services organizations. The PCAOB goes further in its assumptions, and establishes a key factor: any assertions on controls are no longer voluntary, but mandated by the Act, and they must be backed by evidence derived from a recognized internal control framework. It then makes specific reference to a specific framework, and insists that organizations should either adopt this control framework, or have frameworks that cover the competences through internal controls defined within that recommended framework. This is a key factor for compliance with the Act, and the reference model is that of COSO.

What is COSO?

The Committee of Sponsoring Organizations of the Treadway Commission, generally abbreviated to COSO, is a private-sector organization in the United States, created in 1985 to identify and make recommendations on the underlying factors causing fraudulent financial reporting. It is "sponsored" and funded by five influential professional accounting associations and institutes: the American Institute of Certified Public Accountants (AICPA), American Accounting Association (AAA), Financial Executives Institute (FEI), Institute of Internal Auditors (IIA), and Institute of Management Accountants (IMA).

As a result of perceived corporate and political finance malpractices and foreign corrupt practices in the 1970s, the SEC and the US Congress enacted the 1977 Foreign Corrupt Practices Act (FCPA). This instituted law reforms that obliged companies to implement internal control programs. The Treadway Commission was a private-sector response. It was the short name for the National Commission on Fraudulent Financial Reporting. Created in 1985, the Treadway Commission recommended that participating organizations develop a reference model for guidance on suitable internal controls. COSO and Coopers & Lybrand produced a report in 1992, *Internal Control: Integrated Framework*. Over time, and through public consultation, COSO has evolved a definition of internal controls, standards, and criteria against which companies and organizations can measure themselves. As a best-practice reference, it is a de facto standard for US companies evaluating their compliance with the FCPA.

COSO and IT controls

The approach is focused on developing a framework for controls for IT, acknowledging that IT systems are now fundamental to the success of business information systems and business processes. The features of controls we have explored elsewhere are found in the COSO framework, notably that:

- a control is a process; a transient element that provides a conduit for something of value to the organization
- people are the real processing elements in an organization, and setting internal controls is directed at changing or maintaining their behavior
- internal controls are limited in what they can achieve: as mechanisms and processes that provide evidence of effectiveness; but effectiveness is a behavioral issue.

The COSO definition of internal control overlaps with other definitions we have encountered: it is a process under the management of an company's board of directors, management, and other personnel, and is designed to deliver reasonable assurance on the effectiveness and efficiency of operations, and the reliability of financial reporting.

THE FIVE COMPONENTS OF COSO

The Treadway Commission was not concerned simply with the creation and implementation of internal controls. It was interested in practically ensuring that internal controls were effective in the face of legislation that demanded such controls were doing their job. This framework consists of five components which allow an organization to articulate, describe, analyze, and monitor its internal control system. These five components that are central to the framework for delivering effective internal controls:

- control environment
- risk assessment
- control activities
- information and communication
- monitoring.

A brief examination of each of these components affords an insight into the thinking behind the Treadway Commission's perspective.

Control environment

The control environment is the high-level context for internal control. Its scope is the whole company: its management at all levels, its people, its resources, and its processes. In this sense it reflects the culture of the company, the way it likes to do business, and its overall mission. It is also reflected in company policies that influence the attitude of staff and act as a measurable context for implementing change. Most importantly, it provides structure and a reference for decisions for change and the implementation of new business processes. The COSO reference sees this as the foundation for all other components of internal control. Its factors clearly reflect governance issues and the need to manage issues that affect the ethical status of the company, including:

- the operating style and attitude of management to people as well at the business
- the way authority is handled, delegated, and responded to
- the integrity of business and staff activities
- the assumed ethical values of the business.

Table 23.1 indicates key indicators (CE1—CE6) that link the control environment and IT. These indicators are generalized statements that have considerable consequences for the compliance project. They can either be one-off events or processes (0), or represent ongoing activities (1). These consequences are explored as practical compliance points throughout our discussion.

The control environment practical tips or actions listed in Table 23.2 add to our working model of practical compliance.

Risk assessment

The management of risk is a fundamental factor in all business activity. The

Table 23.1 Control environment indicators

Indicator	Statements	Consequences	Freq.
CE1	IT is often viewed as separate from the core business	Managing IT functions as a separate control environment contradicts the reality of the integration of IT and business activities.	[1]
CE2	IT is complex, technically and as the infrastructure for doing business	Seeing IT simplistically as separate (see CE1) and self-contained underestimates the complexity of IT's involvement in business and leads to incomplete compliance assessments and awareness of its place in the overall system of internal control.	[0]
CE3	IT can be a source of new and unaccounted-for risks	All IT change carries risk. This means managing through controls and monitoring activities for effective mitigation.	[1]
CE4	IT skills may be in short supply	IT, as a technology world is skills-intensive. It also has a fast changing skill base, which needs to be replaced or updated regularly. Often regarded as a per-person one-off "investment," it is really a continuous process of investment.	[0]
CE5	IT relies on third parties for processes and components.	Whether fully or partially outsourced., few IT departments are self-sufficient in skills and resources.	[0]
CE6	IT control ownership is often ill defined	The ownership of IT systems is muddied by their integration into overall business processes and activities. Compliance has an essential need to clarify this.	[0]

risk profile of a company is a working reflection of the way the business assesses risk and manages it on a daily basis. This profile is derived from the mission of the company, the business objectives that realize this mission, the potential threats and vulnerabilities to threats of these objectives, and the

Table 23.2 Control environment actions for practical compliance

Indicator	Actions	Ref
CE1	Align IT with business by involving IT management in business planning. Use elements of ITIL/COBIT. IT in risk assessment. Assign role responsibility to IT for analyzing how IT can help business plan more efficiently. Regular involvement of business managers in IT planning Establish "shared budgeting" for compliance activities (define these jointly at board and departmental level). Develop a joint policy based on behavior change (e.g. email use).	[1]
CE2	Top down analysis of IT systems. Use departmental feedback to establish usage of systems (by business functions). Establish scale of IT investment.	[0]
CE3	Review or gap analysis of IT risks identified, and analyze any "new" systems or upgrades for additional risks. Use ISO 17799 processes for this. Manage through ITIL (references).	[1]
CE4	BPM, ERP etc systems have IT-specific skills areas—also ILM—storage, email, document control, networking, systems integration, workflow, access controls etc. Gap analysis on skills needed to identify these for evaluating compliance.	[1]
CE5	Identify outsourced systems and activities. Bring these into or make them aware of corporate or organizational objectives and needs. Include then in the compliance process. Evaluate risks and any changes in relationship (there might be greater risks for third parties).	[0]
CE6	Organizational structure of IT. Who "owns" (is responsible for effective working and maintenance) of IT controls? Note integration of business functions and unclear overlap without defined responsibilities—such as segregation of duties. Need for cooperation and collaboration (define the two). Application-specific controls—dependencies between system and application controls, and blurred ownership.	[0]

degree to which the risks are acceptable or not. However the assessment is carried out, it must be thorough and realistic. It must assess:

■ company level risk: organizational, board-level, strategic
■ activity level risk: departmental, process, or transaction
■ external risk: malicious disruptive activity, market volatility, non-compliance, acts of God
■ internal risk: malicious or accidental staff activities, systemic failures, poor systems and processes.

Managing and treating risk is a valuable consequence of risk assessment, and is made effective through the implementation of a system of internal control.

Using the COSO/ITGI levels of assessment (see Table 23.3), we can show that risk assessment may occur at "company" level, affecting the whole company, and at the "activity" for processes within business units or company functions.

Control activities

The policies and procedures that are implemented throughout the organization are the manifestations of "control activities." These comprise any of

Table 23.3 Risk assessment levels

Risk assessment level	Indicator	Organizational function	Responsibilities
Company level	RA1	IT planning subcommittee subject to the Sarbanes–Oxley task force or steering committee	The review of an IT strategic plan for internal control. The implementation of the plan and its integration with the Sarbanes-Oxley compliance process or project. The assessment of IT risks.
Activity level	RA2	Departmental owners of compliance	Formal risk assessments built throughout the systems development methodology
	RA2	Departmental owners of compliance	Risk assessments built into the infrastructure operation and change process
	RA3	Departmental owners of compliance	Risk assessments built into the program change process

the myriad practices developed to address each control objective that is part of the risk assessment and help mitigate that risk. They ensure that discipline is a reality, in the form of management action at all levels.

In developing its model, COSO recognized that for companies to truly produce reliable financial reports to meet the FCPA, they need to address the integrated nature of IT and business activity. It identified two groupings of controls for decision making and information systems: general controls and application controls.

General controls

These controls are, as their name suggests, controls that affect the organization generally. They ensure that the information generated by the business for the purposes of financial reporting can be relied upon. Table 23.4 explores a number of controls; each one is discussed in a similar manner to Table 23.2.

Application controls

Application controls are controls that are either part of COTS software or written into in-house or outsourced software. In this sense they are not external to the software but part of the software package itself. They may also be controls external to the software but introduced to perform the same function. Such controls need maintenance, and should be adjusted to match software revisions where necessary, and maintained and upgraded accordingly. Much depends on the IPR agreement surrounding the software itself. Responsibility for this may vary:

■ If the controls are part of the software their maintenance may be included in the software maintenance contract.
■ If especially written by an external agency, such as contracted systems integrators, they may be maintained by this agency.
■ If they have been written in-house, then responsibility for maintenance rests with the originating department.

Generally, these controls exist as preventive measures to avoid unauthorized or other actions subject to general controls. Their strength is realized in combination with other controls. They help ensure some key objectives associated with the general internal control process for processing transactions:

■ completeness
■ accuracy
■ authorization
■ validity.

Table 23.4 General controls

Indicator	Statements	Consequences	Freq.
CAG1	General data center controls	Examine existing controls. Job set-up. Scheduling and prioritization of controls. Should reflect business priorities. Actions (operators) part of "cultural" review of staff—trained and aware of compliance needs, e.g. on data retention. Backup: are systems "compliant" and retrieval processes "timely"? Recovery: business continuity, critical controls for the integrity of the business.	[1]
CAG2	General system software controls	System software life cycle database management support systems software for all areas. Prioritization for compliance. Compliance software tools. Software levels—changes and implications for compliance.	[1]
CAG3	General access security controls	These may be built into an existing framework such as BS/ISO 17799, use of system and access to changes—change control user profiles. Review these for risks. Perhaps introduce new software or framework to manage this.	[1]
CAG4	Application system development and maintenance controls	Controls over new products and application introduction. Design and roll-out processes e.g. new desk-top OS roll-outs. Implications for applications for users, for access, for transactions, storage, capital expenditure, third party skills, and so on. Documentation of change management. Approvals, checks, and controls. Oungoing maintenance, contracts, and approvals.	[1]

Examples of application controls indicators are listed in Table 23.5.

Table 23.5 Application controls

Indicator	Control types	Activities	Freq.
CAA1	Balancing controls	Detect data entries—reconciling transactions entered against billing	[0]
CAA2	Check digits	Using part numbers, product codes by product and vendor	[0]
CAA3	Data listings	User selection from forced lists on product selections (versus free selection), criteria to meet conditions of purchase—often web based for call center intranets	[0]
CAA4	Data reasonableness (and testing of this)	Captures exceptions, or improbable sales matches—measuring such as actual against likely scale of an investment, based on disposable income	[0]
CAA5	Logic tests	Reference "standards" (eg SWIFT, crediit card formats). Often automated, known limits of product types, some checks are manual. On the whole, number based.	[0]

Information and communication

An area of focus for control systems is the way information is identified, categorized, processed and used as input for financial reporting. For the financial sector, information is the raw material from which products and packages are produced. The markets are really mechanisms for exchanging information, and the financial report itself is of interest for the Act in so far as it provides information on which decisions can be made. Therefore it is not surprising to see COSO place some emphasis on this. The identification, communication, and management of information is central to the effectiveness of controlling the value of the business. It underpins and supports the other COSO essential components of effective internal control.

This key role of information is underlined by the ITGI comment: "The IT organization processes most financial reporting information." In a sense, information systems are fundamental to internal control systems since information is the raw material for all reports, operational, financial, and compliance-related. For many organizations information not only ensures the running of the business, it *is* the business. Communications are the way information is transferred for the purposes of decision making, either internally, or externally by the customer or investor. Effective communication extends to all parties: customers, suppliers, regulators, and investors.

However, information management for the business is not the focus of the Act. Well managed but inaccurate information can coexist with accurate data. It is the quality of information for financial reporting that is critical. This has been identified by COSO, and the questions asked of such information lead to some fundamental indicators, which are detailed in Table 23.6. These indicators are subdivided into "general," "company," and "activity" levels, in line with previous indicators. For the compliance process, we indicate whether they are strategic (s), tactical (t), or both.

Monitoring

Nothing improves, no activity adds value, to an organization without being monitored, and monitored to match it against a benchmark or agreed ideal to which it aspires. Monitoring for us addresses the most important activity of providing oversight of the internal control system. Broadly speaking, monitoring processes are either continuous in nature, providing ongoing updates on a process through a number of continuous, discrete checks and tests, or they are one-off, separate checks to evaluate the process. Sometimes the distinction is blurred: a continuous process may consist of a number of widely spaced separate checks; a one-off system may look much the same but be treated as separate checks and not part of a continuum. However they are defined, control systems do need to be monitored to ensure the quality and the effectives of the system is reviewed, and its performance is rated for change. Through monitoring, bad practice (as bad habits), deficiencies, and inherent weaknesses in a process can be identified for remediation. Most quality systems are premised on such monitoring. In this sense the compliance project is a quality system focused on monitoring the effectiveness of internal controls.

PERFORMANCE MEASURES

To understand how well a process is operating, there is a need for performance indicators or measures such as key performance indicators (KPIs). Table 23.8 lists a number of these indicators.

Table 23.6 Information quality indicators

Indicator	Description	Activities	
	General indicators		
IC1	Appropriate	Is the information the most relevant?	[s]
IC2	Timely	Is the information able to be made available within defined time periods? This is particularly important for regulatory inspection when information is expected to be made available almost in real time.	[t]
IC3	Current	Is the information up-to-date, reflecting the latest data?`	[t]
IC4	Accurate	Is the information correct? Has it undergone sufficient checks to determine its accuracy?	[t]
IC5	Accessible	Is the information available to individuals who need to access it, in a timely way and with a reasonable degree of ease?	[t]
	Company-level indicators		
IC6	Corporate policies	How well are company policies framed for ease of use, ease of access, and promoted?	[s]
IC7	Reporting requirements	How well are such requirements met for supplying content within formats against deadlines?	[s]
IC8	Financial information	How well is financial information communicated and consolidated for financial reporting?	[s]
	Activity level		
IC9	Standards	How well are established and new standards recognized, and met to underpin corporate activities and policies?	[s], [t]
IC10	Information	How well does the organization manage information in general, through frameworks such as information life cycle management (ILM)?	[s]
IC11	Security violations	How well is the information made secure against misuse, malicious and accidental threats, and suported by business continuity measures?	[t]

Table 23.7 Monitoring indicators

Indicator	Description	Activities	
	General indicators		
MC1	Internal audits	Ongoing and one-off audits of effectiveness and testing of internal controls following change	[1]
MC2	External audits	Generally one-off investigations or snapshots of the state of health of internal controls	[0]
MC3	Regulatory investigations	Generally one-off investigations for testing of compliance or following irregularities	[0]
MC4	Penetration tests and security reviews	Security testing of systems and processes to uncover vulnerabilities	[0] [1 as part of the CP]
MC5	Capacity tests	Internally audited and tested as well as external tests	[1]
MC6	IT effectiveness reviews	Carried out by IT departments (internal)	[1]
MC7	Self-assessments	Ongoing point tests against controls in stages of a process by operators	[1]
MC8	Implementation reviews	Generally part of a roll-out; project plan management	[0]
	Company level		
MC9	Computer operations	Continuous monitoring by departmental and section elements, as well as ad hoc tests	[1]
MC10	Centralized security	IT function-level reviews of security	[0] [1 as part of the CP cycle]
MC11	Internal audit reviews	Audit committee reviews of company as a whole	[0]

Table 23.7 continued

Indicator	Description	Activities	
	Activity level		
MC12	Defect management	Operational noting of weaknesses and poorly working processes or stages of a process	[1]
MC13	Local monitoring	General awareness in everyday operations of security and performance weaknesses	[1]
MC14	Personnel supervision	Person management of IT staff, built into appraisal and ad hoc processes to improve process work through training etc.	[1]

Table 23.8 Performance measures

Indicator	Description	Activities	Benefit
MP1	Process defects	Measuring activities in a process. Comparing and analysing trends.	Isolate weaknesses. Fix weaknesses. Plan upgrades.
MP2	Process security	Assess access and usage. Manage authorization. Checks on availability. Measure IT investment use.	Uncover threats. Isolate vulnerabilities. Fix vulnerabilities. Plan upgrades. Reassign budgets.
MP3	Process integration	Measure process-to-process interaction. Analyze inadequacies such as incomplete integration.	Expose weak links. Expose dependencies. Remediate interfaces between processes.

COBIT

Introduction and summary

The relationship between financial reporting, IT functions, COSO recommendations, and reference frameworks for managing IT and security is meshed together within the concept known as COBIT (control objectives for information and related technology). It bridges the perceived gaps between business risks, controls needs, and technical issues (see Figure 23.1). All three of these linked subjects are pertinent to the compliance process, and COBIT offers a unique approach for managing the complexities of these relationships.

The COBIT mission is stated as:

> To research, develop, publicize and promote an authoritative, up-to-date, international set of generally accepted information technology control objectives for day-to-day use by business managers and auditors.

In its documented form, COBIT is released by the COBIT steering committee and the IT Governance Institute (ITGI).

COBIT evolved as a means of establishing best practice in this arena to help management make good decisions in a practical way. It has the virtue of attempting to relate the abstracts of business discipline to the practicalities of organizational reality. It recognizes that information is a critical business asset, and that this asset is dependent on the quality of the IT function for its security, integrity, and ultimate business value. However, the use of technology aligned to business carries risk; existing and new technologies add to and compound this risk. Regulation, such as the Act, demands tighter control over information and its attendant risks. Managing these risks are now part of enterprise governance (see Figure 23.2).

The significance of IT governance is now such that the health of a business is a reflection of its state of development and the degree to which it delivers effective enterprise processes. This is core to the interest of the Act, and leads to the significance of controls on processes. COBIT positions itself as a mechanism for ensuring that IT governance is an effective link between the interests and objectives of the business as an enterprise, and the interests and objectives of the IT function, expressed through its support for business processes (see Figure 23.1).

IT governance is defined by COBIT as "A structure of relationships and processes to direct and control the enterprise inn order to achieve the enterprise's goals by adding value while balancing risk versus return over IT and its processes." The pressure of regulation bears down on an organization. The response through IT governance is to implement or refine activities through best practice. This is expressed, according to the COBIT model, through attention to IT performance on:

- planning and organizing
- acquiring and implementing
- delivering and supporting
- monitoring.

These areas of activity are translated into "domains" of processes, and these processes are subject to controls in order to achieve best-practice significance. COBIT then sets about delivering "control objectives," with detailed practical controls that offer a comprehensive blueprint for tackling the many technical issues that arise from managing complexity. COBIT does this while offering the concerned manager its focus on business risk, and interest in aligning all that happens to the objectives of the enterprise. In this way it drives IT governance as a unifying "bridge" to link all interested sets of objectives: enterprise, business, IT, and regulatory. These interrelationships are represented in Figure 23.1.

Some key points can be extracted here:

- IT governance is seen as a suite of relationships and processes.
- These relationships and processes are to be governed by best practice, and tied to enterprise objectives as well having to respond to regulatory requirements.
- Best practice, as a consensus on what constitutes the most effective and efficient way of doing something, along with a working framework, is of especial value to management that have to ensure that an internal control system in place to support business processes.
- COBIT establishes how specific control activities satisfy the information requirements of the Act.

The documentation states that "Business orientation is the main theme of COBIT." It is not surprising that its guiding principles are for managers. The central domains are driven by management activities, but COBIT has additional audiences in auditors and general users. Each of the control objectives is accompanied by management guidelines.

COBIT framework tools

COBIT includes guidance and tools that are of real value for the compliance process:[1]

- "Management guidelines" which offer guidance to management on dealing more effectively with IT governance. The advice is generic, as it would have to be to achieve universal endorsement, but it is also practical, and related directly to organizational goals and measuring organizational achievement.
- It also provides "maturity models" for management assessment of where they are on the compliance process.
- In addition it introduces familiar management tools such as critical success factors (CSFs) for prioritizing controls, key goal indicators

(KGIs) for measuring business objective achievement, and KPIs for measuring the processes themselves.

■ It has introduced an "implementation tool set" based on experience of implementing the framework. This include analysis tools:
  – management awareness diagnostic
  – IT control diagnostic.

COBIT and information

Information is the starting and end point of the COBIT project in that it is this that is the subject of processes, business, and IT. It is this that ultimately forms the basis of management decision making and reporting. COBIT places information at the heart of its cycle of activity. In particular it focuses of the integrity of this information, and its:

■ effectiveness
■ efficiency
■ confidentiality
■ integrity
■ availability
■ compliance
■ reliability.

These attributes of information are managed through IT and its resources in terms of:

■ people
■ application systems
■ technology
■ facilities
■ data.

COBIT audiences

The sympathy of those drawing up COBIT is certainly well placed. Management of all kinds now have a range of responsibilities not originally envisioned before the days when ubiquitous IT and allied technologies expanded access to information. The explicated stated COBIT audiences are managers, users of IT, and auditors.

Managers

For managers the primary tasks are linked to decision making. They have to:

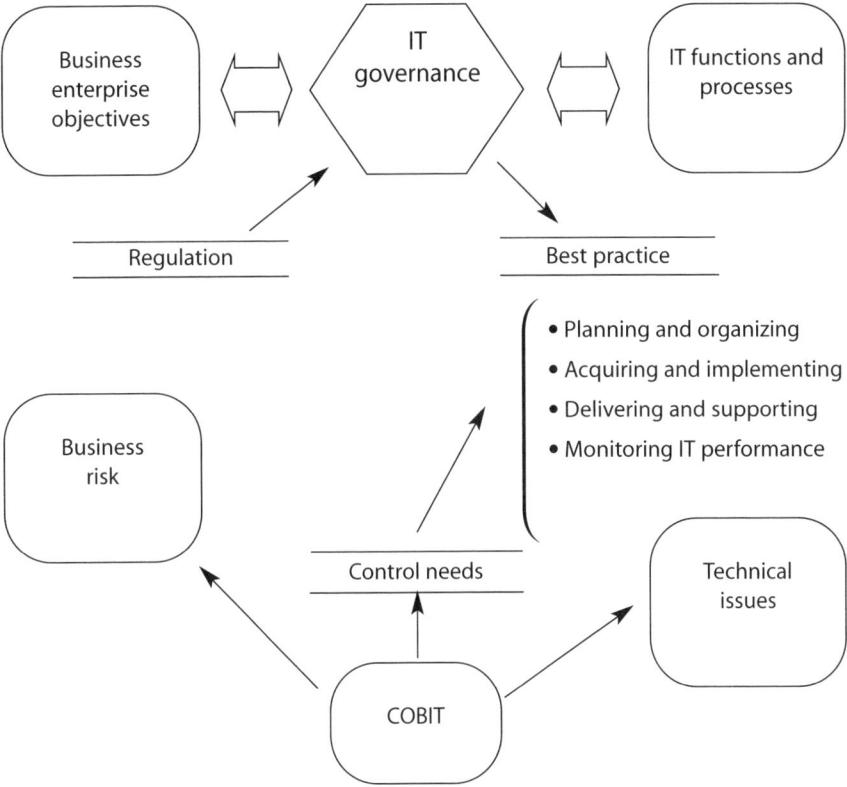

Figure 23.1 COBIT and compliance

- decide what kinds of IT investment to make within budgetary restraints
- anticipate technological change and unpredictable markets which include rapid growth, sudden technological breakthroughs, and sudden collapses, as witnessed by the dot.com boom
- identify risks and reduce them as far as possible with the tools, systems, and skills available
- balance risks against the organization's risk profile for risk tolerance
- be involved in issues of information security, and respond to direction from above to support new initiatives
- be supported in all these activities by a reference model of some kind, if planning and response are to be consistent and achieve measurable targets.

Auditors

A special audience for frameworks is that represented by auditors, who have a double task to perform. They must audit the financial information, and also attest to management's assessment that the controls in place are effective. This should place them in a unique position when it comes to assessing controls, and we might assume that they have a unique ability to involve themselves in the compliance process. However, it is clear that they need to adopt frameworks as a reference. Without an objective reference, stating and verifying an opinion is very difficult. This need is clear from the PCAOB's AS2, which is a reaction to this very need.

Business users

In a sense the control framework is designed around users. They are the users of processes. They interact with IT systems on a daily basis, and in a very practical way link IT support tools with business activity. Best practice translates into policies, which they have to observe. The controls placed on these processes and policies are the measured elements of the compliance system. There is also the pressing requirement to keep practical skills up to date in pursuit of business excellence and efficiency.

IT GOVERNANCE

We have already observed the connection between COBIT and IT governance, and the definition of IT governance espoused by the ITGI. Another way of elaborating on this connection is to position IT governance within the context of enterprise or corporate governance. Figure 23.2 is a diagrammatic representation of this context. The cascade of objectives from board level, which operates at a strategic level, to the tactical level of departmental objectives, captures the hierarchy of instruction and direction that all organizations expect. However flat the organization, this cascade occurs to some extent. Business and IT functions then inherit specific objectives.

In a sense, all staff carry responsibility for the well-being of the organization. However, ownership and responsibility are normally subdivided and refined as the cascade follows stratification. Financial service organizations are not exempt from this. The discipline of IT governance is often separated, and elaborated within "siloed" functional areas for reasons of manageability. One effect of regulation is to reinforce the integration that is inherent in the reality of business. Investment in IT and compliance efforts are coupled. The final decision context is enterprise well-being, and IT is now understood to be critical to this, not just as the keeper of information as business capital, but as the source of risk mitigation.

A critical step is to understand IT as not simply as the delivery mechanism for a company strategy, but an integral part of the strategy itself. Equally, the IT function is not just the way we ensure compliance, it is the subject of compliance as well. As an abstract, IT governance provides the linkage between information and processes, and the objectives of the enterprise. IT governance is an integration mechanism for delivering compliance.

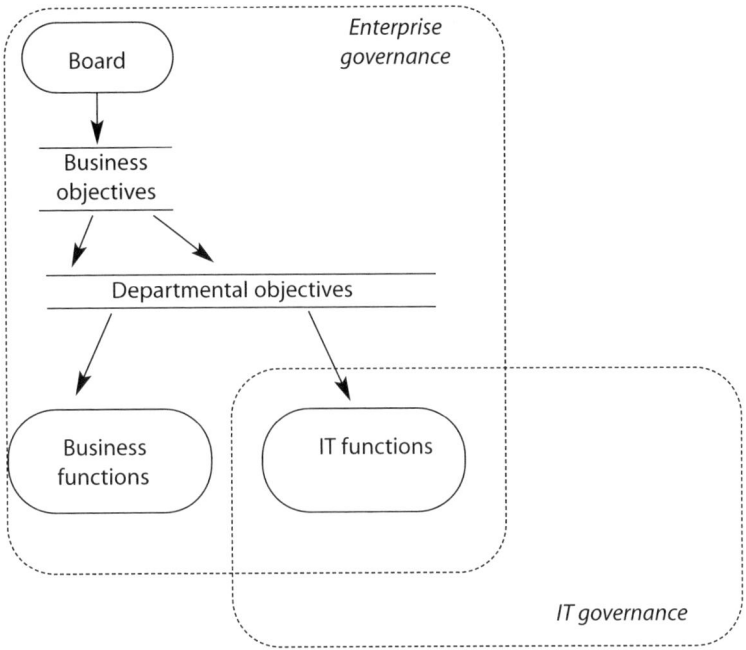

Figure 23.2 Enterprise and IT governance in context

The interplay between these elements is made clear at the point of selecting systems and applications. These are chosen for their value and capabilities in matching the business needs of the organization. However, in very large organizations, such decisions may have a bias: towards cost, for example, or integration capabilities, or perhaps their operational overhead. The specific business need can be met in a number of ways, so how then do we chose a specific solution? Add in compliance as a requirement, and the list of selection criteria can be further imbalanced. Effective IT governance provides a degree of assurance to managers who have to make such choices. We can see this when external consultancies are employed to write tender documents for complex projects. They take on the burden of defining selection criteria.

Dependencies

Enterprise governance provides "direction." The IT function provides resources to the enterprise. This pattern of dependence is common to many organizations. In effect, the controls in place are on resources, if they are defined as processes and policies made real by IT activities. Enterprise governance controls are really those controls absorbed by other governances such as IT governance. In this way, to ensure that objectives are met, management "directs" the IT function in its activities with an eye on the balance of risk and prioritized business activity and interest. To do this it will want a degree of assurance that all is well. To meet this it will need to measure the activities, and place the measurements in the context of a benchmark of some kind.

IT governance fulfils this role as well—providing measurable benchmarks to demonstrate that it is working in the best interests of business information. This sense of a system, controlled, measured, and working towards a goal against a set of business objectives, is an ideal to which COBIT aspires, and to which our compliance process looks when developing an organizational response to the Act.

Management guideline

So significant is IT governance within the COBIT model that a management guideline is provided. At this point COBIT seeks to measure information criteria through KGIs. This is part of hierarchy of tools which includes CSFs and KPIs. These add up to a useful tool set for our compliance project. They are all well-understood industry-acknowledged mechanisms for measuring performance and achievement. These elements can be applied to the controls that are part of the control objectives. COBIT sees KGIs as measuring the delivery of information to the business according to defined information criteria (effectiveness, efficiency, confidentiality, integrity, availability, compliance, and reliability). These enable a "system of process and control excellence." In effect it is a system of internal control. The indication of how far this has been achieved rests on the realization of CSFs, which are measured through KPIs. This system of IT governance is a useful and practical model for our compliance process.

Key goal indicators

The evidence that the correct information is being used in a constructive way for the enterprise is demonstrated by an honest assessment of KGIs. If these are on target and in line with those defined by the business, the IT governance is operating successfully.

Table 23.9 COBIT key goal indicators

COBIT critical success factors	Compliance process comments
Performance and cost management improvements	All continuous improvement efforts are demonstrable evidence of striving for compliance

Table 23.9 continued

COBIT critical success factors	Compliance process comments
Return on major IT investments	ROI criteria should be included in tool selection and overall long-term planning for software solutions and maintenance
Improved time to market	The compliance effort must focus on company-specific objectives; this includes product rollout. Controls should measure product life cycle processes as much as day-to-day customer-facing activities and support processes
Better quality and risk management	Quality, process improvement, and risk management are at the heart of the compliance process.
Integrated and standardized business processes	The formalization of process testing and documentation deals directly with this
New customer base	Revenue growth and market share are ultimate objectives of the business, and should reinforce the company-centric aspect of compliance. Quality systems and shareholder investment underpin this growth
Appropriate delivery bandwidth available	The compliance process will identify constraints in business activity and institute controls where necessary to monitor this
Customer satisfaction	A powerful feedback device through quality systems, capturing poorly executed or designed processes. Generally customer comments are negative, but should be seized on as control testing and hence positive feedback in the compliance process
Compliant organization	The aim of the compliance process is the compliant organization on a continual basis, not just one-off
Maintenance of company risk profile	The risk assessment process at a strategic level is repeated on a "maintenance" basis at tactical level
Benchmarking to IT governance ideal	Benchmarking is part of the reference base for the compliance process and the compliance cycle
New service delivery channels	Opportunities for developing products and organizational capacity will be highlighted in a comprehensive assessment of the business, its risks, and as a result its opportunities. With appropriate controls in place, metrics can support propositions for business growth

Critical success factors

COBIT lists a number of CSFs that indicate whether the organization is on track for IT governance (see Table 23.10). The assumption is that with these in place, IT governance is assured. These are also useful indicators for the likely success of the compliance process.

Key performance indicators

These indicators are the measuring mechanism for how far the overall IT governance effort has been successful. If the ambitions of these can confidently be asserted to be met, the compliance process is going well. The general rule is to look for signs of an increase in or improvement in the indicators (see Table 23.11).

Maturity model

In the end, when we consider the overall impact of the COBIT model we need to understand how far an organization has traveled along an ideal path towards a full governance model. The model purports to provide assurance if its criteria for success are being met. However, in the real world, organizations are in various states of compliance to this ideal, and at any time this state of compliance will further vary according to business success and market conditions. The COBIT model does provide a "maturity model," which enables an organization to map its position on the imaginary road. This is characterized by six stages (detailed in Table 23.12):

0. Non-existent
1. Initial/ad hoc
2. Repeatable but intuitive
3. Defined process
4. Managed and measurable
5. Optimized.

Balanced business scorecards

The prevalence of dashboards in applications that measure anything is present here in the use of color-coded scorecards. These can provide senior executives, managers, and employees with the ability to access a visual, and often real-time, view of performance. They are cross-referenced with business objectives.

One clear advantage is the way the scorecard can deliver a consolidated view of performance across the enterprise. Where possible, users can drill down to investigate the underlying detail of each performance measure. Graphing and reporting highlight trends for planning. Alignment of

Table 23.10 COBIT critical success factors

COBIT critical success factors	Compliance process comments
Relevant activities are part of enterprise governance and reflected in leadership from the top	Senior management involvement is central to the compliance process
The activity reflects enterprise goals for the business and technology is used to keep in step with business demand	Business objectives define the process, software and IT support is fundamental to the continuous process of improvement
There is clarity and purpose to the activities undertaken	The statement of applicability summarizes and communicates the compliance process
These activities are documented as well as implemented	Documentation is mandated by the Act (Sections 302 and 404)
These activities are clearly accountable with defined ownership	Responsibilities and process ownership are measured through audit trails, reviews, and periodic reports
Practices and policies are implemented at management level to ensure the activities are efficient and use resources well	Management who own processes and business activities are responsible for them
Practices should enable a control environment based on risk assessment and standards, where possible, and where deficiencies can be monitored and addressed	The compliance process is about a cycle of control based on a risk-oriented implementation of the regulations, with a special focus on deficiencies, weaknesses, and their remediation
Contingency controls operate when general controls fail	Selected controls in the compliance process go beyond deterrent and preventive to controls that are invoked in contingencies
Complex IT processes (change, problem, and configuration management) are integrated	The IT governance dimension and use of frameworks addresses the complexity of the IT function and its support of business functions
An audit committee appoints an external auditor and audit plans, and reviews and monitors audits and reviews	The audit committee is critical to the way compliance is addressed and approached; this includes liaison with external auditors and internal auditing operations

Table 23.11 Key performance indicators and measurement methods

Performance indicators	Methods
The cost-effectiveness of IT processes	Cost–benefit analyses
Plans for IT process improvements	Raised and budgeted projects
Utilization of the infrastructure	IT reports, trends, and statistics
Satisfaction of stakeholders	Surveys and complaints
Staff productivity and morale	Production increase, surveys, staff turnover
Availability of knowledge and management information	Training programs, coaching, and resource allocation
Linkage between IT and enterprise government	Board-level assessments and reviews
Performance on IT balanced scorecards	Scorecards

individual process activity with business objectives helps develop a sense of working to corporate aims. It introduces the idea of collaborative management. In effect it is a tool in this particular tool set. Ideally, scorecards can involve all staff at the desktop in strategic, tactical, and everyday performance targets.

The "balanced scorecard" defines what should be measured and how.[2] As much as anything else, the process of developing the scorecards helps an organization clarify its vision of what it wants to achieve. It establishes feedback mechanisms on internal processes and their effect on outcomes. The feedback is part of a system of improvement. While the scorecard concept uses traditional financial measures for historic activities, it introduces others that help in planning for future investment in customers, suppliers, staff, technology, and processes. It takes a view of the organization from four angles, developing metrics, data collection, and analysis accordingly:

Learning and growth

Employee training as an aspect of corporate self-improvement. In financial organizations nearly everyone is a knowledge worker. As such, skilled staff are the prime organizational resource. To maintain an edge, staff must be continuously educated and have their skills updated. Measures used to judge who needs training and when are invaluable for management. Skilled trainers who can carry out training needs analyses

Table 23.12 COBIT maturity model and compliance

	Stage	Factors
0	Non-existent	• No IT governance process • No recognition of need
1	Initial/ad hoc	• Some recognition of need • No standardized processes • Ad hoc approach • Inconsistent communication • Some outcome orientation • No standard assessment process • Monitoring is purely reactive
2	Repeatable but intuitive	• General awareness of IT governance • Some KPIs • IT governance is linked to change management • Senior management involvement • Some IT processes marked for improvement and monitored as investments • A defined IT architecture • Measurement and assessment identified but not implemented • No formal training or adoption of standards • IT governance is individually and project driven • Some under-used tools in place
3	Defined process	• A baseline set of indicators exists • Defined and documented links between governance and outcomes • Integrated into strategic planning and monitoring • Procedures standardized • Procedures have been communicated and informal training is in place to support them • Performance indicators are being tracked • Standardized tools in place and current • IT balanced business scorecards are in place and being used • Responsibility for training and implementation is still down to individuals • Root cause analysis infrequently applied • Deviations are not noted by management • Some measurement against metrics remediation is ad hoc • Accountability of performance is detailed • Management rewarded on these measures

Table 23.12 continued

	Stage	Factors
4	Managed and measurable	• Full understanding of IT governance • Supported by formal training • Service level agreements are in full force • Responsibilities are clear • Process ownership is detailed • Quantative understanding of processes • Can monitor and measure compliance with process metrics • Risks are understood • Operational tolerances are defined • Ineffective processes are noted and acted upon, and occasionally improved • Standardized root cause analysis • Continuous improvement introduced though not fully in place • Domain experts are used • IT governance is linked to enterprise, and activities integrated with enterprise processes
5	Optimized	• Characterized by an adventurous view of IT governance and solutions • Training and communications are cutting edge to gain maximum benefits • Processes are refined according to current best practice • Continuous improvement is an operational standard • The organization adapts quickly to change and assimilates new policies as needed • Root cause analysis is routine and action is efficient and effective • IT and IT automation is used for workflow wherever feasible • Monitored processes are the norm, with full reporting and feedback • Benchmarks are used for guidance and external resources used efficiently • Communication on all aspects of IT governance is common and expected • IT governance is fully integrated with enterprise governance • All resources, technological and human are fully exploited for competitive advantage

are in short supply. To meet any of a number of CSFs, learning and growth are required at all levels of the organization. The balanced scorecard ethos also includes mentoring and coaching when it talks of learning. Learning management systems using intranets are also part of a comprehensive learning approach.

Business process

For internal business processes, metrics allow the managers to know how the business, or sub-part of the business, is doing. Two kinds of business processes are discussed:

- mission-oriented processes: these can be difficult to model generically
- support processes: being iterative and common to many services, these are easier to measure and benchmark generically.

The customer

Customer focus and customer satisfaction are leading indicators: dissatisfied customers find other financial service and product suppliers. Consequently, performance is a leading indicator of concerns for the future. Metrics are focused on the classification of customers and the processes that service them.

Financial

Traditionally, financial measures have had pride of place in business self-measurement. However, there is a tendency for this data and its measurement to unbalance the greater picture. It is even argued that the emphasis on financial data leads to an "unbalanced" measurement system. This can be addressed by including other data, such as that stemming from risk assessments and cost–benefit analyses. Automation of this kind of financial data within a balanced mix of interest-driven COBIT and other models is likely to help the compliance process when it comes to a system of internal control and financial reporting.

The balanced scorecard approach borrows from other management ideas, notably total quality management (TQM), and other customer-oriented continuous improvement and employee empowerment-driven processes using measurement-based feedback systems.

An objective of the scorecard is based on the ambition to deal with defects that occur in any step in a production process, with a view to eliminating the defect and improving product quality. To do this, all business processes should be subject to feedback loops. Data from this feedback should be analyzed to:

- determine the causes of any defects
- identify processes with significant problems
- fix the relevant processes.

In this way, the balanced scorecard uses feedback on internal business process outputs and adds a further feedback loop around business strategies. The balanced scorecard thus involves a "double-loop feedback" process.

PRECURSORS AND OTHER MODELS

The steering committee had in mind a number of control models when it constructed the COBIT framework. These are stated in "COBIT Control Objectives." This lists:

- COSO (discussed earlier in this chapter)
- Cadbury (in the UK)
- CoCo (in Canada)
- King (in South Africa).

It notes there are more focused control models such as:

- Security Code of Conduct from the DTI (Department of Trade and Industry in the UK)
- ITCC (Information Technology Control Guidelines) from CICA (Canadian Institute of Chartered Accountants)
- Security Handbook from NIST (National Institute of Standards and Technology, USA).

There are others that we consider such as:

- ITIL
- ISO 17799
- CMMI.

From the perspective of COBIT what these all have in common is a lack of focus on business objectives. They do provide a usable and comprehensive framework for IT control that explicitly supports business processes. COBIT is needed to bridge this gap. It does, however, refer to *SysTrust Principles and Criteria for Systems Reliability* (published by AICPA/CICA). Developed by the Assurance Services Executive of the United States and the Assurance Service Development Board in Canada, SysTrust intuitively, from its title, seeks to provide assurance about systems that support business. It has a focus on external accountancy, providing services for evaluating and testing the reliability of systems against the key principles of:

- availability
- security
- integrity
- maintainability.

Perhaps the recognized originator of this approach is the Information Systems Audit and Control Foundation's Control Objectives. This has been transformed from an auditing tool to a management tool under COBIT.

THE COBIT PROJECT

The emphasis of COBIT is a focus on melding business and IT function objectives so they serve the ultimate aims of the organization, and to introduce a system of controls that enable managers to realize this focus. It does this through introducing best practice using policies and security measures. It is openly compliant with COSO and the importance it places on the business perspective. The control objectives at the heart of the framework are derived form audit objectives.

Specifically, on certification of financial information, it provides certification of efficiency and effectiveness in generating, producing, and using this information. Figure 23.3 takes this picture and points up the salient links between COBIT, COSO, and audit objectives.

It is a fair claim that no other framework so explicitly seeks to represent the interest of the business in managing IT in such a practical manner. Certainly others do stress this, such as ITIL and ISO 17799. But none have the constant reference in the workings of their model so clearly stated.

DEFINITIONS

The language used in the Act and in industry as a whole in response to regulation is limited and often quite precise. COBIT has its own usage. To make progress we need to move on from core ideas and see how far concepts have meanings in common with other models.

Control and IT control objective

This is a central concept which has been defined earlier. COBIT has adapted this from the COSO Report definitions: "the policies, procedures, practices and organizational structures designed to provide reasonable assurance that business objectives will be achieved and that undesired events will be prevented or detected and corrected," and "a statement of the

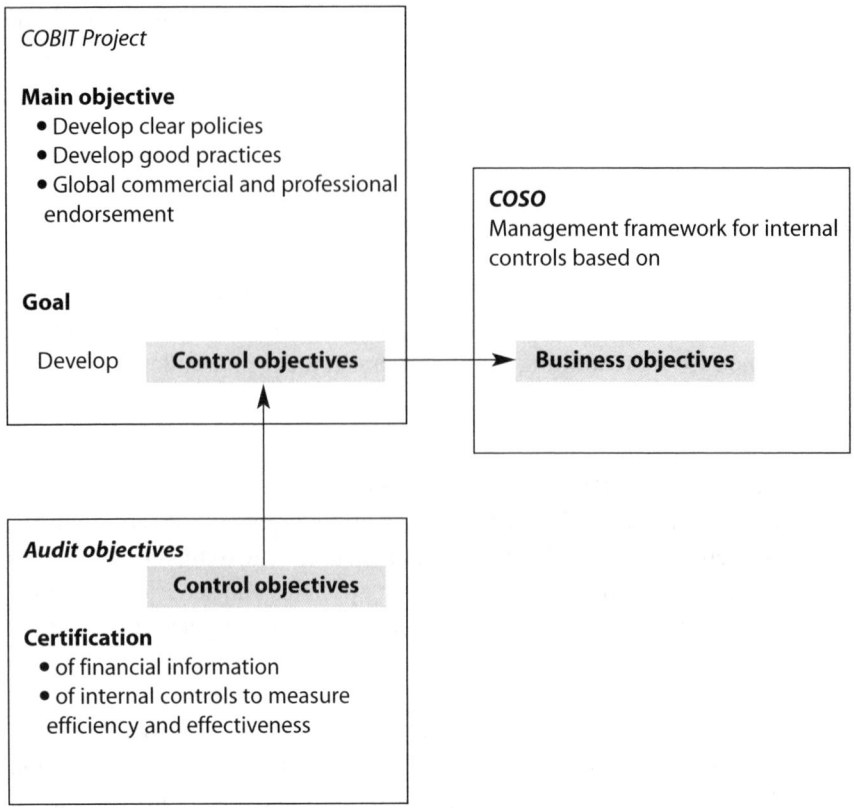

Figure 23.3 The COBIT project

desired result or purpose to be achieved by implementing control procedures in a particular IT activity" (both adapted from IIARF 1991).

COBIT positions itself as the model for IT governance. The definition of IT governance has been explored above. In essence we can summarize the environment in which these elements meet: IT governance is a description of a system in which desired outcomes are defined by IT control objectives realized through controls.

COBIT framework

COBIT talks of domains, which are clearly understood as the realms of management under which control objectives for business fall. The framework identifies 34 high-level control objectives and 318 detailed control objectives. The framework acts as a filter between business objectives, often defined at a senior level in the organization, and information. As such it helps form a basis for making management decisions about IT resources and how they should be used. The framework is discussed as consisting of high-level control objectives and a structure for their classification. At the same time there is an assumption that there are three levels of IT efforts that need to be addressed. These are grouped in a hierarchy:

1. **Activities** that achieve something and can be measured. These are recognized as having a life cycle, which also has to be controlled.
2. **Processes** are defined as a series of joined activities with natural control-base divisions.
3. **Domains** are collections of processes. These are often defined as responsibility domains in an organizational structure which also ties in with the natural life cycles of IT processes.

This domains–processes–tasks framework is the conceptual model on which COBIT hangs its practical approach. COBIT also talks about perspectives on this framework from the point of view of:

■ information criteria (such as quality, fiduciary, and security)
■ IT resources (people, application systems, technology, facilities, and data)
■ IT processes (domains, processes, activities).

The result is a three-dimensional reference translated into a common language close to that used by management rather than by IT or auditors.

Compliance

While the framework principles have three areas of prime interest:—quality requirements, fiduciary requirements, and security requirements—from our perspective the framework has a specific focus on fiduciary requirements at the business level. These are inherited from the COSO model, and focus on the effectiveness and efficiency of operations, the reliability of information, and general compliance with laws and regulations on information and its handling. The framework reuses the COSO definitions. However, it does expand the reliability of information to include not just financial information but all information. The assurance on compliance with the Act is that this includes financial information. There is a degree of overlap with other recognized models as indicated in Table 23.13.

From the discussion of broadly based requirements, COBIT establishes a number of categories that need further definition.

Effectiveness

This is very significant concept for the Act. It is the word on which compliance turns. An ineffective or non-effective system of controls is a statement

Table 23.13 COBIT framework requirement overlaps

Quality requirements	Many stand alone quality systems figure here, notably ISO 9001/2, as well as quality domains within systems, such as ITIL.
Fiduciary requirements	The most obvious model here is COSO and the common interests COBIT shares with it. Other ad hoc models and sub-sets of other solutions are also available.
Security requirements	This is a prime area of activity for IT over time. There are a number of mature models available such as ITIL and ISO 17799. Other sub-sets of frameworks are also in common use.

of failure to conform to the strictures of the Act, and leads to realized risk, public notification, and potential business loss. Under the Act, the system of internal control must be assessed as effective by senior management, and this assessment of effectiveness is attested to by external auditors. There may be a degree of effectiveness, in that there is a sliding scale of effectiveness. A system of internal control may be partially effective rather than wholly effective. How do we arrive at this kind of conclusion, and measure and verify it?

Under COBIT the definition is broad: effectiveness is concerned with the extent to which information is relevant and pertinent to the business process. To be effective it should also be information delivered in a timely, correct, consistent, and usable way. There are a number of concepts in this definition. Effectiveness here is a more matrix of possibilities, with room for weighting according to priorities, interests, and resources. The Act has a narrower vision.

Efficiency

This is a more generally understood term, and this is reflected in its usage under COBIT. Efficiency is the provision of information through the most economical use of resources. This is a fundamental business objective, although not necessarily fundamental to compliance with the Act. It is not stated that the system of internal control must be efficient—that is a separate issue for the organization. There is an assumption, perhaps, that efficiency stems from effectiveness.

Confidentiality

This, along with "integrity" and "availability," is one of the three key concepts in any security system. Generally confidentiality indicates protection of information from unauthorized access, or unauthorized disclosure. COBIT adopts these ideas.

Integrity

Accuracy and completeness of information are central to its integrity. This underlines its validity. The concept can apply to the methods for processing information. COBIT extends this to information's validity for business values and expectations.

Availability

This is the third of the security triumvirate. Again it emphasizes that authorized users must have access to information and assets when required, in a controlled and validated manner. This is especially important for the financial sector, where so much business is e-business, web-based, and electronic in nature.

Reliability

This concept is really a mix of others. For COBIT it ensures that appropriate information is available for decision making, and for compliance and reporting functions to operate.

Other terms are used in a general, intuitive and easily understood manner. These include terms such as "data," "application systems," "technology," "facilities," and "people."

DOCUMENTATION

This vital area for the Act is addressed by COBIT, though the framework offers no additional model elements. It simply states that documentation is so fundamental that if a process or other relevant element is not documented, this must be addressed first. Here there is no suggested parallel activity.

DEVELOPING THE FRAMEWORK

The framework as a whole sees a process encapsulated as an event-driven process: business (and its objectives) creates events (such as business objectives, opportunities, regulatory requirements, and risks), which drive technology with its resources and people (and systems of support for data) to generate information (which should conform to the concept in dimensions such as effectiveness, efficiency, and confidentiality).

The domains introduced in Figure 23.1 form the higher-level part of the framework, and are the starting point for building a COBIT model in practice.

Planning and organization

This concerns the strategic and tactical interests of the organization, and the manner in which IT can address them. These interests are part of the business and organizational plan, and communicated through policies. All this activity is placed within an IT structure.

Acquisition and implementation

IT solutions are identified and acquired to satisfy the strategy and planning. Change management and maintenance is also covered here.

Delivery and support

Implementation, projects, and training are listed under this domain. The definition extends into data processing, which is an arm of delivery.

Monitoring

The assessment of IT processes and continuous monitoring is the role of this domain. It includes management assessment of the internal control process, and is especially relevant to our concerns under the Act. It embraces internal and external audit control.

There is considerable internal overlap between aspects of the framework. Notably, for certain aspects to work they must be effective, and for the business to approve of processes and policies they must be efficient. COBIT recognizes and differentiates between the ways in which processes will satisfy business requirements. A grading is used:

- primary: the extent to which the control objective affects the information criteria applied
- secondary: the extent to which the control objective has a lesser affect on the information criteria applied
- blank: where retirements are likely to be satisfied by another process.

The variation in the way in which controls affect their IT processes and resources is also recognized and accounted for. Each resource should be identified and assessed in a thorough approach.

CONTROL OBJECTIVES AND PRINCIPLES

COBIT control objectives are grouped into domains. Our approach is to align these with our compliance project and understand how they can reinforce the compliance process:

- planning and organization
- acquisition and implementation
- delivery and support
- monitoring.

Principles

The COBIT framework is limited to high-level control objectives for each process. However, it does expand this framework to explicitly include "control objectives." These focus on specific control objectives for each IT process. In this way the 34 IT processes in the framework are each expanded by 30 to total 318 detailed control objectives. COBIT claims that these comprise "the de facto and de jure international standards and regulations relating to IT" (*COBIT Control Objectives*, p. 21), establishing the model as a "clear policy and good practice for IT control throughout the industry, worldwide." With these ambitions and sense of relevance in mind, we can explore the control objectives themselves to see how far they map onto our needs for compliance.

Handling control objectives: navigation

In such a complex structure, managers and owners of processes need some help in working through the controls. COBIT uses indicators for domains that are simple acronyms:

- PO: planning and organizing
- AI: acquisition and implementation
- DS: delivery and support
- M: monitoring.

The perspective adopted when entering this matrix of information determines how the whole structure can be read. It assumes a three-dimensional model based on:

- information criteria: with its seven criteria listed
- IT domains (processes): the four-part domain structure (PO, AI, DS, and M)
- IT resources: the four-part list.

The COBIT three-dimensional approach is used for each of the control objectives, and forms a thorough reference model for practical implementation of any system of control.

Planning and organization

The activities of planning and organizing are characterized by efforts to "define," "assess," and "manage." These establish the framework of action for the organization, and initiatives originate from the top. The processes listed are:

- Define a strategic IT plan.
- Define the information architecture.

- Define the technological direction.
- Define the IT organization and its relationships.
- Manage the IT investment.
- Communicate aims and direction.
- Manage human resources.
- Ensure external compliance.
- Assess risks.
- Manage priorities.
- Manage quality.

COBIT tabulates these activities and cross-matches then to information criteria and IT resources, indicating whether they are of "primary" or "secondary" impact on the information criteria to differentiate the ways in which processes satisfy business requirements. The nature of primary and secondary impacts is not discussed.

SUMMARIZING THE SYSTEM

The COBIT system has value for the compliance process to a varying extent. This is notable when we summarize the processes associated with the domains (see Tables 23.14 to 17). "CP" refers to the compliance process.

PRACTICAL COMPLIANCE SUMMARY

Seek to balance effectiveness and efficiency (regulatory and company emphasis). If using COSO and COBIT:

- Use the five components of COSO to structure a response to the Act and incorporate these into the compliance process.
- Use control "types," such as applications and general controls.
- Implement COBIT as recommended by the PCAOB.
- Use KGIs, KPIs, and CSFs for compliance process activities. Structure these through the CTF.
- Determine which of the maturity models relate to the organization. At a strategic level, map this to the ongoing compliance path for continuous improvement.

NOTES

1. Our examples use COBIT version 3.0. The latest released version is COBIT 4.0. IT is likely that most existing implementations are using version 3.0. The differences between the versions can be implemented as supplements and introduced through the compliance process.

2. The "balanced scorecard" enables an organization to tackle the measurement of systems and processes, especially from a financial perspective. This system was developed by Dr Robert Kaplan and Dr David Norton.

Table 23.14 Planning and organization summary

Domain	Process	Compliance comment	CP reference
P01	Define a strategic IT plan	This process should already be in place and compliance should be a question of demonstrating this and its effectiveness, through documentation. It should be reviewed regularly; the results of reviews are also evidence.	IT strategy
P02	Define the information architecture	The IT strategy (P01) in part defines how information will be used in the organization. An information architecture defines the life cycle of information, how it is secured; in short, from its creation to its destruction. It will develop policies accordingly and may encompass things like use and abuse of email; internal information barriers.	ISMS, ILM, e-mail and unstructured communications management
P03	Determine technological direction	With P01 and P02 in place, the way the company sees itself as an operating mechanism is reflected in decisions on direction. For example, if business is to expand online or be chiefly carried out through the web, then the technological direction will be to invest in intra and extranets, have a strong web presence, and tailor security for external risks.	Web technologies, Supply chain management
P04	Define the IT organization and relationships	A component of IT governance. This process determines how IT will respond to the strategies and architectures agreed upon. The IT function will have to be resourced or refitted to meet these enterprise aims. How IT interacts with and supports the rest of the organization should also be detailed and developed as a set of policies.	IT governance models (such as COBIT)

Table 23.14 continued

Domain	Process	Compliance comment	CP reference
P05	Manage the IT investment	Specifically focused on IT resources: monitor, analyze, and assess the use of IT solutions. This should link to strategic and architectural planning, and be the process whereby the practical administration of these plans is implemented.	ITIL, COBIT
P06	Communicate management aims and directions	Generally implemented through IT solutions such as an intranet; internal awareness training, policy committee communications; interactive desktop information responding to staff actions. Formal meetings, reviews updates. Feedback built into standard business processes.	Intranet, newsletters, meetings, training, business process feedback [CP]
P07	Manage human resources	IT resources are defined as "people" as well as those associated with technology. Roles and responsibilities must be separated appropriately.	Responsibility cascade
P08	Ensure compliance with external requirements	This process involves legal and compliance staff in the setting of enterprise and IT governance objectives. Current requirements must be incorporated in systematic and regular reviews and updates.	[CP]
P09	Assess risks	Risk assessment is carried out at many levels. Strategic and tactical assessments occur within the business function and IT function as part of other frameworks and models. The risk tolerance of the organization should be clarified and adopted as the risk profile. This is used as a benchmark for all planning and organization.	Risk assessment as part of models (COBIT, ISO 17799 etc)
P10	Manage projects	Project management resources, at both the higher level and technical project management level, must be allocated. A formal project management discipline should characterize all budgeted implementations with real stakeholder involvement and tied to enterprise planning.	Project Management training

Table 23.14 continued

Domain	Process	Compliance comment	CP reference
P11	Manage quality	A quality management system may be in place either as a de facto standard along the lines of TQM, or formally as ISO 9001/2, TickIT and so on. The processes of these systems may have their own controls; these should be linked to the model where necessary.	ISO 9001/2, TickIT, TQM

Table 23.15 Acquisition and implementation summary

Domain	Process	Compliance comment	CP reference
AI1	Identify automated solutions	These processes can be business directed or IT directed based on feedback or objectives to resolve cost–benefit interest (automation reducing operational costs, enhancing revenue through speed and accuracy)	Automated workflow and interactive customer web-based solutions. Accuracy for effectiveness.
AI2	Acquire and maintain application software	A set of processes for procurement; policies and guidelines on acquiring and maintaining software solutions. Help-desk processes and general support processes. This may include third party outsourcing; security issues, disaster planning and business continuity.	Procurement; training; help-desk, trouble-ticketing and support. Outsourcing, business continuity. ISO 1799.
AI3	Acquire and maintain technology infrastructure	Based on planning and organization, a process for developing an existing communications infrastructure, both LAN and WAN. Mobile workers and VPN-based offices and staff.	LAN and WAN technologies
AI4	Develop and maintain procedures	Formal models will deliver operational procedures, as well as in-house developed and common usage—ideally based on best-practice. These will include management as well as user procedures. Generally translated into company policies.	Policy-based management; BPM

Table 23.15 continued

Domain	Process	Compliance comment	CP reference
AI5	Install and accredit systems	Accreditation formally acknowledges that best practice is being pursued within the organization. Not all organizations follow this route since there is a considerable, at least initially, resource overhead. It has the benefit of being a continual process. COSO and COBIT are not accredited, but ISO standards are.	ISO 9001/2, ISO1799. Being constantly renewed it is of especial value for compliance which is an ongoing process.
AI6	Manage changes	Change management is a vital business and IT activity. Without it business processes tend to fracture into departmental common usage and the overall links disintegrate. Drivers for change also subject the organization to continuous change, which is largely a management issue. It is especially challenging to manage change for IT resources and human resources.	Change management

Table 23.16 Delivery and support

Domain	Process	Compliance comment	CP reference
DS1	Define and manage service levels`	Service level agreements are common internally as well as externally.	SLAs as reference models
DS2	Manage third-party services	The process of managing external agencies is critical to compliance. Supply chain effects are addressed by this type of process. There should be a direct link to strategic planning and resource management.	Third-party policy management
DS3	Manage performance and capacity	BPM is at the heart of these processes and capacity control is essential to adapting the organization to changing needs.	BPM and ERP

Table 23.16 continued

Domain	Process	Compliance comment	CP reference
DS4	Ensure continuous service	Related to security processes and business continuity planning, the establishment of effective back-up systems is essential for businesses that operate electronically 24/7. This might also apply to staff replacement and mechanisms that ensure the replacement of senior and other management with specific skills are monitored and managed.	Security and continuity planning
DS5	Ensure systems security	Security management underpins a reliable system. Protection from external damage, hacking and so on, and internal malicious or accidental damage is part of the ISMS.	ISMS, ISO 1779
DS6	Identify and allocate costs	Budgeting processes operate as one-off activities, such as projects, or periodic and regular, such as departmental budgeting and at a senior level for divisions or business functions. Compliance is a special project cost which must be seen as an ongoing regular though variable cost.	Financial budgeting policies
DS7	Educate and train users	No system of any kind is likely to perform effectively if it is poorly understood and its users lack the motivation to observe its policies. Education and training is fundamental, though it is often not implemented thoroughly. This may involve specific processes for internal and external training provision. This is large area, and requires a substantial effort to get the maximum benefit from an investment.	Training policies
DS8	Assist and advise customers	Customers are internal and external. Internal customers are users in other departments who share in the activity, but as "consumers" of an internal service. External customers also need to be identified carefully. Effectiveness at this level approximates to satisfaction with the service being delivered, and is measured subjectively by feedback, surveys, and questionnaires as well as compliance. Complaints procedures also qualify as processes here.	Formal feedback mechanisms. Informal feedback

Table 23.16 continued

Domain	Process	Compliance comment	CP reference
DS9	Manage the configuration	A specific process for a specific solution, such as workflow for CRM.	A software application's internal management capability. A solution's self-monitoring features.
DS10	Manage problems and incidents	Processes that are part of troubleshooting. These might be user problems that need support, software issues that need to be addressed, by internal or external suppliers. Incident reporting procedures and escalation procedures.	ITIL, internal incident management
DS11	Manage data	Generally a specific IT function activity: the life cycle processes of capturing, storing, archiving, retrieving, and deleting information for specific groups of users, as well as making this information available and easily accessible as part of business processes. Content management systems figure strongly.	ILM, data storage, content management
DS12	Manage facilities	The physical infrastructure as locations and sub-areas, with their accessibility factored into the security system. The management of these areas is a discipline in its own right, and often these assets represent a substantial part of the overt value of the organization.	Facilities management
DS13	Manage operations	Operational activities are the substance of the business. These range across all business and IT functional areas and consist of many processes.	Operations management

Table 23.17 Monitoring summary

Domain	Process	Compliance comment	CP reference
M1	Monitor the processes	As a process this activity is a generic one, and is really a statement of how we apply controls. Monitoring implies a regularity of inspection and/or testing of a process, and a recorded outcome as input to analysis for further action. This meets all the perspectives and criteria of the COBIT model.	Process management of all kinds
M2	Assess internal control adequacy	A generic process that follows on from observational monitoring and testing. Performed with internal or external help. The assessment is a critical part of the compliance process, and like M1 is essential for compliance with the Act. The processes are focused on the control itself and whether it is appropriate and effective as a monitoring process.	Control assessment
M3	Obtain independent assurance	The action of getting an external verification of a process is an act of self-assurance on behalf of the organization. For true assurance a second or third opinion is invaluable, and enables the organization to demonstrate its sources of assurance on effectiveness.	External auditors; formal accreditation for models and systems
M4	Provide for independent audit	As well as often being a mandated requirement for regulatory bodies, using an independent auditor has many benefits, relating to thoroughness, fresh perspectives, and a means of utilizing specific skills in a cost-effective way. Provision for an audit requires a formal process that can be inspected and monitored. It tends to be tested through regular independent audit use.	Contracts with independent auditors as third-party services

CHAPTER 24

Methodologies and Frameworks

SUPPORTING COMPLIANCE

The support role of IT in the creation, transport, and life cycle of financial information implies that auditors must examine activities across the whole of IT. The challenge for the IT function lies in identifying where technology is vulnerable to causing material weaknesses in the financial process. IT internal auditors may have an approach that is influenced by business needs, but many IT departments have a technical focus, with hardly any awareness of the business functions they support. The department may have considerable controls over its processes, its measurement metrics, and reporting, with efficient auditing of infrastructure performance, capacity, and SLA assurance. However, there may be a very limited grasp of the content of financial data processed, transmitted, and managed through the systems.

To identify deficiencies and weaknesses as part of everyday operations and make the connection with misstatements in financial reports is not generally on the departmental agenda. The danger is that material weaknesses can develop in an environment lacking in business-oriented control of IT processes. IT management must introduce awareness of business functions to its core technical activities. To accomplish this, IT managers need a good grasp of IT governance, and the governance procedures of business functions.

Some models such as ITIL and ISO 17799 offer a great deal to IT functions that use them. They have a confessed interest in linking business objectives with those of IT, and have formalized this through their approach to risk analysis and the mechanisms for managing risk: controls. Through this common interest and focus they fit into the compliance process, reflecting the latter's flexibility, and their practicability. By combining methodologies and frameworks, we find that a framework such as COBIT approaches IT governance from the top down, and ITIL approaches governance from the bottom up. The institution of models such as ITIL can help the organization pass an audit and comply with the Act. However, a combination within a managed cycle is the only way to ensure ongoing compliance.

Other methods, such as Six Sigma and CMMI, focus on the processes, either business or IT. For these methodologies, the business is centered on processes—creation, manufacturing, marketing, support—and through their refinement, in a continuous process of quality improvement, the business becomes more profitable, and its systems more effective.

ITIL

ITIL (IT Infrastructure Library) is a widely accepted approach to IT service management. It is not a standard in the sense that it has been developed by an internationally recognized standards body. It is more a set of guidelines based on best practice from public and private-sector experience. It consists of a series of books that provide IT departments with guidance on implementing quality IT services in an effective and efficient environment. It recognizes the dependency on IT for delivering corporate aims and business needs. ITIL provides the foundation for quality IT service management. Widespread adoption of ITIL has encouraged organizations to develop supporting products.

ITIL has eight core titles, available in three versions: book, CD-ROM and intranet license:

- *Service Support*
- *Service Delivery*
- *Planning to Implement Service Management*
- *Application Management*
- *ICT Infrastructure Management*
- *Security Management*
- *Software Asset Management*
- *The Business Perspective: The IS View on Delivering Services to the Business.*

This body of best-practice guidance is endorsed by standards bodies such as the British Standards Institute's Standard for IT Service Management (BS15000). As a recognizable methodology it emerged in 1989 when the UK government agency the Central Computer and Telecommunications Agency (CCTA) sought to codify IT management practices. The focus of ITIL is the alignment of the IT function, as a service provider, to the real needs of the business. This focus has led to its growing popularity in Europe, the United States, and globally.

Bridging the gap between the business community and the IT function and the forging of business partnerships is central to the importance of effective compliance, and ITIL has a lot to offer IT governance. Internal and external relationships are formalized based on service level agreements

(SLAs). It is also particularly well suited to supporting the separation of responsibilities, with awareness of the accountability of functions throughout the internal service structure. Although appearing at times to be an abstract concept, neither a product nor a standard, it is nevertheless a practical methodology.

Of particular value is the systematic approach adopted by ITIL to the planning, development, delivery, and support of IT services. Its philosophy is summarized by three primary concepts:

- IT functions should align with business goals.
- The focus is on processes to ensure predictability, quality control, and operational excellence.
- IT spending, as a function of service management is conditional on business objectives.

ITIL structure

ITIL places a great emphasis on proactive planning of the business rather than being reacting to events. To achieve this it has developed a comprehensive structure which separates service support and service delivery as the primary activity areas, and subsumes all other IT functions to supporting these:

- Service support concentrates on day-to-day operations and the support of IT services.
- Service delivery looks at the long-term planning and improvement of IT services.

Central to ITIL's best practice approach is the "service desk," as the central point of contact for all IT service management. Each group links to and supports the efficient operation of the service desk.

Structurally ITIL has 11 functional areas or disciplines, divided into the two sections of service support and delivery, and operating as either front-office or back-office support systems. Under service support come management disciplines relating to configuration, change, release, incident, problems, and the service desk. Under service delivery there are the management areas related to service levels, capacity, finance, availability, and IT service continuity management.

SIX SIGMA

In the United States another methodology has emerged, Six Sigma.[1] Developed by Motorola in the 1980s, Six Sigma is a philosophy based on statistics for quality improvement through quantification. Born in manufacturing operations, and mostly used for improving them, it has gained wider acceptance for the general benefits it brings to IT. In particular a service delivery approach uses statistical techniques for improving quality and identifying problems. It is particularly useful for measuring the effectiveness of systems. As a "tool" it is often implemented alongside ITIL as a mechanism for measuring its success.

Six Sigma is a methodology that helps manage processes. It specifically provides techniques for examining variations in processes for their impact. If they are unacceptable, the Six Sigma approach is to work towards managing variation to eliminate defects in a methodical and standardized manner. In effect, it has grown into a quality system for processes.

The effectiveness of Six Sigma for responding to the Act is in the way it offers managers an effective tool for addressing issues that constitute an apparent weakness in the way controls are used, applied, or designed. In an example relating to a US manufacturing process, the plant took an issue to a Six Sigma black belt (advanced practitioner). The company had adopted controls in conformance with the Act. The controls had been introduced several years previously and had worked for a while, but they appeared to have become ineffective, and an audit was due. A discrepancy had occurred. The plant accountant had worked to an agreed SLA of no more than a £100,000 variance in monthly reports, the variance being an expression of goods in, goods out and goods being processed. The plant accountant had noted several variances that were larger than this (see Figure 24.1).

An initial investigation into the statistics showed nothing undue, so working with the accountants and using Six Sigma techniques, efforts were made to reduce common cause variation in the month-end closing. Six Sigma best practice pointed to examining the factors present in the process all the time, and how they influence variation. A Pareto effect was discovered, and the factors contributing the most were analyzed. Root cause analysis and the inclusion of other factors into the month-end closing enabled the variance to be reflected accurately in a way that would no longer generate an auditing issue.

Once the techniques had been applied and the processes involved had been examined, the results were evaluated. Improved processes were introduced to address the issues uncovered. Even with the improved processes, the control limits were not within the range originally agreed, however. The accountant and the internal auditors agreed on a new control plan.

A review with reflection resulted in some key lessons:

■ The Act holds executive management responsible for control.
■ Financial processes are processes; that is, they can be subjected to Six Sigma techniques for process improvement. Statistical process control charts were found to be effective ways of monitoring the performance processes, including those in finance.

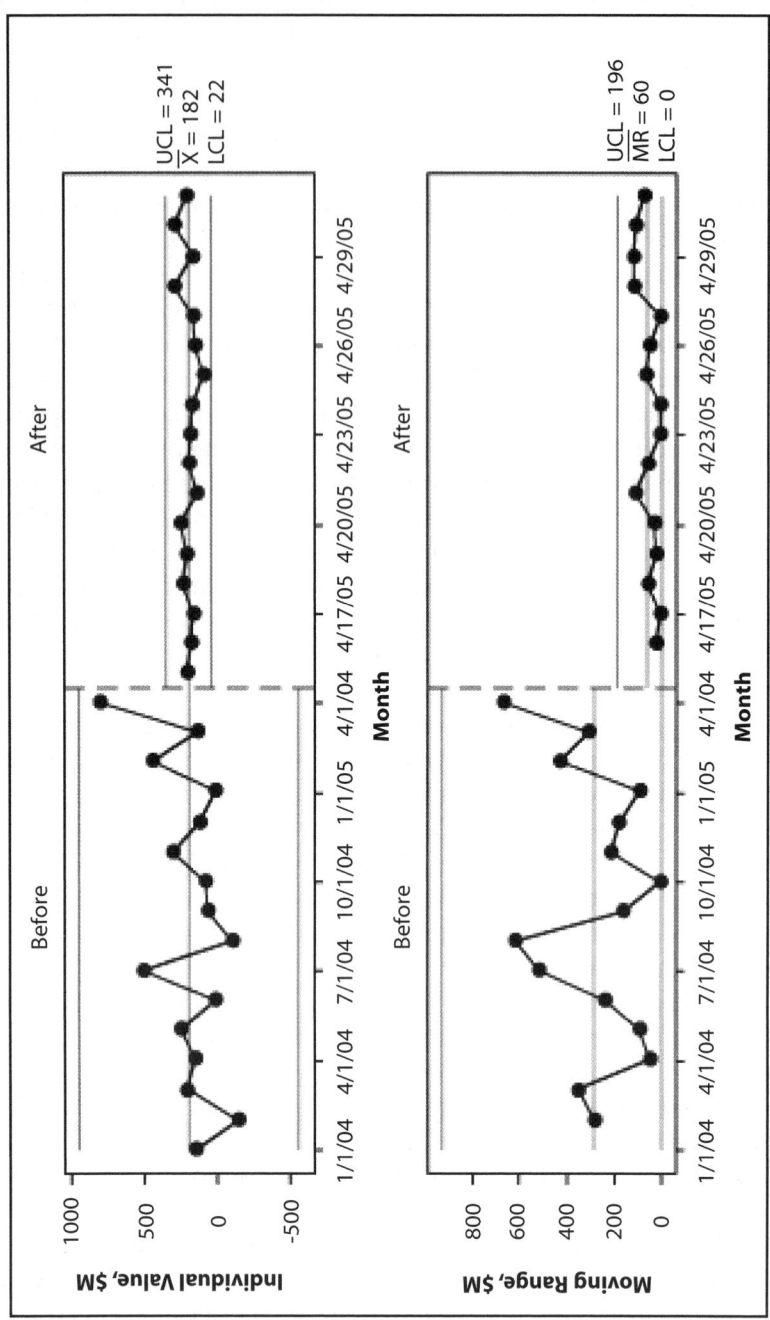

Figure 24.1 Before and after variances using Six Sigma techniques

- Sub-dividing or chunking inputs to financial measures helps identify the key suspect areas.
- There can be confusion in using terms interchangeably between disciplines, such as "variance," and operational definitions are needed for clarification.

The principles at work for this example are applicable to any set of processes that provide inputs to the overall process of financial reporting.

Process mapping is one of the basic quality or process improvement tools used in Lean Six Sigma. It has acquired more importance in recent times, given the complexities of processes and the need to capture and visualize knowledge that resides with operators of processes. Process mapping can result in maps which run into many pages, making them difficult to read and understand, and difficult to modify. Some basic rules can be applied to creating process maps, which make them easier to understand and use. Simplified process mapping is addressing this, and there are a number of practitioners focused on clarifying this area.

The very practical nature of applied Six Sigma is of great value to the compliance process and a useful addition to the compliance tool set.

ISO 17799

Using ISO 17799 as a model for compliance

We have already explored the value of using certifiable systems for the compliance effort, and noted the specific control-centric approach of this standard. Originally a British Standards Institute development, BS 7799, the standard evolved into an international one. (For a fuller discussion of ISO 17799 and the Act, see Chapter 22.) As a reference model for managing information security we can exploit it in two ways:

- As a framework standard to guide a program of compliance for information security, which seeks to comply with the standard and is audited for its compliance.
- As a template in building a specific compliance framework or personal standard for the Act.

In the first option, the organization complies with the standard as part of its own information security process; and in the second, the organization uses the standard as a basis for a do-it-yourself compliance standard.

The scope and focus of the standard embrace the whole security of the organization, including the logical assets (software, documentation, intellectual capital) and physical assets (equipment, premises, PC systems and infrastructure) of the organization. It provides a systematic approach to securing these assets and protecting them against loss, modification, and disclosure. It analyzes risks, identifies vulnerabilities, the potential for successful attacks, and mechanisms and controls to prevent successful attacks. Among other questions, it asks:

■ What is information security?
■ Why is information security needed?
■ How do we establish security requirements?

It then helps in:

■ assessing security risks
■ selecting controls
■ identifying the information security starting point
■ identifying critical success factors
■ developing tailored guidelines.

If we replace "information security" with "compliance," and make other appropriate replacements, what does our new "standard" tell us? One of the most striking messages is that it would portray the requirements of the Act as "threats" which need to be assessed, and compliance as a way of mitigating and treating those threats. This view is not that discordant with the opinions expressed in the past about the Act.

From a practical standpoint, ISO 17799 would consider the "assets" of the organization, which are generally "information assets" that contribute to financial reporting and the processes that support the reporting of workflow, and understand their security requirements. It would then establish their potential vulnerability to threats. This is followed by an assessment of the impact on the business that the realization of any of the these threats would have, and what the sources of these threats might be. The process then adopts an approach that prioritizes and treats these threats, monitoring and managing them through a series of controls. This "threat" and risk-oriented approach sits reasonably well with some of the responses to the Act that are being adopted by companies that have found the systematic approach costly and time-consuming.

As a general comment, although the standard seeks to prevent loss, it is essentially a reactive process, reacting to threats. It is not proactive in the sense it can be used to drive change in business practice to improve business activity, rather than fit business practice to legislative requirements.

A simple paraphrase and substitution in the text for "compliance speak," based on relevance and suitability, illustrates how interchangeable some of the concepts are:

- What is compliance?
- Why is compliance needed?
- How do we establish compliance requirements?
- Assessing compliance risks.
- Selecting controls.
- The compliance starting point.
- Critical success factors.
- Developing your own guidelines.

Following this through and relating it to the recommendations of the Act provides a skeletal framework for developing a compliance process. Clearly it will be shaped by regulatory-specific needs, but it can operate as a supplement. In particular we can note that if we make a substitution in the text of the standard for "Developing your own guidelines" the standard would be revised to state:

> This code of practice may be regarded as a starting point for developing organization specific guidelines. Not all of the controls and guidance in this code of practice may be applicable. Furthermore, additional controls and guidelines not included in this standard may be required. When documents are developed containing additional guidelines or controls, it may be useful to include cross-references to clauses in this standard where applicable to facilitate compliance checking by auditors and business partners.

The spirit of this and the practical focus are very much in line with the overall spirit of the compliance process.

CMMI

The Capability Maturity Model Integration for Software (CMMI) is a model for evaluating and measuring the maturity of software processes.[2] It is also used as an improvement tool, by focusing on the practices that can develop the maturity of processes. It is now a de facto standard for assessing and improving software processes. The Software Engineering Institute (SEI) has instituted a means for documenting, defining, and measuring the maturity of the processes used by software professionals. CMMI measures the maturity of the software development process of organizations on a scale of 1 to 5. The original CMM was created in the mid-1980s and has been superseded by the revised CMMI. The five levels of CMMI allow an organization's software development to be measured in a predictable, effective and controlled manner. The levels represent levels of "maturity."

Level 1: Initial

Maturity level 1 organizations are characterized by a tendency to over-commit, abandon processes in times of crisis, and not be able to repeat their past successes.

Level 2: Repeatable

At maturity level 2, software development successes are repeatable. The status of projects is visible to management at defined points, generally through project management.

Level 3: Defined

At maturity level 3, processes are well characterized and understood, and are described in standards, procedures, tools, and methods.

The difference between levels 2 and 3 concerns standards, process definitions, and procedures. By level 3, these are customized to suit a specific project or company unit.

Level 4: Managed

Using precise measurements, management can effectively control the software development effort. In particular, management can identify ways to adjust and adapt the process to particular projects without measurable losses of quality or deviations from specifications. Now processes are predictable, as is their impact on the overall performance of the development activity.

Level 5: Optimizing

Maturity level 5 focuses on continually improving process performance through both incremental and innovative technological improvements. The effects of deployed process improvements are measured and evaluated against the quantitative process improvement objectives. Both the defined processes and the organization's set of standard processes are targets of measurable improvement activities.

The motivation of the workforce is integral to quality and performance, and workers are aligned to business values. The opportunity to improve is actively looked for. and there are mechanisms to turn opportunity into reality.

WHAT METHODOLOGIES, FRAMEWORKS, AND STANDARDS HAVE IN COMMON

The standards we are considering, COBIT, ISO 17799, ISO 9001, Six Sigma, and so on, have a great deal in common. They have aspirations to address problems and improve a situation so that processes can be transformed from being ineffective to being continually effective. This is a direct overlap of interests with the Act. Each of them and many more make a contribution towards ensuring that the organization and its processes are in good enough shape to manage any regulatory requirements, deal with any risks, and cope with the changes to the market that inevitably occur. They have a common interest expressed in:

- the way they approach their focus
- their common aim of improvement
- their use of processes as the vehicle of implementing compliance
- many of their clauses, and the language used
- the business sectors they deal with.

This overlap is not coincidental. The compliance process is largely an amalgam of processes, techniques, practices, and skills developed for and by these methodologies within frameworks.

Methodologies and the perfect organization

The notion of the "perfect organization" arises again, as it often does in assessments of maturity. Level 5, the optimized organization, has elements of this completeness. Throughout the levels, there is an emphasis on those qualities we associate with the compliance process. The compliance process seeks to move the organization from an ad hoc and arbitrary response to the Act, through a managed approach that becomes repeatable through the compliance cycle, to the ideal of full staff participation in a fully recognized responsibility cascade.

PRACTICAL COMPLIANCE SUMMARY

- Reuse skills and appreciate the value of existing frameworks and methodologies.
- ITIL is especially strong for incorporating the compliance process, notably into the service desk (if implemented).
- Adapt any methodology that adds value to understanding and controlling processes.

NOTES

1. Six Sigma is a registered service mark and trademark of Motorola, Inc. The origins of Six Sigma are in its statistical application around deviation. Sigma

represents standard deviation based on a sample population, and the idea that six of these standard deviations between the mean of a process and its limit will ensure that nothing will be generated that exceeds the specification. Competence in the methodology is associated with "belts"; a "black belt" is an advanced practitioner.

2. The CMM was developed by the Software Engineering Institute (SEI) at Carnegie–Mellon University, Pittsburgh. It has been used extensively in production industry, especially avionics, and for government projects since it was created in the mid-1980s. The SEI has subsequently released a revised version known as the Capability Maturity Model Integration (CMMI).

CHAPTER 25

Professional Service Providers and Best Practice

THE MAJOR PLAYERS: THE BIG FOUR

By the end of the 1980s there were eight large firms dominating this service market. This group form the basis of today's "Big Four." The process towards merger and consolidation has been relentless. Economies of scale mean there are fewer skilled staff available today to work in a more complex and more heavily regulated market than there were during the 1980s. This factor reinforces the need for the compliance process to be supported as best as possible through in-house resources.

In the United States, Ernst & Young and PwC account for about 20 percent of this market each, with KPMG and Deloitte & Touche accounting for about 13 percent each. The rest of the market is accounted for by internal departments, smaller auditors, and agencies.

The market developed and became more competitive until further mergers, such as Arthur Young merging with Ernst & Whinney to form Ernst & Young, and the creation of Deloitte & Touche in August 1990. Local variations saw cross-mergers: in the UK Coopers & Lybrand Deloitte coexisted with Touche Ross. But as the 1990s moved on, further changes simplified even these variants. Finally at the end of the 1990s PricewaterhouseCoopers emerged to simplify the picture further, and stabilize a long period of consolidation. When Arthur Andersen collapsed during the Enron scandal, the Act emerged as a force driving business for the survivors.

A successful filing from these companies is a valuable asset for many large companies affected by the Act. These players are truly global operations and dominate their market. Because of their importance in auditing and their expertise in compliance, the following briefly illustrates their approach to compliance, summarizing the way they adopt best practice to ensure that clients gain the most from the compliance effort. It is as well to understand how their compliance strategies have evolved.

Ernst & Young

As a major financial and accounting service provider, Ernst & Young (E&Y) has developed considerable experience and expertise with the Act. Its website opens with the thought:

> The passage of the Sarbanes-Oxley Act has caused an abrupt reawakening for business—altering the landscape and forcing a new atmosphere of accountability. At Ernst & Young we view the Act as a positive opportunity to review our own practices and to emerge as an even better organization.

This is a positive message to financial services in the face of the Act, and the bulk of the library and information services offered by the firm follow this theme. It is also looking beyond the immediate issues of even Section 404, and trying to anticipate further stages of action to "404+1". E&Y talks of post-implementation issues:

- the level of effort required
- embedding "control consciousness" in business units
- how to avoid being locked into "implementation-only" strategies that are costly in the long run.

E&Y makes the point that requirements of the Act will continue to be heavy, despite the workload achieved. Like all the Big Four, E&Y has carried out a number of surveys (see Ernst & Young 2004), and based on the information they provided, it has concluded that:

- Ongoing compliance effort will be significant, with an ongoing spending rate of 50 percent to 75 percent of first-year implementation costs.
- Over 70 percent of companies are planning some form of control self-assessment as part of their future compliance strategy.
- The role of internal audit in the ongoing process is still evolving.
- Technology solutions and other tools can reduce the cost of compliance.

Its assumptions regarding the longer term are borne out by many reports across the industry. They underline the nature of the commitment that must be made to compliance, and reinforce the value of undertaking a full compliance process with an inbuilt compliance cycle.

KPMG

KPMG includes service solutions for the Act among its range of offerings. One area it looks at is the way to address internal controls as part of an integrated solution to manage the whole business. KPMG suggests, for example, the upgrading of an enterprise resource planning (ERP) system to realize business value and sustain compliance. The requirement is to ensure that compliance is part of the business in the same way as any other business activity, and seen as a process, not a one-off project. This activity calls for integrating software control capability into the organization's internal control and compliance program. The objective is to integrate controls within an ERP solution. This offers:

- optimized controls within business processes
- process and control efficiencies
- cost reductions
- effective compliance management.

The emphasis is on ERP integration as a differentiator. As in all things, getting controls right first time is cheaper than retrofitting them. Staff implementing systems focus on functionality rather than control and security. There is an opportunity to build in good controls from the beginning. Ineffective controls fitted later can lead to reporting of significant deficiencies and material weaknesses, with the risks of an adverse audit opinion. This also applies to the design of controls. In this design process the organization must balance:

- risk and controls
- process optimization
- organization and people
- technology.

The emphasis moves from manual to automated solutions under the ERP umbrella. A design–test–build–deploy process delivers integrated controls. In the design phase key questions generate the activity (KPMG, 2006):

- What are the key risks and controls for each business process, and how are they configured in the ERP system?
- What gaps exist between current key controls and the newly identified key controls?
- What control procedures are required?
- What is the security control strategy?
- Are controls being identified and linked to process definition documents?

■ How does the organization ensure that its project documentation will satisfy regulatory compliance and monitoring needs?

The build phase lists some key questions such as:

■ Who are the users of the new system?
■ What are their access and security rights?
■ What are the IT change management procedures?
■ How are the key controls configured or customized, and who is responsible for monitoring them?
■ How do controls interact with processes?

Some of these questions would be answered through a framework such as ITIL.

Test questions link to the other phases:

■ Are controls testing end-to-end business processes?
■ Are business roles being assessed in line with segregation of duty (SOD)?
■ Have interfaces been tested to ensure consistency and accuracy across multiple databases?
■ Are trial conversions being executed and reconciled?
■ What are the user acceptance test (UAT) criteria and sign-off procedures?

Again a formal framework relating to IT and software management, including test procedures, will form the backbone of this work. Following launch of the integrated system, the need to monitor and evaluate performance leads to ongoing monitoring. In deploying, the following questions act as guides:

■ What is the structured plan to assess control and security performance?
■ What is the review process for risk and monitoring compliance?
■ How is documentation being updated?
■ How are treatments being included in the compliance process?
■ How is ownership and control accountability being monitored throughout this process?
■ Are there plans to train users effectively on controls?

Through this process of integration with an ERP system, the formal documentation and process feedback is fed into the compliance cycle to ensure ongoing compliance.

PwC

PricewaterhouseCoopers declares that "Without a doubt, the Sarbanes-Oxley Act is the single most important piece of legislation affecting corporate governance" (PWC 2005a). Recognizing this gravitas and providing solutions to help companies achieve compliance has been a critical activity for the company. In one of its guidance reports it details a specific approach to the Act, which mirrors our concept of compliance as a process rather than a project. It notes that its perspective sees a sustainable approach to Sarbanes-Oxley as requiring a transition from a "one-time project" approach and into a way of working where compliance is integrated into daily operations. Two factors drive this transition:

- quarterly reporting under Section 302 aligned with annual reporting under Section 404
- the need for organizations to proactively address change in business processes and internal controls and the ability to sustain compliance with the Act.

For this approach to be successful there must be a defined program that operates year on year as a part of the business. To embed compliance in ongoing operations requires:

- clear accountability
- an efficient operating structure
- effective enabling technology.

This overall process is a repeatable one, and the best option for really addressing compliance costs. The PwC guidelines are positioned as an effective path for companies to follow as they seek to achieve sustainable compliance. A key part of this is staffing the organization with the right skills. This theme is further explored in the PricewaterhouseCoopers *2005 State of the Internal Audit Profession Study* (PWC 2005b), conducted in the third quarter of 2005. It includes responses from a cross-section of the internal audit community. The study identified six trends that are affecting the internal audit profession specifically as a consequence of the Act:

- The requirements of the Act continue to have a significant effect on the priorities of internal audits.
- The internal audit is seen to develop relationships with key company stakeholders.
- Risk management and corporate governance have gained greater visibility.

- The demands on internal audit resources are causing resourcing problems.
- Chief audit executives are asked to provide formal opinions on internal controls.
- The perceived value of continuous auditing and monitoring is growing.

The PwC approach is clearly based on seeing the compliance effort in its totality, and aligns with the approach of the other members of the Big Four in stressing compliance as a process that is part of the bigger business picture and not an isolated activity.

Deloitte & Touche

Deloitte & Touche has evolved a range of services for compliance. One service set, Sarbanes-Oxley Section 404 Readiness Services, is designed to assist companies in complying with Section 404 of the Act. It provides help in documenting, evaluating, testing, and reporting on the effectiveness of internal controls over financial reporting, using the COSO internal control framework as a reference. This set of services offering extends into working with clients to develop processes and technologies relevant to management's ongoing assessment of internal control. The specifics of these services are part of a wider view that sees the Act as an opportunity for change.

This is centered on the experience of Deloitte & Touche with its client base. In this approach a structured internal control program can provide much more than compliance. It:

- enables better business decisions
- improves relations with and encourages investors
- prevents loss of resources
- provides competitive advantage.

The Deloitte & Touche approach widens the advantages to business through:

- increased stakeholder, CEO, and CFO confidence in the company's internal control, documentation, and evaluation
- remediation and monitoring process
- reduced potential risk for fraud
- enhanced risk management practices
- improved financial reporting
- improved governance practices.

The Deloitte & Touche approach is founded in the structures of COSO, and a methodology that is practically focused on the Act in detail. However, the above benefits derive from the larger compliance picture. For companies that see the Act as a specific set of obligations and no more, these approaches are controversial. But for the organization that understands the need to maintain compliance, the Big Four can offer a great deal of support and practical experience.

A complication for listed companies, as we have seen, is the separation of auditing activities from other non-audit activities. Whereas before the Act the same firm, with perhaps a substantial history of cooperation with the client, used to manage auditing and other tasks, even consulting internal auditing and process development as well as managing IT projects, now the Act specifically forbids such an overlap in activities. This is seen as in the interests of eliminating potential conflicts of interest and maintaining transparency in service–client relationships. This has:

- created recruitment issues for organizations trying to recruit skilled staff with Big Four backgrounds
- driven up costs, as consultants with specific skills become rarer in a period of high demand
- made servicing auditing and other functions problematic through lack of competition in the marketplace among auditors
- forced companies to use smaller and sometimes less experienced auditors with a lack of skills in such large environments.

PRACTICAL COMPLIANCE SUMMARY

- Recognize that controls integration is critical.
- Consider controls related to the whole organization.
- Begin with the design stage and continue throughout the implementation.
- Get system implementers to focus on controls as well as transaction processing efficiency.
- Emphasize the importance of controls to ERP project teams.
- Ensure that related documentation is updated and can be exploited.
- Develop manual (detective) controls towards automated (preventive) controls.
- Decide on control integration early in the design stage to reduce costs.
- Ensure ownership and accountability extend to external suppliers.

CHAPTER 26

The Benchmark Solution

AN IDEAL SOLUTION?

How far is an "ideal" response to the Act possible? Most legislation recognizes that corporate behavior is liable to stray from the ideal, or is at best flawed. The assumption of corporate governance is that we need to be vigilant in managing our activities so that they conform to a social ideal and operate within acceptable limits. What these limits are is often a point of considerable debate, one that is not generally resolved. Overall, such legislation is subject, like socio-political attempts at behavioral reform, to interests within society operating through pressure groups which attempt to sway legislation in one direction or another. Having recognized the pragmatic nature of regulation, the Act does however imply an ideal, as we have observed. It appears to assume a perfect organization, however impractical that concept might be. Attempts to comply must somehow be measurable against such an ideal.

A practical approach might be to establish a standard based on a form of benchmark. This benchmark can incorporate the compliance process, including its reformatory cycle of activities, industry best practice, and the organization's own personal standards expressed through internal policies and publicly stated standards of corporate governance and board-level ethics. This combination establishes a benchmark against which the compliance process can operate and be measured. The measurements can be both qualitative and quantitative. The conclusions about the state of the organization in relation to this benchmark can operate as clear, demonstrable evidence that inputs to the management assessment of control effectiveness, and underpins the credibility of the non-financial as well as financial aspects of the periodic financial report. So what does this benchmark look like?

BENCHMARKS IN GENERAL

Benchmarking as a concept has evolved into a necessary part of business life. It helps key managers in their decision making, and shapes their approach to their areas of responsibility. In all aspects of business there is a need to understand how we are doing, in order to make improvements and to identify where we may be failing. Benchmarking is a process that enables strategic managers, such as chief executive officers (CEOs), to compare and contrast the performance of their organization with that of others in their industry. It is closely aligned to the idea of best practice, and assumes there is a likely better method or approach to an activity than the one currently being pursued.

Best practice assumes that there is something closer to an ideal, where with appropriate application of processes and methods, using tests, assessments, and feedback mechanisms on performance, the unpredictability of events can be contained and progress can be made. As its name suggests, this is often a set of techniques that:

- are observable
- are practical
- are testable
- have a track record in delivering measured success.

Benchmarking operates with best practice to give senior management a reference model for delivering with a degree of predictability against the goals and objectives set by the organization. Like most planning and decision-making activities, benchmarking is a process that reduces business risk by ensuring current business practice is improved or held to a measurable standard. It may refer to a single project, but generally operates within the context of a strategic, ongoing process. The compliance process is such a process. Figure 26.1 illustrates the context for benchmarking, emphasizing the variation in benchmarking according to sector and sector type. Ultimately an organization's benchmark will be unique to itself.

Sometimes there is some confusion over the terminology, since in computing benchmarking is very test-intensive. It is also project-specific in that it describes activities that test a program to assess performance, either one-off or as part of quality assessment project. This is not strategic in the business sense, and can be applied to quite discrete aspects of a program. From the point of view of the Act, benchmarking is a useful concept that adds an industry-wide dimension to the compliance process. It also introduces the accumulated experience of best practice through solutions available on the market from:

- software vendors
- consultants
- auditors
- regulators.

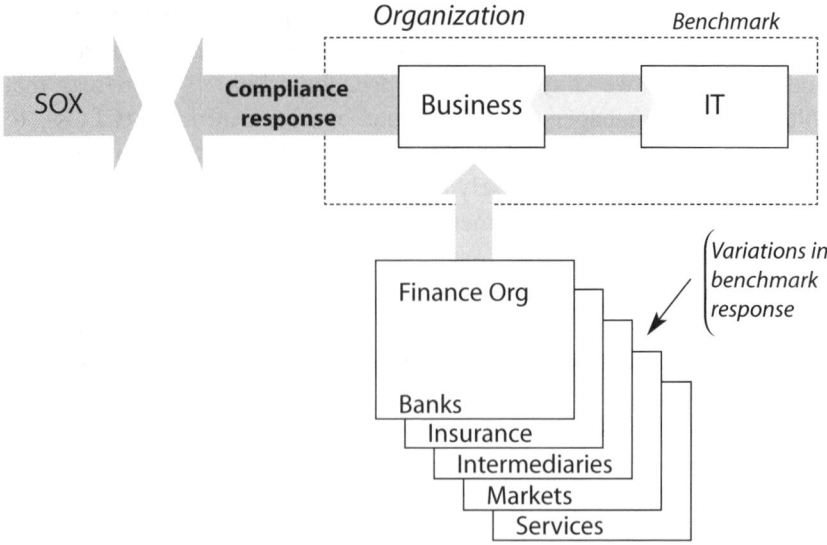

Figure 26.1 Benchmarking and compliance

Strategic management

Benchmarking in business is generally associated with strategic management. This is about giving direction to the company, and the direction chosen is reflected in the periodic reports as chairperson's reports and other non-financial statements. Strategic management entails:

- defining the organization's objectives
- creating policies to achieve the objectives
- allocating resources such as budget and skills for implementing the policies
- assigning responsibility for using the resources and following through on implementation.

These are all aspects of the initiation phase, or the first part of the compliance process. These activities can be benchmarked by reference to the industry by examining what do other companies do, and by exploring the methods recommended by consultancies. The compliance cycle, the second part of the compliance process, is also subject to a number of benchmarks. Some of these, notably the recommendations of the large audit consultancies, have been indicated elsewhere in this book.

Corporate strategies and compliance

Corporate strategy is about having a clear mission, and a sense of how effectively and efficiently the organization is carrying out its core objectives. While the compliance process appears to be tactical in its practical application, its roots are strategic. By linking corporate direction with effective benchmarking, the business can ensure that:

■ it is line with market developments that are common to its sector
■ it allows for issues and challenges that all companies in its sector face
■ it has referenceable models for responding to these challenges.

In this context, understanding sector trends is vital, and regulatory trends are part of the overall picture. Benchmarking against common best practice in regulatory compliance is part of the strategic perspective; it is an activity within the corporate strategy world. It also ensures that senior executives sharpen their focus on the key questions:

■ Where are we now?
■ Where do we want to get to, or in which direction do we want to go?
■ How do we get there?

The answers to these questions form the core elements of a strategic plan. The planning activity refines these questions, tests assumptions, draws conclusions based on evidence, defines and scopes a planning process, and details how it is to be done.

ONGOING PROCESSES AND FLEXIBILITY

Strategies, however, are not one-off concepts either. They are, and must be, subject to change. They are ongoing, and last as long as the business is viable. While it is important to have consistency in overall purpose, the way that objectives are achieved may have to be redefined, and if the objectives are not changed as a result then the way that they are realized will be. A static organization is doomed to atrophy. Profit drives a company to seek new and diverse paths, but new initiatives must be integrated into existing processes and structures if change is not to become destabilizing. In this sense the organization is "dynamic." It must view regulation not simply as much like any other aspect of business: it must anticipate it and plan accordingly. By maintaining a flexible compliance process in the compliance cycle, an organization can respond to new developments quickly and still maintain existing strengths, such as skills and investments in processes and controls. The dynamic nature of such planning has been captured as part of an analysis that indicates critical moments (sometimes called strategic inflection points) at certain points in business planning.[1]

TIMESCALES

Since the business planning process is ongoing, and the compliance process runs in parallel, there are complexities that result from the confluence of existing processes and the current of change and new processes. There is a tension between them, and a tendency to move in parallel worlds. The critical points at which business options change and functional activity takes a new departure are not always consciously recognized until well after the event. There is a sense in which there are different timescales at work: the surface timescale, conscious and measured by everyday activity, and a sub-surface timescale in which longer-term processes are being worked through. Influenced by events in the surface timescale, the events that occur here are not necessarily visible unless they are really looked for, or are uncovered as part of a thorough assessment. Information security offers a example of this confluence:

- A backdoor loophole in an otherwise secure server environment left by a disgruntled employee might sit unused for a long time, and then act as the conduit through which a successful attack is made. The attack itself might remain hidden for some time. It could be a trojan or a malware program set to trigger at a date in the future, either with minimal effect but some frequency, and perhaps unnoticed, or with a devastating eruption into vital business processes.
- A closer example in the world of regulatory evidence might be stored non-compliance information living within the life cycle of information as "hidden," but discovered as part of a regulatory investigation. Surface events might trigger the investigation in present time. The non-compliance evidence would have been laid down at an earlier stage and left to await a longer-term point for its destruction.

What matters is the point at which such an event occurs and the impact it has.

Short and long-term planning (tactical versus strategic)

Timescales are also relevant to planning, both short and long term. The nature of what is planned will depend on the strategic direction discussed above. Manifestation is the important point, where information is revealed or discovered.

BENCHMARKING AND THE COMPLIANCE PROCESS

Although benchmarking is a considerable activity in its own right, it does not have to be onerous for the organization. Benefits can be gained by simple benchmarking based on low-cost, quick to implement approaches. Since it is likely to be part of a cycle of activity, benchmarking can be updated and broadened as and when appropriate, as long as it is a controlled process in its own right.

Costs

Although it is an expensive activity, benchmarking contributes real cost benefits. As a supplementary decision-making tool it provides a reference that can save considerable sums in the short and long term. For compliance, effective benchmarking allows the project to keep within reasonable bounds, focusing always on the criteria for which a benchmark is created. The costs are generally:

■ Cost of time and materials: for drawing up surveys, questionnaires, interviewing customers, suppliers, partners. These costs will include:
  – travel and subsistence costs, underlying the importance of setting a budget for the exercise
  – any capital expenditure on software, and other materials or equipment.
■ Skills costs, for the specific skills involved in building and implementing benchmarks, such as:
  – marketing skills
  – IT support skills
  – interviewing and customer relationship skills.
■ Assuming these skills come from within the organization, their cost must be accounted for to the departments from which the staff are drawn.

Initial assessment of scope and resources

As part of the first stage of the compliance process any opportunity to benchmark control activities or compliance activities should be examined and taken up. Decisions can be made to include or exclude benchmarking, but any inclusions must take account of the time it takes to benchmark. There are a number of approaches that can be adopted:

■ Use existing benchmarked information, if it exists. This might come from previous or other compliance programs.
■ Informal discussions with managers and other employees, especially those in key positions with domain knowledge.
■ Discussions with customers who have insights into common practice among suppliers.
■ Discussions with suppliers and service providers.

Research

This is generally a time-consuming activity, and greatly benefits from either buying in a base of knowledge, from consultants or industry-specific knowledge brokers, or exploring and consolidating the knowledge already within the organization in areas such as finance, legal departments, IT, and business functions. One valuable aspect of a cross-functional compliance task force (CTF) is the involvement of these departments and access to their resources.

Research can take a number of forms, and can be interactive or traditional. Techniques include:

- **Surveys**: that are focused on the most relevant staff, such as those responsible for using company policies when managing or enacting transactions.
- **Questionnaires**: that can be as broad or narrow as required. These are effective for gaining a quantity of information, but less reliable than face-to-face techniques.
- **Marketing research**: this might be either internally derived or externally captured. By and large its emphasis is on promotion of products, and it is not as useful as internal surveys, or surveys conducted across the industry by consultancies. An alternative is to purchase existing surveys that are relevant to the subject. However, these are generally conducted with specific objectives in mind, and may not reflect the right kind of information. A better approach is to commission a bespoke survey on behalf of the company. Employing a consultancy or marketing company is a costly but very effective means of establishing both quantitative and qualitative data.
- **Quality control data**: this should exist for the organization. It may well be accessible for other organizations through quality institutes. The objective is to establish differences in performance over time, and differences in quality, defined within the scope of the compliance process. Internal quality assessments, for ISO 9001 for example, provide good demonstrable evidence.

Comparisons with the rest of the industry

This activity should involve a direct comparison, if at all possible, with market leaders, innovators, and those organizations recognized to be among the best in the sector. Again, initial surveys and questionnaires, as well as commissioned surveys, can be useful inputs to this activity. Once the key players and competitors, or partners, have been identified, the information can be corroborated with evidence from customers, suppliers, and financial analysts, professional institutes and organizations, trade associations, and others in the market.

Benchmarking can be a comparison between the existing state of affairs and a future ideal for the organization (comparing now and an ideal future), or between the organization and peer organizations in the industry (comparing the organization's "now" and a peer's current state).

For financial markets benchmarking is well established. There are a number of recognized areas where benchmarking plays a prominent role. Benchmarking financial systems involves a number of steps. Activities include comparing aspects of financial intermediaries and markets for the size and mix, and the efficiency, of the activities of these entities, such as banks, insurance companies, pension funds, development banks, and stock markets, at similar stages of development.

This is a labor-intensive set of activities requiring:

- considerable research
- access to the right information
- up-to-date statistics
- techniques such as sampling and statistical analysis
- effective, supported databases.

These are all resources that must be backed with:

- expertise in the domain being benchmarked
- expertise in the use of systems and techniques
- additional support from IT functions responsible for supporting databases, applications, and workgroups.

All of these elements have an associated cost, and these costs must be factored into any project of activity that includes benchmarking.

Cooperative benchmarking within the industry

Benchmarking was originally invented as a formal process by Rank Xerox, and is usually carried out by individual companies. Sometimes it is carried out collaboratively by groups of companies. One such venture is the NYSE eGovDirect.com initiative. This provides a password-protected website and an interactive, web-based tool, acting as a secure platform for listed companies which need to register governance documentation to the NYSE. A specific feature is the ability for listed companies to compare their corporate governance structures against similar NYSE companies using a benchmarking tool. As of year-end 2005, nearly 1,100 listed companies were registered for the website. Typical documentation includes annual and interim affirmations, CEO certifications, information on governance relating to company officers and board members, and required information on dividends, shares, and shareholder meeting dates. The system is fully interactive and acknowledges filings.

From our perspective the governance tools are examples of how to implement industry-wide benchmarking efficiently. The governance tools available include a comparison tool, which offers objective quantitative analysis of a board's structure versus its peers, including market value, industry, and company peers, and a comprehensive database offering a unique search feature which identifies experienced candidates for board compatibility.

An advantage of the finance sector is its willingness to use and exploit solutions to gain efficiencies in the way it operates. It is likely that benchmarking will be a feature of compliance activities, as the Act matures and regulation is refined.

SAMPLE COBIT MODEL MAPPED TO A GENERIC FINANCE COMPANY

One way of summarizing and bringing together a number of the features examined in the compliance process is to establish a simulation that allows benchmarking. This introduces FinOrg as our fictional, generalized reference model.

FinOrg International

FinOrg is a fictional finance organization with a US HQ and a substantial operation in Europe which provides its primary retail customer base. Its European headquarters are in the United Kingdom. By examining COBIT mapped to its activities, we can tease out some of the issues associated with compliance, and examine them with a view to detailing practical solutions.

FinOrg: the compliance perspective

As a large international company, FinOrg has a number of separate but mutually dependent operations and internal divisions. It is not our intention to define an ideal organization, with detailed business activities. Rather the aim is to suggest a structure that is familiar to the reader, and that can act as an example for the purposes of illustrating approaches to the compliance process. The nature of this imaginary organization will only be sketched in as needed; the rest of the picture is one the reader can provide. As such, the construct can carry a number of views on how the organization should respond to the Act, as well as follow some of these through to demonstrate their value.

Each organization is unique, and so will be its response. FinOrg's response is a mixture of well-thought-out best-practice solutions, existing unreviewed practices, and ad hoc expedient reflections on what it can do within time constraints. It provides a narrative to allow a larger view of the many dimensions of compliance to be explored, and some observations and conclusions to be made.

A vital set of policy documents center on a major review which defined FinOrg's strategy over a three-year period. This strategy review encompassed many aspects of the business, including its IT function. This strategy view is known as F3, an abbreviation for "FinOrg 3 year plan," and contains a full plan for the business. Many relevant policies and bodies relate to this.

The board has a number of bodies and committees that report to it as well as the normal divisional structure. The central drive is towards a twenty-first century company, fully engaged with changing electronic markets for financial services, and the productization of financial instruments for a larger retail market that has become more sophisticated in its understanding and selection of services, and more diverse in its needs. F3 is FinOrg's master plan for achieving an increased market share in the United States and European markets, with potential expansion to new business opportunities in Asia, especially China and South-East Asia.

The documents include:

- "FinOrg 3 Year plan," the main reference documents, owned by the board and reviewed by the management forum.
- "Information First," a set of statements and policies about how information, as the core business asset, is to be handled by the organization. This has substantial IT input and relevance. It is jointly owned by IT and Business Development, and details a full information life cycle management structure.
- "FinOrg Operational Rule Book (FORB)," which covers company policies and is constantly updated. The rule book is owned by the Management Forum.
- "The IT Future," which defines the IT function in terms of the F3 plan.

Relevant main internal management bodies are:

- a board of directors: with the usual structure, led by CXOs such as the CEO and CFO, and including a CIO
- the Management Forum (MF): a cross-functional forum that reports to the board through the CFO
- a Quality Task Force (QTF), which reports to the Management Forum (MF)
- Transforming Business, an irregular body that represents all business divisions and includes the IT function
- a Compliance Forum, a mixture of legal, operational (business and IT), and administrative management, with the CEO as board champion, which manages the organizational response to financial and other regulation

■ an Accreditation Committee, an older group, responsible for seeing FinOrg through its repeated accreditation for standards such as ISO 9001:2, which also looks at how the organization can standardize more of the company processes.

We can examine a selection of control objectives to see how they might be structured. Each control has a definition, which is a statement about what is desirable as an outcome, the goal, and the frequency of the review of action around the control. The "factors" help add weight to the control, and indicate elements and activities that will affect the control and its effectiveness. COBIT presents the control at two levels: high-level objectives and detailed control objectives.

P01 Planning and organization

Define a strategic information technology plan

High-level objective

This control looks at the process that defines the plan. This plan should balance the interests of IT and the business against a background of IT change and opportunity.

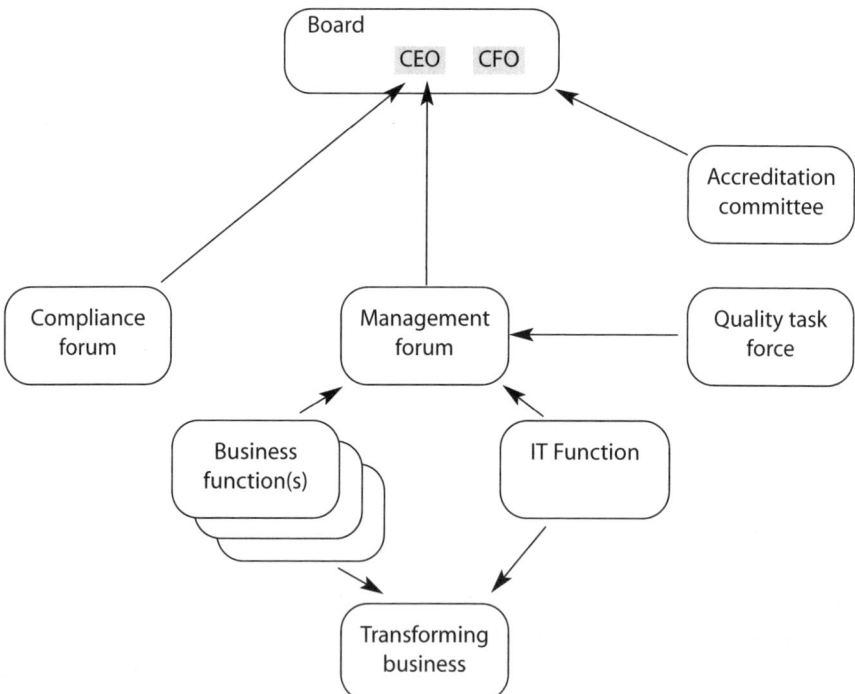

Figure 26.2 FinOrg relevant internal management bodies

Table 26.1 FinOrg domain planning and organization

Domain process(es)	ID	FinOrg reference
Define a strategic IT plan	P01	F3[1]
Define the information architecture	P02	"Information First." A project to establish information as the core asset of the organization. This is documented and defines a full ILM structure for information
Define the technological direction	P03	Also part of F3. The company has decided to evolve to a fully online model. This is planned over a six-year period. F3 is phase 1 of this process. The e-finance planning is fully defined and includes a detailed technological architecture and implementation plan
Define the IT organization and its relationships	P04	Covered in F3 under "The IT future"
Manage the IT investment	P05	"IT marker system" in-house developed management policy includes measurement criteria
Communicate aims and direction	P06	Covered in F3 under "Developing our key asset—communicating to all"
Manage human resources	P07	Covered in F3 under "Developing our key asset—staff development and retention"
Ensure external compliance	P08	"Governance and FinOrg." A five-year plan for achieving the "responsible organization." This includes organizational responses to local regulation, such as the FSA in the United Kingdom, directives in the European Union and the Act in the United States. The complex internal aspects of this are managed through the newly set up Compliance Forum (CF).
Assess risks	P09	Covered in F3 under "Planning for success." A subsidiary interest of the Risk Assessment Group," a cross-functional team reporting to the CFO
Manage projects	P10	Policies are covered in the "FinOrg Operational Rule Book" (FORB)
Manage quality	P11	Policies are covered in FORB). FinOrg is ISO9001/2 compliant and accredited. There is a Management Forum that reports to the board through the CFO and a Quality Task Force (QTF) that reports to the Management Forum (MF). The FORB is owned by the MF

1 F3 is theFinOrg three-year plan, which contains a full plan for the business. The references to it indicate that the plan includes the elements of planning and organization listed.

- Level: strategic. The process itself is undertaken at a strategic level.
- Frequency: regular. This will depend on the organization. Being strategic it might be driven by events in the market, sales circumstances, and so on.
- Goal: to generate long-term plans which are the basis for operational initiatives with specific goals.
- Factors:
  - business strategy
  - IT and how it supports the business
  - an inventory of IT assets and solutions
  - a system of checks and feasibility assessments
  - systems assessments
  - risk associations and business risk considerations
  - board-level buy-in and support (board-level champion) through reviews.

COBIT lists eight detailed control objectives associated with this high-level control objective (see Table 26.2).

Domain acquisition and implementation

Acquisition and implementation

See Table 26.3.

Delivery and support

See Table 26.4.

Maturity issues

We can comment on the position of FinOrg within the COBIT IT governance maturity model, and the COBIT management guidelines might improve its overall process management. Currently it is somewhere between levels 1 and 2. It has a system of compliance which is "repeatable," and its processes are designed and documented to a level where they can be reproduced. It is moving towards level 3, "Managed and measurable." Level 4, "Optimized" takes us closer to the ideal or perfect organization. Touching that status is the aspiration of all compliance, even if it proves impossible from a practical point of view.

INTERNAL AUDITING IN PRACTICE

FinOrg's auditing function offers a number of insights into the way we can practically approach internal auditing.

Table 26.2 FinOrg strategic information technology plan control objectives

		Control objective	CP
1.1	IT as part of the organization's long and short-term planning	The responsibility for such planning resides with senior management. IT must be reflected in this kind of planning and aligned with the interests of the business.	A strong statement that links directly with the Act and its emphasis on senior management responsibility for planning and implementing strategic plans
1.2	IT long-range plan	IT management and business process owners also play a part in the planning. Ensure planning includes ways of representing the interests of all those affected by the plan. Structure this, preferably around standards.	This aligns with the responsibility cascade, and embraces all stakeholders where possible
1.3	Plan: approach and structure	The plan evolved by 1.2 should address what, who, how, when, and why. It should account for risk and the way the company itself is structured, its formation, its geographical dimension, the requirements made upon it, its business model, and relationships with third parties. The rationale for choices should be made clear and performance indicators included. It should cross-reference any other relevant plans and policies (such as quality and information security).	Responsibilities are extended to ownership and the rationale for plan components. This satisfies the need to demonstrate how the plan will be effective. Inclusion of indicators for monitoring delivers a degree of proof of efficacy. It is also an example of documentation that fulfils the mandates of the Act. It is a prime source for senior management assessment of the effectiveness of the system of internal control.
1.4	Plan: changes	A separate process must be in place for modifying the plan in reaction to changing IT conditions without introducing inaccuracies.	Change control over time to reinforce the accuracy of financial information is essential for transparency
1.5	Short-range planning for the IT function	A process is needed for the long-term plan to be translated into short-range plans. Resources must be assigned to meet this and the objectives of the long-range plan. The short-range plan must be reassessed and amended when necessary.	The mechanisms for managing short and long-term planning are not part of the Act, but they are part of an effective control system.

Table 26.2 continued

		Control objective	CP
1.6	Communication of IT plans	Management have the responsibility to communicate plans.	Clear communications are essential for effective compliance. This control is a vital one.
1.7	Monitoring and evaluating IT plans	A process must be in place to capture feedback from users and those affected by planning and plans. This feedback is to act as input for amendments and future planning.	Feedback processes are part of the compliance loop. They are essential for manual and automated systems. For planning they underscore its credibility as well as effectiveness.
1.8	Assessment of existing systems	The process of assessing the planning for the purposes of amendment and direction should account for business automation, complexity, costs and relevance to the business requirements.	These criteria for assessment cover the essentials for effectiveness.

Internal auditing staff

The chief auditing officer (CAO) has board-level contact through an immediate reporting line to the CFO and the board. This visibility has been built up over the years as the auditing function has amassed skills and experience. The Act has helped boost its internal image as a "must-have" and "must-help" resource.

The CAO oversees the Auditing Department, which consists of six financial auditors and three IT systems auditors. This group is scheduled to expand over the next three years to ten financial and business process auditors and five IT systems auditors. This expansion is a direct result of legislation such as the Act and the likely expansion of the organization into new markets. As part of the expansion planning, the department has a policy of hiring graduates for intensive training and longer-term promotion to operational management.

The internal auditing function has a great deal to offer the compliance process beyond its specific auditing skills. Some additional functions auditors are able to manage are:

■ Lead project management: auditors are often skilled at leading large projects and complex ones.

Table 26.3 FinOrg acquisition and implementation

Domain process(es)	ID	FinOrg reference	CP
Identify automated solutions	AI1	The ambition is to introduce as much automation as possible to achieve the three-year plan. Automation also enables staff reductions and simplifies training. For IT it adds a specific skills requirement since many processes will now be part of "black box" workflows. Documentation is prepared by IT largely on an ad hoc basis.	(c)
Acquire and maintain application software	AI2	Software acquisition is managed in conjunction with procurement. There have been a set of policies on software purchase, but these are under review as part of "information first" initiatives. Third-party contracts and outsourcing are part of the remit of the Contracts and Legal department, and handled centrally.	(s)
Acquire and maintain technology infrastructure	AI3	The FinOrg network uses a mixture of in-house build and maintenance, and support from external suppliers. The international network is outsourced to a major international carrier. National networks are a mixture of self and third-party administered. There is a move in the three-year plan to outsource all activities that are not core to the business, but this is a point of debate centered on the security of information. Security has become a big issue as the financial industry measures up to significant increases in fraud. The web-oriented planning also complicates this picture. with initiatives to enable access to FinOrg financial services through mobile platforms such as PDAs and cell phones, as well as triple play options such as home IP TV services.	(s)
Develop and maintain procedures	AI4	Procedure development and documentation is very ad hoc despite the relevant bodies in place. IT assigns staff to write procedures, which are submitted to the MF for inclusion on the FORB. The FORB is reviewed but its processes are not well monitored: there is not real control system in place. Many procedures do not go through this route and exist as separate and unmonitored. Moves to expand a limited BPM structure have not been successful.	(t) (c)

■ Training: this is especially so on internal controls. They are an excellent resource for communicating these issues as part of he compliance education program. Many have undergone "train the trainer" and one-to-one skills development.

Table 26.3 continued

Domain process(es)	ID	FinOrg reference	CP
Install and accredit systems	AI5	The Accreditation Committee oversees formal accreditations in FinOrg. However, this supervision tends to be limited to quality systems such ISO 9001/2. Efforts by IT to introduce ISO 17799 have not fared well because of a lack of internal expertise and training. This has been identified as a critical area for the future within the "information first" plan. Security is a key issue. Other accreditation is centered on efforts by the Compliance Forum to standardize its processes, especially in relation to the Act.	(t)
Manage changes	AI6	As FinOrg is an organization in transition, change management is important. However, change management practices have not evolved, nor have they been extended to the whole organization. Many functions are left to create their own systems and practices. Some of these are captured in the FORB; most are not. Compliance and accreditation are notable examples. A central change management system is part of the three-year plan and has been given to the Transforming Business group (in conjunction with HR) to develop.	(c)

■ Facilitators for CSA: this is another common capability, where internal auditors have the combined skills of facilitation and domain knowledge of working control self-assessment.

Departmental mission

The objectives for the department were defined some years ago at board level. They are "to develop as a center of excellence in internal audit as a resource for the whole company and generate value through expertise in risk assessment, business processes and risk treatment." An important consideration for the organization which combines internal auditing regimes with compliance monitoring is the matter of internal auditor objectivity. While the team may have a range of transferable skill, use of auditors in other functions can undermine their objectivity in the audit process. Transparency is something that should be valued internally as well as externally. It is something external auditors will want to discover, and the Act has expectations about the role of all internal staff in maintaining demonstrable propriety.

Table 26.4 Delivery and support

Domain process(es)	ID	FinOrg reference	CP
Define and manage service levels	DS1	Service levels are part of the arrangements in place	SLAs as reference models
Manage third-party services	DS2		Third party policy management
Manage performance and capacity	DS3		BPM and ERP
Ensure continuous service	DS4		Security and continuity planning
Ensure systems security	DS5		ISMS, ISO 1779
Identify and allocate costs	DS6		Financial budgeting policies
Educate and train users	DS7		Training policies
Assist and advise customers	DS8		Formal feedback mechanisms. Informal feedback.
Manage the configuration	DS9		A software application's internal management capability. A solution's self-monitoring features.
Manage problems and incidents	DS10		ITIL, internal incident management
Manage data	DS11		ILM, data storage, content management
Manage facilities	DS12		Facilities management
Manage operations	DS13	Operational activities are the substance of the business. These range across all business and IT functional areas and consists of many processes.	Operations management

Internal audit approach

The approach is characterized by the adoption of:

- industry best practice in auditing, which is maintained through an ongoing training program and encouragement to belong to trade and professional bodies with active participation in them
- ongoing training as part of the induction process and career progression planning
- regular personal reviews, reflected in practical reviews as part of auditing projects.

Continuous auditing and monitoring

FinOrg has instituted steps towards a continuous auditing and monitoring regime. It is looking at automating monitoring tasks, especially for internal policy checking. In line with a number of companies in the sector, it is moving beyond an annual to a more continuous internal audit model. Surveys in 2006 noted that nearly half of polled companies had continuous auditing, with a substantial further number intending to introduce the practice. Many still had quarterly cycles, but others had monthly and even daily cycles. This change was a direct result of the Act and the need to monitor risk directly and consistently, and the costs involved. However, such monitoring had an overhead, and skilled auditing staff were an issue.

FinOrg auditing challenges

FinOrg found itself with several auditing challenges, including managing the variety and quantity of auditing now required, and balancing the requirement of business and IT functions for auditing. Business functions were historically prioritized according to a scheme laid down by the board many years ago. This historical view of priorities no longer matches the reality of revenue and value generation within the business. A series of responses reflect changing priorities for the business.

A replacement scheme matched frequency of audit with a simple metric based on revenue generation. However, this did not properly reflect risk to the organization—some lesser revenue-generating departments represented far greater risks than higher-value departments. Yet they were only audited once every four years, as against every two years for many lower-risk entities. Overtly high-risk entities were audited every year regardless of revenue.

The switch to a risk-based model was in progress when the Act became a significant factor. While it does not appear to contradict this model, nevertheless there was a conflict between the poorly understood or appreciated interests of the Act and the well-understood interests of the company.

The third, and current, phase has been to adapt the internal auditing activities to reflect the impact of the Act. This scenario assumes a prioritized audit every one to three years for a business area. The number of audits undertaken can be significantly reduced by integrating or consolidating audits, where possible. Frequently audits are carried out separately for business areas, because of historical practice, not best practice. A better approach is for audits to reassign themselves according to the need on an ongoing basis. This feedback on prioritization fits well with our developing model of a compliance process that has at its heart a feedback mechanism and a review loop which takes compliance into a cycle of continuous improvement and refinement.

Internal audits and the Act

The Act has had an influence on business organizations greater than that of any other recent legislation, and the momentum is such that internal audit functions can think and act beyond the constraints of past practice. The benefits of the Act here are reflected in FinOrg's approach to maintaining critical auditing skills and domain knowledge. There are several actions FinOrg can take that originate in the weight of the Act:

- Hire additional skilled staff to bolster its existing complement of specialists—a useful development to meet early timescales. Hiring staff buys in specialisms. However, there is likely to be a shortage of skilled people at a time when they are most needed, so this might not be as practical an approach as it first seems.
- Training internal staff. This investment in skills is a cheaper practical measure. It should be part of a bundle of measures adopted at any stage to build a reference body of knowledge and experience.
- Using third party consultants is common and well understood across the financial services industry. There is a higher cost associated with this method but it does address initial issues. However, considering the long-term implications of the Act, and compliance as a whole, it can be no more than a stop-gap measure. To use consultants year on year is not a cost-effective way of addressing the compliance challenge.
- Build a database of audited knowledge, similar to a risk register, which is available and accessible to a wide range of staff. Couple this with policy developments that are pushed out to all staff, whatever their function, as another objective that supports the compliance process. Using this with CSA sees the organization really beginning to use its own resources most effectively.
- Tightly link corporate governance initiatives, such as codes of ethics and board-level education, with auditing activity.
- Use time efficiently. Put some projects on hold and review milestones to allow the redistribution of skills to build a compliance process that can be sustained with lower skill levels.

FinOrg and the CTF

In FinOrg, the CAO is a member of a newly created CTF. The CTF may consist of senior executives, IT, project management, and compliance staff, and business function managers. For internal auditing the CTF can perform a number of important tasks:

- Ensure that auditing efforts feed into a cross-functional team to get the maximum buy-in across the organization for the support of internal auditing. The collaboration of internal auditing teams, business and IT oriented, should generate benefits by delivering ad hoc gap analyses from their experience, which feed into a formal assessment of the state of compliance.
- Review and adopt a formal framework as a model for the CTF activities, but also for internal auditing of internal controls. The COSO model is a likely contender, with COBIT providing control objectives and control instances.
- Refine this framework, with reuse of existing documentation templates, assessment methods, testing processes, and policies. If possible, pilot any framework and review it for effectiveness. At this point, time is the greatest challenge, and external expertise may be needed.

PRACTICAL COMPLIANCE SUMMARY

- Reuse as much existing compliance benchmarked work as possible.
- Consider a budget and adopt benchmarking measures that fit within that budget.
- Time spent in conversation with staff and informal sessions can form the basis for intuitive or qualitative rather than quantitative benchmarking.
- Model scenarios for significant processes. This is useful for clarifying internal issues over which there might be dispute.
- Research and establish industry benchmarks, and use these as a compliance baseline for performance measurement.
- Ensure strategic and tactical issues are not separate but coincide within the compliance process. Have senior management buy in to this.

NOTES

1. The idea of "inflection points" as complex but strategic opportunities to change course or direction and accelerate change is explored on www.inflectionpoints.com.

A Summary of Practical Compliance

The following is an outline guide based on the practical compliance tips associated with the chapters in this book. It provides a quick guide to the elements that contribute to an effective compliance process. Figure A.1 is an overview of how these elements fit together as a set of compliance relationships. The tables are taken from the practical compliance summaries. Each point has a value for the organization, and can be used as a structure for developing a comprehensive analysis for the preparatory and strategic stages of the compliance process, as well as offering indicators for the compliance cycle. Although these pointers are generalized, each organization will select actions and values suited to its specific circumstances.

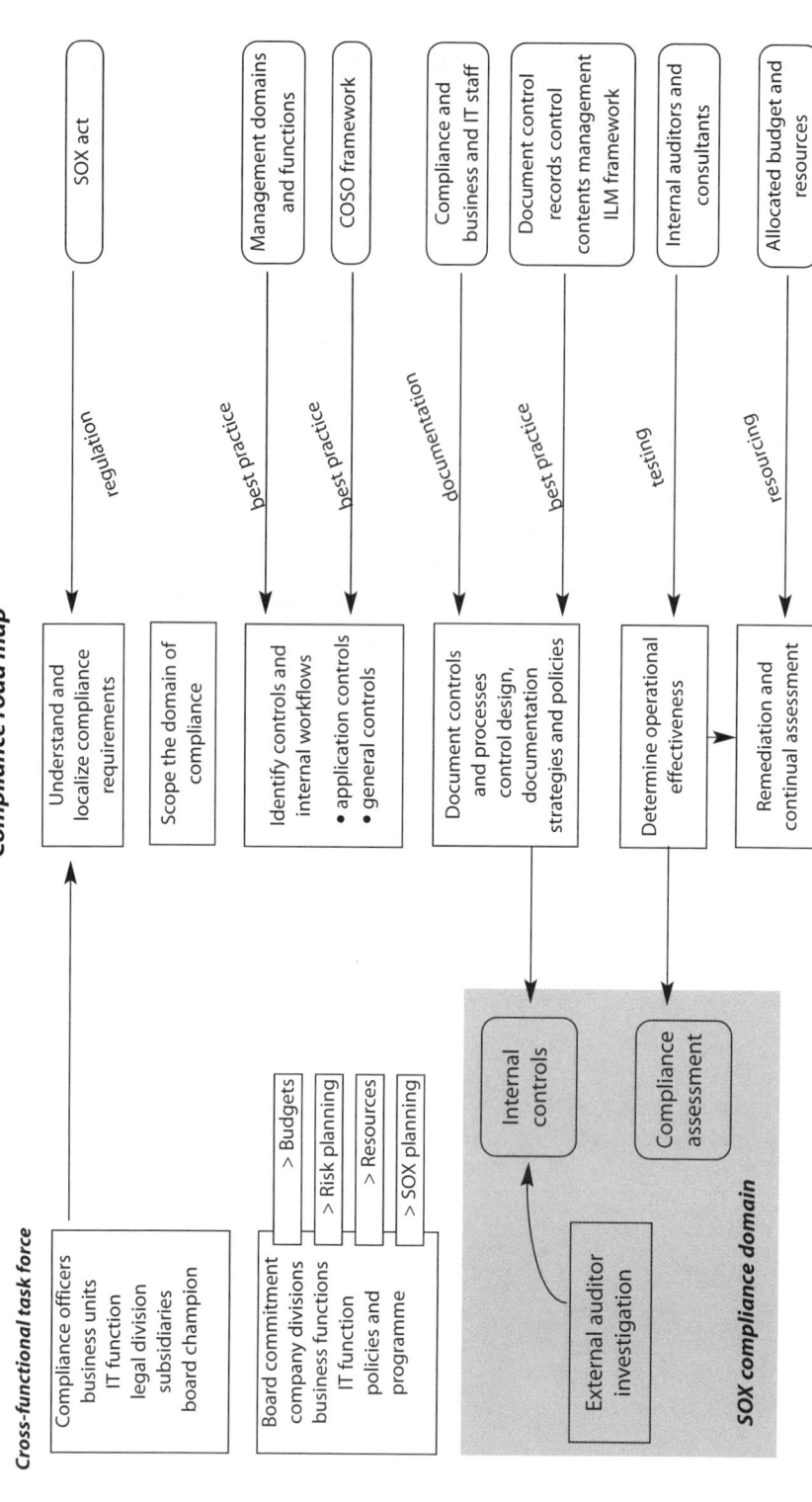

Figure A.1 Compliance process road map

Table A.1 What is Sarbanes-Oxley?

Action	Description
Understand the Act	Ensure your response is thorough and relevant
Determine the best response for your organization	Establish the interests of your organization as the basis for your response
Explore available solutions	Understand what is possible based on your needs
Apply best practice	Best practice and the experience of others is a short cut to effective solutions

Table A.2 Background and legislative trends

Action	Description
Be aware of industry and technology trends affecting the short-term response	Trends are indicators of how the industry has responded and what is driving the sector, building a picture of best practice and helping to plan future activity
Improve the overall quality of financial reporting	This is a general but overriding goal
Reduce costs, internal and external	Negotiate with suppliers and contractors and invest in internal skills and resources to minimize longer-term costs. Focus on ROIs for any of these investments, stressing the interests of your organization.
Improve the support of the IT function	As the underlying base on which compliance succeeds or fails, IT should be supported appropriately
Automate manual processes wherever possible	Automation achieves a number of objectives: reducing operational costs long term, speeding up processes for increased revenue, and enabling complex controls to be managed error-free

Table A.3 Perspectives for the financial sector

Action	Description
Establish clear lines of communication within the organization	Without effective communication, processes are error-prone and subject to localized changes independent of centralized control. This is a strategic priority.
Educate the workforce	A vital step for the spread of accountability for compliance—and for a working strategy to be effective.
Reduce confusion over roles and responsibilities	Clarifying responsibilities is an important part of the "setting guidelines" aspect of the strategic phase. The responsibility cascade is central to real behavioral change.
Develop a cross-functional approach to meeting the Act	By involving as many functions as is feasible across the organization, compliance becomes an entity-wide issue. This broadens the scope beyond financial reporting. The approach should include key functional areas, as a minimum.
Maintain real-time control	To be effective, the organization must be able to respond quickly to match the timescales required of it, especially for Section 409. This is an objective for the CTF to deliver on.
Balance between manual and automated processes	The ideal is an automated environment; the reality is a mixture. Getting the balance right will make a big difference to the costs and practicalities of developing an effective response.

Table A.4 Why financial services?

Action	Description
Define sector-specific issues for your organization	Every organization is unique. This uniqueness should be factored into the compliance process. This is expressed through the organization's risk profile, based on its general activities, size, and business ambitions; national and geographical location; company culture; key person-alities; and sector-specific activities which will especially determine the extent of its compliance effort.
Tailor compliance to your needs	This follows from the previous point. Once defined, these needs determine the detailed activities of the compliance process.
Combine information management with informa-tion security	Manage information for compliance with a view to its security, exploiting security techniques and structures where possible. This is especially relevant to financial services organizations as information economy entities.
Factor your reputation into a risk assessment	The reputation of a financial services company is para-mount. Its maintenance must be a primary objective.
Examine key processes for overlaps or conflicts	Reduce duplication of effort by uncovering common elements and common control opportunities.
Build a picture of your compliance regimes and identify common elements	Any financial services organization will have compliance regimes. Use these as practical inputs to the compliance process.

Table A.5 Financial reporting

Action	Description
Audit the financial reporting process	A standard internal audit activity; part of the overall assessment.
Assess the value of the existing process	Assign a value to the organization (financial or otherwise) to every process. This helps to prioritize activity.
Consider external resources and expertise for remediation	Find resources as needed externally, and capture the experience and knowledge for further internal use. Negotiate a train the trainer arrangement or other value-add to the relationship.
Exploit best practice as a basis for action	Research best practice in financial reporting.
Consider software solutions from known vendors	To speed up software solution acquisitions use existing vendors with a track record, especially if they are used for active compliance programs.
Assess existing skills in: managing projects, data gathering and analysis, and financial closing	Use the internal skills of generic project program managers and internal analysts.
Define and implement policies and procedures for financial reporting activities	These may already exist: if so, review and update accordingly.
Use auditable processes	Ensure that all processes have fully documented audit trails. This should be instituted at the practical, tactical level as a matter of common practice, and summarized in a statement of applicability.
Exploit the financial report, publicize the compliance process, and stress the ongoing program for investors' protection	Make the most of all the hard work by publishing its success; ensure investors know that your organization is serious about good governance and active in its pursuit.

Table A.6 The impact of cost

Action	Description
Support multiple regulations	This helps gain the most from any investment. The common elements are effectively combined within the compliance process. For example, use the documentation requirements of ISO 9001 for the compliance process, and reuse tools to reduce costs.
Support as much of the business as possible	Broaden the scope to include back and front-office activities to spread the cost burden.
Use automation to trim costs	The initial extra cost of automation will deliver a good return on investment, in terms of staff and operational maintenance costs, if handled properly.
Widen the scope of the compliance process	Include budgets on security, legislation, internal policies, business-driven IT projects.
Turn exception reports into work programs	Focus remediation on the areas where errors and mistakes occur, to reduce resource expenditure.
Centralize on an ERP or other central storage	An effective way to consolidate and centralize support costs, skills, and other capital expenditure.
Reuse system assets	High-cost items in the infrastructure can be reused, and identified "spare" capacity in the exsiting infra-structure should be used to support more tools or development projects.
Retain compliance skills	Preserve the value of the spend on skills as a real longer-term investment.

Table A.7 Responsibility

Action	Description
Ensure the signatories to the financial report and those that report on internal control know their responsibilities	These are responsibilities mandated under the Act.
Ensure the audit committee is suitably staffed and educated	To establish that their responsibilities and those of the organization and other staff are understood. The audit committee, as the accountable body, is central to successful compliance.
Ensure key operations and support staff know their responsibilities	All key staff should have specific briefings on what they, and their staff, are expected to contribute to the compliance process.
Introduce a compliance dash-board	This acts as an early warning system for senior executives, and can act as a monitor to anticipate significant qualifying changes on the state of the company that should be reported.
Institute and publish a code of ethics	This is mandated for the board and senior executives; it could extend to all staff.
Educate senior executives	Not just on the 'signing' obligations but also on the evaluation activity for the assessment process on internal controls.
Define a responsibility cascade for the organization	This clarifies who does what and why, and to whom everyone reports. It is the basis for a clear communication chain, and helps in the assignment of responsibilities. It also allows the organization to note who has too much responsibility, so that realistic adjustments can be made.
Review the status of non-executive directors	Review their skills and responsibilities, and recruit or hire necessary skills at this level.

Table A.8 Internal auditing

Action	Description
Use the audit process to maintain a constant review of the audit activity itself	Use the audit process to reinforce the compliance process.
Focus on some key activities	As a general rule across all compliance efforts, ensure priorities are maintained to manage cost and resource allocation.
Make knowledge accessible and shareable across the organization	Help the internal auditing activity by educating staff on its value and how they can contribute to it. Hold lunchtime training sessions.
Internally market compliance	To motivate and encourage staff use internal marketing resources. Incentivize, if necessary, to ensure policies are observed. Market through internal bulletins and the company intranet. A learning management system (LMS) can push information to the desktop.
Use 'pilot' projects to test the compliance process	This draws together resources from multiple departments in a dry-run test of the process as well as control items. Center this effort on a real problem to gain the maximum ROI from the effort.

Table A.9 External auditing

Action	Description
Minimize the risk to external auditors of working with you	Define cooperative measures; provide a comprehensive assessment of the state of compliance through the statement of applicability, and demonstrate this with evidence and walkthroughs.
Ensure documentation is accurate	To simplify the auditing process and build confidence in the systems of the company.
Continuous monitoring	With this in place the auditing activity is more transparent.
Educate the CTF on external auditing	Use external sources to educate the CTF; think like an external auditor.

Table A.10 Building the strategy

Action	Description
Set up the CTF	This is the prime resource of the organization. It concentrates the skilled assets and represents the body of expertise.
Publicize the compliance process	Make the process known and canvass opinion on approaches and implementation.
Identify pragmatic parts of the systematic process	This gives the organization the flexibility to go for quick solutions where necessary.
Prioritize around the risk assessment	Risk should be linked to compliance at every stage. Perhaps the most important step is the risk assessment. The more thorough it is. the greater the chance of realizing an effective system of internal control through the compliance process.
Use a preparatory checklist	Get as many stakeholders as possible to contribute to documented preparatory assessments.

Table A.11 The compliance process

Action	Description
Canvas advice from legal sources on senior management exposure	Reinforce the value of the compliance process by engaging board-level interest and commitment.
Initiate the compliance activity	Follow the compliance process—strategic phase.
Gather information from seminars, training events, and vendor presentations	Build a library of materials that contribute the biggest picture possible of the implications of the Act and approaches to managing compliance.
Establish links between the CTF and the audit committee	Make clear the lines of reporting and accountability as well as ownership of key activities.
Explore existing compliance programs	Borrow from compliance programs for working solutions and part solutions.
Detail resources needed	Build a case for a budget to meet the resource requirement, especially for external resources. Build in support for ongoing research.
Establish a benchmark for the behavior of staff at all levels	Measure this against policy adherence, notified compliance issues, non-conformities (for certified activities).
Build a set of guidelines	Cover behavior, reporting practice, codes of ethics, attorney rules, and whistleblowing rules. Ensure senior management buy in and accept these modes of behavior.

Table A.12 Compliance with Section 302

Action	Description
Observe compliance details	Ensure that the form of the certification prescribed by the SEC is followed. Prioritize around Section 302 to cover any exposure.
Include all known deficiencies and weaknesses	Anticipate future problems in this area. In particular maintain incident plans and follow-on post-evaluation reports to keep control of likely future problems.
Use tools in which there is a high level of confidence	Support the image of the organization by establishing a track record of the tools and processes in delivering successful compliance.
Document all relevant processes and controls	Reinforce this through a flexible document management system that is detailed and comprehensive enough to manage compliance, and easily accessible by all those who need access in the CTF.

Table A.13 Compliance with Section 404

Action	Description
Give this section as much resource as it needs, if prioritizing	Section 404 is the dominant section for compliance activities. The compliance process is built to manage it as much as anything else.
Give senior management support in their assessment by keeping the statement of applicability up to date	Use the resources of the CTF to work on management's assessment (internal control report).
Use 'walkthroughs' on a regular basis	Combine internal audits with the pilots suggested elsewhere. Support with project management skills.
Determine test methods that add value to the business process	Focus on areas for testing that are strictly relevant to identified business issues. Vary the testing over time to include a spectrum of processes. Build a trend analysis by revisiting certain key controls.
Acquire industry best practice	Allocate resource and time to a research effort. Keep this up to date.

Table A.14 Compliance with other sections

Action	Description
Allocate resources that are not involved in the Sections 302 and 404 efforts to other sections	The CTF will have some variation in workload. Build in time for the other sections. Use peer-reviewing of cross-sectional work whenever possible.
Prepare for 409 compliance. Put an 'early warning' system in place.	Research possible software solutions that can help automate and simplify processes and are event-driven to trap likely 409 events.
Provide strategic guidelines for Sections 802 and 1102	In the strategic phase, establish clear and well-understood guidelines for these sections. Also institute a staff retention plan to preserve the investment in skills, and encourage staff training.
Conduct a review of Section 201 prohibited activities	Research and clarify the use of external resources to prevent Section 201 breaches.

Table A.15 Compliance in the supply chain

Action	Description
Conduct a study of supply chain dependencies	Build a picture of the exposure of financial misstatement as a result of supply chain obscurity or weaknesses.
Review SLAs	Factor non-compliance as a risk factor into SLAs.
Assign controls to supply chain processes	If these have not already been assigned. Review them for suitability for meeting the requirements of the Act.
Review the scale and impact of outsourced services, and review reports from users of these services	Where necessary, negotiate additional clauses for documentation and appropriate timing of supplier reports.
Review leasing agreements	Assess how they affect financial reporting and whether they are covered by suitable controls.

Table A.16 The impact of cost

Action	Description
Select an approach to compliance	Prioritize for quick and systematic compliance within an overall compliance process.
Identify key controls and focus costly efforts there	These are the controls with the greatest impact on the business and financial reporting.
Ensure the AS2 is understood and information on PCAOB decisions is kept up to date	Allocate a training budget to ensure this. Make this available on a CTF intranet site.
Define and use control types suitable for the organization	Select controls and cost them according to criteria important to the organization (such as the supply chain and the procurement of external skills and resources).

Table A.17 Documentation, testing, and evaluation

Action	Description
Use a document management system, preferably an existing one	Ensure there is standard for documentation (use one such as ISO 9001). Inadequately documented processes and controls are a potential deficiency in their own right.
Determine an effective email and unstructured communications strategy	Be aware of the issues surrounding instant messaging (IM) and unstructured communications such as email (see Appendix B).
Manage document retention	Use or implement a strategy for managing the life cycle of documentation.
Identify significant processes as a basis for the documentation effort	The CTF to identify significant processes. The CTF should help management detect deficiencies and material weaknesses for remediation (using quick compliance).
All documentation should be considered for its use in the management assessment and how it contributes to it	In designing controls and process documentation allow for this perspective.

Table A.18 Process and the organization: policies and behavior

Action	Description
Review the process management system	Incorporate the compliance process and cycle into the company policy system.
Identify workflows, processes, and tasks	Distinguish these, determining their significance using project management techniques.
Support staff in developing behavioral change	Provide desktop solutions at the customer interface. Use software solutions to help prompt for correct actions according to defined internal policies. Combine e-learning with formal training to build awareness of policies and compliance (see Appendix B).
Manage the issues around IM* and email	Provide filtering and interactive help systems to ensure staff avoid violations at source (see Appendix B).

* Instant messaging (IM) is part of the arena of unstructured communications that is proving to be a significant challenge for both organizations and regulators. The latter are now including IM and even voice mail as admissible evidence in investigations. This, along with email, broadens significantly the amount of documentation that has to be stored, archived, and available for retrieval. Behavior that meets defined policies is an effective and practical way of reducing the considerable risks in this area.

Table A.19 Risk management

Action	Description
Re-examine existing risk assessments	Use existing risk assessments as a starting point but be aware of the need to expand these if necessary.
Use certified risk management processes as models (such as ISO 17799)	Exploit known models, especially those with which the CTF is familiar.
Determine how risk will be modeled for your organization	"Top down" or "bottom up." Strategic and tactical: the approach can be decided by the CTF or more strategically at board level.
Distinguish between organization risk and personal risk	Identify early on the types of risk, especially strategic and tactical. Consider risk at the fringes of the organization.

Table A.20 Intellectual capital

Action	Description
Include an information security framework in compliance efforts	
Protect effective financial reporting inputs with a secure system.	Adopt or move toards a certified security systems (information security management system)

Table A.21 Information security

Action	Description
Adapt ISO 17799 where possible	Use controls beyond preventive and detective to strengthen the control structure and broaden control options.
Have a sign-off process for the compliance process	Helps link responsibilities with tactical activity and clarify the status of activities as either separate sub-projects or cycles of activity.
Use a "statement of applicability" to summarize the compliance process	This documents the system of internal controls, their status, their effectiveness, and remediation issues, along with risks and resources needed to reduce risk.
Institute an "incident management" process	This tracks an event (non-compliance) and links it to the compliance dashboard to make it visible. This is also linked the responsibility cascade.
Exploit ISMS structures and controls	To help simply control introduction. Test scenarios are good for developing awareness in training.

Table A.22 COSO and COBIT

Action	Description
In using COBIT, balance company and regulatory interests	Balance effectiveness (the regulatory objective) against efficiency (the company objective), using the organization's risk profile and other criteria.
Use COSO as a reference framework (recommended by the PCAOB)	Use the five components of COSO to structure a response to the act and incorporate these into the compliance process as best practice.

Table A.23 Methodologies and frameworks

Action	Description
Reuse existing frameworks and method-ologies	Brings rapid costs reductions on skills and resources. Adapt any methodology that adds value to understanding and controlling processes.

Table A.24 Professional service providers and best practice

Action	Description
Review the policies on use of external contractors	Establish a clear policy for management on hiring contractors for compliance work.
Make suppliers accountable within the process	Ensure ownership and accountability extends to external suppliers. This is vital for the "extended enterprise" organization that sees financial reporting issues overlap with supply chains: in this case, external contractors supplying skills, but also other firms supplying outsourced services.
Ensure systems integrators and other contractors work to the best interests of compliance	Ensure system implementers focus on controls as well as transaction processing in their projects. This can greatly reduce work on introducing controls at a later date, and keeps compliance absolutely up to date. These considerations could be factored into a contract by procurement. Decide on control integration early in the design stage to reduce costs.

Table A.25 The benchmark solution

Action	Description
Determine what benchmarks exist for this work	Reuse as much existing compliance benchmarked work as possible.
Assign a budget for introducing a benchmark for the organization	This should be a natural aspect of the compliance process, and a realistic budget should exist or be allocated; benchmarking measures must then fit within that budget.
Set up meetings to assess benchmarking opportunities and inputs	Time spent in conversation with staff and informal sessions can form the basis for intuitive or qualitative rather than quantitative benchmarking. This can include scenario modeling to draw out issues and conflcting views.
Use industry benchmarks as a model	Research and establish the relevance of industry benchmarks for your compliance baseline. Develop a perfomance measurement system on the back of this work, with realistic measures and goals.
Use benchmarking to align the compliance cycle (tactical) with the strategic level	Ensure strategic and tactical issues do not separate but coincide within the compliance process. This is especially valuable for clarifying issues for senior management and acquiring new budgets or resources.

Vendor solutions

When the strategic work has been carried out and the compliance cycle is active, there is an inescapable need for tools to deliver the practical aspects of making the organization compliant. These tools are software tools and they are available from a number of sources:

- **In-house solutions**: developed by the software development capabilities of the organization, in-house analysts, programmers, and systems engineers who operate as part of the IT function.
- **Integrated frameworks**: solutions constructed from a range of products which need to be integrated into a coherent whole. These are generally supplied by systems integrators, who introduce independent "best of breed" products or their own software set.
- **Vendor products**: these are the independent software vendors (ISV) solutions, which dominate the marketplace. Usually stand-alone solutions, they deliver competency in a core function.

Each option has its pros and cons. And in the case of large financial organizations, all have a presence. The diversity of functions that have to be addressed in the contemporary organization is such that no one solution can provide a comprehensive answer to all of the issues raised by the compliance process:

- Some frameworks will scale in function and capacity to meet many of the challenges.
- Specific in-house solutions are often constructed in response to specific and often time-bound problems.
- Vendor solutions offer an effective way to pick off problems as they occur.

We now briefly explore examples from the range of vendor solutions available to meet the functional requirements of the compliance process, with a more in-depth exploration of one area that is particularly difficult to manage: unstructured communications. This is not a comprehensive comparative survey of vendors and their solutions, but rather an introduction to the types of product that might be a starting point. Nothing substitutes for thorough due diligence on the reality behind the marketing, and a track record is usually the best indicator of effectiveness.

COMPLIANCE AT THE DESKTOP

The emphasis of the Act appears to be on controlling the behavior of the most senior staff in the organization: the signing officers, such as CEOs and CFOs, the audit committee, and managers throughout the organization responsible for ensuring their company is compliant with regulations. But the nature of compliance is more all-embracing. We have seen it stretch through the organization, through business functions, the IT function, and even through the extended enterprise into the supply chain. Paramount in this drive to compliance is the way that staff at the coalface of the business react. It is at the extremities of the organization, where it touches customers, clients, and other intermediaries and markets, that the issue of compliance is resolved. The mistakes of a broker, an advisor, an analyst, a branch officer, or a call-center staff member can start the trail of investigation and disruption that can have a dire impact on the business.

Internal policy making is largely about controlling this behavior, especially for staff at the lower end of the responsibility cascade. Compliance at the desktop is every bit as important as compliance in the boardroom. But whereas directors can be targeted and brought into the compliance process based on self-interest driven by penalty and financial loss, the ordinary staff member might not have such a pressing motivation. Practical approaches to compliance at this level are reflections of the overall effort to maintain compliance through internal controls. However there are complex issues here, of human behavior, motivation, knowledge, skills, and investment. From our perspective we can consider a twin approach that delivers a high degree of confidence in the compliance process for senior managers: compliance awareness and education on policies, and policy enforcement at the point of customer interaction.

Compliance awareness and training

vcContact from Atrium

The experience of many financial organizations that have a mass-market client base is that regulation poses real challenges for:

■ making staff aware of regulation

- being able to demonstrate that staff are aware of regulation and act accordingly
- providing information so that front-line staff sell the right product to the right customer
- allowing for agent churn, where high staff turnover imposes a constant demand for re-skilling and education programs.

To address these challenges, a number of solutions have emerged from the combination of training expertise and technological innovation. Traditional face-to-face training may not be an effective way of conveying the information that has to be pushed out to staff on a regular basis. It might not be scalable nor deliverable in the right timescale, and it could be too costly to implement across a large company. Alternatives are now available through variations on e-learning, learning management systems (LMS) and "blended learning".[1]

Atrium Communications Ltd, a UK provider of online training, is an example of a vendor that has developed contact center solutions that allow staff to update themselves, monitored by management, with this controlled approach integrated into a compliance process. Staff can have a learning environment at the desktop, their place of work, with training divisible into chunked or bite-sized amounts to absorb across a working day. Interactive testing generates scores that translate into quantifiable measures to test the effectiveness of controls, and allow mangers to audit trail and manage compliance awareness and competence.

Systems such as Atrium's vcContact, include content authoring. This enables the organization to tailor the content to suit the specific interests of the organization, and operate within its cultural and policy-based approach to compliance. This allows consistency, with easily modified content to reflect changes to compliance and refinements to the compliance process as an ongoing activity. The distribution platform is generally web-based, with branding possibilities to maintain a consistent, authoritative image, supported by the existing IT controlled environment. Ideally the solution is multimedia-based, integrating audio, text, presentations, animations, broadcast media, and recorded video footage. Such a solution is a highly interactive, very visible demonstration of the organization's effort to introduce and maintain compliance. The solution should be able to be scaled across a large organization, and allow for differentiated content to match all levels of staff.

UNSTRUCTURED COMMUNICATIONS

A strategy for compliance: avoiding violation

At a common-sense level, the need to comply and at the same time eliminate the reason for compliance can only truly be resolved by preventing a violation. Without violation, there is no regulatory investigation; no digging into the corporate inner life and unearthing of evidence that leads to further investigation.

The solutions that attempt this present themselves in many ways, within many contexts. The concept of filtering at source is positioned as a proactive check on email and IM sessions before data is transmitted. As a consequence, whatever passes the filtering process is compliant and archived. When this data is stored it poses no threat to the wellbeing of the organization. This satisfies the interests of regulation and the organization. The latest "pre-review" techniques go beyond standard key word searches to the point where they understand the nature and purpose of every email, its context, and where an information boundary might be breached.

Given the difficulty of monitoring unstructured communications it is vital that a strategy establishes exactly what the organization wants from a solution, and defines the maximum return on investment. This approach allows unstructured communications to be addressed in the context of the real intentions of the Act, married with core business requirements. Compliance has relied upon capturing all correspondence and reviewing a representative sample. At the heart of this is a dilemma: archiving, while required, cannot modify user behavior or enforce compliance at the point of creation. The characteristics of a solution that attempts to deal with this might include:

- pre-review to eliminate corporate liability at source
- block review–release/retain, to catch any high-risk events that slip through filters
- active archiving, to maintain ongoing compliance and coordinate with internal records and content management systems
- budget balancing, to minimize archive costs
- speed of retrieval, to ensure compliance for legal discovery
- coordination with internal IT storage strategies such as storage area networks (SANs), to manage storage costs.

There is a need for a flexible model, under constant review to reflect the changing priorities of business growth, and strategies for the use of text messaging, multimedia messaging, e-commerce, and the fundamental shift towards information as the "value" of business.

Looking at email as workflow, we can recognize that most organizations would be paralyzed without it; along with browsers and IM, it picks up where other systems end, defining a de facto process and acting as a tool for collaboration and communication for installed customer management, document management, or underwriting systems. The downside is that process inefficiencies and workarounds are hidden within the daily volumes of mail. At the sharp end of all this, legal and compliance professionals are faced with a long list of internal policies to maintain:

- information boundaries that electronically separate research and investment banking activities
- adequate supervision and review to audit, review, and approve activities without disrupting the real-time nature of communications
- the ability to stay current with changing legal disclaimers, which vary according to audience and activity.
- disclosures, or the release of confidential information or company assessments on controlled or restricted lists
- inappropriate content, covering the use of inappropriate or insensitive language in correspondence.

More complex is the use of web browsers as alternative email and IM platforms. Managing these is a akin to managing voice system transactions, which is even more taxing issue, since the opportunities to do this are specific and limited. Yet the SEC and the Act see many of these methods of communications as of equal value when it comes to capture, storage, and retrieval.

Distributed compliance

While regulation evolves, on a daily basis organizations are implementing a strategy based on available compliance infrastructures, which vary according to internal factors such as:

- departmental policies
- classes of user
- scoping exercises
- the risk profile of the organization.

Financial services companies have always displayed great flexibility in the way they manage these challenges. An advantage of another approach is that it enables a compliance infrastructure that provides organizations with the ability to distribute compliance effort among their end-users. This compliance is built on two simple principles: do something before an action becomes a problem, and engage the user in the solution.

PREVENTIVE COMPLIANCE

Real Time Prevention™, Intelligent Review™, Smart Tagging™ from Orchestria Corporation

A player in the advanced messaging compliance solutions, Orchestra illustrates how the user-oriented approach to compliance can deliver practical benefits. The nature of business communications is universally electronic. Electronic transfers and transactions in near real time are the basis of nearly all financial services activities. The pressure to turn securities certification electronic (see Chapter 6) will complete this picture. The approach of the Orchestria solution is to apply policy controls at the point of sending, and perform an immediate compliance check. In this way non-compliant actions are prevented from occurring, and no improper communications enter the archive.

PolicyPaks[2] are regulation-specific and can be tailored by the organization as plug-ins to the active solution. For compliance officers, the onerous process of sifting through filtered queues of transactions as either spot checks or as the result of large numbers of false positives being identified is now reduced to problem-only events.[3] Out of every million emails sent, around 10,000 are policy violations of some kind. Most are unwitting, but to regulators they are all equally worthy of investigation. By greatly reducing this burden of filtering and checking, a solution based on immediate policy inspection can operate at the edge of the organization where it is most vulnerable. Software agents sit on the desktop monitoring transmissions. When a user creates a message that contains a policy violation, the agent prompts the user to reconsider and suggests the reasons for the reconsideration. This is both a preventive measure and an educational measure. Depending on the compliance process control, this message might be allowed to be sent, be stopped, be placed in a review queue for management consideration, generate alerts, or a combination of actions. The sheer volume of traffic is daunting. As information economy entities, most large financial companies transmit millions of messages every day. The potential for hundreds of thousands of violations is great. A system that can pre-empt violation has a dramatic impact in terms of:

- resource costs to filter and review
- storage and retrieval costs of tagged data (tagged for review)
- potential liability as violations.

Solutions such as Orchestria's also analyze messages in real time, understanding the context of the message in terms of date, size, sender, recipient, and the presence of an attachment. This contextualization transforms the message from data to information which has meaning within the context of the organization. Real-time assessment and detection, and meta-information for context, are two valuable components for the compliance process when it comes to dealing with the mandates of Section 409 of the Act.

USEFUL CONTACTS FOR COMPLIANCE SOLUTIONS AND COMPONENTS

Table B.1 lists a cross-section of solutions available on the market. In addition to these there are a great number of integrated solutions from major software houses and systems integrators.

Table B.1 A cross-section of solutions available on the market

Company	Solution	Website
Diagonal Solutions Ltd	Wisdom	www.diagonal-solutions.co.uk
Trillium Software	Trillium Software System® and Trillium Software Discovery	www.trilliumsoftware.com
NetEconomy	ERASE® Compliance Manager™	www.neteconomy.com
Respond	Product Suite	www.respond-uk.co.uk
Qumas	QUMAS Compliance Framework	www.qumas.com
FaceTime	FaceTime Enterprise Edition™	www.facetime.com
RuleBurst	Oasis (Compliance Assessment module)	www.ruleburst.com
Orchestria Corporation	APM Platform (Real-Time Prevention™, Intelligent Review™, Smart Tagging™)	www.orchestria.com
Symantec	Symantec BindView Policy Manager, Control Compliance Suite	www.symantec.com
Cendura	Cohesion	www.cendura.com

NOTES

1. "Blended learning" combines web technology and its unique accessibility with interactive face-to-face sessions and workshops allowing for pre-course preparation and post-course follow-up.
2. PolicyPaks are field-ready policies for Orchestria's solutions, covering regulatory requirement and including Sarbanes–Oxley.
3. False positives are the consequence of filtering processes that identify possible violations. Uncertainty leads to large queues of possible infringements that have to be investigated or reviewed by compliance staff. By improving the accuracy of selection from "possible" to "certain" violation, these queues are greatly reduced.

Bibliography and References

American Institute of Certified Public Accountants (AICPA)/Canadian Institute of Chartered Accountants (CICA) (1999) *SysTrust Principles and Criteria for Systems Reliability*, New York: AICPA.

Board, J., Sutcliffe, C. and Wells, S. (2002) *Transparency and Fragmentation: Financial market regulation in a dynamic environment*, Basingstoke: Palgrave Macmillan.

BOC (2005) "Implementing our strategy effectively, Chairman's Statement," *Annual Report and Accounts 2005*, BOC Group plc.

Bookal, L. E. (2003) "Internal auditors: integral to good corporate governance," *Directors Monthly*, March.

Buckle, M. and Thompson, J. (2004) *The UK Financial System*, Manchester: Manchester University Press.

Calder, A. and Watkins, S. (2004) *IT Governance*, 2nd edn, London: Kogan Page.

Committee of Sponsoring Organizations of the Treadway Commission (COSO)/Coopers & Lybrand (1992) *Internal Control: Integrated Framework*, New Jersey: AICPA.

Confederation of British Industry (CBI) (2005) "Comments on Sarbanes-Oxley Act," April, London: CBI.

Curtis, G. A. and Stone, L. S. (2006) "Understanding the cost of Sarbanes-Oxley compliance," *Outlook*, January.

Dresdner Bank (2005) "Corporate governance statement," *Corporate Profile,* Dresdner Bank.

Ernst & Young (2004) *Section 404 Post-Implementation: What you should be thinking about now*, Internal Controls Summary Library, www.ey.com.

Goodhart, C., Hartmann, P., Llewellyn, D., Rojas-Suarez, L. and Weisbrod, S. (2001) *Financial Regulation: Why, how and where now?* London: Routledge.

Gorrod, M. (2004) *Risk Management Systems: Process, technology and trends,* Basingstoke: Palgrave Macmillan.

GTNews (2004) *Sarbanes-Oxley Snapshot Poll, January 2004*, www.gtnews.com.

Herring, R. J. and Litan, R. E. (1995) *Financial Regulation in the Global Economy*, Washington: Brookings Institution.

Howells, P. and Bain, K. (2004) *Financial Markets and Institutions*, London: FT Prentice Hall/Pearson Education.

Institute of Internal Auditing (IIA) (1998) "A perspective on control self-assessment," Professional Practices pamphlet 98-2, Florida: IIA.

Institute of Internal Auditors Research Foundation (IIARF) (1991, rev. 1994) *Systems Auditability and Control*, Florida: IIARF.

KPMG (2006) *ERP Controls Integration: Sustaining Compliance While Implementing Change*, advisory document, USA: KPMG International.

Lander, G. P. (2004) *What is Sarbanes-Oxley?* New York: McGraw-Hill.

Liebenberg, L. (2002) *The Electronic Financial Markets of the Future*, Basingstoke: Palgrave Macmillan.

McGill, R. and Sheppey, T. (2005) *The New Global Regulatory Landscape*, Basingstoke: Palgrave Macmillan.

Oversight Systems (2006) *Financial Executive Report on Sarbanes-Oxley 2006*, USA: Oversight Systems, Inc.

PricewaterhouseCoopers (PwC) (2005a) "How to move your company to sustainable Sarbanes-Oxley compliance—from project to process," white paper, Hong Kong: PwC.

PwC (2005b) *2005 State of the Internal Audit Profession Study*, USA: PwC.

Public Company Accounting Oversight Board (PCAOB) (2004) *Auditing Standard No. 2: An audit of internal control over financial reporting performed in conjunction with an audit of financial statements, approved by the Securities and Exchange Commission on June 17, 2004*, USA: PCAOB.

Rasmussen, M. with Hunt, S. and Lambert, N. (2004) *Deciphering the*

Dual Meaning of Compliance Monitoring, Forrester Research Report, June 7, USA: Forrester.

Securities and Exchange Commission (SEC) (2005) "Notes at a U.S. Securities and Exchange Commission roundtable, April 13, 2005, on the implementation of reporting requirements of Section 404 of the Act," USA: SEC.

Servaes, H. and Tufano, P. (2006) "Ranking risk and finance," research conducted with Deutsche Bank and Global Association for Risk Professionals, news.ft.com.

Sparrow, M. K. (2000) *The Regulatory Craft: Controlling risks, solving problems, and managing compliance*, Washington: Brookings Institution.

Steinberg R.M., Everson M. E.A., Martens F. J. and Nottingham L. E. (2004) *Enterprise Risk Management – Integrated Framework, Executive Summary*, USA: PwC and COSO.

Stewart, T. A. (1997) *Intellectual Capital: The new wealth of organizations*, London: Nicholas Brearley.

Turner, C. (2000) *The Information e-conomy: Business strategies for competing in the digital age*, London: Kogan Page.

US Senate (2002) "Financial statement restatements—trends, market impacts, regulatory responses, and remaining challenges," GAO Report to the Chairman, Committee on Banking, Housing, and Urban Affairs, US Senate, October.

Wilhelm Jr., W. J. and Downing J. D. (2001) *Information Markets*, Boston, Mass.: Harvard Business School Press.

Index

accelerated filer, 60, 84
access
    control, 285, 291
    roaming, 204
accountability, 14, 41, 58, 116, 158, 164,
        177, 181, 202, 240, 243, 259, 266,
        268, 275, 294, 344, 354–9
    criminal fraud, 53, 56
accounting firms, 52, 53
    foreign, 34
    public, 5, 33–4, 52, 127, 138
    registered, 40
accounts
    consolidated, 81
    immaterial, 210
Act, 1, 3–28, 33–40, 43–60, 67–88, 93, 98,
        101–33, 136–9, 141, 145, 148, 149,
        152–64, 166, 168, 170–2, 176, 181,
        185, 188–91, 194–5, 199, 201, 203–7,
        209–14, 221, 223–7, 232, 238, 240,
        245, 253–60, 262–78, 299, 307, 308,
        312, 313, 318, 327, 329–34, 342, 345,
        347, 351, 353–61, 368, 374, 376, 378,
        400, 402–4
    see also sections of the Act
ADR, 3, 6
ADS, 6
adverse selection, 66
AICPA, see American Institute of Certified
    Public Accountants
amendments, 6, 10, 38, 44, 52–6, 59, 83,
        102, 176, 226
    conforming, 52
American Accounting Association (AAA),
    299
American Depositary Receipts,
    see ADR
American Depositary Shares, see ADS
American Institute of Certified Public

Accountants (AICPA), 84, 204, 299,
    326
archive
    costs, 273
    management, 186
archiving, 5, 186, 195, 227, 273, 402
Arthur Andersen, 8, 99, 353
AS2, 92, 138, 165, 208, 222, 316
assertions, financial, 78, 81, 233
assessment
    management, 71, 83, 131, 137, 180,
        193, 205, 313, 332, 360
    preparatory, 158, 162, 165, 168
asset, 8, 12, 17, 65–78, 79, 92, 95, 103,
        114, 119, 136, 140, 155, 171, 193,
        217, 246, 253, 254, 276–8, 281, 285,
        293, 296, 312, 331, 347, 353, 369, 372
asymmetrical information, 67
audit
    and scale, 230
    committee, 5, 14, 36–40, 45, 49, 102,
        110–15, 120, 128, 139, 140, 160,
        170, 180, 189, 190, 195, 197, 201,
        232, 400
    trail, 86, 92, 186, 223, 226, 282, 401
auditing, 7, 8, 32–6, 38, 40, 92, 97, 103,
        110–38, 141, 146, 160, 172, 179, 195,
        198, 208, 211, 282, 327, 342, 345,
        359, 372, 376, 378–80
    continuous, 358, 378
    department, 374
auditor, 4, 7, 8, 16, 26, 36, 38, 39, 43, 48,
        52, 71, 82, 86, 90, 102–4, 110,
        115–19, 124, 127–39, 141, 156, 165,
        189, 191–3, 198, 205, 210, 219–22,
        230, 231, 242, 246, 278, 281, 312–15,
        329, 342, 349, 353, 359, 361, 374
    external, 5, 36, 81, 110–15, 127, 130,
        131, 141, 157, 161, 177, 179, 190,

193, 195, 197, 201, 205, 264, 278, 330, 376
independence, 82
internal, 90, 112, 114, 125, 129, 199, 238, 342, 345, 376
IT systems, 374
prohibited activities, 36, 199
automation, 15–17, 20, 21, 68, 81, 89, 96, 103, 124, 219, 240, 280
controls, 231

balanced business scorecard, 320, 322, 325, 326, 335
banking, 20, 21, 68, 75, 112, 403
wholesale, 68
banks, 14, 17, 20, 66–9, 79, 87, 224, 367
behavior
corporate, 13, 40, 78, 360
risk-averse, 267
training, 247
benchmark solution, 360
benchmarking, 129, 267, 360–8, 380
cooperative, 367
project-specific, 193, 361
best practice, 9, 13, 69, 84, 91, 107, 117, 125, 148, 163–6, 173, 181, 199, 230, 237, 260, 267, 277, 278, 282, 312, 316, 327, 343–5, 354, 361, 379
industry, 6, 35, 163, 194, 267, 360, 378
BI, 11
black box, 231, 240
black-out periods, 44
blended learning, 401
board
of directors, 4, 8, 40, 45, 107, 110, 125, 139, 140, 158, 168, 190, 195, 208, 212, 232, 245, 300, 369
see also PCAOB
BPM, see business process management
brokers, 20, 51–3, 66, 70, 72, 74, 90, 204, 224, 366
BS 7799, 296, 347
business
continuity, 101, 282, 293
function, 160, 378
process management, 223, 239, 242

call center, 22, 87, 206, 243, 282, 291
CAO, see chief auditing officer
Capability Maturity Model Integration for Software, see CMMI
Central Computer and Telecommunications Agency (CCTA), 343
Certified Public Accountant, (CPA), 129
change management, 163, 332

Check 21, 17
chief auditing officer, 374, 380
chief executive, see officer
CMMI, 76, 326, 343, 349, 352
coaching, 325
COBIT, 25, 76, 92, 97, 102, 123, 157, 164, 239–42, 278, 299, 311–18, 320, 325–34, 342, 350, 368, 370, 380
domains, 313, 328, 331–4
Codification of Statements on Auditing Standards, 208
companies, 3–17, 29, 33, 40, 48, 53, 60, 74, 75, 79, 82, 84–90, 93, 97–101, 104, 107, 115, 140, 148, 155, 161, 173, 181, 188, 195, 204, 214, 227, 236, 243, 255, 265–9, 300, 305, 348, 353–9, 362, 367, 378, 403
publicly traded, 55, 83
policies, 161
compliance, 3–9, 11–22, 24, 40, 44, 45, 50, 53, 60, 65, 67–71, 74–82, 88, 90–132, 136, 141, 145–50, 154–61, 163, 164, 165, 166, 167, 168, 170, 172, 173, 174, 176, 177, 178, 179, 180, 181, 185, 186, 187, 188, 189, 191, 192, 193, 194, 195, 197, 198, 199, 201–11, 220, 222–48, 289, 290, 291, 293, 294, 351–69, 372, 374–6, 379–81, 400–5
active linear, 149, 150
awareness, 400
chain, 157, 165
and completeness, 123, 152–4, 305, 331, 351
cost of, 97
cycle, 76, 132, 152, 163, 167, 170, 174, 177, 179, 189, 191, 194, 201, 232, 234, 235, 243, 270, 281, 294, 351, 354, 362, 381, 399
cyclical, 151
degrees of, 152
demonstrating, 4, 265
frameworks, 299
good faith, 44
iceberg, 146–9, 156, 164
ideal response, 154
mapping, 76
model, 151, 152
monitoring, 191, 376
ongoing, 97, 132, 164, 193, 201, 276, 334, 343, 356, 402
passive linear, 149
pragmatic approach, 149, 157, 211
process, 4, 6, 14, 17, 41, 74–7, 82, 88, 90, 99–105, 107, 110–41, 145–52, 157–63, 165–70, 176, 180, 185,

186, 191–5, 197, 201, 203, 211,
220, 222, 228, 230–3, 238, 241–8,
254, 268, 270, 278, 280–2, 285,
291, 293–6, 308, 312, 316, 320,
325, 332, 342, 347, 349, 351, 356,
360–8, 374, 379, 399–401, 404
program, 6, 9, 75, 76, 128, 160, 259,
355, 365
quick, 211
specific response, 154
state of, 16, 25, 129, 149–53, 164, 230,
254, 320, 380
systematic, 211
systematic approach, 156, 165, 173,
344, 348
task force, *see* CTF
timetable, 60, 192
training, 400
conflict of interest, 46, 51, 108, 112, 127,
161, 199, 226, 255, 359
conforming amendments, 52
content authoring, 401
contingency
management, 282
planning, 203
control
activities, 264, 304
application, 305, 307
automation, 231
company-level, 213
deficiency, 214
detective, 136, 219, 233, 291, 296, 359
further, 220
general, 207, 221, 305, 334
internal, 5, 14, 21, 25, 33, 47, 71, 77,
81, 94, 97, 99, 106, 107, 110–16,
121, 124, 127, 129, 130–40, 146,
147, 153, 160, 163–5, 171, 176,
179, 185–9, 191, 193, 194, 203,
205–16, 219, 229–35, 242, 254,
256, 259, 261–7, 282, 294, 299,
304–8, 313, 325, 330, 332, 355,
375, 380, 400
objectives, 97, 116, 124, 131, 242, 278,
285, 311–13, 318, 327–33, 370,
380
preventive, 219, 280, 403
risks, primary and secondary, 229
significant deficiency, 214
types, 231, 278
control environment, 16, 102, 208, 221,
301
controls, IT, 221, 300
COO, *see* officer
Coopers & Lybrand, 300, 353

co-opetition, 204
corporate
accountability, 51
behavior, 13, 40, 78, 360
governance, 3, 9, 13, 24, 48, 82, 94, 98,
102, 114, 115, 125, 126, 163, 204,
245, 249, 261, 266, 316, 357, 360,
367, 379
COSO, 10, 25, 33, 76, 80, 123, 129, 135,
157, 189, 208, 211, 222, 232, 253,
261, 265, 299, 300–8, 311, 326–29,
334, 358, 380
Integrated Framework, 208
CP, *see* compliance process
CPA, 129
crime, 56
see also accountability, fraud
critical success factor, *see* CSF
cross-functional, 25, 159, 170, 176, 186,
211, 244, 291, 366, 380
CSF, 129, 189, 194–9, 201, 313, 318, 320,
325, 334
CTF, 112, 125, 131, 141, 158–62, 170,
194, 199, 201, 222, 231–4, 235, 242,
248, 278, 282, 291, 294, 334, 366, 380
currency exchange rate, 155, 257
custodians, 3, 68
customer care, 247

D3P, 224
decision making, 11, 22, 116, 151, 167,
254, 260, 268, 271, 276, 305, 314,
331, 360
deficiency, 140, 214, 218
evaluating, 219
remediate, 171, 172, 193
significant, 140, 217–19
demonstrating compliance, 4, 265
dependency chain, 204
designated third party, *see* D3P
deterrence, 5
director, 44, 47, 59, 112, 116, 159, 221
disclosure controls, 207–11
documentation, 21, 53, 72, 94, 102, 123,
127–9, 141, 172, 181, 186, 191, 206,
223, 225–9, 232–8, 243, 259, 274,
282, 296, 313, 331, 347, 356, 358,
367, 380
electronic records, 53, 224, 275
as evidence, 223, 228
as proof, 95, 123, 223, 228, 274

e-business, 248, 331
e-commerce, 83, 245, 248, 402
EDGAR, 83, 84

electronic records, 53, 224, 275
email, 116, 186, 224, 226–8, 235, 273, 282, 402
   management, 227
Employee Retirement Income Security Act, 44, 56
endowment mis-selling, 22
Enron, 7, 8, 105, 227, 255, 353
enterprise governance, 317
enterprise risk management (ERM), 186, 255, 261–8, 272
enterprise resource planning (ERP), 103, 223, 275, 355, 359
ethics, 7, 13, 33, 82, 108, 199, 244, 360, 379
   code of, 48, 108, 113, 164, 170, 246
EU, 102
evaluate
   effectiveness, 171, 247
   operational effectiveness, 171
executive officer, see officer
extended enterprise, 203, 400
eXtensible Business Reporting Language, see XBRL
external auditor, see auditor, external

FAS, see Financial Accounting Standards Board
fast-moving consumer goods, see FMCG
FCPA, 300, 305
feedback, 33, 116, 120, 128, 151, 167, 173, 177, 186, 258, 264, 281, 322, 325, 356, 361, 379
financial
   assertions, 78, 81, 233
   business intelligence, 11, 88, 245
   instruments, 21, 66, 156, 203, 369
   markets, 15, 65, 75, 89, 104, 367
   reports and marketing, 82
   sector, 16, 24, 65, 74, 101, 181, 254, 269, 299, 307, 331
   statements, 13, 17, 46, 79–89, 105, 135–40, 211–12, 215, 219–21, 272, 362
Financial Accounting Standards Board, 84, 215
Financial Executives Institute (FEI), 299
financial services
   retail, 21
   trends in, 4
   wholesale, 21
fines, 5, 56, 73, 105, 259
FMCG, 21, 22
Foreign Corrupt Practices Act (FCPA), 10, 300

framework, reference, 137, 253, 277, 311
fraud, 8, 14, 51, 54–9, 187, 219, 220, 233, 358
   corporate, 7, 58
   criminal, 53–6
function
   business, 160, 378
   IT, see IT function

G30, 25
GAAP, 7, 17, 80, 84, 88, 91, 112, 136, 140, 212
GAO, 7, 17, 52
gap analysis, 122, 131, 158, 168, 175, 180
General Accounting Office, see GAO
Generally Accepted Accounting Principles, see GAAP
Global 1000, 227
global warming, 255
governance, 4, 5, 11, 48, 65, 92–157, 167, 245–7, 254, 264, 268, 301, 312, 316–20, 328, 342, 358, 367
   corporate, 3, 5, 9, 13, 14, 24, 48, 82, 94, 98, 102, 114, 125, 163, 164, 204, 245, 249, 261, 266, 316, 357, 360, 379
   IT, 76, 95, 102, 163, 312–13, 316–20, 342, 343, 372
   transformational, 246
Group of Thirty, see G30

ICC, 245, 249
IFRS, 6, 85, 86, 92
ILM, 197, 201, 225, 265, 271
immaterial accounts, 210
imprisonment, 5, 56, 105, 256, 259
incident
   management, 281–4, 296
   response, 282
independent software vendors, 399
India, 22, 87, 206
informant, 60
information, 4, 10, 12, 14, 16, 20–6, 34, 40, 46, 51, 54, 60, 65–8, 77, 81–91, 94, 100–4, 114, 123, 129, 139, 146–8, 158, 163, 179, 181, 185, 193, 197, 204, 208–10, 214, 219, 220, 222–6, 229, 236, 240–4, 247, 254, 258, 262, 263, 285, 291, 300, 305, 312–18, 327–34, 342, 347, 348, 354, 364–7, 369, 370, 401–4
   as transformed data, 271
   asymmetrical, 67
   economy, 10, 65, 94, 101, 181, 236, 247, 276, 404

lifecycle, 197, 223, 271
lifecycle management (ILM), 197, 223, 271
management, 185, 204, 223, 248, 265, 308
meta, 404
security, 12, 21, 77, 100, 197, 219, 223, 229, 254, 276, 285, 291, 315, 347
sharing, 275
value, 272
Information Technology Control Guidelines, see ITCC, 326
instant messaging (IM), 273
Institute of Internal Auditors (IIA), 114, 125, 299
Institute of Management Accountants (IMA), 299
insurance, 20, 65, 75, 89, 99, 255, 367
intellectual capital, 11, 79, 271, 274–7, 347
intermediaries, 21, 65, 66, 67, 89, 104, 204, 254, 400
financial, 65–9, 75, 367
US, 74
internal control
as a process, 211, 214
definition, 39, 77, 121, 128, 138, 189, 204, 211–14, 221–8, 236, 238, 239–41, 245, 260, 300, 316, 328–32, 355, 370
report, 48, 189, 193
see also control, internal
Internal Revenue Code, see IRC
internal security management system, see ISMS
International Chamber of Commerce, see ICC
International Financial Reporting Standards, see IFRS
International Organization of Securities Commissions, see IOSCO
intranet, 121, 125, 130, 185, 199, 222, 247, 282, 291, 343
Investment Company Act, 48
investor, 9, 14, 17, 21, 27, 36, 40, 45, 49, 53, 80, 82, 85, 89, 101, 104, 107, 125, 139, 204, 209, 212, 254, 258, 271, 308, 358
confidence, 5, 12–14
IOSCO, 10, 17
Principles, 10
IP, see intellectual capital
IRC, 44
ISMS, 12, 155, 197, 254, 277, 280, 296
ISO 17799, 117, 119, 126, 128, 157, 163,

173, 194, 220, 254, 277–85, 291–3, 296, 326, 327, 342, 347–50
ISO 9001, 128, 161, 197, 203, 226, 247–8, 350, 366, 370
issuers, 6, 29, 33, 49, 53, 188, 199
ISV, see independent software vendors
IT, 11, 17, 20, 22, 76, 91–7, 102, 106, 116–25, 129, 159, 160, 168, 176, 179, 201, 203–6, 221, 224, 227–30, 239, 257, 260, 265, 272–6, 300, 301, 305, 308, 311–20, 326–34, 342–5, 356, 359–70, 372, 374, 378, 380, 399–402
controls, 221, 300
and financial services, 20
function, 11, 17, 22, 91, 102, 106, 116, 160, 168, 179, 203, 224, 240, 272–6, 311, 312, 316–18, 327, 342–4, 367, 378, 399
governance, 76, 95, 102, 163, 312–18, 320, 328, 342, 372
process, 239, 272, 329, 332, 342
systems auditors, 374
IT Governance Institute, 312
IT Infrastructure Library, see ITIL
ITCC, 326
ITGI, see IT Governance Institute
ITIL, 76, 102, 117, 163, 221, 242, 326, 342–5, 351, 356
service desk, 242, 344, 351

key goal indicator (KGI), 313
key indicators, 79, 301
key performance indicators (KPI), 193, 308, 314, 318, 334
KYC, 21

learning
blended, 401
e-learning, 401
management systems, 125, 401

management
assessment, 47, 71, 83, 107, 131, 180, 188, 193, 205, 313, 332, 360
email, 227
incident, 281, 284
strategic, 362
material weakness, 111, 139, 189, 217–19, 231–5, 342, 355
maturity
issues, 372
model, 313, 320, 334
mentoring, 325
metaprocess, 277, 278
misstatement, financial assertion, 234

model, cyclical, 152
monitoring, continuous, 15, 120, 124, 132, 141, 194, 231, 332
moral hazard, 68

NASDAQ, 3
National Institute of Standards (NIST), 194, 326
national securities exchanges, 51
non-audit services, 36, 199
non-compliance, 5, 14, 22, 45, 53, 69, 94, 99, 107, 110, 128–32, 149, 152, 154, 170, 176, 180, 194, 199, 253, 259, 267, 276, 304, 364
non-US entities, 3
NRA Regulations, 19
NYSE, 3, 7, 112, 367
    eGovDirect.com, 367

officer
    chief executive, 5, 44, 45, 47, 57, 59, 71, 105, 107, 115, 130, 159, 160, 361, 400
    chief financial, *see* chief executive
    executive, 44, 57, 59, 71, 105, 107, 115, 130, 159, 400
organization
    meta-model, 238
    the perfect, 152, 164, 351, 360, 372
outsourcing
    China, 22, 369
    India, 22, 87, 206
oversight board, 5

PCAOB, 23, 26, 28, 32–6, 39, 40, 48, 60, 81, 92, 99, 101, 131, 133–40, 157, 165, 189, 195, 207, 211–15, 217, 222, 232, 261, 267, 299, 316, 334
PDCA, 173, 176, 211, 282
penalties, 5, 14, 34, 44, 53–7, 59, 99, 108, 128, 179, 181, 195, 224, 246, 257
    punitive considerations, 51
personal risk, *see* risk
phase
    strategic, 179
    tactical, 179
Plan-Do-Check-Act, *see* PDCA
policies
    company, 161
    distribution, 185
    violation, 404
preparatory assessment, 158, 162, 168
PricewaterhouseCoopers, 8, 262, 353, 357–8
problem solving, 148, 167, 173

procedure, incident response, 282
process
    business, 16, 21, 25, 95, 121, 161, 191, 203, 210, 221–5, 239, 240–4, 254, 259, 266, 272, 278, 293, 300, 301, 312, 325, 330, 355–7, 364, 374
    as end-to-end work, 239
    and error, 243
    event-driven, 331
    IT, 239, 272, 329, 332–3, 342
    management, 94, 242, 259, 372
    manual, 17, 21
    mission-oriented, 325
    owner, 110, 186, 266
    redesign, 243
    significant, 192, 233, 380
    task-oriented, 241
    undocumented, 238
prohibited activities, *see* auditor
project control, 186
project management, 193, 268, 350, 374, 380
Public Company Accounting Oversight Board, *see* PCAOB
Public Company Accounting Reform and Investor Protection Act, *see* the Act
PwC, *see* PricewaterhouseCoopers

quality
    control, 32–4, 197, 199, 248, 344
    system, 161, 199, 223, 308, 345

Radio Frequency IDentification, *see* RFID
records, 53, 67, 81, 128, 224, 259, 271, 274, 402
    electronic, 53, 224, 275
    live, 81
    maintenance of, 136, 140, 212
records management, 259, 274
regulation, electronic, 83
regulators, 8, 10–14, 22–4, 40, 89–91, 108, 114, 125, 139, 160, 204, 214, 223–7, 255, 259, 265, 274, 308, 361, 404
report, 8, 39, 45–8, 51, 52, 53, 77, 80–4, 90, 94, 101, 103, 107, 110, 128, 133, 134–8, 140, 146, 147, 154, 165, 172, 179, 188, 193, 197, 200, 209, 215, 228, 230, 231, 258, 261, 268, 300, 307, 369
    audit, 33, 103, 199
    financial, 4, 5, 14, 16, 24, 33, 40, 46, 56, 67, 70, 71, 77–90, 92, 107, 110, 127, 129–40, 146, 153, 158, 177, 179, 181, 185, 188, 193, 204, 207, 210–14, 219, 220, 221, 222, 226,

231, 232, 235, 243, 256, 258, 266,
269, 272, 276, 300, 305, 307, 311,
325, 342, 347, 358, 360
key indicator, 79, 301
and marketing, 82
non-periodic, 259
periodic, 46, 79, 84, 108, 139, 153, 170,
189, 199, 209, 214, 233, 264, 362
reporting out, 45, 77
reporting up, 45
reputation, 67, 69, 70, 71, 77, 78, 99, 108,
226, 268
research, 127, 175, 194, 201, 366, 380
responsibility, 8, 33, 37, 40, 45, 56, 105–9,
116, 122, 126, 135, 140, 145, 158,
189, 202, 206, 212, 240, 246, 267,
275, 289, 294, 305, 316, 329, 351,
361, 362, 400
attorneys, 45
cascade, 109, 113, 126, 159, 202, 240,
294, 351, 400
hierarchy, 240
and organization, 246
separation of, 240
retrieval, 21, 22, 186, 224–8, 273, 274,
402–4
RFID, 16, 17
risk
appetite, 262, 263
enterprise, 255, 261, 262
identification, 80
implicit, 226
management, 3, 80, 114, 126, 190, 194,
228, 259–70, 273, 275, 358
matrix, 22
mitigating, 259
personal, 259
primary and secondary controls, 229
profile, 99, 115, 148, 153–7, 166, 173,
180, 253, 270, 281, 302, 315, 403
reducing, 237, 254
reputational, 67
systematic, 119, 155
systemic, 10
threshold, 268
tolerance, 96, 260, 262, 264, 268, 315
treatment, 132, 277, 280, 296, 376
unsystematic, 155
roaming access, 204
root cause analysis (RCA), 175, 282, 296,
345
rules, 45, 141
SEC, 224

SAG, 26

Sarbanes-Oxley, see Act
SAS 70, 193, 194, 203, 204, 205, 206, 222
scorecard, balanced, 320, 322, 325–6, 335
SEC, 3–10, 27, 35–9, 44–53, 56, 60, 81,
83, 89, 92, 97, 104, 108, 112, 128,
140, 181, 187, 208, 211–14, 224–6,
256, 274, 300, 403
sections of the Act, 28
Section 103, 32–3, 197
Section 108, 35, 83
Section 1102, 54, 58, 195, 197
Section 201, 36, 199, 201
Section 302, 40, 42, 81, 106, 111, 140,
181, 185, 187, 193, 199, 207, 214,
221–2, 256, 357
Section 404, 6, 15, 33, 47, 97, 102, 104,
107, 114, 124, 138, 188–94, 199,
207, 208, 221, 354, 357–8
Section 409, 23, 50, 79, 153, 193,
199–201, 256–60, 264, 404
Section 802, 53, 109, 195, 225
see also Act
Securities Exchange Act of 1934, 5, 35, 50,
52, 59, 83, 141, 181, 188, 224
Securities Exchange Commission, see SEC
Security Code of Conduct (DTI), 326
segregation of duties, see SOD
senior executives, 5, 8, 38, 43–7, 55, 78,
82, 90, 105–15, 140, 157, 164, 181,
201, 214, 224, 246, 270, 320, 363, 380
see also officer
service level agreement (SLA), 203, 343
service providers
Big Four, 353, 358, 359
Deloitte & Touche, 353, 358
Ernst & Young, 353–4
KPMG, 353, 355
PwC, 8, 262, 353, 357–8
share value, 5, 69, 129, 256
significant deficiency, 140, 214–19
sign-off, 192, 294, 296, 356
single sign-on (SSO), 293
Six Sigma, 76, 242, 343–7, 350
lean, 347
SLA, see service level agreement
sliding window, 153
SOD, 16, 197, 356
Software Engineering Institute (SEI), 349,
352
solution
benchmark, 360
vendor, 399
SOX, 3, 5, 63
see also Act
standards, 5, 17, 32–5, 40, 48, 56, 69, 75,

78, 82–92, 103, 107, 114, 116, 121, 124, 135, 136, 148, 160, 173, 194, 197–9, 203, 247, 249, 277, 300, 333, 343, 350, 360, 370

Standing Advisory Group, *see* SAG

statement of applicability, 131, 141, 278, 282, 289, 291, 296

Statement of Auditing Standards (SAS), 204

storage, 21, 88, 103, 117, 186, 195–7, 225, 227–9, 234, 240, 248, 257, 272–5, 402–4

    area networks (SANS), 402

    non-rewritable, 224

straight-through processing (STP), 86, 204

strategic inflection points, 363

strategic management, *see also* management

strategy, risk-based, 156

studies

    credit rating agencies, 53

    violators and violations, 53

supply chain, 15, 18, 21, 128, 179, 202–6, 222, 257, 266, 400

SWOT, 168

SysTrust, 326

tax returns, 57

technology, 20, 24, 242, 326, 354

test, strategy, 230

text messaging, 402

timescale, 20, 99, 120, 128, 156, 187, 192, 245, 364, 379, 401

sub-surface, 364

surface, 364

titles, 5, 28, 51, 60, 343

tools, 7, 19, 24, 97, 117, 119, 123–5, 129, 131, 163, 174, 177, 179, 185–7, 224, 237, 242, 247, 260, 265, 275, 313–18, 347, 350, 354, 368, 399

total quality management (TQM), 325

transformation, 13, 14, 66, 152, 227, 241

transparency, 27, 33, 38, 46, 65, 76, 88–90, 98, 105, 149, 204, 232, 245–7, 268, 359

Treadway Commission, 137, 253, 299–301

UAT, 356

underwriters, 204

US Code, 9, 53–60

user acceptance test, *see* UAT

user access, 292

vulnerability, 119, 229, 253, 348

weakness, material, 111, 139, 140, 189, 215–19, 231–5, 342, 355

whistleblower, 55, 77, 111

withholding tax, 70–3

workflow, 94, 186, 203, 223, 226, 234, 239–43, 248, 348, 402

WorldCom, 7, 8

XBRL, 81, 88–92, 186